AF843996

UX AND DESIGN THINKING HANDBOOK

Kruger Brentt
Publishers

UX AND DESIGN THINKING HANDBOOK

Derek Doran
Jacob Sorber

Kruger Brentt
Publishers
2025

Kruger Brentt Publishers UK. LTD.
Company Number 9728962

Regd. Office: 68 St Margarets Road, Edgware, Middlesex HA8 9UU

© 2025 AUTHORS

ISBN: 978-1-78715-304-2

Disclaimer:

Every possible effort has been made to ensure that the information contained in this book is accurate at the time of going to press, and the publisher and author cannot accept responsibility for any errors or omissions, however caused. No responsibility for loss or damage occasioned to any person acting, or refraining from action, as a result of the material in this publication can be accepted by the editor, the publisher or the author. The Publisher is not associated with any product or vendor mentioned in the book. The contents of this work are intended to further general scientific research, understanding and discussion only. Readers should consult with a specialist where appropriate.

Every effort has been made to trace the owners of copyright material used in this book, if any. The author and the publisher will be grateful for any omission brought to their notice for acknowledgement in the future editions of the book.

All Rights reserved under International Copyright Conventions. No part of this publication may be reproduced, stored in a retrieval system, or transmitted in any form or by any means, electronic, mechanical, photocopying, recording or otherwise without the prior written consent of the publisher and the copyright owner.

For information on all our publications visit our website at http://krugerbrentt.com/

PREFACE

"UX and Design Thinking Handbook" is a comprehensive guide to understanding and applying user experience (UX) principles and design thinking methodologies in the development of products, services, and systems. This handbook serves as an essential resource for designers, engineers, product managers, and anyone interested in creating user-centric solutions that delight and empower users.

User experience design and design thinking have emerged as essential approaches for creating products and services that meet the needs, preferences, and aspirations of users. By putting users at the center of the design process, organizations can create innovative solutions that not only solve problems but also foster meaningful and engaging experiences.

As editors of this handbook, we have endeavored to compile a diverse array of perspectives, methodologies, and case studies from leading experts and practitioners in the fields of UX design and design thinking. Through a blend of theoretical insights, practical advice, and real-world examples, this handbook covers a wide range of topics, including user research, ideation, prototyping, usability testing, and iterative design.

Our overarching goal in presenting this handbook is to provide readers with a comprehensive and practical guide to UX design and design thinking, empowering them to create impactful and user-centered solutions. By offering actionable guidance, best practices, and tools for innovation, we aim to inspire creativity, collaboration, and excellence in the design process.

We extend our sincere gratitude to all the contributors who have generously shared their expertise, experiences, and insights in the field of UX design and design thinking. It is our hope that this handbook will serve as a valuable resource and inspiration for designers, innovators, and problem-solvers as they strive to create products and services that delight users and drive success in today's competitive landscape.

Derek Doran
Jacob Sorber

CONTENTS

Part I: Introduction to UX and Design Thinking

CHAPTER-1

UNDERSTANDING USER EXPERIENCE (UX)

INTRODUCTION TO UX AND DESIGN THINKING

User experience (UX) design is the process design teams use to create products that provide meaningful and relevant experiences to users. UX design involves the design of the entire process of acquiring and integrating the product, including aspects of branding, design, usability and function.

Design thinking is an ideology and process in UX design that has a user-centred approach to solving problems. Within UX design, the user's interactions and experience are at the centre. Similarly, design thinking places the user at the centre of the process to understand their needs and requirements.

Explore the powerful realm of Design Thinking in our UX/UI Design Course. Design thinking is accessible to UX designers of all levels, ranging from beginners to advanced.

The 5 Stages of Design Thinking

- **Empathise** is about understanding the problem from others' perspective. It helps designers know what users need.
- **Define** – we use the information we learned in the empathise stage to figure out what problems we need to solve. It's like making a list of the things we need to fix.
- **Ideate** – you're ready to generate ideas to solve the problems found.
- **Prototype** – we can design a mock-up of our product to see how it looks and works.

- **Test** – now we put the product to the test. It's important to note that the testing stage doesn't always mean we're done. It often gives us new insights and ideas to keep improving the product.

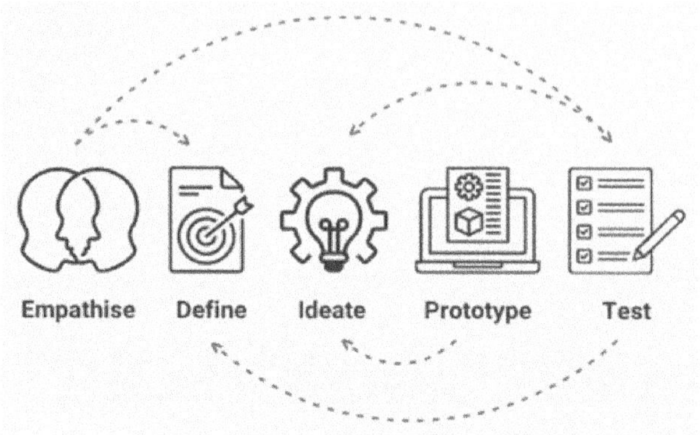

Fig. 1.1 Stages of Design Thinking

UNDERSTANDING USER EXPERIENCE (UX)

Ever wondered why you find some websites more intuitive than others? Or why do some mobile apps seem to anticipate your needs perfectly, while others get you endlessly clicking in frustration? Welcome to the world of User Experience, often abbreviated as UX.

At its core, user experience is all about how a person feels when interacting with a system, be it a website, a web application, or desktop software, and in general terms, any device or service. Aspects such as usability, accessibility, system performance, design/look and feel, utility and ergonomic properties all commonly fall under the umbrella of user experience.

Although it might seem like a trendy buzzword, the concept of user experience is deeply rooted in human-computer interaction theories that date back to the 1980s. As technology continues to evolve, so too does our need for making digital systems more user-friendly. Isn't it fascinating?

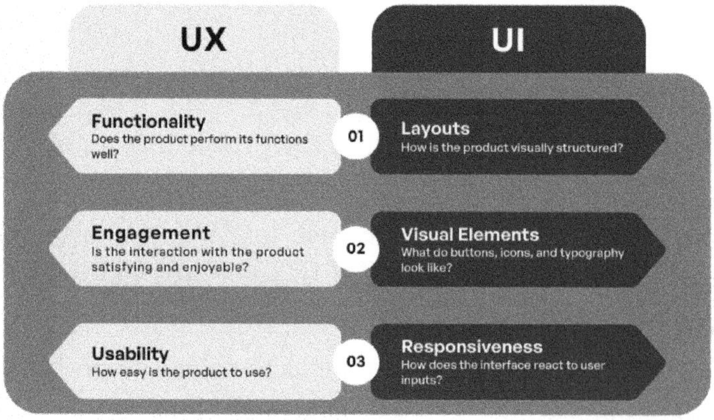

Fig. 1.2 User Experience(UX) vs User Interface(UI)

Now, you might be wondering, why is UX so essential, especially in product development. How can you enhance the user experience? What is its impact on the bottom line? Continue reading to unwrap the answers to all these questions and dive into the intriguing world of user experience. Shall we?

User Experience(UX) vs User Interface(UI)

Have you ever wondered about the difierence between User Experience (UX) and User Interface (UI)? While they seem to be used interchangeably in conversations, in fact, they hold distinct roles in product development. Let's uncover what each term signifies. **User Experience (UX)**, as the name suggests, encompasses all the interactions and experiences a user has with a product. UX concentrates on the product's usability, functionality, and how users perceive, interact, and feel about the product. Think of UX as the whole journey: from the moment a user discovers your product, to their interactions, feelings, and thoughts that transpire as they navigate through it.

UX covers:

- **Usability:** How easy is the product to use?
- **Engagement:** Is the interaction with the product satisfying and enjoyable?
- **Functionality:** Does the product perform its functions well?

On the other hand, **User Interface(UI)** is the specific asset users interact with. Essentially, UI is the point of interaction between the user and a digital product or service. This covers all the screens, buttons, icons, and visual elements that facilitate user interaction.

UI includes:

- **Layouts:** How is the product visually structured?
- **Visual Elements:** What do buttons, icons, and typography look like?
- **Responsiveness:** How does the interface react to user inputs?

In essence, while UX is about how the product *feels*, UI is about how the product *looks*. Both are essential to the product and work closely together. But remember, a product with an excellent UI can fail if it provides a poor UX, and vice versa. Therefore, a harmonious balance between UX and UI is crucial for a product's success. Makes sense, isn't it?

User Experience: Matters in Product Development

So why does user experience matter in product development? Have you ever wondered why some products fiy ofi the shelves while others stagnate? Often, it comes down to how users feel about the product – and that's where user experience steps in.

User experience (UX) encapsulates all the interactions a person has with a product. It's also about how they feel throughout the entire process, from the moment they first hear about it, to the point they try it out, and even when they stop using it. Translated to the world of product development, UX is about empathy and understanding your user's needs, wants, and expectations.

Here are a few reasons why user experience is so critical to product development:

- Your product needs to be intuitive. A product that's dificult to use will put people ofi, no matter how beautiful or innovative it may be.
- Good UX design can make your product stand out from the competition. In today's saturated markets, a well-designed user experience can be the defining factor that sets your product apart.
- An excellent user experience helps retain users and foster loyalty. If users enjoy using your product, they're more likely to continue using it and recommend it to others.

It's important to remember, though, that understanding your users' needs and translating them into a functional, enjoyable product isn't always clear-cut. You'll need to listen carefully, research thoroughly, and iterate constantly - but more on that in a bit. For now, just remember: the best products are those that put users first.

When developers understand how users will interact with their product, they can create a more user-friendly solution. It helps to identify potential issues and roadblocks early on, which can save time and resources in the long run. Moreover, optimizing your product based on the user's perspective can increase sales and profits, but we'll get to that later. The takeaway here? Investing in user experience isn't just about aesthetics or usability; it's about creating a product that truly meets your users' needs.

How Does UX Affect Product Development?

The best products out there didn't just happen by accident. They are the result of careful planning, perfect execution, and meticulous attention to user experience (UX). UX design iteratively improves the overall quality of the product, ensuring the final outcome is not only functional but also user-friendly and appealing.

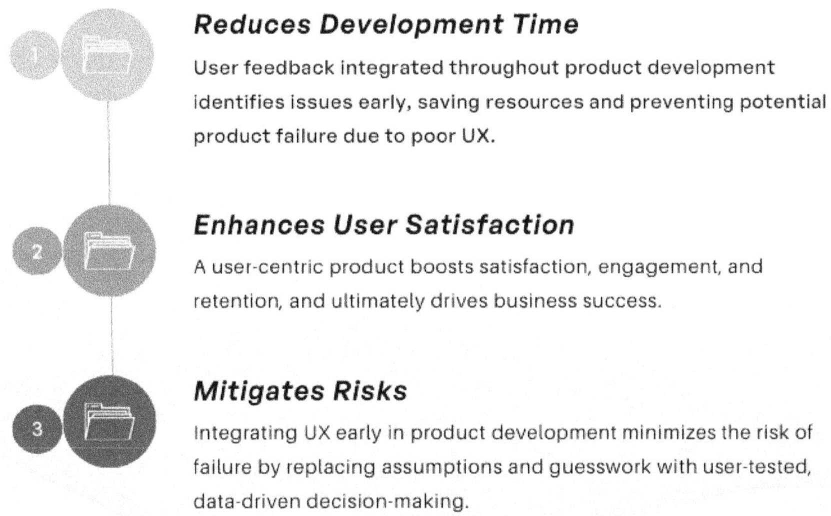

Fig. 1.3 How Does UX Affect Product Development?

But how, specifically, does UX injection into product development enhance its quality?

- **Reduces Development Time:** When user feedback is integrated at every stage of product development, it helps identify issues earlier, saving precious resources and time. This could mean preventing a product release that may fail due to poor UX.
- **Enhances User Satisfaction:** A product developed with user experience in mind is more likely to satisfy the users' needs, leading to higher user engagement, retention, and ultimately, business success.
- **Mitigates Risks:** Incorporating UX in the product development process from the get-go reduces the risk of product failure drastically. It eliminates assumptions and guesswork, replacing them with user-tested, data-based decideci-making.
- Ways to Enhance User Experience (Fig. 1.4)

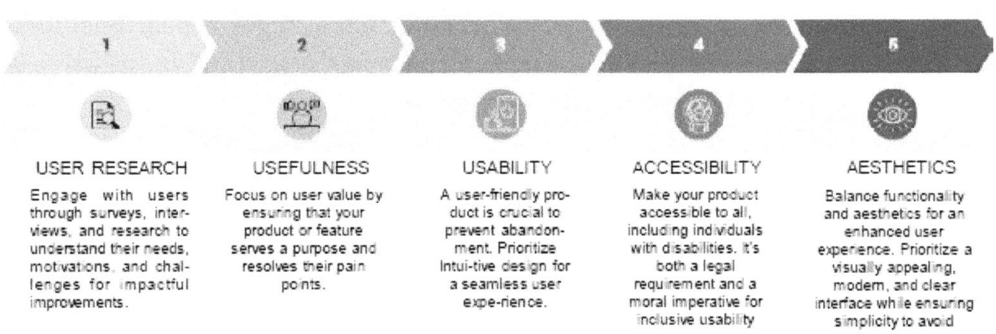

Fig. 1.4 Ways to Enhance User Experience

Following are some techniques that can help you improve user experience:

- **User Research:** Nothing beats hearing straight from the users themselves. Conduct user surveys, interviews, and research to understand their needs, motivations, and challenges. Use this information to make the necessary improvements.
- **Usefulness:** Ask yourself, "Is the product or feature useful to the user?" If it doesn't serve a purpose or resolve a pain point, it may not enhance the user experience. Focus on creating value for your users.
- **Usability:** This pertains to the ease of use of the product. If users struggle to use the product or find the information they need, they're more likely to abandon it. Make sure your product is intuitive and straightforward.
- **Accessibility:** Your product should be accessible to everyone, including those with disabilities. Accessibility is not only a legal requirement but also a moral one, ensuring that everyone, regardless of ability, can use your product eficiently.
- **Aesthetics:** While functionality is king, "looks" still matter. A visually appealing, modern, and clear interface can significantly enhance the user experience. But remember, simplicity is key; you don't want the design to be distracting or confusing.

Keep those tips in mind, and you're on your way to creating a product that not only meets your users' needs but also provides an outstanding and enjoyable user experience.

The Impact of User Experience on Profits

You're likely asking, "But how exactly does user experience play into my bottom line?" Well, it's simple. The better a customer's experience with your product, the more likely they are to use it, stick with it, and recommend it to others. This increase in user satisfaction and advocacy directly impacts your profits. Let's break this down a bit further.

First and foremost, a positive user experience encourages repeat business. If you're able to provide a product that meets a customer's needs in an intuitive and pleasant way, they're more likely to come back to you in the future. It saves them the time and effort of looking for an alternative to fulfill the same need. Can you see how this directly contributes to increased revenue?

Secondly, happy customers become brand advocates. Word of mouth is an incredibly powerful tool in business, and customers who have had a positive experience with your product are far more likely to recommend it to their friends and family. This organic promotion is priceless and can significantly bolster your profits.

DEFINITION AND CORE PRINCIPLES OF LUX

The primary sensor data type for ambient light sensors is illuminance in lux (lumens per square meter). The principles outlined in this topic are based on taking lux values as input and reacting to that data in a program.

Lux readings are directly proportional to the energy per square meter that is absorbed per second. Human perception of light levels is not so straightforward. Human perception of light is complicated because our eyes are constantly adjusting and other biological processes are affecting our perception. However, we can think of this perception from a simplified perspective by creating several ranges of interest with known upper and lower thresholds. The following example data set represents rough thresholds for common lighting conditions, and the corresponding lighting step. Here, each lighting step represents a change in lighting environment.

Lighting condition	From (lux)	To (lux)	Mean value (lux)	Lighting step
Pitch Black	0	10	5	1
Very Dark	11	50	30	2
Dark Indoors	51	200	125	3
Dim Indoors	201	400	300	4
Normal Indoors	401	1000	700	5
Bright Indoors	1001	5000	3000	6
Dim Outdoors	5001	10,000	7500	7
Cloudy Outdoors	10,001	30,000	20,000	8
Direct Sunlight	30,001	100,000	65,000	9

If we visualize this data by using the mean values from this table, we see that the lux-to-lighting-step relationship is not linear, as show in the following graph Fig. 1.5).

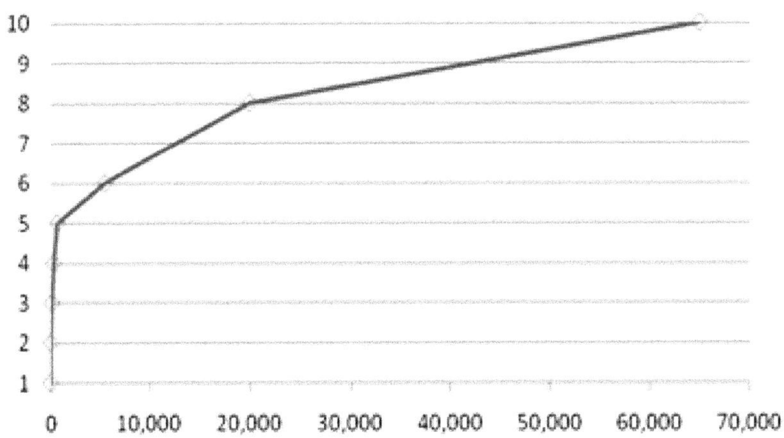

Fig. 1.5 Illuminance (lux) vs lighting-step

However, if we view this data by using a logarithmic scale on the x-axis, we can see that a roughly linear relationship emerges (Fig. 1.6).

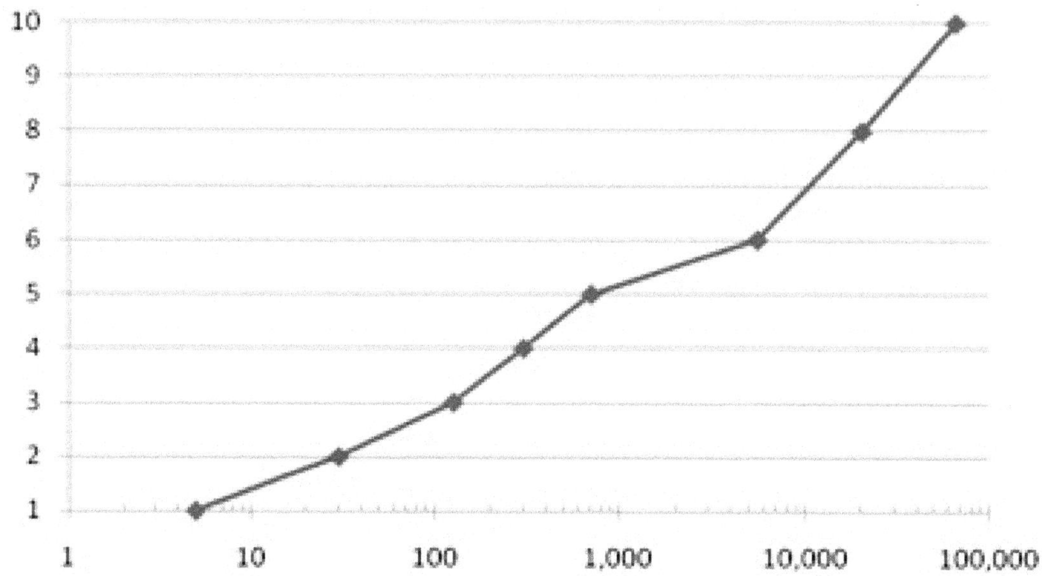

Fig. 1.6 Illuminance (lux, $\log_{(10)}$) vs lighting-step

An Example Transform

Based on the sample data set for ambient light sensors previously provided, you could arrive at the following equation to map lux values to human perception. In this example, the expected values range from 0 lux to 1,000,000 lux.

$$Light_{normaluzed} = Log_{10}(x)/5.0$$

This equation results in values that vary in a roughly linear fashion between 0.0 and 1.0. This result indicates how human-perceived lighting changed based on the example data set that was shown previously.

Core Principles of Lux

The working principle of a lux meter revolves around the fundamental concept of illuminance, which is the measurement of the amount of light falling on a surface. Lux meters, also known as light meters or illuminance meters, operate based on this principle to quantify the brightness level in a given area.

Lux meters typically consist of a photodiode sensor, a lens, and electronic circuitry. The photodiode sensor is the key component responsible for detecting and converting light energy into an electrical current. It is designed to be responsive to the visible spectrum of light, which is the range of light wavelengths that human eyes can perceive.

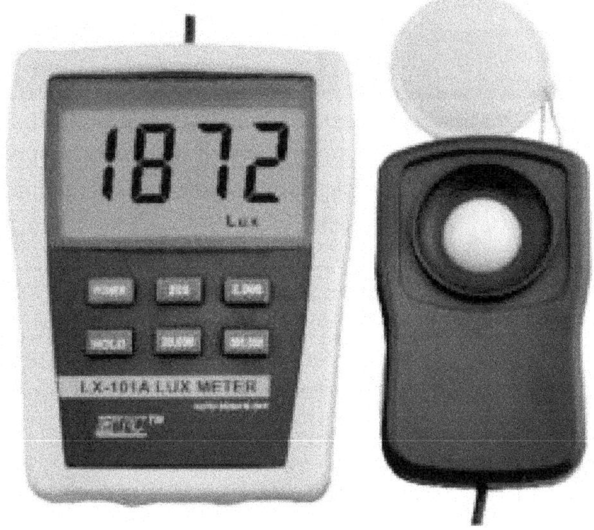

Fig. 1.7 Lux meter

When a lux meter is exposed to light, the lens collects and focuses the incoming light onto the photodiode sensor. The photodiode absorbs the photons, generating an electrical current proportional to the intensity of the incident light. This current is then converted into a voltage signal by the electronic circuitry within the lux meter (Fig. 1.7).

The voltage signal is further processed and calibrated by the internal circuitry to obtain a lux value. Lux is the unit of measurement for illuminance, representing the amount of light that falls on a unit area. The lux value is calculated based on the sensitivity of the photodiode sensor and other factors such as the distance between the light source and the sensor.

To ensure accurate measurements, lux meters are often calibrated against known reference standards or calibrated light sources. This calibration process helps align the lux meter's readings with a standardized scale, enhancing the reliability and accuracy of the measurements.

Lux meters can be used to measure light intensity in various environments, such as indoor spaces, outdoor areas, photography studios, workplaces, and more. They provide a quantitative assessment of the brightness level, allowing users to determine whether the lighting conditions meet specific requirements or standards.

In summary, the working principle of a lux meter involves the detection of light by a photodiode sensor, the conversion of light energy into an electrical current, and the subsequent calculation of illuminance in lux units. By utilizing this principle, lux meters enable professionals in different industries to evaluate and optimize lighting conditions for various applications.

Specifications and features of Lux meter

Specification/ Feature	Description
Measurement Range	The smallest increment of illuminance that the lux meter can detect and display. The higher resolution allows for more precise measurements.
Resolution	Lux meters may offer various measurement modes, such as lux, foot candles, or other specialized units. Choose the mode that suits your application.
Accuracy	The degree of closeness between the measured value and the true value. Look for a lux meter with high accuracy to ensure reliable results.
Display	The type of display on the lux meter, such as LCD, LED, or OLED. Consider factors like readability, backlighting, and digit size for ease of use.
Measurement Modes	Lux meters may offer various measurement modes, such as lux, foot-candles, or other specialized units. Choose the mode that suits your application.
Data Logging	Some lux meters have built-in memory or storage capabilities for recording and retrieving measurement data over time. Useful for long-term monitoring and analysis.
Connectivity Options	Lx meters may offer connectivity features like Bluetooth or USB for data transfer to external devices or computer software for further analysis.
Auto-Ranging	This feature allows the Lx meter to automatically adjust its measurement range based on the detected light intensity, ensuring optimal measurements without manual range selection.
Calibration	The range of light intensities the Lx meter can measure, typically in lux or foot candles. Make sure it covers your desired measurement range.
Power Source	Check the power source requirements, whether it's batteries, rechargeable batteries, or AC power, and consider the expected battery life for prolonged use.
Size and Portability	Consider the size, weight, and portability of the Lx meter to ensure it fits your needs, especially if you require a compact and easily transportable device.
Additional Features	Look for any additional features that may enhance functionality, such as data hold, min/max readings, auto-off, backlight control, or integration with other measurement tools.

Lux meter uses

Use/Application	Description
Lighting Design	Lx meters help assess and analyze lighting conditions in architectural and interior design projects to ensure optimal illuminance levels and create the desired ambiance.
Workplace Safety	Lx meters are used to measure and monitor light levels in work environments to comply with occupational safety standards and provide adequate lighting for employee well-being and productivity.

Use/Application	Description
Photography and Cinematography	Lx meters aid in achieving proper exposure and lighting ratios in photography and cinematography, ensuring accurate and consistent lighting conditions for capturing high-quality images and videos.
Energy Efficiency	Lx meters assist in energy audits and efficiency assessments by measuring and optimizing lighting levels to reduce energy consumption and improve sustainability in buildings and facilities.
Horticulture and Plant Growth	Lx meters are utilized in agriculture, horticulture, and indoor gardening to determine the ideal light levels for plant growth, photosynthesis, and optimizing artificial lighting setups for greenhouse cultivation.
Research and Scientific Studies	Lx meters are employed in research studies related to light sensitivity, visual perception, circadian rhythm, and other areas where precise measurements of illuminance are required.
Facility Management	Lx meters help facility managers monitor and maintain appropriate lighting conditions in various settings such as offices, retail spaces, schools, and hospitals to create comfortable and visually pleasing environments.
Art and Museum Lighting	Lx meters aid in preserving artworks and artifacts by measuring light levels to prevent excessive exposure and potential damage caused by UV radiation and inappropriate lighting.

Use of a lux meter

Using a Lx meter is a straightforward process that involves a few simple steps. Here's a general guide on how to use a Lx meter effectively:

- **Familiarize Yourself with the Lux Meter:** Read the user manual provided with your specific Lx meter model. This will help you understand the device's features, functions, and operation.
- **Prepare the Lux Meter:** Ensure that the Lx meter is in good working condition and properly calibrated. Check the battery level and replace it if necessary to ensure accurate measurements.
- **Select the Measurement Mode:** Some Lx meters offer different measurement modes, such as lux (lx) or foot candles (FC). Choose the appropriate method based on your region's preferred unit of illuminance.
- **Determine the Measurement Area:** Identify where you want to measure the light intensity. Ensure that the Lx meter's sensor is unobstructed and facing toward the light source.
- **Position the Lux Meter:** Hold the Lx meter at the desired location in the measurement area. Keep the sensor parallel to the direction of the incoming light for accurate readings.

- **Take the Measurement:** Activate the Lx meter and allow it to stabilize for a few seconds to obtain a steady reading. The digital display or readout will show the lux value corresponding to the measured light intensity.
- **Record and Analyze the Results:** Note down the lux readings or use any data logging feature available in your Lx meter to record the measurements. Compare the results against recommended or desired illuminance levels for your specific application.
- **Repeat Measurements (If Needed):** If you need to assess light levels at multiple points or different times, repeat the process by repositioning the Lx meter accordingly.
- **Ensure Proper Maintenance:** After each use, clean the lens and sensor of the Lx meter using a soft cloth to remove any dirt or debris. Store the Lx meter in a safe and dry place.

Best Lux meter

Choosing the best Lx meter depends on your specific requirements and intended use. Here are a few factors to consider when selecting a Lx meter:

- **Accuracy:** Look for a Lx meter that offers high accuracy in measuring light intensity. Check the specifications or user reviews to ensure that the Lx meter provides reliable and precise readings.
- **Range and Resolution:** Consider the Lx meter's measurement range and resolution. The range should cover the expected light levels in your application, and the resolution should be sufficient to capture subtle variations in brightness.
- **Display:** Opt for a Lx meter with a clear and easy-to-read display. A digital display with backlighting or large digits can enhance visibility, especially in low-light conditions.
- **Functionality:** Assess the Lx meter's additional features and functionality. Some models offer data logging, memory storage, auto-ranging, or connectivity options like Bluetooth or USB for data transfer and analysis.
- **Build Quality:** Look for a lux metr that is durable and well-built. It should be able to withstand regular use and possible environmental conditions associated with your application.
- **User-Friendly Interface:** Consider the ease of use and intuitive interface of the lux metr. A well-designed interface and intuitive controls can make operating the device more convenient and efficient.
- **Calibration:** Check if the lux metr can be calibrated or has a calibration certificate. Calibration ensures accurate measurements and allows for periodic recalibration as needed.

- **Budget:** Consider your budget and select a lux metr that offers the best value for money without compromising essential features or accuracy.

SIGNIFICANCE OF UX IN PRODUCT DEVELOPMENT

User experience done right can benefit a lot. The first step, most often, is to have the UX strategy in place. Take a moment to think of all the pain points—it can help to turn them around for a superior product and user experience.

Everyone wants their products to provide excellent user experience, but this is not what all the products end up achieving.

While designing and development of the product for the users, the effort must be to provide them with the solution to their problems in an easy as well as efficient way. It is vital to pay adequate heed to design the system so that users get what they need.

In the case of e-commerce sites, people visit the site to buy products. The interface of the product needs to meet product goals. If you have a good user experience, they will come back and shop again. (Fig. 1.8)

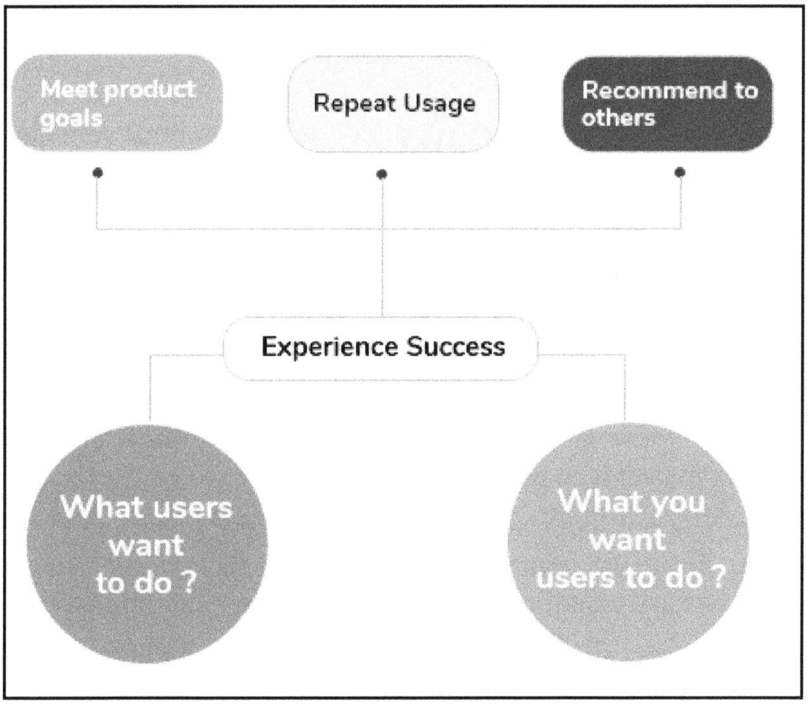

Fig. 1.8 Significance of UX in Product Development

According to a survey published in the "Net" magazine (Issue 283 Summer 2016), 78% of the business that one can get is from word of mouth. A solid reputation among past clients takes you a long way.

Let's examine some use cases for a not-so-good user experience (UX):

Confusing to use where the users don't understand how to navigate or understand the features

- Inaccessible, for example- when the app isn't curated for accessibility, leaving behind a few users who struggle to work around the product
- Lacking visual appeal, when the product isn't a visually appealing experience
- Inefficiency, when it is taking too long to do things
- As a product owner, you want to work around the pain points and beyond to create a great user experience. A good product then would augment the user experience and have some of these facets:

- Increased accessibility, where users can access it on various devices; plus enable users with a range of abilities and disabilities to perceive, understand, navigate, and interact easily
- Pleasant, attractive, and fun experience
- Easy to learn and figure out the app/product features
- Helps users with a more engaging experience and, in turn, feel more connected to the product
- To achieve a successful user experience, designers must consider seven key factors that shape the overall perception of the product:

The Seven Factors that Influence User Experience

- **Valuable:** A product must provide real value to its users. Understanding their needs and addressing their pain points is crucial to offer something that genuinely improves their lives or solves a problem.
- **Useful:** Beyond being valuable, a product must also be useful. It should serve its purpose effectively and efficiently, fulfilling the primary tasks that users expect it to perform.
- **Usable:** The product's usability is vital to ensure users can easily interact with it. Intuitive navigation, clear interfaces, and straightforward interactions are essential to prevent frustration and improve engagement.
- **Findable:** Users should have no trouble finding what they need within the product. A well-organized and searchable interface allows users to locate information or features effortlessly.
- **Credible:** Trust is a crucial component of UX. Establishing credibility through clear communication, transparent policies, and a professional appearance helps build user confidence.

- **Desirable:** Aesthetics and emotional appeal play a significant role in user satisfaction. A visually appealing product that evokes positive emotions creates a desire to engage with it repeatedly.
- **Accessible:** Ensuring that the product is accessible to all users, regardless of their abilities or limitations, is essential for inclusivity and reaching a broader audience.

Balancing the Factors for Optimal User Experience

To create an outstanding user experience, designers must strike a delicate balance between these seven factors. Neglecting any one of them can lead to a subpar product experience and alienate users.

User experience design involves a multidisciplinary approach that encompasses user research, information architecture, interaction design, visual design, and usability testing. By incorporating these practices into the design process, designers can gain valuable insights and iteratively improve the product's UX.

Let's see transformative power of UX with real-life examples of startups that have flourished by prioritizing their users' needs and desires.

1. Swiggy - Satisfying Hunger and Users Alike

Swiggy, a renowned food delivery startup in India, redefined the way people order food online. By offering a seamless and intuitive mobile app, they ensured that customers could effortlessly browse restaurants, customize orders, and track deliveries in real-time. Their obsession with UX helped them gain an edge over competitors, making Swiggy the go-to choice for millions of foodies across the country.

2. Razorpay - Simplifying Payments for Businesses

Razorpay, a fintech startup, recognized the pain points that businesses face while dealing with payment gateways. They crafted a developer-friendly interface with smooth integration and robust security features, empowering businesses to accept online payments with ease. Razorpay's dedication to UX not only attracted a vast customer base but also garnered industry recognition, driving their rapid growth.

3. BYJU'S - Learning, Simplified

BYJU'S, an edtech unicorn, revolutionized the way students learn by offering interactive and engaging educational content. Their app's user-friendly design, coupled with gamified learning experiences, captivated young minds, and made learning enjoyable. As a result, BYJU'S became a household name and a leading edtech player in India.

4. Dunzo - Delivering Convenience

Dunzo, a hyperlocal delivery startup, positioned itself as the 'go-getter' for its users. Their app's simple interface allowed users to get almost anything delivered with just a few taps. From groceries to medicines, Dunzo's commitment to UX earned them a loyal customer base and expanded their services to multiple cities.

5. Freshworks - Empowering Customer Support

Freshworks, a SaaS company, built its success around empowering businesses to deliver top-notch customer support. Their intuitive and easy-to-navigate helpdesk software simplified the customer support process, enhancing the overall experience for both businesses and their clients. As a result, Freshworks has grown into a global player with a suite of successful products.

Challenges in getting the right UX

Although every product owner wants to have a good user experience for its product, it's not so easy to have good UX. One of the reasons why UX is difficult is that we are not the actual users of the product.

Might be the product you are developing is useful to you also in your daily lives, but still, you are not the actual user. The actual users may be different. Their needs and use of the product is different. It is important to get to know about all these things before actually making the product.

Secondly, the difference between human intelligence and computer intelligence. Making something understandable to computer-based interactive systems and users at the same time is quite challenging.

Another most important reason is that, in today's technology world of programming, we can create as much complex functionality and system as we want but it is important to understand and filter the exact functionality that the user needs.

Solution for getting the right UX

Although UX is a critical work, there are techniques that UX designers use to make the user experience process easy.

How UX research solves problems in the product development process?

The business needs to focus on user research from the very start of the project. Through early research, a business can identify customer pain points and how their products can solve all these issues.

User research can begin at the very start of product development, or it can be part of its ongoing lifecycle.

Start with user research – By focusing on the end-user from the very start of the project can help you reveal the customer's pain points and how your product can solve these problems.

By conducting a thorough UX research with the target audience through contextual interviews, prototyping, etc. we can design journey maps, user personas, and user scenarios. It will simplify our design and decision-making process.

Ongoing research – If you already have a product in the market, then ongoing research is the best way to fine-tune your offerings. This feedback is more valuable as it is coming from the actual users. This type of research can be conducted through A/B testing, surveys, heuristic evaluations, etc.

If the product is being developed on a feature-by-feature basis, then it becomes easy to be blinded by the initial solution pitched by the product manager.

So, UX research is most effective when the UX designer is brought to the product development lifecycle at a very initial stage.

Benefits of introducing UX designer in the product development process

- UX designer gets a better view of the complete product and not the current deliverable. It allows the UX designer to keep the UX consistent across all the product features.
- It gives extra time to the UX designer to study new features, conduct early user research, and bring new ideas to accelerate the design process.
- It allows better work management and allows UX designers to plan all the tasks ahead of time.

Getting started with UX design process

The ideal UX designer will not jump to a solution straight away. The UX researcher will start by identifying the problem and come up with the ideas that will solve that problem.

The UX researcher in the course of looking for the solution will start by answering these questions –

- Who has the problem?
- What is the problem?
- How will we solve the problem?
- What will the solution achieve?
- What features are required to accomplish the objective?
- What will the product look like, and how will it function?

Methods of the UX design process

User personas

The very initial step is to understand your target audience, who will be using your product. You can start creating user persona, which will help you develop experiences keeping in mind the emotions of your users.

Interviews

Interview your existing or potential users to gain insights into the most effective design for your product.

Job stories

It is a short, simple description of the product feature as described by the person who wants that feature.

Functionality map

After studying the job stories, the UX researcher will start by building a functionality map for the pages. A functionality map is nothing but an organized hierarchy of pages and subpages in the product.

Wire frames

Wireframes are visual guides that give an overview of the product. It is like the skeletal structure of the product. Visuals are equally important as the site structure, so it is important to invest time in wireframes.

Prototyping

It is a mockup version of the final product which can be used for user testing before the actual product launch.

Usability testing

Usability testing is the testing of the product with actual users to identify any issues the user might face while interacting with the product.

CHAPTER-2

INTRODUCTION TO DESIGN THINKING

Design thinking is an innovative and human-centered approach to problem-solving that has revolutionized the way organizations tackle complex challenges. It goes beyond traditional problem-solving methods by placing users' needs and experiences at the process's core. Design thinking empowers individuals and teams to think creatively, collaborate effectively, and generate innovative solutions. In today's competitive landscape, organizations are constantly faced with the need to adapt and innovate. Design thinking provides a structured framework that encourages a deep understanding of users, fosters creativity, and embraces iteration. By approaching problem-solving from a user-centric perspective, design thinking enables organizations to develop solutions that truly meet the needs and desires of their target audience.

The End Goal of Design Thinking: Be Desirable, Feasible and Viable

The design thinking process aims to satisfy three criteria: desirability (what do people desire?), feasibility (is it technically possible to build the solution?) and viability (can the company profit from the solution?). Teams begin with desirability and then bring in the other two lenses.

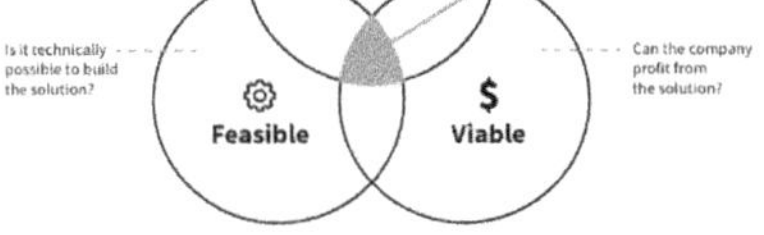

Fig. 2.1 Three Lenses of Design Thinking

Desirability: Meet People's Needs

The design thinking process starts by looking at the needs, dreams and behaviors of people—the end users. The team listens with empathy to understand what people want, not what the organization thinks they want or need. The team then thinks about solutions to satisfy these needs from the end user's point of view.

Feasibility: Be Technologically Possible

Once the team identifies one or more solutions, they determine whether the organization can implement them. In theory, any solution is feasible if the organization has infinite resources and time to develop the solution. However, given the team's current (or future resources), the team evaluates if the solution is worth pursuing. The team may iterate on the solution to make it more feasible or plan to increase its resources (say, hire more people or acquire specialized machinery).

At the beginning of the design thinking process, teams should not get too caught up in the technical implementation. If teams begin with technical constraints, they might restrict innovation.

Viability: Generate Profits

A desirable and technically feasible product isn't enough. The organization must be able to generate revenues and profits from the solution. The viability lens is essential not only for commercial organizations but also for non-profits.

Traditionally, companies begin with feasibility or viability and then try to find a problem to fit the solution and push it to the market. Design thinking reverses this process and advocates that teams begin with desirability and bring in the other two lenses later.

EXPLORING THE DESIGN THINKING PROCESS

Design thinking follows a structured framework that encourages creativity and iteration. While different variations exist, the following five-step process, with example is creating a new mobile banking app

1. Empathize

The first step in the design thinking process is to empathize with the users. This involves conducting in-depth research, interviews, and observations to gain a deep understanding of their needs, desires, and challenges. By putting ourselves in their shoes, we can uncover valuable insights that inform the subsequent stages (Fig. 2.3).

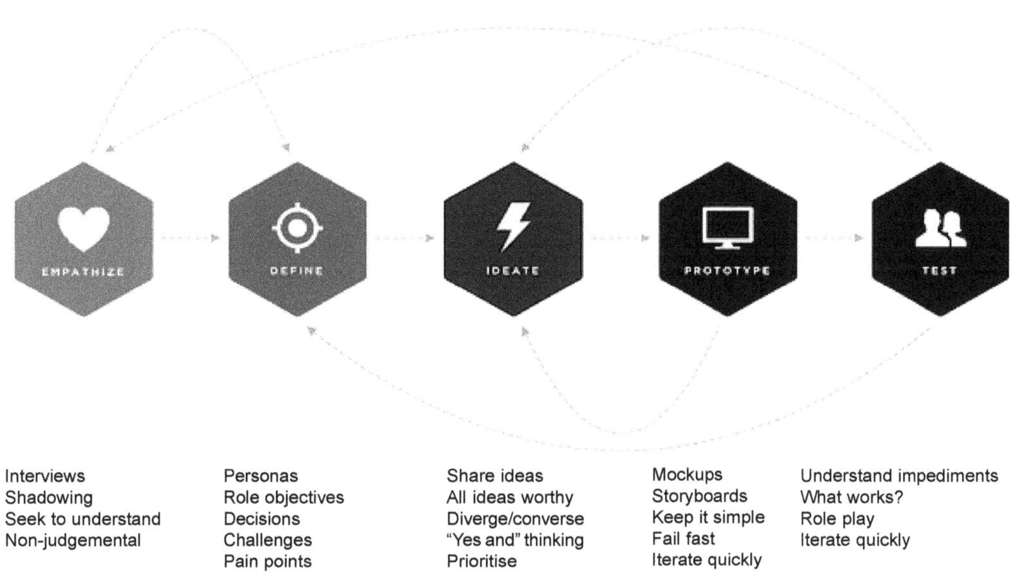

Fig. 2.2 Design Thinking Framework and Process

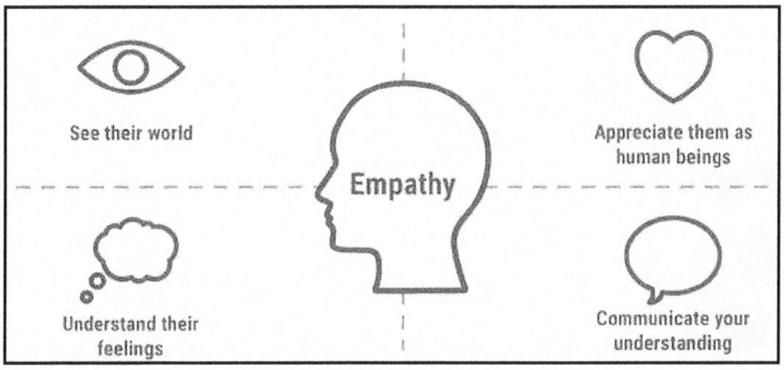

Fig. 2.3 Empathize

Let's consider a team developing a new mobile banking app. They spend time shadowing and interviewing potential users to understand their frustrations with existing banking applications. Through this process, they identify pain points such as complex navigation, lack of personalized features, and difficulty managing finances effectively.

Define

Once we have a clear understanding of the users, we move on to defining the problem. This involves synthesizing the research findings and identifying the core issues that need to be addressed. The problem statement should be framed in a way that inspires innovative solutions.

Building on the insights gained, the mobile banking app team defines their problem statement as: "How might we create a user-friendly and personalized banking app that simplifies financial transactions and empowers users to manage their finances effectively?"

Ideate

In the ideation phase, teams brainstorm a wide range of ideas without judgment. This encourages creative thinking and opens up possibilities. Techniques such as brainstorming, mind mapping, and sketching are employed to generate a diverse pool of ideas (Fig. 2.4).

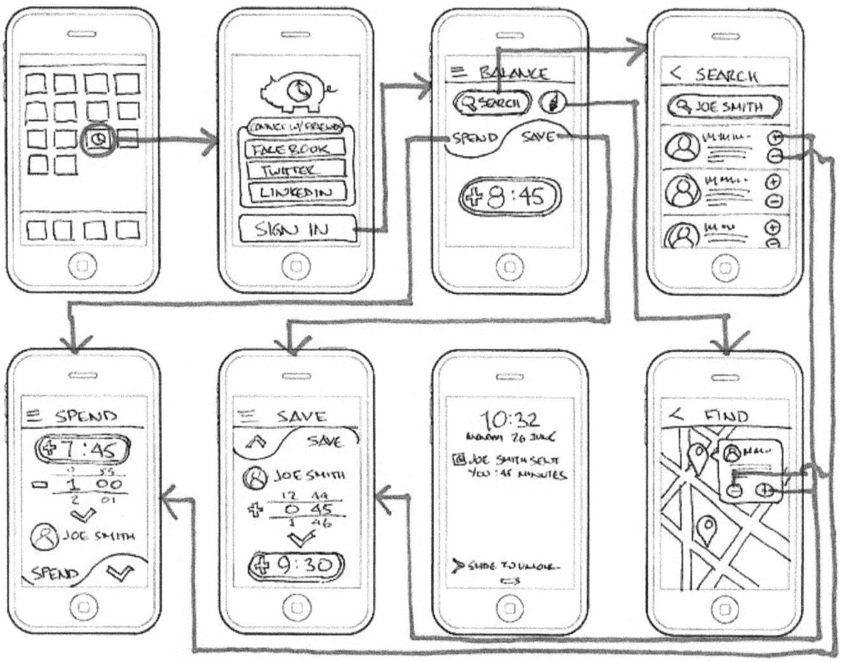

Fig. 2.4 Sketching: The mobile banking app team conducts an ideation session, generating ideas such as voice-activated commands, personalized spending trackers, interactive tutorials on financial literacy, and gamified savings features.

Prototype

Prototyping involves transforming ideas into tangible representations. The goal is to create low-fidelity prototypes that can be quickly and inexpensively tested with users. Prototypes can be anything from simple sketches to interactive digital mock-ups.

The mobile banking app team creates a paper prototype with basic screens and features. They conduct usability tests with potential users, gathering feedback on navigation, layout, and overall user experience. This iterative process helps refine the design and identify areas for improvement.

Test

The final stage of design thinking involves testing the prototypes with users and gathering feedback. This feedback informs further iterations and improvements. The process is repeated until a refined solution is achieved.

Based on user feedback, the mobile banking app team makes iterative changes to the design, streamlining navigation, incorporating personalized features, simplifying the registration process, and enhancing the overall user experience.

The Purpose of Design Thinking

Design thinking serves a twofold purpose: solving specific problems and fostering a culture of innovation within organizations. By adopting a user-centric approach, organizations can develop products and services that truly resonate with their target audience, leading to increased customer satisfaction and loyalty.

The iterative nature of design thinking encourages teams to challenge assumptions, embrace ambiguity, and think creatively. This approach allows for rapid experimentation and testing of ideas, reducing the risk of investing significant resources in solutions that may not meet user needs. Through collaboration and interdisciplinary teamwork, design thinking fosters an inclusive environment that leverages diverse perspectives and expertise.

Moreover, design thinking extends beyond product development. It can be applied to various organizational challenges, such as improving internal processes, enhancing customer service experiences, and fostering a culture of innovation. By ingraining design thinking principles and practices into the fabric of an organization, it becomes a driver of continuous improvement and a catalyst for innovation.

The Double Diamond Process

The Double Diamond is a visual representation (Fig. 2.5) of the design thinking process, showcasing the divergent and convergent stages. It consists of four phases: Discover, Define, Develop, and Deliver. The Discover and Define phases correspond to the initial problem exploration, while the Develop and Deliver phases involve solution implementation.

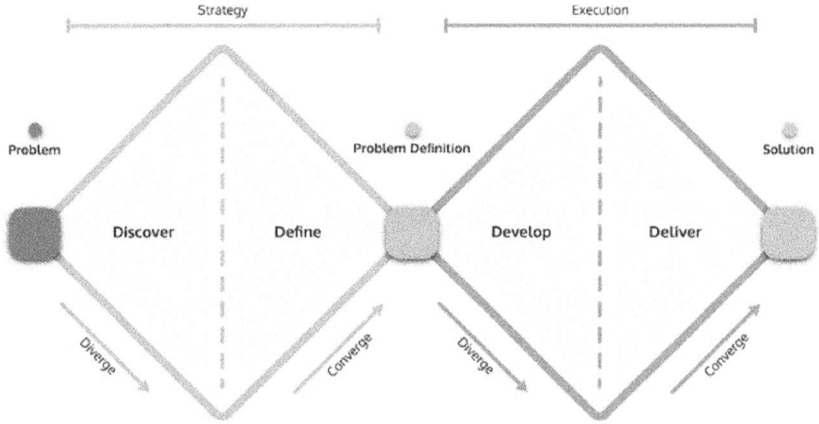

Fig. 2.5 Double Diamond is a visual representation

Let's revisit the team improving a company's customer service experience. They would go through the Discover phase by conducting user research, interviews, and analyzing customer feedback. In the Define phase, they would synthesize the findings and identify the main pain points or opportunities for improvement. The Develop phase would involve ideating and prototyping potential solutions, and the Deliver phase would encompass testing and implementing the chosen solution.

Design Thinking: A Non-Linear Process

We've outlined a direct and linear design thinking process (Fig. 2.6) here, in which one stage seemingly leads to the next with a logical conclusion at user testing. However, in practice, the process is carried out in a more flexible and non-linear fashion. For example, different groups within the design team may conduct more than one stage concurrently, or designers may collect information and prototype throughout each stage of the project to bring their ideas to life and visualize the problem solutions as they go. What's more, results from the Test stage may reveal new insights about users which lead to another brainstorming session (Ideate) or the development of new prototypes (Prototype).

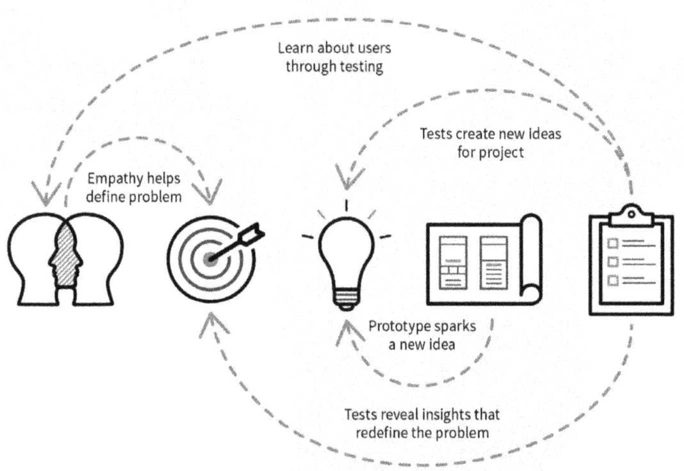

Fig. 2.6 Design Thinking: A Non-Linear Process

It is important to note the five stages of design thinking are not always sequential. They do not have to follow a specific order, and they can often occur in parallel or be repeated iteratively. The stages should be understood as different modes which contribute to the entire design project, rather than sequential steps.

The design thinking process should not be seen as a concrete and inflexible approach to design; the component stages identified should serve as a guide to the activities you carry out. The stages might be switched, conducted concurrently or repeated several times to gain the most informative insights about your users, expand the solution space and hone in on innovative solutions.

This is one of the main benefits of the five-stage model. Knowledge acquired in the latter stages of the process can inform repeats of earlier stages. Information is continually used to inform the understanding of the problem and solution spaces, and to redefine the problem itself. This creates a perpetual loop, in which the designers continue to gain new insights, develop new ways to view the product (or service) and its possible uses and develop a far more profound understanding of their real users and the problems they face.

The Benefits of Design Thinking

Design thinking offers numerous benefits to individuals, teams, and organizations. By embracing design thinking, you can:

- Understand the Unmet Needs of Users: Design thinking helps you gain a deep understanding of users' needs, allowing you to develop products and services that truly address their pain points and aspirations.
- Reduce Risk in Innovation: The iterative nature of design thinking allows for early and frequent testing and feedback. This reduces the risk associated with launching new ideas, products, and services, as potential issues can be identified and addressed early in the process.
- Generate Revolutionary Solutions: Design thinking encourages thinking beyond incremental improvements and challenges the status quo. It fosters an environment where revolutionary ideas can be generated, leading to innovative and transformative solutions.
- Learn and Iterate Faster: Design thinking promotes a culture of continuous learning and iteration. By testing and gathering feedback early and often, design thinkers can quickly identify what works and what doesn't, allowing for faster iteration and improvement.

Making use of these information will help designing easy for you, following these stages you will get to understand how design thinking works and how to Empathise, Define, Ideate, Prototype,

Different Design Thinking Models

Double Diamond

The Double Diamond is a Design Thinking framework designed by the British Design Council. It was created by interviewing several leading design authorities about their processes.

Similar to the Stanford Design Thinking process, its steps are:

- Discover
- Define

- Develop
- Delivery

It's an incredibly effective framework for navigating ambiguous or complex design challenges. One fundamental tenet is the idea of diverging and converging thought, where we go through a process of going wide to explore before going narrow to define.

IDEO Design Thinking Process

IDEO – an agency co-founded by Stanford Professor David Kelley along with Tom Kelley – are well-respected Design Thinking practitioners that publishes ideas, tools, and techniques through IDEO U to help others learn and practice the process effectively. They emphasize that the design thinking approach isn't linear; its fluid. And although we depict the steps of the process in a linear sequence, in reality, we might go back and forth as we gather learnings throughout the process.

IDEO's Design Thinking Process is as follows:

- Frame a Question
- Gather Inspiration
- Generate Ideas
- Make Ideas Tangible
- Test to Learn
- Share the Story

Design thinking can unleash a whirlwind of creativity, taking you on an ever-evolving journey to the cutting edge. Through iterative cycles and backtracking between steps, possibilities are explored until a revolutionary new product or innovation emerges.

The MYB Design Cycle

The Design Cycle was developed to teach middle-year students how to apply the design process. It's a simple, structured problem solving approach that can be used in various fields.

The graphic (Fig. 2.7) explains the process best, but broadly the phases are:

- Inquiring and analyzing
- Developing a new idea
- Creating the solution
- Evaluating

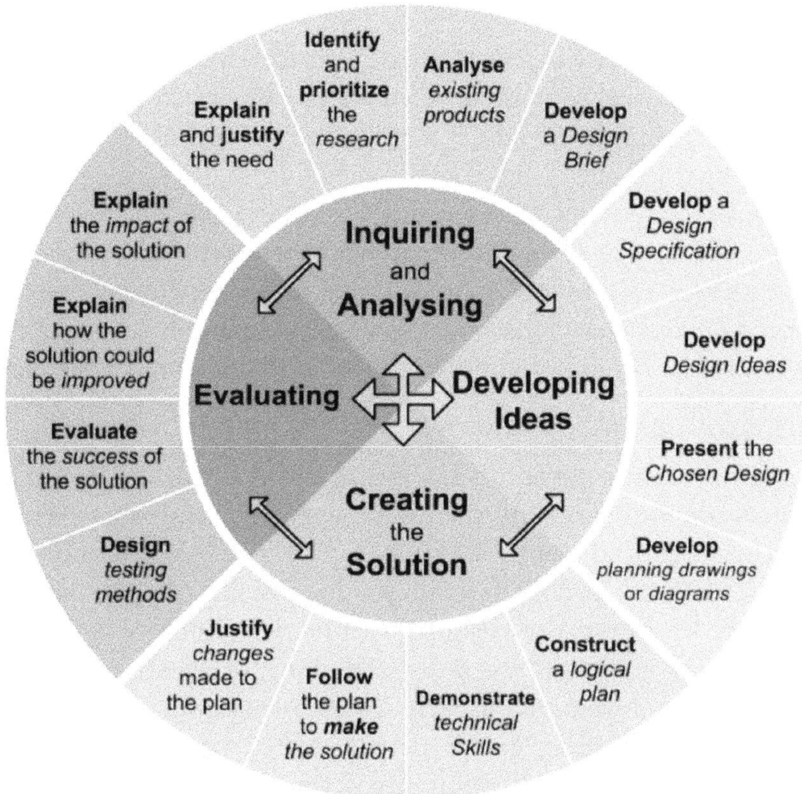

Fig. 2.7 The MYB Design Cycle

The Design Cycle (Fig. 2.7) is a step-by-step system combining research, problem solving, and collaboration in 4 critical phases broken down for easy implementation. From creating innovative products or features to tackling challenges in science, education, healthcare, and technology, this design process helps guide us in various areas.

Alternatives to Design Thinking

Analytical Thinking for Complex Technical Problems

Well suited to solving complex technical issues – The analytical approach to problem solving is analyzing a situation and finding the most effective method to tackle it. It considers all of the relevant information surrounding a problem, such as historical context and current phases, as well as any necessary changes that need to be implemented to reach an ideal solution. By breaking down the elements of a problem and looking at each component carefully, one can make educated decisions on the best course of action. This analytical approach allows us to take on a wide range of issues confidently and efficiently, which is an invaluable asset in today's ever-changing world. Understanding this method of thought can give us the mental agility needed to tackle any obstacle standing in our way.

Lean Startup for Building and Validating MVPs

A popular method within the startup community: The Lean Startup method is an approach for entrepreneurs and business owners to get their businesses off the ground and rapidly produce a new innovation. Many companies have succeeded in using this approach by launching a minimally viable product that has been continuously tested and modified with customer feedback as they go along. This lets entrepreneurs receive real-time customer feedback, which helps them validate their ideas before investing in complex development processes. The Lean Startup method encourages "failing fast" so that valuable learning can be quickly implemented into the product to improve its effectiveness and customer impact.

Design Sprint for Continous Improvement of Digital Products

The Design Sprint is useful in UX Design and Product Design to quickly design, prototype, and test new products, services, and ideas. This synthesis of disciplines ensures that teams stay focused on the essential objectives while rapidly solving complex problems in days, not weeks. As popularized by Jake Knapp and Google Ventures, the Design Sprint model combines agile development principles with fresh insights into design thinking to create an accelerated yet collaborative product development cycle. Every Design Sprint involves the same core steps: Understand, Define, Sketch, Decide, Prototype and Test. Together these are the foundation of turning intuition into actionable solutions that can be used to iterate and improve existing products.

RELATIONSHIP BETWEEN UX AND DESIGN THINKING

Over the past decade, Digital Services have become an increasingly common part of our daily lives, often augmenting or even replacing, traditional channels with digital ones. Think about the last time you visited a bank branch, paid an electricity bill over the phone, or booked your plane ticket at a high street travel agency. How many of those experiences are now predominantly digital?

Today with over two billion people using smart devices, Digital Services provide customers increased levels of convenience and businesses with opportunities to deliver better customer experiences at a significantly reduced cost.

These days, pure digital companies effectively deliver meaningful digital service experiences. Companies like Apple have used those learnings to improve their physical service experience through initiatives like the Apple Store.

The rise of digital services

By comparison, many traditional businesses have struggled to modernise their in-store or phone services, and are using digital only as a self-service cost cutting exercise, rather than a means to craft a deeper and more intimate service experience.

Brands like Monzo and Starling are examples of companies offering purely digital banking experiences, replacing traditional touchpoints such as branches and phone support. Companies such as Uber, Airbnb and Zipcar deliver physical services (taxis, hotel rooms and car hire) in a digital first way, eschewing customer service centres, check-in desks and car rental depots in favour of digital equivalents.

Exploring the shared space

The exact definition of Service Design has been widely debated due to its fluffy edges that border on multiple disciplines. Common themes within definitions include adopting a holistic approach to the design of interactions that occur throughout the customer journey, taking into consideration business departments, actors, platforms and touchpoints.

With technology being pivotal to the digital service's value proposition, digital touchpoints become a much more important part of the overall service experience and in some situations, replacing the entire service experience. So much so that it is increasing helpful for Service Designers to have a deep understanding of UX principles, methods, and practices when approaching Digital Service projects.

Don Norman defined UX Design as "encompassing all aspects of the end -user's interaction with the company, its services, and its products" whereas recent definitions point to UX Design as the design of an "experience between a person and a single touch point".

UX Design & Service Design Comparison.

When designing digital products and services, UX designers are increasingly required to adopt a holistic approach to their work. Often this approach requires digging deeper into the wider context of the problem and how the solution may relate to the wider organisation, its business goals and the end-to-end customer experience.

A Wider Comparison

Good UX designers are always looking at the context. That inevitably means stepping outside the screen to understand how their products are being used in the real world. Often with digital products and services, the wider context of the project has been neglected, requiring UX designers to take on this service component out of necessity. Similarly, Service Designers often need to delve into the details of a digital touch-point to create meaningful specifications that can be handed over to a UX designer. With the rise of Digital Services, the boundaries between the disciplines and the role of the designer are becoming increasingly blurred. As Service Design becomes more digitally focused and UX projects become more and more service oriented, a shared space between the disciplines emerges.

Importance of Design Thinking in UX

Importance of Design Thinking can be understood under following points:

- **User-Centric Approach:** Design Thinking puts the user at the center of the design process. By emphasizing empathy and understanding the user's needs, motivations, and pain points, UX designers can create solutions that genuinely solve pain points of their target audience. This user centric approach increases the likelihood of developing better and more engaging user experiences.
- **Design Innovation:** Design Thinking encourages divergent thinking and creative problem solving. By breaking free from traditional constraints and exploring unconventional ideas, UX designers are able to come up with innovative solutions that set their products or services apart from the competition. This innovative mindset is crucial in today's rapidly evolving design industry.
- **Iterative Experimentation:** The iterative nature of Design Thinking allows UX designers to rapidly prototype and test their ideas with users. This continuous feedback loop enables them to identify and address issues early in the design process that could later have costed a lot of resources and time, this ultimately leads to more refined and user-friendly solutions.
- **Collaboration:** Design Thinking promotes collaboration across different disciplines and functional areas. By bringing together diverse perspectives and expertise, UX designers can gain a a better understanding of the problem and develop better solutions that address multiple aspects of the user experience.
- **Solving Complex Problems:** Many modern day challenges in UX design involve complex and interconnected problems that require a deep understanding of human behavior, emotions, and motivations. Design Thinking provides UX designers the tools and mindset to tackle these complex challenges, enabling them to develop innovative solutions that meet the user's needs while addressing the underlying complexities of design.

Best Practices

Best Practices for Integrating Design Thinking in UX are as follows:

- **Empathy:** Encourage your team to put the user in the center of the design by the help of observation, interviews, and direct engagement. This empathetic understanding is crucial for identifying the real problems and creating meaningful solutions.

- **Embrace Diverse Perspectives:** Involve cross functional teams with diverse backgrounds and expertise in the Design Thinking process. This diversity of perspectives can lead to more creative and comprehensive solutions.
- **Ideation and Experimentation:** Create an environment that promotes divergent thinking and encourages calculated risks. Encourage your team to explore unconventional ideas and experiment with rapid prototyping and iterative testing.
- **Engage Users Early and Often:** Involve users throughout the Design Thinking process, from empathy building to prototype testing. Their insights and feedback can help in validating assumptions and refining the solutions that you and your team come up with.
- **Flexible Approach:** Design Thinking thrives in an agile and flexible environment. Be prepared to pivot and adapt your solutions based on user feedback and changing market conditions.
- **Learn from failure:** Learn to take your failures as opportunities for learning and growth. Encourage your team to analyze and learn from unsuccessful experiments, as these lessons can lead to improved solutions in the future.

Conclusion

By embracing a human centric, iterative, and collaborative approach to problem-solving, UX designers can create innovative and user-friendly solutions that truly resonate with their target audiences. Design Thinking is a systematic and user-centric approach to problem solving that focuses on empathy, creativity, and iterative experimentation for coming up with a user friendly and user centered design. It is a mindset and a process that encourages designers to immerse themselves in the user's world, understand their needs, and develop innovative solutions that address those needs in a meaningful way.

CHAPTER-3

USER-CENTERED DESIGN (UCD)

User-centered design (UCD) is a process that focuses on the needs of users throughout the design process, from the beginning to launch. UCD involves research and design techniques to create products that are accessible and usable. The concept of designing products based on user needs was introduced in 1986 by Donald A. Norman and Stephen W. Draper in their book User-Centered System Design: New Perspectives on Human-Computer Interaction.

User-centered design (UCD) is an iterative design process in which designers focus on the users and their needs in each phase of the design process. In UCD, design teams involve users throughout the design process via a variety of research and design techniques, to create highly usable and accessible products for them.

In UCD, design teams involve users throughout the design process via a variety of research and design techniques, to create highly usable and accessible products for them.

Example: When a product team develops digital products, it takes into account the user's requirements, objectives, and feedback. Satisfying users' needs and wants becomes a priority, and every design decision is evaluated in the context of whether it delivers value to the users. The user-centered design gives you a way of adding an emotional impact to your products.

USER-CENTERED DESIGN PRINCIPLES:

User-centered design is based on a few fundamental principles that can be applied to the product design process:

- Users are involved in the design process from the very beginning. Critical design decisions are evaluated based on how they work for end-users.

- Importance of requirement clarification. The product team always tries to align business requirements with users' needs.
- Introducing user feedback loop in the product life cycle. The product team collects and analyzes feedback from users regularly. This information helps the team to make more user-focused decisions.
- Iterative design process. The product team constantly works on improving user experience; it introduces changes gradually as it gains more understanding about its target audience.

The Essential Elements of User-Centered Design

- **Visibility:** Users should be able to see from the beginning what they can do with the product, what is it about, and how they can use it.
- **Accessibility:** Users should be able to find information easily and quickly. They should be offered various ways to find information for example calls action buttons, search options, menu, etc.
- **Legibility:** Text should be easy to read. As simple as that.
- **Language:** Short sentences are preferred here. The easier the phrase and the words, the better.

Focus areas of UCD

- Identify the primary users of the product.
- Why they will use the product?
- What are their requirements?
- Under what environment they will use it?
- Collect information about their users' needs.

Phases of UCD

The following are the general phases of the UCD process (Fig. 3.1):

- **Specify the context of use:** Identify the people who will use the product, what they will use it for, and under what conditions they will use it.
- **Specify requirements:** Identify any business requirements or user goals that must be met for the product to be successful.
- **Create design solutions:** This part of the process may be done in stages, building from a rough concept to a complete design.
- **Evaluate designs:** Evaluation – ideally through usability testing with actual users – is as integral as quality testing is to good software development.

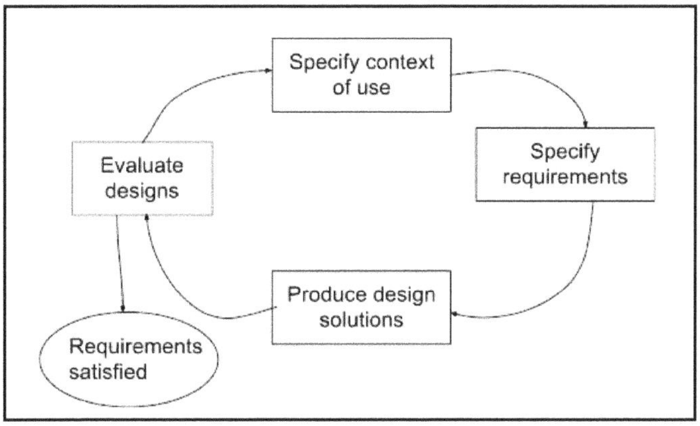

Fig. 3.1 Phases of UCD

Implementation of the UCD process

Generally, the UCD approach involves 4 steps, which typically start from understanding the context of the problem and evaluating the designs. Let's understand each step in detail:

- **Understanding context of use:** The primary step is to understand the problem as well the context in which the product that is being designed later would be used. How the product would solve the problem. Learning about the users and their problems would mark the first step of the user-centered design process.
- **Specifying user requirements:** Once the big picture is clear about what is the problem and what is to be designed, now it's time to understand the requirements that need to be fulfilled to make the product succeed. What users want and expect from the product is essential to be known. Through surveys and user interviews, designers would get to know about the key user's requirements. Based on the user requirement, a design strategy is created. This is a plan of how to proceed further looking into all the nitty-gritty of the whole process.
- **Ideating and designing solution:** After all the data is collected and evaluated, the team proceeds to work on the ideation. New ideas are explored, discussed, and carried out along with cross-functional teams to check on the feasibility and timelines. This way collaboration and communication help keep everyone aligned on the work. A lot of different ideas are explored and based on alignment and discussion, a single idea is taken up for further design.
- **Evaluation against Requirements:** Evaluation is of utmost importance to check whether the app/product is fulfilling the requirement. A usability test is also carried out with the user to check the:

- Does the product/app meet user requirement
- Does the app have the expected behavior
- Is everything aligned with the user's mental model
- Is the user able to navigate and interact with the app/product

ISO Standard Definition of UCD

ISO stands for International Organisation for Standards, which released ISO - 13407 in 1999 that is for UCD. According to ISO standards UCD is defined as - "The active involvement of the user and a clear understanding of the user and task requirement along with an appropriate allocation of functions between user and technology carried out as the iteration of design solution known as multi-disciplinary design." As per the current standard and update of the ISO standard definition now also focuses on - user understanding, user tasks, and environments, validation testing with users,s and developing design while encompassing the whole user experience.

ISO standard definition is something that is now being used as a benchmarking definition to follow the UCD approach. To understand every element of the ISO standard definition, let's look into these elements in detail.

Element of UCD-based on ISO Standard

From the ISO standard definition, there are 7 different elements around which the whole UCD revolves. Understanding each step would help designers to use the UCD approach more appropriately and positively.

1. Active Involvement of User

It says to have active user involvement during the design process. Taking user input from the beginning, and using those inputs to validate the design would make the design robust and easier for users to relate with.

Active involvement means when you involve users in an iterative, interactive process at every single stage of the complete design cycle.

While planning to actively involve users in the process, keep in mind:

- **Technique:** By technique, here it means - User interviews, data gathering, usability testing, surveys, and contextual inquiry. All these techniques could be used to get user inputs during the complete design process.
- **Purpose:** By purpose, it means to say when are we collecting data and for what. Such as - collecting data to understand users' needs, behavior, and expectations, as well as collecting user data both quantitative and qualitative data collected to measure usability criteria.

- **Stage of Design Cycle:** At what stage of the design cycle are you going to apply a certain technique to collect data for a particular purpose? Like the midpoint of the design cycle, the start of the process, or the end of the process.

Combining all three 3 steps, the designer first selects a technique(i.e. User interview) for the purpose(i.e. collecting user's needs and expectation data) during the stage(i.e. beginning of the process).

2. Clear Understanding of User Requirements, Tasks, and Environment

Getting a clear understanding of the user's requirements, what task they'll perform to meet those requirements and in what environment will those tasks be performed. All this information would come from the previous step, which is purely dedicated to getting the user information through different techniques.

- **Requirement:** This would include all the key needs of the user, for which they'll use the product. Knowing the requirement would help designers to think is a way of solving the core issue. Key needs of the user when catered properly, would increase the chances of users sticking to the app and the app being more useful to them.
- **Task:** Task Bucks included all the core tasks that a user would be performing to meet the end goal. For example, a user needs to shop for a product, to do so he/she needs to select the product, add it to the cart, proceed to buy, select an address, and make the payment. All these tasks would fall under the bucket of core tasks required to be performed to achieve the end goal.
- **Environment:** Getting to know about the environment is also an important input for designers. Knowing where the user would perform core key actions would add a lot of value to the end product. For example, Google Maps – users would mainly use maps while on the go. So it is very important to understand how users would manage the app, the vehicle, and the directions at the same time. Showing only the relevant element on the interface is crucial, other than too much information would hinder the chance of users to effectively use the app. Therefore only directions are shown on the app while the user is in the navigation mode.

3. Allocation of function between User and Technology

By saying the appropriate allocation of function, it means to say be mindful of the fact that what actions would be best suitable to be performed by whom?

Designers should evaluate what action is better performed by whom, this would avoid the clash between machine and human interaction. For example: While using Microsoft team, the best thing a user could do is set his/her calendar as per how they want their day to be. What a machine or technology could do better is find a common slot for meetings. Now if we compare both scenarios and reverse them concerning who is doing it, it would be messy. Why?

Because a machine can't plan your day, better than you. Also, you can't sit and find a free slot for a meeting when inviting 100 people to the meeting.

This is what the allocation of function between user and technology meets, it seems a small point but is very crucial for designers to deeply understand.

4. Iteration of Design Solution

Almost every designer is aware of the fact that design is an iterative process. The whole idea seems very easy but when it comes to implementing the whole iteration concept it is very difficult. Picking the right requirements, flaws to work on, updates to be made and features/functionality to be added before getting started with iteration would be very helpful as it will save a lot of time and effort. Getting started with iteration without anything to work on would waste a lot of time. Including the stakeholders and users before and after each iteration would also help validate the changes.

5. Validation Testing with User

Validation of the designs would be based on the iteration carried out till now. Every iteration should be thorough. Validation includes testing with low-fidelity, high-fidelity as well as the final designs. Whenever the team thinks, iteration and work are 80% done, try to start validating what has been done already.

Always take a go-ahead from your actual user – not through a word but the way they interact with the app would be a sign for you to either work more on the same design as an iteration or that it for the final updates before launching.

6. Multi-Disciplinary Design

By saying a multi-disciplinary design, it means including people from all the other dependent cross-functional teams as well. Including teams that are co-dependent would add a lot of value to the product. Before launching, whenever designs are tested, add developer and product to check the feasibility and accessibility of the feature. For example when thinking of a new feature, have a word with developers concerning time, effort, and the possibility of having that feature in the product.

Cross-functional teams that the designer should be actively involved in during the design process are:

- Engineering
- Visual/communication design
- Marketing & Brand
- Operations

- Copywriters
- Content strategist

Invlving the team in the process at the right time would help designers explore crucial use cases, brand identity, and market standards before launching the product.

7. Encompasses the Whole User Experience

Designing while keeping in mind the complete user experience involves, encompassing all channels with which the user interacts. There are many channels of a product through which the user interacts, and by encompassing the whole user experience it means that there should be a maintained consistency for each channel.

For example, Amazon is a big brand that encompasses a lot of products like the Amazon shopping app, Amazon Music app, Amazon Prime Video, and Amazon Alexa, etc. All these products are different touch points with which the audience/user of Amazon interacts.

All these channels maintain consistency and one unique brand identity of Amazon. This is what a designer as well as the whole design team should think while working on products associated with a brand.

Importance of UCD

User-centered design is an approach that is important for all, not just the designer.

- For users, it is a chance to check whether a product can solve their problem and get them what they need.
- For designers, it is an approach that is used to put the user front and center, understand users' requirements, and work on a product to fulfill user needs.
- For developers, it determines the success or failure of the product based on how users are interacting with the app.
- For the product, it determines the product's market value based on metrics like conversion rates impressions, etc.
- For stakeholders, UCD saves time, cost, and effort.

INTEGRATING UCD INTO DESIGN THINKING

User-centered design

The term user-centered design was first coined in 1977 by computer scientist Rob Kling. It gained further attention and popularity as it was featured in Don Norman's books *User-Centered System Design: New Perspectives on Human-Computer Interaction* (1986) and *The Design of Everyday Things* (1988).

In short, user-centered design is an approach to design that puts users' needs front and center, and follows an iterative design process that focuses on the user's needs every step of the way. While there is some focus on the requirements of the company, a majority of design decisions are made with the user's expectations and needs at the forefront. The main goal of UCD is to create a product that is highly desirable and functional to the user.

There are five key principles that guide user-centered design and four main steps that make up the UCD process.

The main principles of UCD are:

- Early involvement of end-users
- A clear understanding of the context of use and user needs
- Regular collection, analysis, and incorporation of user feedback
- Employing a user-centric approach to product development and delivery procedures
- Utilizing an iterative design process with a continual goal to improve user experience

Fig. 3.2 UCD process

The four steps of the UCD process (Fig. 3.2) are as follows:

- **Understand the user and context of use:** This first step is all about researching your users' behaviors, problems, and goals as well as how they might interact with your product.
- **Specify user and business requirements:** Here, you establish why the product is beneficial for both the users and the business, and find metrics to measure what success looks like to the company and the users.
- **Create design solutions:** Step three is all about storyboarding, journey mapping, wireframing, designing mockups and user flows, testing out different UI elements, as well as determining effective information architecture to design a product that solves users' problems.
- **Evaluate designs:** Finally, you conduct usability testing (preferably with actual users) to test the effectiveness of preliminary designs, and determine what is working well and what needs improvement

Once the UCD process has been completed, there's usually a need for multiple rounds of iteration until the design is complete and ready for release.

Design thinking

Design was first thought of as a science or way of thinking by Nobel Prize laureate Herbert A. Simon in 1969. This concept has been accepted and expanded upon widely by a variety of designers, scholars, and practitioners over the years, but IDEO has been credited with bringing design thinking into the mainstream—they even coined their own terminology and step-by-step process.

Design thinking is a creative approach to innovation and problem-solving that takes design perspectives and processes and applies them to problems that designers don't typically encounter.

According to IDEO, design thinking looks for solutions to "wicked" (or complex) problems that are feasible (technologically possible), desirable (to the end user), and viable (cost-effective to the business).

Design thinking is an iterative process consisting of five steps (Fig. 3.3):

- **Empathize:** Develop an understanding of the challenges the system/users are facing through observation (ie. interviews, surveys, etc.).
- **Define:** Analyze data and clearly articulate the problem you want to solve.
- **Ideate:** Brainstorm a large quantity of diverse ideas that could serve as potential solutions to the problem.
- **Prototype:** Build a simulation of your ideas as prototypes to test as possible solutions.
- **Test:** Share and test the prototype with end-users for assessment then implement feedback into rapid iteration.

Design thinking is a non-traditional approach to problem solving and can be applied to a variety of industries to help strengthen their services, products, policies, or design processes. It can be used to develop solutions for end-users but can also help organizations reinforce innovation, boost creativity, and implement new strategies and concepts for better overall function.

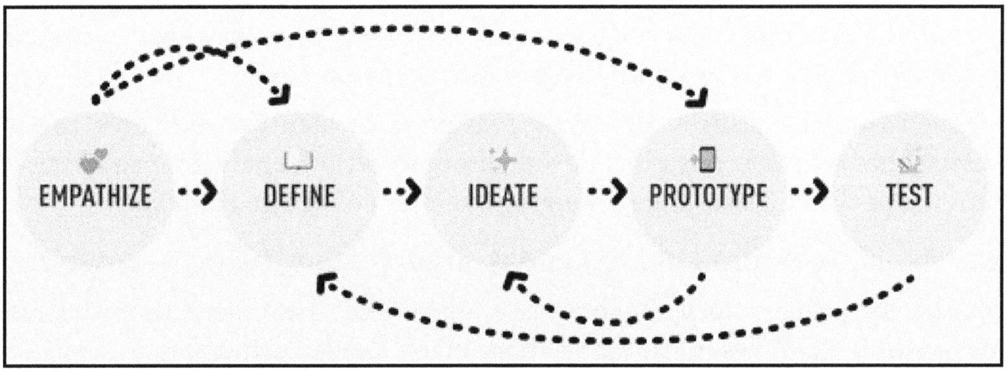

Fig. Five Stage Design thinking iterative process

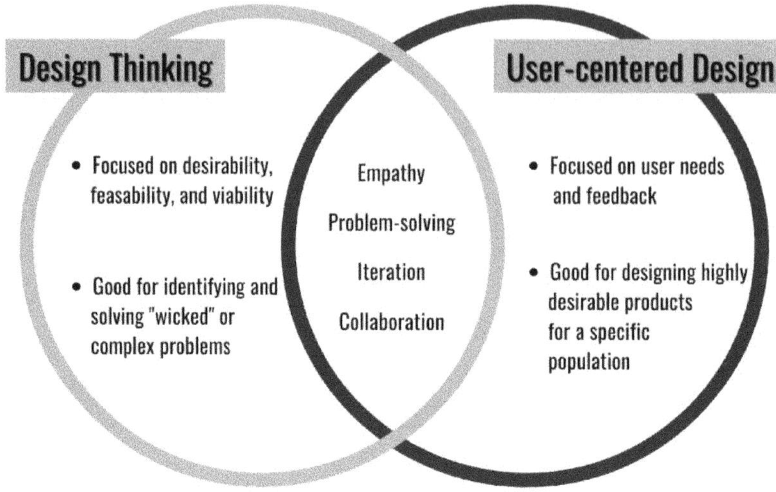

Fig. 3.4 Differences between user-centered design and design thinking

Differences between user-centered design and design thinking (Fig. 3.4)

Since user-centered design and design thinking both help find solutions to people's problems, you may be wondering what the big differences between these two design methods are. While the steps and general mindset of each are quite similar, the most notable difference is their primary focus.

User-centered design focuses on fostering deep empathy with the population you are designing for. The goal is to create solutions with users' needs and feedback at the forefront of all design decisions.

User-centered design is a great approach when you want to design a highly desirable product for a specific audience.In the UCD process, the user is the focus from first ideation to development and release. Check out these great examples of user-centered design.

While design thinking also requires great knowledge of the user, it also takes technological feasibility and business goals into consideration. This is a method that can be applied to more than just product development.

Design thinking utilizes abductive reasoning to identify and solve complex problems that may affect product design or organizational policies, processes, and function. Check out these game-changing examples of design thinking.

What do user-centered design and design thinking have in common?

While the primary focus of these two approaches are indeed different, user-centered design and design thinking share many similar principles and concepts. Let's take a look at what these design methods have in common.

Empathy

Empathy is key for UX designers. The ability to feel for your users and understand their behaviors as well as the challenges they face is a crucial part of any design process. So, whether you are using UCD to create a stellar mobile app or design thinking to revamp employee training, you'll need to have great awareness of the population you are designing for and what their needs are.

Problem-solving

Both UCD and DT view problems as opportunities for improvement. Each method takes an optimistic approach to problem-solving and uses structure, action, and design to take the issue at hand and turn it into a positive experience for both the company and their users.

Iteration

The process for both UCD and DT is a cyclical one that relies on learning from mistakes and incorporating user feedback into future designs. At the end of each cycle, designers assess what went well, what needs work, and how to use past failure to generate new and improved solutions.

Collaboration

Each design method works best when a team of people across organizational silos work together. Both approaches are optimized when designers, high level executives, developers, accountants, customer-facing employees, researchers, etc., all work together towards a common goal.

Part II: UX Research and Discovery

CHAPTER-4

USER RESEARCH METHODS

INTRODUCTION

Discovery: A preliminary phase in the UX-design process that involves researching the problem space, framing the problem(s) to be solved, and gathering enough evidence and initial direction on what to do next. Discoveries do not involve testing hypotheses or solutions.

Discoveries are crucial to setting design projects off in the right direction by focusing on the right problems and, consequently, building the right thing. They are often referred to as 'product discoveries' (although I'm not keen on this name because it can set the expectation that this phase is about discovering requirements for a given product).

In order to be effective, a discovery should be broad and technology- or solution-agnostic. When teams carry out a discovery on a product they have already decided to build, it no longer is a discovery, but, instead, it becomes a requirements-gathering exercise or a validation exercise where teams seek to confirm that their solution is the best. The discovery is off track when teams are asked "How do we make [insert name of solution] work for users?" or told to "Go find out what the user needs are for [insert name of solution]".

A discovery should start with a broad objective such as like: "Go find out about this problem, just how big it is, and what the opportunities might be."

Well-done discoveries ensure that any solutions proposed later are desirable to users, viable for the organization, and feasible with the technology made available.

A discovery should result in the following:

- **Understanding of users:** Through user research, the project team achieves an understanding of who the users are and how they are affected by a particular problem, as well as what they need, desire, and value from a solution (and why).
- **Understanding of the problems to be solved and of the opportunities:** Through investigative work, the team understands how and why the problem(s) occur, what effect the problem has on users, as well as on the organization. It understands the magnitude of the problem and opportunities for the organization, product, or service.
- **Shared vision:** During discovery, the team works with stakeholders to understand overarching business objectives and desired outcomes and get answers to questions such as 'what do we want to achieve?', or 'what does success look like?'. This approach, in turn, focuses the team on the problems (and later the solutions) that will have the greatest impact on that outcome. The team should also have an idea of what to measure going forward, to understand whether the solution is working towards the desired outcome.

A discovery starts broad and requires team members to investigate the context of the problem. The double-diamond diagram introduced by the UK Design Council — and reproduced below — illustrates the high-level process of a discovery: first, the team expands its understanding of the problem by researching its full context; armed with this knowledge, the team agrees on what the problem is, before moving to the next phase of ideating and testing in the *Develop* stage.

User Research Methods

There is a long, comprehensive list of UX design research methods employed by user researchers, but at its center is the user and how they think and behave—their needs and motivations. Typically, UX research does this through observation techniques, task analysis, and other feedback methodologies.

There are two main types of user research: quantitative (statistics: can be calculated and computed; focuses on numbers and mathematical calculations) and qualitative (insights: concerned with descriptions, which can be observed but cannot be computed).

- Quantitative research is primarily exploratory research and is used to quantify the problem by way of generating numerical data or data that can be transformed into usable statistics. Some common data collection methods include various forms of surveys – online surveys, paper surveys, mobile surveys and kiosk surveys, longitudinal studies, website interceptors, online polls, and systematic observations.

This user research method may also include analytics, such as Google Analytics.

Google Analytics is part of a suite of interconnected tools that help interpret data on your site's visitors including Data Studio, a powerful data-visualization tool, and Google Optimize, for running and analyzing dynamic A/B testing.

Quantitative data from analytics platforms should ideally be balanced with qualitative insights gathered from other UX testing methods, such as focus groups or usability testing. The analytical data will show patterns that may be useful for deciding what assumptions to test further.

- Qualitative user research is a direct assessment of behavior based on observation. It's about understanding people's beliefs and practices on their terms. It can involve several different methods including contextual observation, ethnographic studies, interviews, field studies, and moderated usability tests.

Top UX Research Methods and When to Use Them

Here are some examples of the types of user research performed at each phase of a project.

- **Card Sorting:** Allows users to group and sort a site's information into a logical structure that will typically drive navigation and the site's information architecture. This helps ensure that the site structure matches the way users think.
- **Contextual Interviews:** Enables the observation of users in their natural environment, giving you a better understanding of the way users work.
- **First Click Testing:** A testing method focused on navigation, which can be performed on a functioning website, a prototype, or a wireframe.
- **Focus Groups:** Moderated discussion with a group of users, allowing insight into user attitudes, ideas, and desires.
- **Heuristic Evaluation/Expert Review:** A group of usability experts evaluating a website against a list of established guidelines.
- **Interviews:** One-on-one discussions with users show how a particular user works. They enable you to get detailed information about a user's attitudes, desires, and experiences.
- **Parallel Design:** A design methodology that involves several designers pursuing the same effort simultaneously but independently, with the intention to combine the best aspects of each for the ultimate solution.
- **Personas:** The creation of a representative user based on available data and user interviews. Though the personal details of the persona may be fictional, the information used to create the user type is not.

- **Prototyping:** Allows the design team to explore ideas before implementing them by creating a mock-up of the site. A prototype can range from a paper mock-up to interactive HTML pages.
- **Surveys:** A series of questions asked to multiple users of your website that help you learn about the people who visit your site.
- **System Usability Scale (SUS):** SUS is a technology-independent ten-item scale for subjective evaluation of the usability.
- **Task Analysis:** Involves learning about user goals, including what users want to do on your website, and helps you understand the tasks that users will perform on your site.
- **Usability** Testing: Identifies user frustrations and problems with a site through one-on-one sessions where a "real-life" user performs tasks on the site being studied.
- **Use Cases:** Provide a description of how users use a particular feature of your website. They provide a detailed look at how users interact with the site, including the steps users take to accomplish each task.

SURVEYS, INTERVIEWS, AND FOCUS GROUPS

UX Surveys, or User Experience Surveys, gather information about users' feelings, thoughts, and behaviors related to UX design, product, or service. These online surveys form a part of the broader field of usability surveys. They focus on understanding how users interact with a system, application, or website to create a user-centered design.

Customer Effort Score Surveys (CES)

CES surveys assess how simple it is for customers to complete tasks with your company. Think of it like this: It's a score that tells you if using your product or getting help from your service team was a breeze or a struggle for the customer.

Many people value quick, straightforward answers to their questions. Time is precious, so spending less effort resolving issues is better. Ease of experience can be more revealing than overall satisfaction. Experts now use the Customer Effort Score.

For instance, after a customer service interaction, the question could be:

"How easy was resolving your issue with our customer support?"

- Very Difficult
- Difficult
- Moderate

- Easy
- Very Easy

This format helps companies understand the ease of interaction from the customer's viewpoint. It can be an excellent tool for identifying areas for improvement.

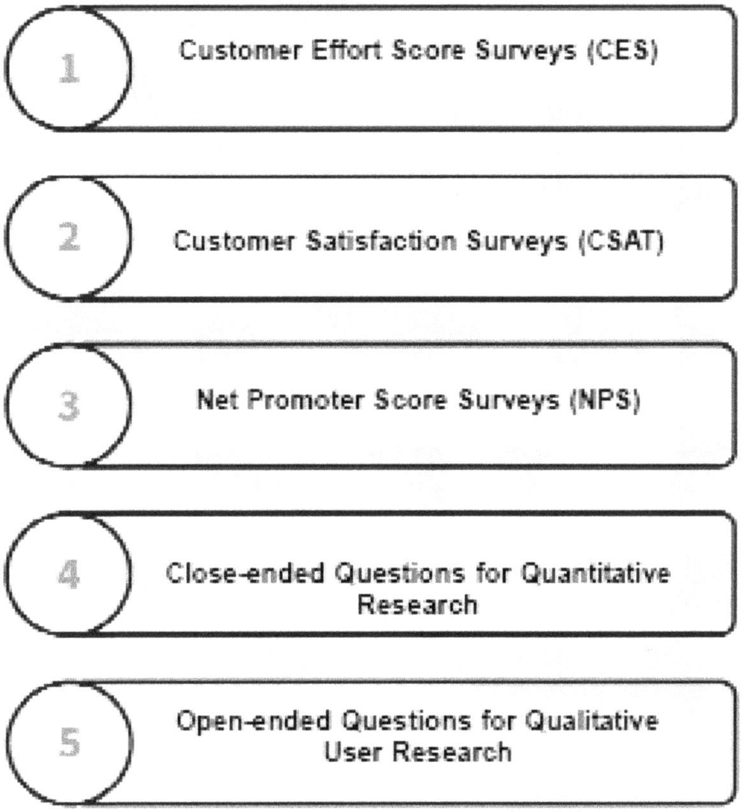

Fig. 4.1 Types of UX Surveys

Customer Satisfaction Surveys (CSAT)

A CSAT survey measures how happy customers are with your company.

- The main question is, "How satisfied are you with our service?"
- Answers range from 1, meaning "very dissatisfied," to 5, indicating "very satisfied."

CSAT surveys focus on individual interactions, like purchasing or using customer support. They use numeric scales to track satisfaction levels over time. These surveys help you understand your customers' needs and pinpoint issues with your products or services. They also allow you to categorize customers based on their satisfaction levels, which helps with targeted improvements.

Net Promoter Score Surveys (NPS)

NPS surveys are simple and quick since they use just one question: "On a scale from 0 to 10, how likely are you to recommend this product/company to a friend or colleague?". Based on the score, you can do respondent segmentation into one of three categories:

- **Promoters** (Score 9-10): These are your biggest fans, and they are likely to recommend your product.
- **Passives** (Score 7-8): These folks find your product/service satisfactory but could easily switch to competitors.
- **Detractors** (Score 0-6): These unhappy customers could harm your brand through negative word-of-mouth.

You can calculate the NPS score by subtracting the Detractors' percentage from the Promoters'. This gives a snapshot of customer loyalty and areas for improvement.

Close-ended Questions for Quantitative Research

Well-designed, close-ended questions are easy to answer. Users pick from predefined options like checkboxes, scales, or radio buttons. These surveys are suitable for gathering data. You'll see these in exit surveys asking users about their shopping experience. The answers provide actionable data, like customer preferences or standard problems.

Get more insights on quantitative research in this course on Data-driven Design.

The options could be:

- Very Satisfied
- Satisfied
- Neutral
- Dissatisfied
- Very Dissatisfied

Here, users don't need to type out their thoughts. They select an option that best describes their feelings. It's quick for the user and easy for the company to analyze.

While closed-ended questions offer fixed options for quick responses, open-ended questions allow for more detailed, free-form answers. These questions ask for written responses. They dig deeper into how users feel and what they expect.

It may take more time to analyze the responses you gather from this type of survey. But they're valuable because they offer nuanced insights.

For example, questions like "What feature do you wish we had?" can lead to ideas for product enhancements that meet users' needs.

When and Why Should One Conduct a UX Survey?

Conducting a UX survey is a strategic decision to understand various aspects of user interaction with a product or service. Here are vital scenarios and reasons for implementing them:

1. Feature Evaluation and Enhancement

You may find UX surveys better suited to assess existing products than development ones. These surveys can gather insights on how well your target audience receives a feature or service. Feedback from such surveys can guide adjustments or additions to your product.

For instance, if customers believe an existing feature lacks functionality, you can focus on enhancing it. UX surveys offer valuable data to refine a product to better align with customer needs and expectations.

2. Identifying Pain Points

Spotting pain points is essential for creating a user-friendly experience. UX surveys provide direct feedback from users about what's troubling them. These could be issues you're unaware of that make the customer experience less enjoyable or efficient.

For example, users might point out that they find your checkout process too complicated or that they have trouble finding specific information on your website. These insights are like gold; they give you specific areas to focus your improvement efforts. Addressing these issues helps you fix problems and show users you value and act upon their feedback.

3. Assessing Customer Satisfaction

Customer satisfaction is crucial for any business. A well-timed UX survey can gauge how well you meet customer expectations after a critical interaction, such as a purchase or customer service call.

Positive feedback helps identify vital areas, while negative feedback highlights issues that need attention.

4. Evaluating Customer Loyalty

Long-term success hinges on customer loyalty. NPS surveys, a type of UX survey, help gauge this.

Identifying promoters, passives, and detractors can help you tailor customer retention and referral strategies. If you see a dip in loyalty scores, it's an alert to dig deeper into potential issues.

5. Journey Mapping

Journey mapping visually represents a user's interactions with your product or service. It tracks the entire experience, from the first touchpoint to the final interaction. A well-designed UX survey can provide insights at multiple stages of this journey.

For example, you can use CES surveys at various checkpoints to measure ease of use. Are customers finding it simple to navigate from one section of your website to another? CSAT surveys can check satisfaction at critical touchpoints like purchase or support.

Open-ended questions can offer qualitative insights into why users make specific choices. These answers fill gaps in the journey map that analytics data might lack.

6. During Major Transitions or Updates

If you're planning a significant change, such as a rebrand or major update, a UX survey becomes invaluable. It helps assess customer sentiment and expectations before you roll out the differences.

Collecting survey data allows for adjustments that align with customer needs. This way, you can reduce the risk of negative backlash.

7. Continuous Improvement

The need for improvement never stops. Regular UX surveys create a feedback loop to help you track user sentiment and performance metrics. They allow for ongoing adjustments based on real-world usage.

For example, if you notice a slight dip in satisfaction scores related to app usability, you can investigate and make adjustments before it becomes a significant issue.

Continuous improvement through regular UX surveys keeps your product aligned with users' needs and expectations. It helps you sustain your success.

UX Survey Best Practices from Experts

Conducting a UX survey requires careful planning and execution to achieve actionable insights. Here are five best practices from experts in the field:

1. Make it Quick

People value their time, and long surveys can deter participation. A quick and concise survey ensures that the participant remains engaged. Focus on the essential questions and remove any unnecessary ones.

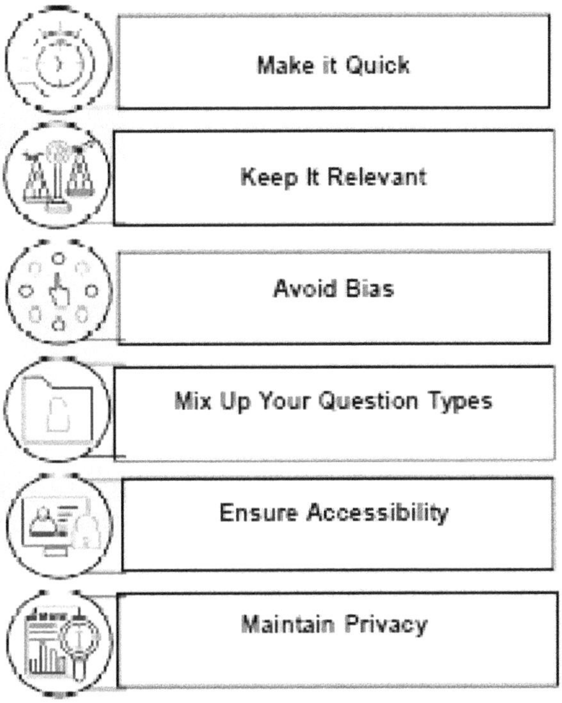

Fig. 4.2 Sic UX Survey Best Practices

Steps you can take:

- Limit your survey to 5-10 essential questions
- Use clear and concise language
- Preview the survey with a friend or colleague to get feedback on the length.

2. Keep It Relevant

Ensuring relevance in your survey questions is crucial for collecting valuable data. If questions stray off-topic, they risk irritating or baffling participants. Keep questions focused to ensure you get the insights for your goals.

Steps you can take:

- Define your target audience and goals before writing questions
- Avoid generic questions that don't relate to the product or service
- Focus on specific user experiences that align with your objectives.
- Provide not applicable/don't know answers for all closed questions.

3. Avoid Bias

Bias can distort the results and lead to misguided conclusions. The objective framing of questions helps in collecting unbiased responses. Some of the common biases include:

- **Question order bias**: Affects responses based on the sequence of questions.
- Confirmation bias: Only ask questions that affirm what you already believe.
- Primacy bias: People choose the first options given.
- Recency bias: People are more influenced by their last experience.
- Hindsight bias: Respondents say events were foreseeable.
- Assumption bias: Assumes respondents know certain information.
- Clustering bias: People see patterns where none exist.

Steps you can take:

- Avoid leading questions
- Use neutral language
- Consider asking an expert to review your questions for potential bias
- Test the survey on a small group before launching it.

4. Mix Up Your Question Types

While multiple-choice and rating scales excel at gathering numerical data, open-ended questions offer rich, qualitative insights. The blend can give you a more comprehensive view of customer sentiment.

Steps you can take:

- Use a mixture of types of questions according to the information you need
- Utilize open-ended questions for in-depth insights and multiple-choice for quick feedback
- Consider using scale questions to gauge user satisfaction or preferences

5. Ensure Accessibility

Making your survey **accessible** helps you capture a wide range of perspectives. If you create an accessible survey for everyone, including those with reduced abilities, you'll get a more complete and diverse set of insights. This comprehensive view can enhance the quality of your data and decision-making.

Steps you can take:

- Utilize easy-to-read fonts and adequate color contrast
- Provide alternative text for images
- Ensure that users can navigate the survey using keyboard controls
- Test the survey's accessibility features
- Avoid complex layouts and matrix-style questions

6. Maintain Privacy

Prioritizing participants' privacy is critical to building trust. When people feel confident that their data is safe, they're more likely to engage fully in your survey. A strong privacy policy meets legal standards and boosts participation rates. It enriches the quality of your insights.

Steps you can take:

- State your privacy policy at the start of the survey
- Use secure platforms for conducting the survey
- Assure participants that their responses will remain confidential
- Put sensitive or personal questions towards the end

Following these best practices, you can make UX surveys effective for gathering insights and improving the user experience. The actionable steps outlined above make creating an engaging, unbiased, and insightful survey possible.

The Ultimate Guide to Conduct a UX Survey

Conducting UX surveys is essential for understanding user interaction with your product. Follow these steps to design, distribute, and analyze surveys for actionable insights.

Step 1: Define Your Objectives

Defining clear objectives sets the stage for a successful UX survey. It helps you understand the key insights you are seeking. To zero in on what you're aiming to discover, consider these questions:

- **What is the main goal?** Understand if you want to measure user satisfaction or you want to focus on something else.
- **Which user behaviors are relevant?** Is the survey targeting frequent users, new users, or both?
- **What are the key metrics?** Do you want to look at completion rates, time spent, or other indicators?
- **New feature opinions:** Are you seeking input on new rolled-out features?
- **Pain points:** Are you trying to identify user frustrations and roadblocks?

Clarity in the objectives will guide every next step and ensure you align the results with your project goals. Well-defined goals will streamline the survey's structure and help craft relevant questions. The sharper focus also helps in analyzing the data you collect later on.

Step 2: Identify Your Target Audience

Identifying your target audience is a pivotal step in creating a survey. Here's why:

- **Product awareness:** Gauge how much your audience knows about your product. This shapes the depth and detail of questions.
- **Interests:** Understand what topics engage your audience. Use that insight to make questions interesting.
- **Language:** A professional audience may understand industry jargon. A general audience may not. Choose words carefully.
- **Region:** Geography can affect preferences and opinions. Localize questions if needed.

Understanding your target audience helps you write questions that they can relate to. It leads to higher engagement and more accurate data in user research. You can also create customer personas and a user journey around them.

Step 3: Craft Engaging Questions for the Questionnaire

Questions are the heart of your survey. Writing engaging, clear, and unbiased questions will provide the insights you need.

Step 4: Select a Tool For the UX Research Survey

Selecting the right tool for your UX survey is crucial for data collection and analysis. A Google Form provides a quicker way to get started with UX surveys. Here's why:

- **Ease of use:** Google Forms is user-friendly. Even if you're not tech-savvy, you can create a survey quickly.
- **Customization:** It offers various themes and allows question branching based on prior answers.
- **Integration:** Google Forms integrates with other Google services like Google Sheets for real-time data tracking.
- **Free:** For basic features, it's free of charge.
- **Data analysis:** Offers basic analytics like pie charts and bar graphs for quick insights.

You can also use specialized UX research tools like SurveyMonkey with more advanced features. Consider what your objectives and target audience need. Then, choose a tool that best serves those needs.

Step 5: Pilot the Survey

Pilot testing is an invaluable step in refining the UX survey. It provides an opportunity to uncover unforeseen issues with the survey design, questions, or technology.

Recruit participants in small numbers to test the survey. You can ask internal team members for help or contact professionals via LinkedIn. Use this test survey to understand their experience and make necessary adjustments. This can make the difference between a good survey and a great one. It helps iron out the kinks and ensures a smoother product experience for the primary audience.

Step 6: Launch the Survey

Launching the survey is more than making it live. It involves choosing the proper channels, timing, and even incentives. Promoting the survey ensures that it reaches your intended audience and encourages participation.

Consider the time of day, week, and even platform that aligns with your audience. You must plan every aspect of the launch to maximize participation.

Step 7: Analyze and Interpret the Results Data analysis transforms raw data into valuable insights. Use analytical tools to sort, filter, and interpret the data in the context of your objectives. Look for patterns and correlations but also for unexpected discoveries.

Your interpretation should lead to actionable insights that guide product or service improvement. This step transforms the effort of surveying real value for your project.

Step 8: Share Insights and Implement Changes

Finally, sharing your findings and implementing changes completes the process. Create comprehensive reports and engage stakeholders with the insights. Sharing fosters a shared understanding and sets the stage for informed decisions.

Plan and iterate on improvements based on the insights and use the learnings for continuous enhancement.

Each step is a building block that contributes to a successful and insightful user experience survey. Following this roadmap helps ensure that you create an engaging, relevant, and actionable UX research survey.

Interviews

User interviews (also called in-depth interviews) are 30- to 60-minute conversations with a single participant, in which a researcher asks questions about a topic of interest to gain a deeper understanding of participants' their attitudes, beliefs, desires and experiences.

Because interviews are live (either online or in-person), moderators are able to pick up on and respond to verbal and non-verbal cues, ask followup questions, and probe into topics more deeply. The candid, interactive nature of interviews often leads to serendipitous nuggets of insight that is hard to achieve by other methods.

This UX research method is a relatively quick and easy way to collect qualitative user data, and interviews pair well with just about any other research method—use them to follow up with usability testers, understand decisions made during card sorting studies, or flesh out feedback from ongoing listening surveys.

Types of user interviews

Generative interviews

Generative interviews are the most common type of user interview—they are the best way to answer the question "what don't I know?".

Like other generative or discovery methods, generative interviews are used early in the design and development process when you're looking for opportunities and ideas.

But these are not simply brainstorming sessions—interviews are structured conversations used to gather the information you need to answer clear, specific, and actionable research questions (even if, at this stage, your research questions are fairly broad).

Note that this chapter is primarily focused on generative interviews.

Contextual interviews

Contextual interviews (or contextual inquiry) are a special type of semi-structured interview that gives researchers insight into the context of use. These interviews take place in a user's environment (in *context*), which can make them feel more natural than interviews conducted in a lab or a staged virtual setting.

During contextual interviews, researchers ask participants questions while they complete tasks. This could involve shadowing a participant in their physical workplace, or moderating a usability testing session and asking questions as users interact with a site.

Continuous interviews

Continuous interviews are interviews you do on a regular basis by setting aside a chunk of time each week to connect with users. The goal of continuous interviewing is to keep you in touch with the people that matter most—your customers.

Continuous interviews are especially important for people who may not have regular research contact with users. They can also be used to keep teams in touch with users in between research projects.

What decisions do user interviews enable?

User interviews are used to inform vision decisions, allowing you to get clarity on a participant's big-picture beliefs and philosophies in order to determine a potential company, product, or service direction.

They can also be used to inform strategic decisions, allowing you to understand participants' current behaviors, expectations, or frustrations to determine a plan for a product or service.

What are the outputs?

Interviews generate a large amount of qualitative data, including detailed notes, transcripts, and videos. All of this data then needs to be synthesized into artifacts such as: personas, scenarios, thinking styles, or journey maps.

Because interviews capture the voice of the participant, they often provide powerful first-hand testimonials that support research-backed recommendations for improvement or change.

When to choose interviews

User interviews, as we mentioned, can be used throughout the product development cycle—from ideation to testing to post-launch listening.

Interviews are used:

- During initial discovery (before you have a product to test) to uncover broad patterns and themes relating to people's experiences, problems, behavior, and opinions.
- To test concepts and early ideas for possible solutions, before heavy design work gets underway.
- As a followup to usability tests or other evaluative methods, when it's important for you to have users articulate their decisions or experiences.
- After a product has launched, as a means of understanding evolving customer needs and expectations.

Why are user interviews so important?

We've mentioned contextual and continuous interviews, and have also explained how interviews can be used alongside methods during the testing and validation phase.

But the truth is user interviews *really* shine during discovery, when you still don't really know exactly the problem you're trying to solve or how. You might have a general idea about what a problem is, in which case generative interviews can help you refine your understanding. Or, you may simply want to develop a product in a given space, and you need to generate ideas about what problems exist before you can imagine their solutions.

Generative interviews are a fantastic method for uncovering opportunities for innovation and illuminating solutions to problems. And what's more, this method allows you to build up a nice bed of rich information about your user base from which you can pull ideas—both for brand new project builds or improvements to existing products.

Limitations and potential pitfalls of user interviews

Interviews, like every user research method, have their limitations and drawbacks. None of the potential pitfalls are big enough to outweigh the benefits, and most can be offset with mindful research design and planning.

Some things to be aware of:

- Interview data is largely self-reported. Although researchers can record observations about nonverbal responses and make inferences, the bulk of interview data comes straight from the participants' mouths. And participants, like all humans, are flawed and prone to misremember facts and experiences.
- Participants may leave out important information because they take it for granted that the interviewer already knows or is not interested in the minor details.
- Not every participant will share the same amount of information or be as forthcoming about their thoughts, feelings, and personal experiences. Some people are just more private or shy than others.
- Interviewing takes practice and skill. From writing effective, non-leading interview questions to moderating (but not leading) a conversation to qualitative analysis—a lot rests on the abilities and preparedness of the researcher

User interviews can help you answer just about any qualitative research question you can think of. Qualitative means it's answered with words, not numbers. So while user interviews can't tell you how many people bought your competitor's product, they can help you understand why people made that purchasing decision.

Typically, user interviews are just one piece of your research puzzle. For most projects, you'll want to supplement interview data with quantitative methods like product analytics, usability tests, or surveys.

How to plan and conduct user interviews

We covered how to set research goals and come up with effective research questions in depth in the Planning UX Research module—definitely give the chapters in that module a read if you're struggling to clarify your goals or uncover stakeholder needs. Very briefly...

Define your research goals

Talk to your stakeholders. Conduct stakeholder interviews to find out what it is they want to learn, what decisions they need to make, and what they hope to achieve. You won't be able to satisfy every stakeholder wish in one research project—look for the core, concrete goals that can practically be answered through UX research.

Ask yourself (and your stakeholders) the following questions:

- What do I want to know?
- How will I know when I've learned it?
- What company goals will this work support?
- What decisions will this research enable?

From there, you should be able to answer the key question: *What do I want to learn through user research?*

User interviews, like all the research methods discussed in this Field Guide, should start with a research question that is specific enough to know when you've found the answer, actionable in that you can do something about it, or practical in that you can reasonably answer it within the scope of a research project.

For example, you can't reasonably answer "Why don't people buy my product?" There could be many different reasons people aren't buying your product, and covering them all in one study wouldn't be practical or give you actionable results.

A better question may be, "Does my pricing page accurately answer my users questions?", or "Why do people in my target market choose X competitor over my product?".

Both of these questions could be answered with user interviews, and your team would have a clear path to action once the study was complete.

How to write an interview guide

Next, prepare a set of questions to ask participants. Having a list of questions helps keep the conversation flowing and serves as a good framework for notetaking and organizing data during and after the interview.

Some of these interview questions should spring directly from your core research question.

For example, if you want to learn how people research travel destinations, you could plan to say "Tell me about your last vacation" followed by the question "What prompted you to choose X as a destination?"

But remember: This is an interview, not an interrogation—a good moderator guide should also incorporate get-to-know-you questions, and leave room for spontaneous, open-ended responses and followup questions.

Tips for writing user interview questions

- **Ask questions that focus on past behavior vs. hypothetical scenarios.** "What would you do if..." can be a useful question, but in many cases, it's not as useful as "How did you handle it when...". It's a golden rule in job interviews, too: past behavior is the best indication of future behavior. So begin in real life scenarios where the subject has prior experience.
- **Ask open-ended questions.** Give your participants the opportunity to elaborate on their answers and take the conversation in new and interesting directions. Questions like "What is your opinion on Neoclassical architecture?" are much more likely to produce unexpected insights than closed questions such as "Do you agree that people built far too many dang columns between the late 18th-mid 20th century?" (That is also a leading question, which makes it doubly bad.)
- **Mitigate your own biases and presumptions.** Generative interviews can be glorious in how they meander and illuminate areas you might not have even considered. Still, generative interviews can suffer from interviewer assumptions or bias. To keep yourself accountable for your own presumptions and preconceived ideas, try to keep questions open-ended and aligned around words like how, why, and what. This will guide your interviewee toward their own answers, rather than leading or prompting them toward the areas where you want or expect them to go.
- **Be willing to have your assumptions challenged.** It helps to come in with some idea of what you think is true, but generative interviews are only useful if you allow ideas to be generated. So don't be overly attached to the rightness or wrongness of your preconceptions.
- **Create a list of possible followup questions.** Anticipate different responses to your key questions, and make a list of possible followup questions that will help you dig deeper and steer the conversation down interesting avenues. It can also be useful to think about how you'd keep the conversation flowing if a participant didn't have an answer to your question at all.
- **Be prepared for different conversation styles and personalities.** Some participants will talk your ear off—others might need to be asked several followup questions to elicit the same amount of information. Identify your most important interview questions (the must haves) to keep talkative

participants focused. To account for the reticent types, make sure you've prepared more questions than you think you'll have time to ask.

- **Avoid leading questions.** Leading questions prime the participant to answer in a certain way by suggesting a 'correct' response. A (glaringly, obviously) leading question would be something like "Why do you love sugary food so much?" Less obviously, "What is your biggest dietary challenge?" could also be considered leading question as it assumes a negative relationship with food, which may not be true for all participants.

Moderator guide vs. script

We purposely this set of questions a 'discussion guide' or 'moderator guide', rather than a 'script'.

That's because although its good to prepare a loose questionnaire to guide the interview, you should feel free to deviate from it when it makes sense. You don't want the interview to feel stilted—you want it to flow, and you want your interviewee comfortable. If the interview is taking a useful turn, follow it where it wants to go.

For discovery interviews, where the scope of your inquiry might be quite broad, consider a list of topics in lieu of a questionnaire.

If you identify a handful (3-6) of larger topics you'd like to cover, and identify a handful of subtopic, you've got yourself a nice loose guideline for an interview that won't be overly confining.

For example, say your area of interest is snacks (because who isn't interested in snacks?). You might come up with larger topics like cookies, popcorn, charcuterie, and healthy snacks. And beneath each main topic, you might have a few subtopics. In the end, your list of topics might look like...

- Cookies: gooey, crunchy, layered
- Popcorn: instant, savory, sweet
- Antipasto: meats, cheeses, olives, nuts
- Fruits: fresh fruit, dried fruit, pureed fruit

And you can use this list of presumptions as a guideline for understanding how, why, and what your interviewee looks for in a snack without locking yourself into a prescribed list of questions.

Examples of good user interview questions

We put together a list of sample interview questions in **this handy sheet**. Here are a few examples of different types of interview questions you can ask:

Getting-to-know-you questions

- Tell me about your role at work
- What did you do last weekend?

Digging in questions

- When was the last time you did [activity]?
- Tell me about how you currently solve [problem].

Product/market fit questions

- Have you used any other tools in the past to solve [problem]?
- What's your team's current budget for [activity]?

Usability testing questions

- Please describe your experience with [tool].
- If you were looking for [information] where would you expect to find it?

Customer interview questions

- Tell me about how you and/or your team uses our product.
- What do you wish our product could do that it can't today?

Surveys

Survey is a set of questions you use to collect data from your target audience.

Surveys are appealing because they're cost effective while having the potential to reach large numbers of people quickly and easily. You can ask almost anything, and the results are easy to tally.

However, these are the exact same reasons why surveys are so dangerous; surveys are deceptively simple. Although they're relatively easy and inexpensive to implement, you can't let this ease fool you into cutting corners. Getting valid and valuable data from a survey still requires strict adherence to best practices.

Surveys vs. questionnaires vs. polls

What's the difference between a survey, a questionnaire, and a poll? The terms 'survey' and 'poll' can be used interchangeably, while a questionnaire refers to the content of the survey/poll you're conducting:

- **Survey (aka Poll):** The task or process of collecting data in order to gather insights from a specific set of respondents.
- **Questionnaire:** The content—a list of questions—that you are asking respondents to answer.

Using surveys for UX research

In UX research, surveys are typically used as an evaluative research method, but they can also be used in generative research and as a continuous research method. In-product surveys, for example, are an easy and effective way to automate ongoing data collection.

There is a variety of approaches you can take to designing and implementing a survey. Here's an overview of the different types of survey methods in UX research.

Types of survey methods in user research

Quantitative vs qualitative research surveys

Quantitative surveys collect a large number of responses to questions that can be answered using checkboxes or radio buttons. These types of surveys are designed to answer "how many" questions; like all quantitative research methods, these types of surveys are meant to deliver statistically meaningful results representative of the broader population.

Quantitative survey types include descriptive and causal:

- **Descriptive surveys** provide insight into behaviors, attitudes, or opinions.
- **Causal surveys** are designed to define the cause-and-effect relationship between two or more variables.

Qualitative surveys use open-ended, ***exploratory*** questions to collect more detailed comments, feedback, and suggestions. While these types of responses cannot be as quickly and easily tallied as the data from quantitative surveys, the insights they provide can be very valuable. Researchers often run a qualitative survey with a small group to gain a deeper understanding of the respondents and identify the best questions and answers to include in a quantitative survey aimed at a larger group.

Cross-sectional vs. longitudinal vs retrospective surveys

Cross-sectional surveys look at a specific, isolated situation and solicit a single set of responses from a small population sample over a short period of time. The aim is to get quick answers to a standalone question. This method is purely observational, and does not measure causation.

Longitudinal surveys collect a series of responses from a larger group of participants over a longer period of time (from weeks to decades). This observational method helps researchers study change over time, and includes three types of studies: trend, cohort, and panel. These long-term studies are most successful when designed around short, frequent sessions, instead of lengthy interviews that can be burdensome for participants.

Retrospective surveys combine longitudinal and cross-sectional elements by looking at change over a long period of time via a one-time survey. This approach helps reduce the time and money needed to perform the survey, but can introduce accuracy issues depending on participants' memory recall.

Ultimately, choosing the right research method for you will depend on your goals and the questions you're hoping to answer.

The advantages and disadvantages of surveys for user research

Surveys are a popular and advantageous research method for many reasons:

- They are inexpensive.
- They are scalable.
- They are usually less susceptible to the Hawthorne effect (the phenomenon of study participants changing their behavior based on the knowledge that they are being observed and tailoring responses to meet assumed expectations).
- They give your team confidence in making survey-informed design decisions.
- They provide statistically meaningful data that is reassuring to business stakeholders.

When should you use surveys in UX research?

It can be tempting to use surveys for all kinds of quantitative research, but that's not always the best use of the method. While surveys are undeniably a relatively fast, unmoderated, and low-cost way to compile a lot of data on a lot of people, there are many ways that data can be skewed to deliver biased or otherwise compromised results.

A better use of a survey is as a qualitative tool that helps you explore and define the area of investigation. Using open-ended survey questions as a starting point can help you gain a much deeper understanding about the subject at hand and the end users you're surveying. And that understanding is invaluable for mitigating the risk of designing subpar solutions as well as increasing your ability to design better products more efficiently.

How to design an effective research survey

Thorough and thoughtful planning and preparation are crucial to survey success. You need to be clear and explicit about your goals. One of the most common mistakes new researchers make is to cast a wide net, asking for responses to a wide range of questions, and then try to reverse-engineer a central goal from the resulting data.

A strong survey explores a very specific and clearly defined research question via well-written, bias-free survey questions and an optimized survey flow.

Defining the research question and scope

The research question is different from the individual questions that you eventually include in your questionnaire. A research question defines the topic you are exploring. It is the 'big idea' at the heart of your survey.

Identifying your research question typically starts with brainstorming to develop a list of all the possible suggestions. From there, you refine the question to its essence. Caroline Jarret does this by running each possible question through a series of four challenges (Fig. 4.3):

- What do you want to know?
- Why do you want to know?
- What decision will you make based on the answers?
- What number do you need to make the decision?

Look for your most crucial question (MCQ)

As you run your various questions through this 4-part challenge, you're looking for your Most Crucial Question (MCQ), which Caroline defines as, "the one that makes a difference. It's the one that will provide essential data for decision-making." She suggests stating your question in two parts:

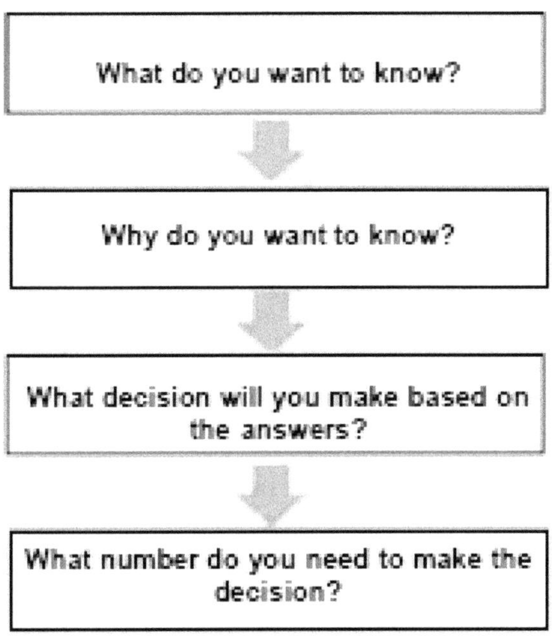

Fig. 4.3 Four challenges

- "We need to ask _______."
- "So that we can decide ___________."

And don't stop there. Before you settle on your MCQ, you want to really pick it apart by questioning what you mean by each word. You want to wind up with something that is incredibly clear and doesn't require any interpretation.

Remember, in order for your research to make a meaningful impact, it needs to be designed to enable decisions for your company, product, or service. **R**

Writing great survey questions

Clarity and specificity are the two most important characteristics of effective survey questions. With that in mind, here are our top tips for creating questions that help you get the answers you need:

- Use the first person to encourage people to focus on their experience rather than their opinions.
- Replace UX jargon with simple, familiar words.
- Use language that a child could understand.
- Use straightforward syntax.
- Choose words with clear, unambiguous meanings that don't require any interpretation.
- Be as specific as possible with your wording.
- Eliminate any double-barreled questions that ask two questions at once.
- Avoid the use of single or double negatives.

Types of survey questions

Mixing up the types of questions on your survey can help you collect the most insightful data. There are two main types of questions: open and closed.

Open-ended survey questions allow participants to respond in their own words. This type of question typically generates a great deal more qualitative detail and can uncover unexpected responses. Open-ended questions help you get at the "why" behind people's answers. However, it can be difficult and time-consuming to analyze and draw conclusions from open-ended responses.

Closed survey questions have pre-populated response options that participants choose using tools like checkboxes or radio buttons. Closed survey questions have higher response rates since they require less effort from the respondent. Because the response options are standardized, closed questions deliver data that is easier to analyze and which provides statistically significant findings.

There are several different types of response options for closed survey questions:

- Multiple choice (radio buttons)
- Checkbox (select as many as apply)
- Rating scale
- Ranking order
- Dichotomous (Yes/No)
- Matrix
- Image Choice
- Likert scale (e.g., strongly disagree to strongly agree, never to always, very dissatisfied to very satisfied, etc.)

Avoid bias and leading questions

It is very easy to **accidentally insert bias** into your survey questions. And it's also possible for participants to be biased in their responses. We already mentioned the Hawthorne effect, which causes people to change their behavior when they know they are being observed. There is also **acquiescence or agreement bias,** which causes survey respondents to agree with research statements in an effort to be more agreeable or to give the answer they think you want.

Here are a few different kinds of bias that can sneak into your questions:

- ***Confirmation bias*** happens when all your questions are geared to support your existing hypothesis.
- ***Implicit bias*** relates to subconscious and/or unspoken attitudes and associations about different stereotypes.
- ***Framing effect*** has to do with how question presentation can influence responses.
- ***Hindsight bias*** can distort memories by giving people the sense that they "knew it all along" and could have easily predicted events that have already happened.
- ***Clustering bias*** is a cognitive bias that causes people to see patterns where none exist.
- ***Serial position effect*** refers to how it's easier to remember the first and last items in a list.

OBSERVATIONAL RESEARCH AND USABILITY TESTING

To understand exactly why the structure of user tests is so important (and why we so strongly recommend observational research), you first need to have an understanding of biases as they relate to UX research methods.

All people are naturally biased. That's no surprise; a quick scroll through the news feed on your favorite social media app will likely bear this statement out. But in the context of user testing, biases are much subtler than things like political preferences and religious affiliations. In fact, the biases that impact user testing are so subtle that the people involved likely won't perceive them at all.

Users are often eager to please, eager to seem smart, and quickly forget when things have gone wrong if they achieve a goal. If we as testers aren't careful, these very pleasant tendencies can give way to misleading biases. The following three biases are especially important to understand since they often cause users to unwittingly change their behavior in a testing environment.

- **Social Desirability Bias:** Users don't want to be judged for not understanding something or for using a product "incorrectly," so they may unintentionally modify their behavior in an attempt to look more proficient. The best way to minimize this bias is by putting your test users at ease and reassuring them they aren't the ones being tested. Remind them that you are testing your own interface, so if something isn't working, it's a problem with the interface and not the user. Stay neutral as test participants move through the test session, and make sure to ask open-ended questions that don't imply right and wrong answers.
- **The Hawthorne Effect:** While observational research is key for a number of reasons, the very act of being observed can cause participants to change their behavior in subtle ways. Since the effect of this bias often goes down over time, the best way to reduce it is to plan for longer observation sessions in the hopes that users will forget you're there. You can also attempt to ameliorate the Hawthorne Effect by directly addressing it with test takers. Tell users to pretend you aren't there as they go through the testing session. You can also ask them how they might handle things differently if they weren't being watched. You may be surprised at how much insight users can bring to this question once it's brought to their attention.
- **Hindsight Bias:** Hindsight bias refers to the fact that people tend to subconsciously filter memories of past events through the lens of present knowledge. In the context of user testing, self-reporting is less reliable than observational research because of this very phenomenon, with users often reporting that an interface was easier or more manageable than it actually was. Only by observing users during testing does this important gap come to light. What people say isn't always what they mean, so we need to watch them in action to collect a broader range of data points and help fix experiences that aren't reported as issues.

It would be impossible to eliminate all the biases that might come into play in a testing environment. Still, having an awareness of the existence of the most common biases—and how best to counteract them—goes a long way toward reducing the problem.

The Importance of Observational UX Research Methods

By now it should be pretty clear that you don't want to make UX decisions based on verbatim and self-reporting alone. But hindsight bias isn't the only reason to prioritize observational studies as part of your UX research methodology.

We want our products to fit into the lives of our users. People won't change their behavior to use your product, and there's a lot more that goes into someone's day than their strict interaction with your software. You need to understand how your product fits into users' lives by watching them in action.

Observing Users in Their Own Environment

We can't know how users live their lives unless we observe them, ideally in their own environments and contexts. For example, if your product is used to help manage coursework and assignments, then you need to have an understanding of how and when it's being used by instructors and students. Only by observing your product in action might you learn that instructors typically assign coursework while looking at an on-screen calendar, meaning that your product's screen needs to be responsive enough to work alongside another app. Careful observation allows variables like this one to become known entities that your product can then accommodate.

In-person, in-context observation is the gold standard for user testing. But, of course, there are a number of reasons why it's not always feasible, from budgeting to timing and logistics. The good news is that a lot can be learned by simply observing users click through prototypes in remote moderated sessions. And this is all the more true when you have an understanding of how to coach testers in a way that reduces bias.

CHAPTER-5

PERSONA DEVELOPMENT

A "Persona" is a fictional representation of an actual user and is applied in the early stages of product development or product redesign. Personas are vital to the success of a product because they drive design decisions by taking common user needs and bringing them to the forefront of planning *before* design has actually started. Personas provide the team with a shared understanding of users in terms of goals and capabilities. Once Personas are defined, going through a task analysis exercise with scenarios will offer an inexpensive way to test and prioritize features throughout the development.

As opposed to designing products, services, and solutions based upon the preferences of the design team, it has become standard practice within many human-centered design disciplines to collate research and personify specific trends and patterns in the data as personas. Hence, personas do not describe real people, but you compose your personas based on actual data collected from multiple individuals. Personas add the human touch to what would largely remain cold facts in your research. Creating persona profiles of typical or atypical (extreme) users will help you understand patterns in your research, which synthesizes the types of people you seek to design for. Personas are also known as model characters or composite characters.

Personas provide meaningful archetypes which you can use to assess your design development against. Constructing personas will help you ask the right questions and answer those questions in line with the users you are designing for. For example, "How would Peter, Joe, and Jessica experience, react, and behave in relation to feature X or change Y within the given context?" and "What do Peter, Joe, and Jessica think, feel, do and say?" and "What are their underlying needs we are trying to fulfill?"

Personas in Design Thinking

In the design thinking process, designers will often start creating personas during the second phase, the Define phase. In the Define phase, Design Thinkers synthesize their research and findings from the very first phase, the Empathise phase. Using personas is just one method, among others, that can help designers move on to the third phase, the Ideation phase. The personas will be used as a guide for ideation sessions such as Brainstorm, Worst Possible Idea and SCAMPER.

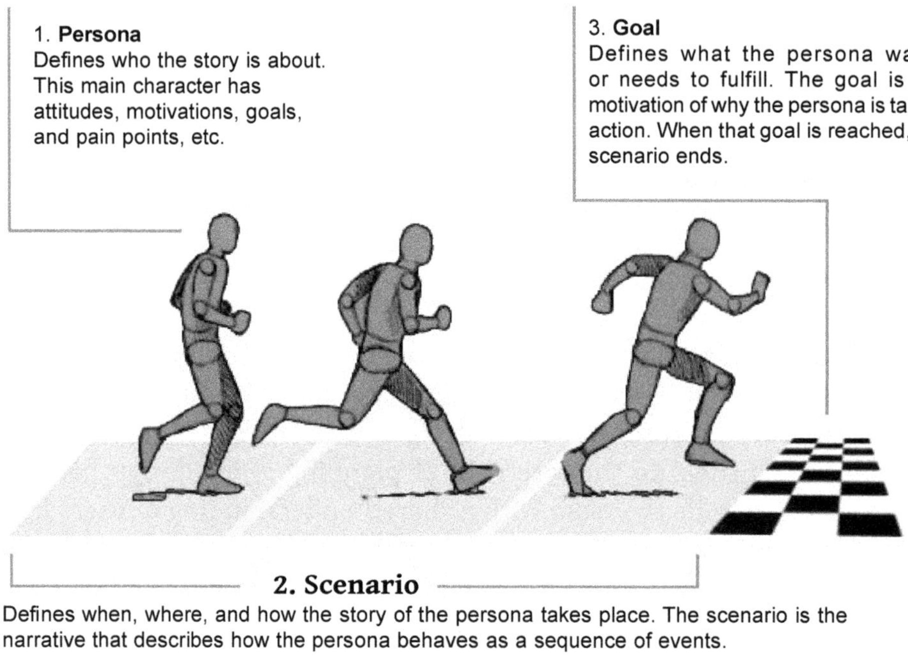

Fig. 5.1 Persona, Scenario and Goal

Four Different Types of Personas

In her Interaction Design Foundation encyclopedia, Personas, Ph.D. and specialist in personas, Lene Nielsen, describes four perspectives that your personas can take to ensure that they add the most value to your design project and the fiction-based perspective. Let's take a look at each of them:

Goal-directed Personas

This persona cuts straight to the nitty-gritty. "It focusses on: What does my typical user want to do with my product?". The objective of a goal-directed persona is to examine the process and workflow that your user would prefer to utilize to achieve their goals in interacting with your product or service. There is an implicit assumption that you have already done enough user research to recognize that your product has value to the user and that by examining their goals, you can bring their requirements to life. The goal-directed personas are based upon the perspectives of Alan Cooper, an American software designer and programmer who is widely recognized as the "Father of Visual Basic."

Role-Based Personas

The role-based perspective is also goal-directed, and it also focuses on behavior. The personas of the role-based perspectives are massively data-driven and incorporate data from both qualitative and quantitative sources. The role-based perspective focuses on the user's role in the organization. In some cases, our designs need to reflect upon the part that our users play in their organizations or wider lives. An examination of the roles that our users typically play in real life can help inform better product design decisions. Where will the product be used? What's this role's purpose? What business objectives are required of this role? Who else is impacted by the duties of this role? What functions are served by this role? Jonathan Grudin, John Pruitt, and Tamara Adlin are advocates for the role-based perspective.

Engaging Personas

Engaging personas can incorporate both goal and role-directed personas, as well as the more traditional rounded personas. These engaging personas are designed so that the designers who use them can become more engaged with them. The idea is to create a 3D rendering of a user through the use of personas. The more people engage with the persona and see them as 'real', the more likely they will be to consider them during the process design and want to serve them with the best product. These personas examine the emotions of the user, their psychology, backgrounds and make them relevant to the task at hand. The perspective emphasizes how stories can engage and bring the personas to life. One of the advocates for this perspective is Lene Nielsen.

One of the main difficulties of the persona method is getting participants to use it (Browne, 2011). In a short while, we'll let you in on Lene Nielsen's model, which sets out to cover this problem through a 10 step process of creating an engaging persona.

4. Fictional Personas

The fictional persona does not emerge from user research (unlike the other personas), but it emerges from the experience of the UX design team. It requires the team to make assumptions based upon past interactions with the user base and products to deliver a picture of what, perhaps, typical users look like. There's no doubt that these personas can be deeply flawed (and there are endless debates on just how flawed). You may be able to use them as an initial sketch of user needs. They allow for early involvement with your users in the UX design process, but they should not, of course, be trusted as a guide for your development of products or services.

CREATING USER PERSONAS FOR DESIGN INSIGHTS

The role of user personas in design

User personas are essential to creating a strong product design. They help us gain more insight into our target audience and influence our design decisions.

By creating personas, you can build empathy with users and align your design team and stakeholders around a shared understanding of user needs and behaviors.

In turn, this ensures your design is user-centered and relevant to your audience.

Personas are more than just pretty faces; they represent the most important user groups of your product, allowing you to focus on their pain points, needs, and preferences.

They can also bring user research findings to life, ensuring your design decisions are grounded in real data and not just gut feelings.

The Significance of User Personas

- **Insightful Understanding:** Personas provide a human-focused representation of users, allowing teams to comprehend and empathize with their needs.
- **Guiding Design Decisions:** They serve as guiding beacons, ensuring design choices are aligned with the identified user requirements.
- **Enhanced Communication:** Personas facilitate communication across teams, fostering a shared understanding of the user base.

Components of Effective User Personas

- **Demographics:** Age, gender, location, occupation, etc.
- **Behaviors:** Usage patterns, preferences, goals, and frustrations.
- **Goals and Motivations:** Objectives, needs, and aspirations.

Creating Impactful User Personas

- **Research Phase:** Conduct thorough user research through interviews, surveys, and analytics to gather insights into user behaviors and needs.
- **Data Analysis:** Identify commonalities and patterns among user groups to formulate representative personas.
- **Persona Development:** Create personas with detailed descriptions, incorporating demographics, behaviors, and motivations.
- **Validation:** Validate personas through user testing sessions and refine them based on feedback and real user interactions.

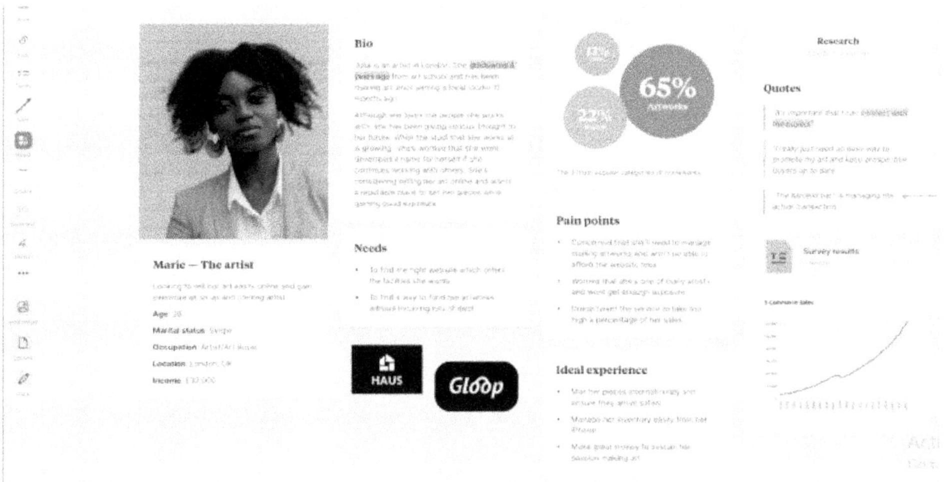

Fig. 5.2 Example persona

Tools for Persona Creation:

- **Empathy Maps:** These visual tools aid in understanding user behaviors, emotions, and motivations, fostering empathy with the user. Examples - **Miro** and **Mural**
- **Journey Maps:** Diagrams illustrating user experiences throughout their interaction with a product or service. Examples - **UXPressia** and Smaply
- **Persona Templates:** Predefined templates providing a structured framework for persona development. Examples - Adobe XD, Sketch, and Figma offer **Explore more tools**

Implementing Personas:

- **Reference Points:** Utilize personas as references during design discussions and decision-making processes.
- **User-Centric Approach:** Frame user stories based on personas to guide design iterations and feature development.
- **Validation and Iteration:** Continuously validate design choices against user personas, iteratively improving the user experience.

Challenges and Solutions:

- **Data Collection Challenges:** Gather diverse data sources for comprehensive personas. Combine qualitative and quantitative data for a holistic view.
- **Maintaining Relevance:** Regularly update personas based on evolving user needs and behaviors.

Step-by-Step Guide to Creating User Personas

Understanding your target audience is the foundation of successful UI/UX design. User personas, fictional representations of your ideal users, provide invaluable insights into their needs, preferences, and pain points. In this comprehensive guide, we will walk you through a step-by-step process to create effective user personas that will not only elevate your design process but also help your website rank higher on Google. Let's dive in!

Step 1: Define Your Project Scope

Before delving into user persona creation, clearly define your project's scope and objectives. Identify the purpose of your website or application, the specific features you plan to offer, and the problems you aim to solve. Understanding the project's context will help you create user personas tailored to your unique design goals.

Step 2: Conduct Extensive Research

Gather data through comprehensive research to form the foundation of your user personas. Utilize various sources, such as user surveys, interviews, website analytics, and market research reports. Focus on demographics, behaviors, motivations, and pain points of your potential users. The more data you collect, the more accurate and reliable your user personas will be.

Step 3: Segment Your Target Audience

Divide your audience into segments based on their shared characteristics, goals, and preferences. Each segment will represent a unique user persona. For example, if you are designing an e-commerce website, segments could include "Tech-Savvy Shoppers," "Budget-Conscious Buyers," and "Fashion Enthusiasts." Tailor your personas to the specific needs of each segment.

Step 4: Name and Personalize Your Personas

Give each user persona a name, age, occupation, and a brief personal background. This humanizes the personas and makes them more relatable. Include a photo or illustration to add a visual element. The goal is to make these personas feel like real people, enabling your design team to empathize with their needs and preferences.

Step 5: Describe Goals and Objectives

Outline the primary goals and objectives of each user persona. What are they trying to achieve by using your website or application? Understanding their intentions will guide your design decisions and help prioritize features that align with their goals.

Step 6: Identify Pain Points and Challenges

Pinpoint the pain points and challenges that each user persona faces in their interaction with your platform. This insight will help you address potential usability issues and create intuitive solutions that resonate with your target audience.

Step 7: Define User Behavior and Preferences

Describe how each user persona behaves when using your website or application. What are their typical user journeys? What features do they prioritize, and what design elements appeal to them? Understanding user behavior will enable you to optimize the user experience based on their preferences.

Step 8: Analyze Motivations and Expectations

Understand the motivations and expectations of your user personas. What drives them to engage with your platform, and what are their expectations regarding functionality, aesthetics, and content? Aligning your design with their motivations will foster a deeper connection and increase user satisfaction.

Step 9: Create User Persona Scenarios

Craft scenarios that depict how each user persona interacts with your platform in specific situations. These scenarios simulate real-life experiences and help identify pain points or areas for improvement in your UI/UX design.

Step 10: Share and Utilize Your User Personas

Share the finalized user personas with your entire design and development team. Encourage team members to refer to the personas throughout the design process to ensure that all decisions align with the needs and preferences of your target audience.

APPLYING PERSONAS IN UX AND DESIGN

User personas are research-based, archetypal representations of your ideal customer. Personas can take on many different forms, but typically they are one-page documents that outline the context, motivations, and needs of specific user audiences.

Personas can be used by people in many different disciplines, including marketing, design, product management, and user research. Because they are such flexible tools, different departments within an organization may have different sets of personas, or may create personas that look entirely different from each other.

Whether you have one persona or many, personas are important because they help teams and stakeholders empathize with users and keep the correct audiences in mind when creating products and campaigns.

Because personas are used broadly, across disciplines, and for a variety of reasons, let's clarify:

- The difference between design (or UX) personas and marketing personas
- The difference between user personas, empathy maps, and other mental models
- Types of user personas for UX, product, and design teams

Design personas vs. marketing personas

One of the biggest misconceptions people have about *user* personas is that they're interchangeable with *marketing* personas. They're not.

Yes, design teams and marketing teams both commonly use personas - but the persona documents they create are **not** interchangeable. If you get them mixed up, you won't get (much) value out of them.

1. Understand your users.

UX personas represent real people - their likes, dislikes, attitudes, habits, pain points, and more. The descriptive nature of these personas enables designers to understand their ideal customers.

They also help designers empathize with the issues their users face and how these issues affect how they interact with the product.

2. Make better product decisions.

UX personas highlight what's important to your users and what they need from your product. This helps designers craft a UX strategy that's centered around features and solutions that users will appreciate.

Understanding your users' pain points, goals, and motivations will help you figure out what changes will make the most positive impact on your users' experience with your product.

3. Improve user-centric design.

Think of UX personas as a compass that alerts you when you're making the wrong decisions and steers you back on the right path.

When you consult your UX personas often, you won't design a product based on what you think it should look like. Instead, you'll design a product that is tailored to your ideal customers, their capabilities, and their needs.

For example, having a clear understanding of your customers' behaviors and preferences can help you create a user-friendly interface that your users can operate easily. This user-centric design makes all the difference between an app that just looks attractive and one that meets customers' expectations and fulfills their needs - the latter being crucial for attracting and retaining users.

4. Align your UX strategy.

To ensure alignment across all aspects of your design process, you need a well-crafted UX persona.

By creating detailed and research-based UX personas, designers are better equipped to understand the behaviors, needs, and pain points of their target audience. This informs their decisions on which features and functionalities to prioritize, how to structure their site hierarchy, what color palettes to use, and other design elements that will impact user experience.

UX personas ensure that everything the design team does contributes to the ultimate goal of satisfying the end users in every way possible.

Creation of UX Persona

Crafting UX personas is an iterative process. You create them before you start designing and then update them as you gather new data.

Below are the main steps you need to follow to create a foundational UX persona.

1. Conduct user research.

The first step to creating a UX persona is to collect data about your users (or prospects). You can do this through qualitative and quantitative research methods.

Qualitative research methods include user interviews, contextual interviews, focus groups, and usability tests - all of which give you the chance to ask your target audience some questions about your product (or watch them use the product) and receive in-depth information about their experience with it.

Quantitative research methods include sending out online surveys and analyzing web analytics, including the number of page visitors, time spent on site, and the journey visitors go on before they convert to paying customers.

The responses from the surveys give you deeper insights into the demographics, psychographics, behavioral patterns, challenges, and needs of your customers, which is vital information you need to make the best design decisions.

Pro tip: If you have enough time and resources, use both research methods to get a more accurate and balanced result.

2. Organize your research.

After conducting your market research, try to find commonalities and patterns that allow you to identify different types of users, i.e., how different user types behave and use your product.

This process will vary depending on the kind of research you conducted. With qualitative research, you can use a Notes app or a word frequency counter to visualize data and group users who follow similar themes.

For example, if you notice that a large number of users you spoke to have the same pain point or goal, you can put them in one category. Or you can analyze the written answers from your survey respondents to find commonalities in the words they use, their interests, hobbies, or personal information, such as age or gender.

For quantitative research, however, you can visualize your data with charts and graphs. These will clearly show you any trends or patterns you should consider as you create your UX persona.

3. Decide on a number of personas

Now that you have a better understanding of your user groups, identify which ones are the most important and prioritize them throughout the development process.

Ideally, you should have 1-4 main user groups. For each one, create a clearly defined UX persona that's distinguishable from the others. You can define each one by their ages, backgrounds, technical ability, or even their motivations for using your product.

A great way to distinguish between multiple UX personas is to place them in primary and secondary categories. A primary persona is the most relevant persona that represents users who actually interact with your product.

Secondary personas, on the other hand, are users that may have additional needs that you need to adjust your product to meet. The adjustments, however, should not affect the experience of primary users.

For example, users who are disabled or have limited technical abilities are secondary users because you need to make your website accessible to them.

4. Describe your UX persona

Now it's time to actually set up the UX persona. Use your research to define the key details about your ideal user as they relate to your product. You can structure your findings in several ways, but ensure you include the following elements:

- **Name:** Instead of something vague like "User 1", create a fictional name to make your persona feel more realistic and memorable.
- **Image:** Use a stock photo or a digital illustration of a person to represent your persona. This helps you empathize with them and makes it easier to imagine them in various product-related use cases.
- **Demographics:** Specify the age (or age range), family status, employment status, education, background, and technical ability of your persona. This information should be based on research.

- **Psychographics:** Here, specify the behaviors, pain points, goals, and needs of your persona. This will help you understand your users' motivations and reasons for using your product.
- **A quote:** This is a concise statement that sums up the most important thing to your user persona as it relates to your product. Base this quote on research by imagining how your persona would describe themselves if they were a real person.

Pro tip: Put your UX personas in a well-designed document to make it accessible to your team members and other teams that need it.

5. Share (and use) your UX persona(s).

Once you're satisfied with your UX persona(s), share it with other teams so that other people can get to understand the users they're trying to serve.

During the design process, refer back to your persona(s) and include it in discussions about the product. Before making a critical design decision, ask yourself, "Will this benefit my UX persona?" Doing this helps you put your users first and create a product that meets their needs.

As your product evolves, revisit and tweak your UX personas to keep them current. This may mean adding new personas, scrapping existing ones, or just making small changes accordingly.

Examples of UX Personas

Now that we've covered the process of creating a UX persona, here are two UX persona examples that can inspire your own.

These personas are for a healthy food delivery app that delivers to Illinois residents.

1. John Michaels, a University Student

Fictional Name

John Michaels

Occupation

Part-time coffee barista, undergrad University student

Demographics

- 20 years old
- Lives in Chicago
- Single, no children
- Has two roommates who work part-time

Goals and Needs

John doesn't know how to cook. But he's health-conscious, so instead of eating junk food, he prioritizes eating healthy foods, especially proteins, fruits, and salads, at optimal times throughout the day.

John's schedule is tight, and he mostly spends time at school or at the coffee shop where he works. Leaving the shop to get food can disrupt his schedule (and pay), so he needs a way to get healthy food without risking those things. His best bet is to order it.

Pain Points

John isn't tech-savvy, so he needs an app that clearly displays the available dishes, along with the prices and any add-ons. He'll also appreciate a quick and easy payment process and fast delivery.

Personality

"Doing hard things favors no one. If there's an easy way out, take it. It's all the same in the end."

2. Hannah McCoy, software engineer

Fictional Name

Hannah McCoy

Occupation

A full-time software engineer who works from home, a part-time business consultant

Demographics

- 42 years old
- Lives in Chicago with her 44-year-old husband
- Married with two young children
- Has a high-income level and a profitable business

Goals and Needs

Ever since she started reading about the lack of quality ingredients in processed foods and juices, Hannah tries to make time each day to cook healthy meals for her family. However, she just started her consulting business while working a full-time job as a software engineer, so she's really busy.

Despite her tight schedule, Hannah refuses to give her family junk food and processed meals. She needs a reliable restaurant that can deliver healthy foods in bulk to her Chicago residence.

Pain Points

Most food delivery apps that Hannah has checked out don't offer healthy salad bowls, and the few that have salads on their menu don't deliver in bulk. Hannah would appreciate a restaurant that can deliver healthy meals that can last at least four days.

She'd also love it if they could deliver pre-made veggies to her so she won't have to go to the grocery store often.

Personality

"Doing everything all at once saves time and stress, especially if you're a busy bee."

Tips for Creating a UX Persona

As you create your UX persona, here are some tips you should keep in mind.

1. A UX persona goes beyond demographics.

While demographics are an important part of creating a UX persona, it shouldn't be your entire persona. UX personas should be based on your users' behaviors, goals, and motivations, rather than their age and job title.

Knowing that your ideal buyer is a middle-aged full-time project manager who runs a side hustle is useless if you don't know what's stopping them from subscribing to your product.

2. Don't make up personas.

It can be tempting to just whip up a UX persona based on your (or your superiors'/colleagues') understanding of your product and the market. But this can be detrimental because you'll end up creating a product that's for you (or the person whose ideas you're basing your persona on) and not for your users.

Good UX personas should be based on real insights you get from communicating with your target audience.

3. Keep an open mind.

This ties nicely with the previous point. During your research, you might be surprised by the answers your target audience is providing, especially if they don't coincide with the company narrative. In cases like this, you need to keep an open mind.

4. Talk to your user base in person.

Sending out online surveys for your target audience is a great way to get detailed answers to your questions. But if you want to get a deeper knowledge of your users, your best bet is to speak directly with some of your actual customers (or site visitors) face-to-face or via video chat.

This helps you get raw, unedited answers you can use to expand on what you have already built.

5. Collaborate with other teams.

While UX personas are mostly used by the design team, other departments, like marketing and product, may need to reference them while creating business strategies. So make your UX persona(s) available to them.

Steps to building user personas

1. Define your user research plan

First up, you'll want to set the goals of your personas. What are your business problems right now, and how are user personas able to solve them? These goals will help keep you on track through every step that follows.

User persona goals will help determine the kind of information you need to collect and display.

You'll probably want to take all your current data points and user research, and throw it out of the digital window. However, there's no need to take such a strong approach - some of your data may be valid or recent enough to support this research phase.

Equip yourself with the data sets you need, or establish where you can find them, before you start to build your user personas. Doing the above should give you a good idea of the amount of personas you'll need to do your product justice and encompass every type of user.

Lastly, identify where you're able to conduct this research. What avenues do you have available? Now's a good time to create a stellar user research plan.

Consider existing customers, potential customers and prospects, referrals, and user research groups for your research groups.

2. Create questions to help map your personas

You'll want to ask questions that truly showcase who your users are. We're building archetypes, not stereotypes. Only rich questions are going to help flesh out your personas. Rich questions are questions that provoke thought, and generate in-depth qualitative responses you can spot trends in, build on, and learn from.

The top three things you want answering are:

- Who are they?
- What is their goal?
- What's their main barrier from reaching that goal?

Think of these three bulleted questions as chapters, and each will have its own subsections to help you further identify your personas.

"We're not our users, even if we're adjacent to them. For example, I'm a designer, but I'm just one designer. Context helps frame your understanding. The more context we have, the broader picture we can illuminate. It helps us get a better understanding of what daily life looks like for users."

Ash goes on to explain the importance of rich, open-ended questions over closed questions focusing on quantitative data: "They weave in storytelling, to better allow UX designers to step into the minds of those users and experience the product from their point of view."

How you get those answers is determined by the rich questions you put together and how they enable you to segment. This is such a crucial stage of your user research that it's deserving of its own chapter. Jump ahead to explore how to create a persona map and further benefits of undergoing this process.

Examples of rich questions are:

- What are you currently using to get your job done? Why is it no longer serving you?
- What other challenges are you facing in your role that you need help with?
- What's your profession and responsibilities?

3. Send out your questions

It's important that no matter where you're delivering your user research questions, you're delivering the same question set, so every user goes through the same experience. This way, their answers are less likely to hold experience bias.

For example, you can't take the responses of an Instagram poll as having the same weight as those that have completed a ten-minute survey. When creating personas, the slightest divergence in survey experience can impact the overall accuracy of your data.

It's a good idea to target users by setting up an invite to your user research survey on a popular page, either in-app with a product modal, or on your website with a banner or modal.

Lastly, look at other resources you have: email, social media, Slack communities, or recruiting participants from a SaaS business providing user testing opportunities. If you already have a participant group in the works, then consider Maze to help you manage this feedback step.

4. Segment your data and map your personas

You've now sent all of your questions and can start collecting, organizing, and segmenting this data! Next, you'll want to build a knowledge base of sorts to help organize your user personas. By doing this, you'll be able to identify trends and turn qualitative responses into quantitative data points to help flesh out multiple personas.

It may sound old school, but the best tool to do this is Google sheets or Excel. If you're not a whizz with either, this may be a good time to level up, or find the talent to manage this for you.

Read through your data, and start segmenting answers based on trending keywords - they'll be easy to highlight and group in Excel or Google Sheets. From there, you can start sorting answers into sub-groups of those groups - this will help your next step.

5. Clarify how many personas you need

Keep repeating the above process until you've covered the large trends. If you still have a lot of ungrouped information, consider ways you can further segment: look for micro-communities within larger communities.

Even if this information doesn't aid design, it can prove useful for other areas of your business, like your product marketing efforts, customer success teams and sales.

By the end of this step, you'll have a clear idea of how many user personas you need to cover all your data trends. Try not to leave anything ungrouped, as you could potentially be missing a new persona opportunity.

There's no right or wrong answer for the number of personas you need. Most businesses tend to go for three-five, however, that's not to say this needs to be the case for you.

6. Find or create a persona template that fits your needs

Your research should not be dictated by how you're going to display it. That's why we introduce this stage later in the process. If you're already collecting and segmenting your data with a specific template in mind you'll be biased to the information you choose to collect and how you give it preference.

Once you've got your data sorted, look for a user persona template that can help you showcase what you want to put out to your business, and which areas of each persona need spotlighting.

There are a lot of templates out there for marketing personas that you can tweak for your own purpose. Or, jump to chapter four to learn how to create a user persona template in-house.

7. Create your personas

Now comes the fun part: it's time to start building out each user persona that perfectly encapsulates your target audience. Start doing this with a very low-fi frame of mind, just get a few ideas onto paper for those predetermined groups of data.

Don't worry about putting names to them yet, you're more so looking for grouping principles that relate to each other.

For example, note if those with the same job title also have the same job to be done, or the same stale way of doing their job. Perhaps within this group, you have two data sets, one that's aware of your product or niche and already using competitive tech, and one that isn't, and is doing their job manually.

Group your data together, then you can start adding your creative flair to bring these user personas to life.

Remember: personas are mostly data-driven, however, you'll definitely need to add some creative freedom to bring these ICPs to life, and make them memorable.

8. Prioritize your personas

Identify the personas that provide the biggest opportunity for your business. Perhaps they're easy wins, or they're a particularly large customer cohort. This will help you prioritize your product backlog, and perhaps even inspire a new feature or two. You'll most likely walk away from this step with a primary persona that dominates your data. However, you'll also have smaller user personas that can provide valuable insight and potentially highlight a new opportunity for your product marketing efforts.

In this step, consider your product team's maturity, resources, and time. Prioritization may be limited by what you're physically able to achieve in the near future, and what is more of a long-term goal.

9. Name and distribute your personas

Lastly, give your personas their names. It's important to do this last so you're not tailoring information to fit a name or profile you have in mind. Alliterations help people remember who is who - for this, you can find their core problem or goal and place it in their name.

Take this step with a pinch of salt. It's not uncommon for product teams today to agree that naming, gendering, assigning an image, and essentially stereotyping your personas does not lead to usable ones - they can even be damaging.

However, the argument is that some of these demographic labels help your team to remember and differentiate your user personas, getting everyone on the same page and keeping them there.

So, when it comes to naming and distribution of each ideal customer, do so in a way that enables your team, while allowing - not limiting - your user personas to still be able to do their job.

Ash Oliver, UX Designer & Design Advocate at Maze explains more.

"This is where the creativity of UX designers can shine, it's where you push past the one-pagers, and think about how your personas can live on in a fluid state, rather than being static. We're not thinking about personas with a start and end date. Your sharing process should be ongoing and not a one-time share."

Ash goes on to explain how UX designers need to take all of their users into account when building personas, and this includes internal teams as users of their research.

"As a designer you have to think about who your internal users are, and how you can display your user persona data in a way that creates a positive learning experience. You can give on-going digestible artefacts like PDF one-page templates, but you also need to give people self-serve tools if they want to learn more."

We asked Ash what else needs to be considered when sharing personas company-wide.

"Part of your distribution process needs to be around matching the ethos and culture of the company with your research, and the way you share this information. It's important to know you're not trying to create a new learning muscle or habit - stick to cultures your teams already know.

At Maze, we layer in artefacts with workshops, and create a diverse learning experience. The overarching theme of on-boarding teams to new user personas leans heavily on traditional storytelling tactics - they make information memorable and sticky."

CHAPTER-6

JOURNEY MAPPING

A journey map is a visualization of the process that a person goes through in order to accomplish a goal.

In its most basic form, journey mapping starts by compiling a series of user actions into a timeline. Next, the timeline is fleshed out with user thoughts and emotions in order to create a narrative.

Journey Maps are a UX visualization document that showcases the steps that a user takes in a process to accomplish a goal. Personas are created with information gathered from user and stakeholder interviews. As a result of these activities, you can identify the most important functionality an audience needs.

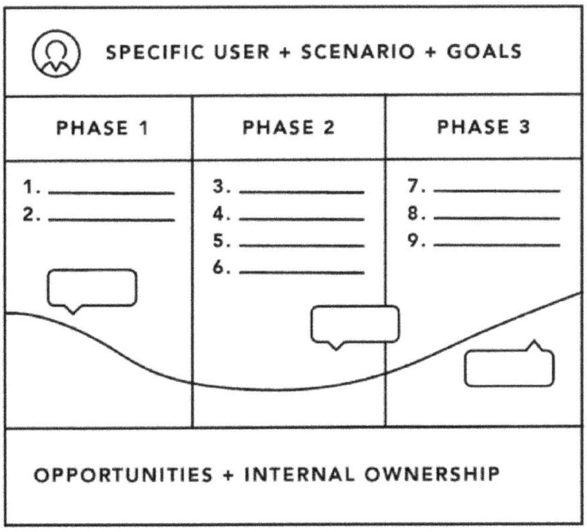

Fig. 6.1 Customer/User Journey Maps

The terms ‘user journey map’ and ‘customer journey map’ can be used interchangeably. Both reference a visualization of a person using your product or service.

While the argument can be made that the term ‘customer’ does a disservice to the method (because, especially for certain business-to-business products, not all of end users are technically customers, i.e., product buyers), alignment on what you call the map is far less important than alignment on the content within the map.

Key Components of a Journey Map

Journey maps come in all shapes and sizes. Regardless of how they look, journey maps have the following 5 key elements in common:

- Actor
- Scenario + Expectations
- Journey Phases
- Actions, Mindsets, and Emotions
- Opportunities

Actor

The actor is the persona or user who experiences the journey. The actor is who the journey map is about - a point of view. Actors usually align with personas and their actions in the map are rooted in data.

Provide one point of view per map in order to build a strong, clear narrative. For example, a university might choose either a student or a faculty member as actor — each would result in different journeys. (To capture both viewpoints, the university will need to build two separate maps, one for each of the two user types.)

Scenario + Expectations

The scenario describes the situation that the journey map addresses and is associated with an actor’s goal or need and specific expectations. For example, one scenario could be switching mobile plans to save money, and expectations for it include to easily find all the information needed to make a decision.

Scenarios can be real (for existing products and services) or anticipated - for products that are yet in the design stage.

Journey maps are best for scenarios that involve a sequence of events (such as shopping or taking a trip), describe a process (thus involve a set of transitions over time), or might involve multiple channels.

Journey Phases

Journey phases are the different high-level stages in the journey. They provide organization for the rest of the information in the journey map (actions, thoughts, and emotions). The stages will vary from scenario to scenario; each organization will usually have data to help it determine what these phases are for a given scenario.

Here are some examples:

- For an ecommerce scenario (like buying Bluetooth speakers), the stages can be discover, try, buy, use, seek support.
- For big (or luxury) purchases (like buying a car), the stages can be engagement, education, research, evaluation, justification.
- For a business-to-business scenario (like rolling out an internal tool), the stages could be purchase, adoption, retention, expansion, advocacy.

Actions, Mindsets, and Emotions

These are behaviors, thoughts, and feelings the actor has throughout the journey and that are mapped within each of the journey phases.

Actions are the actual behaviors and steps taken by users. This component is not meant to be a granular step-by-step log of every discrete interaction. Rather, it is a narrative of the steps the actor takes during that phase.

Mindsets correspond to users' thoughts, questions, motivations, and information needs at different stages in the journey. Ideally, these are customer verbatims from research.

Emotions are plotted as single line across the journey phases, literally signaling the emotional "ups" and "downs" of the experience. Think of this line as a contextual layer of emotion that tells us where the user is delighted versus frustrated.

Opportunities

Opportunities (along with additional context such as ownership and metrics) are insights gained from mapping; they speak to how the user experience can be optimized. Insights and opportunities help the team draw knowledge from the map:

- What needs to be done with this knowledge?
- Who owns what change?
- Where are the biggest opportunities?
- How are we going to measure improvements we implement?

MAPPING THE USER EXPERIENCE JOURNEY

User journey mapping, also known as customer journey mapping (CJM), maps a website visitor's experience from their perspective. Presented through a visual diagram, the customer journey map charts the user's path as they seek information or solutions, starting at the homepage and tracking their routes across other menus and links. To create a customer journey map, you begin by researching who users are, what they want from your site, and how positive or negative their experiences have been.

There are two main purposes for mapping your customers' journey.

Improve customer experience

This is the ultimate goal of CJM. Site navigation can be especially tricky to assess because you're already familiar with the layout. A fresh perspective on your site often uncovers overlooked details such as navigation issues or broken links.

By conducting research on UX trends and visually mapping your results, you'll identify any parts of your design that confuse or frustrate visitors. This process also reveals areas that work well, which you can repurpose elsewhere in the design.

Maintains ease-of-use as your site grows

A customer journey map can make even a simple site more straightforward to navigate. When your website or business grows, you may need to add content and features to accommodate the expansion. Implementing customer journey mapping ensures your website's fundamental flow remains intuitive and that new material and features are easily discoverable and usable.

Primary user journey map types

There are various ways to approach customer journey mapping based on the specific insights you're seeking. The end result of each map will look similar, but the focus of each is different - which changes the information it offers. Here are three standard types of maps to get you started.

Current state

The current state map is the most common type. It evaluates your website's present state to better understand visitors' current experiences, helping identify improvement opportunities for its existing design.

Future state

A future state map explores a hypothetical "ideal" website, considering the visitor's experience if every site component were optimized. This map is helpful when planning a total redesign or a specific change. When you collect user research and translate the results into your map, you can present a visual outline to your client or company for a straightforward explanation.

Persona-based

A persona-based map lays out the journey of a single designated type of user, or persona (which we will define below). This type of diagram is useful when optimizing your website for a specific sector of your audience with particular needs.

The 5-step customer journey mapping process

Once you've set clear goals for your map's achievements, you can select the appropriate diagram type. To begin visualizing your user journey, follow this five-step process.

1. Define the map's scope

Your map may focus on just one customer interaction or outcome, such as finding the newsletter sign-up sheet or making a payment, or it could cover the entire website's navigation. A focused scope helps you troubleshoot a problem area or ensure an especially critical element functions properly. Alternatively, a larger-scope map provides a big-picture perspective of how the site works as a whole.

Creating a comprehensive map is more complex, but high-level mapping helps comprehend the entire user experience from beginning to end.

2. Determine your user personas

A persona describes a particular type of visitor using your site. When imagining and defining these users, you can assign a name to each and include details about who they are, what they're looking for, and why.

Focus on users who contribute most to your business goals, consulting your marketing or sales teams for insights. To define your customer personas, explore current user behavior through surveys, online reviews, and email list responsiveness.

For example, if you're creating a website for a store that sells artisanal coffee-making tools, your personas could be:

- **The gift giver.** This user only knows a little about coffee but wants to select an impressive gift for someone else. They'll need help with purchase decisions, so they might interact with an FAQ or chat feature before visiting the products page. They may also leave your site if overwhelmed by options, so it's important to offer helpful information proactively. This will keep them engaged and more likely convert them to paying customers.
- **The coffee nerd.** This person is knowledgeable and always seeks the highest-quality tools, so easily accessible product details and customer reviews are important to them. To support their user experience and encourage them to purchase, ensure these elements are easily discoverable.

- **The tourist.** This user is on vacation and looking for a cute brick-and-mortar shop to visit. They aren't interested in your online store, but an appealing photo of your physical store with easily accessible hours and location information may convince them to come by in person.

These three types of users have very different needs and goals when visiting your website. To capture all of their business, create a map for each of them to ensure you accommodate their specific wants and circumstances.

3. Give the personas context

User context is the "when" and "how" of each persona visiting your site. A user will have a different experience loading your site on a mobile device than on a laptop. Additionally, someone in no rush may use your website differently than someone looking more urgently with a specific purpose.

Figure out when, how, and in what mindset your personas most commonly visit your site to map their experience accurately. This context has very concrete impacts on your finished design. If visitors tend to look for one specific page whenever in a hurry (like contact or location information), placing those details on the front page or prominently linking to it will smooth the user experience for those users.

Here's an example of how to place a persona in context.

- **Persona:** Jo is an apartment hunter in her early 20s and is still in college. She's looking for off-campus housing for herself and some roommates. The collective group values location and cost more than apartment features.
- **Context:** Jo is in a hurry and trying to visit as many apartments as possible. She's looking at property rental websites that clearly state apartment addresses in each listing.
- **Method:** Jo is browsing the sites on her iPhone.

4. List persona touchpoints

Touchpoints mark when the user makes a purchase decision or interacts with your user interface (UI). They include visitors' actions to move toward their goals and consider each associated emotion. The first touchpoint is how they reach your website — such as tapping a social media ad, clicking on a search result, or entering your URL directly.

First, list each action the visitor took and their corresponding emotional reactions. Subsequent touchpoints include instances when they navigate a menu, click a button, scroll through a gallery, or fill out a form. When you diagram the route through your site in an A-to-Z path, you can place yourself in the persona's mind to understand their reactions and choices.

A met expectation - for example, when clicking a "shop" button takes them to a product gallery - will result in a positive emotional reaction. An unmet expectation - when the "shop" link leads to an error page - will provoke an adverse reaction.

5. Map the customer journey

Illustrate the user journey by mapping these touchpoints on a visual timeline. This creates a narrative of users' reactions across your entire service blueprint. To represent your users' emotional states at each touchpoint, graph their correspondences like this:

The map helps you understand the customer experience as a whole.

For example, based on the diagram above, touchpoint 3 is the largest navigation challenge on the website. The graph also shows that the user's mood eventually rebounds after the initial setback. Improving the problem element in touchpoint 3 will have the biggest impact on elevating the overall user experience.

Customer journey mapping best practices

Now that you understand the mapping process, here are some best practices to implement when charting your customer journey.

- **Set a clear objective for your map:** Define your CX map's primary goal, such as improving the purchase experience or increasing conversions for a specific product.
- **Solicit customer feedback:** Engage directly with customers through surveys or interviews so you can implement data-driven changes. Ask users about their journey pain points and invite both positive and negative feedback on the overall navigation.
- **Specify customer journey maps for each persona:** To specifically serve each customer persona, consider charting separate paths for each based on their behaviors and interests. This approach is more customer-centric, as not all user types interact with your website the same way.
- **Reevaluate your map after company or website changes:** As your business scales, your website must evolve — and so will your customer's path. Review your map when making both large and small website adjustments to ensure you don't introduce new user challenges. Navigational disruptions can frustrate visitors, causing would-be customers to leave your site and seek competitors.

Current state customer journey maps

As their name suggests, current state customer journey maps help you visualize a user's experience *as it is today*. These are fact-based journey maps—to create an accurate current state journey map, you'll need to start by gathering data around actual, current customer interactions.

Current state mapping is a useful approach when your goal is to identify existing pain points and create a shared understanding of the end-to-end customer experience. A current state map—or at least the research that is required to create one—is also a valuable starting point for a future state map (see below), which focuses more on the customer experience as you'd *like it to be*.

1. B2B customer journey map from Bright Vessel (Fig. 6.2)

This is a relatively simple example of a B2B customer journey map, which focuses on the emotions and typical questions a customer experiences throughout their journey. This map also includes recommendations for interacting with the customer at each stage.

2. Persona-based CJM from a USA.gov case study (Fig. 6.3)

This journey map is based on the real-life experience of a specific customer, but you could also create a similar persona-based journey map to visualize the nuances of different customer journeys.

CUSTOMER JOURNEY MAP

	RESEARCH	COMPARISON	WORKSHOP	QUOTE	SIGN-OFF
TYPICAL QUESTIONS	How do I make an app? What platform should I use? How much does it cost? How do I protect my ideas?	What should I look for in an app developer? Cost vs quality? Who have they worked with before? What are their capabilities?	How do I know the app will be successful? Who will be the product owner/decision maker?	How does this compare? What other business opportunities do I have? Do I really want to take this leap? How will I fund this?	What else do I need to do to set up the business? When will I get my finished product?
EMOTIONS/ FEELINGS	Curious. Protective. Enthusiastic. Keen to rush in.	Discretionary. Subjective. Unsure. Weighing up pros and cons - usually focused around time, money and quality.	Eager. Inspired. Has a new comprehension of the workload required.	Revisioning prior ideas or options. Justifying their decisions with business partners or family. Validating internally that it is the right move to make.	Optimistic. Nervous/anxious. Keen to see results ASAP.
WE NEED TO...	Be present, ensure that we are found. Give confidence in us as a company and give them reason to contact us.	Explain the process of app development, best practices and show our past success stories. Be open, honest.	Get them to really understand what is involved - that nothing is an overnight success. Establish that we will be there to guide them through the process.	Display why we are the best team for the job and justify our pricing with substantiated information. Welcome questions.	Set clear expectations. Keep them informed with relevant information. Communicate frequently. Ask for feedback on how we're doing to ensure everyone is happy and on the same page.

Fig. 6.2 B2B customer journey map

In the example above, each stage of the customer journey has been broken down into activities. This level of detail allowed the creators to identify specific (rather than high-level) opportunities for improvement, like merging the domains grants.gov, benefits.gov, and govloans.gov to streamline customer journey.

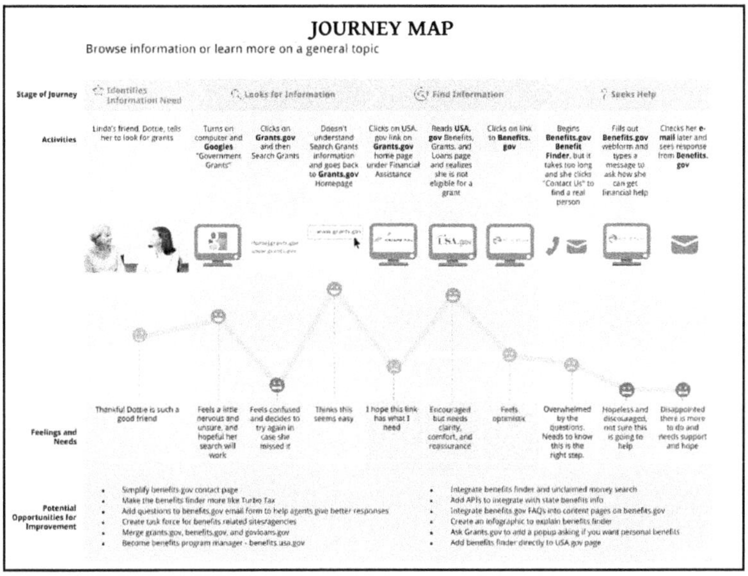

Fig. 6.3 Persona-based CJM from a USA.gov case study.

3. Customer journey map example by Customer Thermometer

This journey map depicts the several phases of a customer's buying journey, plus the degree of various emotions the customer may experience during each phase. Another important aspect of this map is the section that outlines important actionable opportunities to improve the customer's journey.

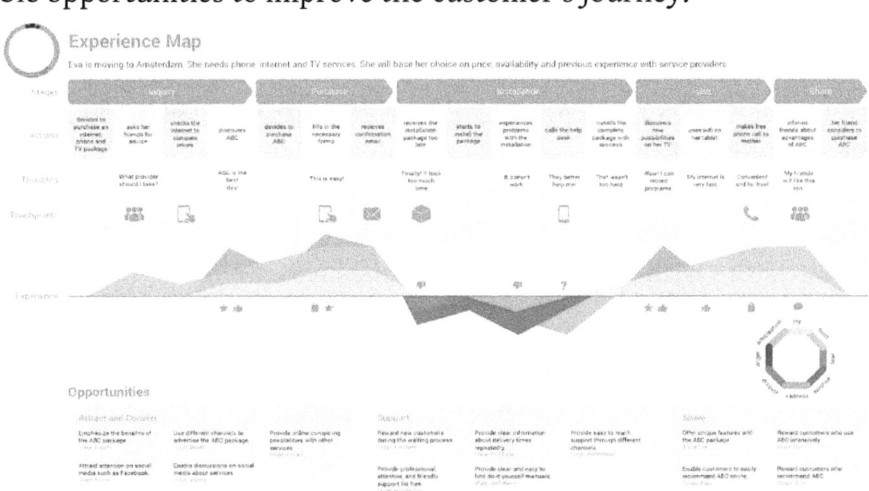

Fig. 6.4 Experience Map

4. Multi-channel journey map by Adaptive Path via UX Mastery

Customer journey maps can also be complex, like this multi-channel journey map made for Rail Europe (Fig. 6.5), which is notable for its scope—a customer base of "everyone"—and the intricately detailed thought processes and behaviors.

This experience map is informative, but dense. Depending on your goals, this level of complexity may actually be counterproductive.

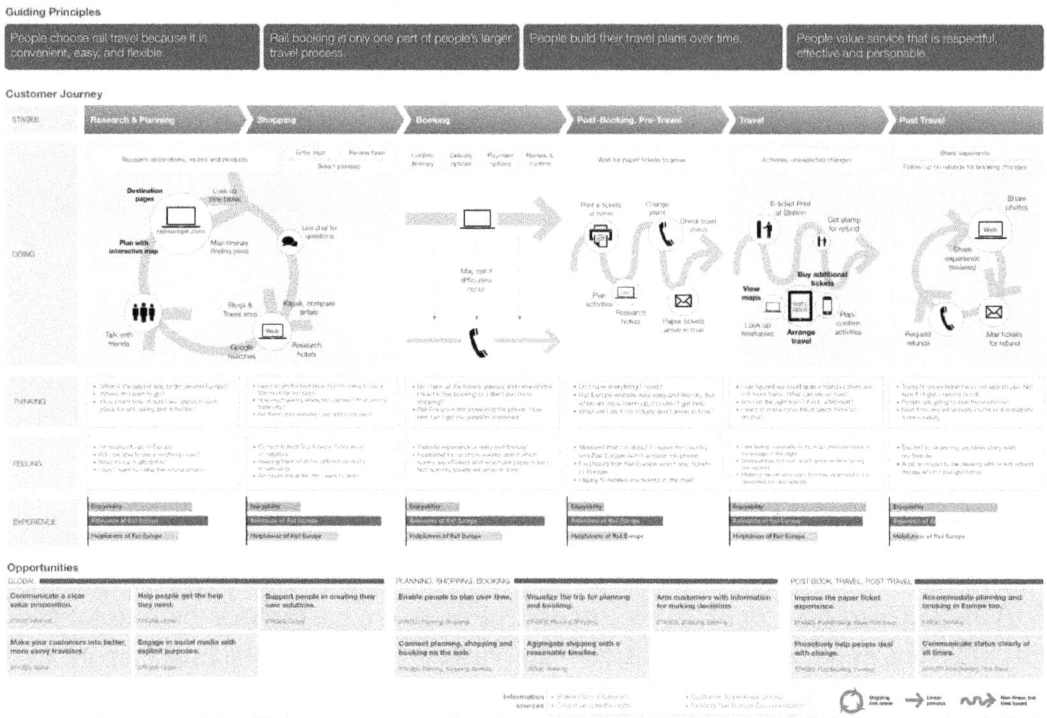

Fig. 6.5 multi-channel journey map made for Rail Europe

5. Customer journey map infographic example by Paul Boag

For some audiences, you may even decide to turn your customer journey map into an infographic (Fig. 6.6).

This customer journey map infographic has both style and substance. It maps out the digital experience journey of Sammy, a "chocoholic", who comes across a new chocolate store with new digital media displays.

Future state customer journey maps

While current state maps look at the customer journey as it exists today, future state maps focus on what the customer journey can and should look like in the *future.* Although data (like that contained in a current state map) is certainly an important input, future state journey maps also involve a fair amount of creative speculation and interpretation. These customer journey maps also focus on customer hopes and wants (future feelings), in addition to experiences and reactions.

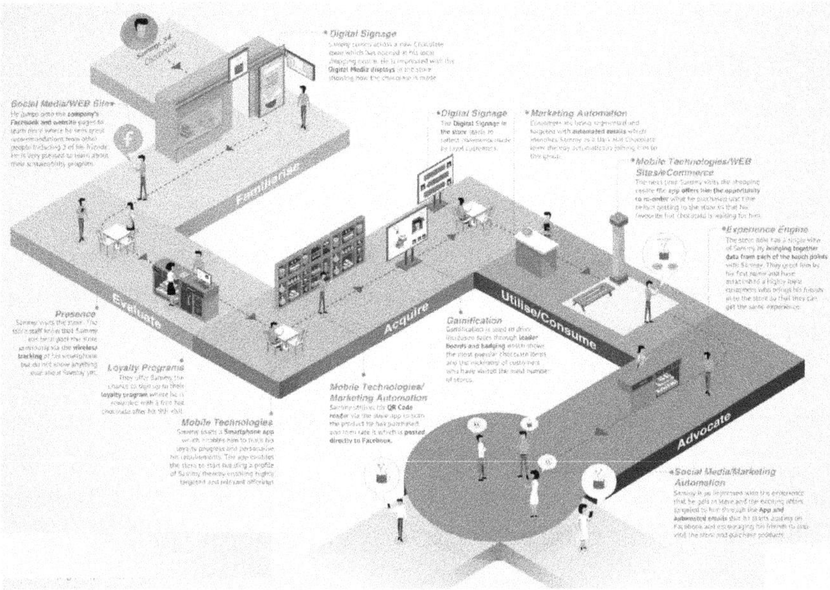

Fig. 6.6 Digital Experience Journey

Future state journey mapping is a useful approach when your objective is to explore possible customer expectations and to create new experiences and value. Mapping out a future customer journey helps teams align around a common goal.

Future customer journey map from Bright Vessel (Fig. 6.7)

In this example, the company has mapped out what they would like or expect their customers to feel in the future. It's a map of a future, yet-to-be-realized customer journey, including the touchpoints, devices, and environments involved.

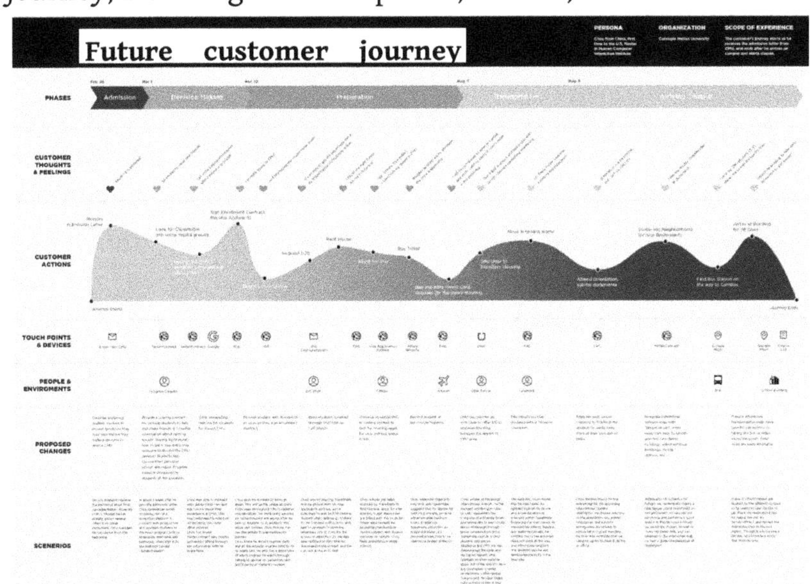

Fig. 6.7 Future customer journey map

Future state customer journey map for Carnegie Mellon University

Here's that same format again, used to map out the journey Carnegie Mellon University wants students to have, along with proposed changes to optimize each step.

Day in the life customer journey maps

A day in the life map helps you visualize your customer's entire daily routine—interactions with family, their commute, work meetings, afternoon coffee, etc—regardless of whether or not the activities are related to your company. It should be organized chronologically.

This type of customer journey map is great for providing context and giving you insights into all the thoughts, needs, and pain points a customer experiences throughout their day. You can use a day in the life map to identify moments in a customer's day when your product or service will be most valuable.

Day in the life journey map example by by Pedro Marroquin

The example above from Dribbble highlights the day-in-the-life experience of patients with secondary progressive multiple sclerosis. It shows how a patient might feelor act during various daily activities because of their condition.

Creative day in the life customer journey map designed by Chiara Galiano

Here's an interesting example that shows all the activities in a dyslexic child's typical day. This map not only visualizes the customer's day (the child's day, in this case), but also the days of the people they interact with (here, the child's parent or caregiver and their classmates).

Service blueprint customer journey maps

A service blueprint is a useful counterpart to a classic CJM. Whereas a customer journey map focuses on the thoughts, needs, and actions of the customer, a service blueprint reflects the perspective of the organization and its employees.

Essentially, service blueprinting helps visualize all the things that need to happen behind the scenes in order for the customer journey to take place. (Sort of like peeking behind a clock face.)

You may create a blueprint when making organizational or procedural changes, or when trying to pinpoint solutions to particular roadblocks in the customer journey.

A service blueprint example for an appliance retailer from NN/g

The example above shows a typical service blueprint: It's chronological and hierarchical, and is split into four layers—the customer journey, frontstage employee actions, backstage actions, and supporting processes.

A hotel service blueprint example from Miro

A hotel service blueprint example from **Miro**. (You can actually download and edit this template with a free Miro account.)

Here's another, simpler example of a service blueprint map showing the behind-the-scenes actions and processes that are needed to support a successful customer journey. You can actually download and edit this template with a free Miro account.

Circular customer journey maps

For some businesses—for example, SaaS companies with a subscription model—it may be useful to visualize the customer journey as a circle or loop. A non-linear map can help reinforce the importance of retention and advocacy for companies that rely strongly on recurring revenue, or for products that are meant to have a strong viral element.

Customer journey map flywheel example by UX Firm

In Fig. 6.8, the stages of the customer journey are shown as a loop, which is annotated with customer activities and emotions.

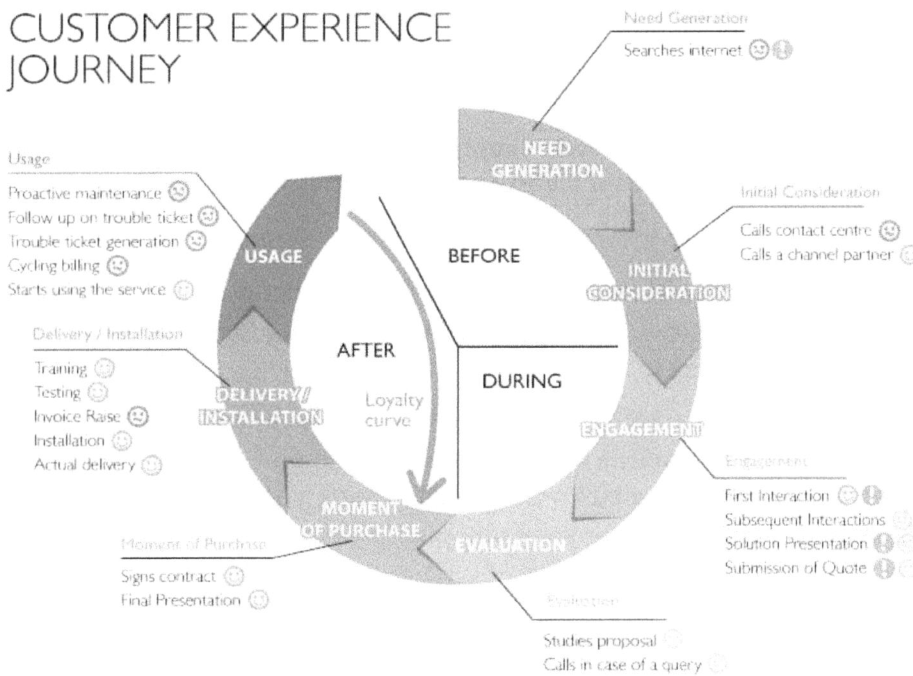

Fig. 6.8 A customer journey map

Customer journey circle map

This customer journey map example from Zendesk (Fig. 6.9) accounts for customer churn and reconsideration. It doesn't include details about the customer's activities, thoughts, or feelings, but it is notable in that it accounts for many different outcomes—including churn and reevaluation. If these are important considerations for your team, you could adapt this format to provide more insights into the customer's state of mind at each stage in their journey.

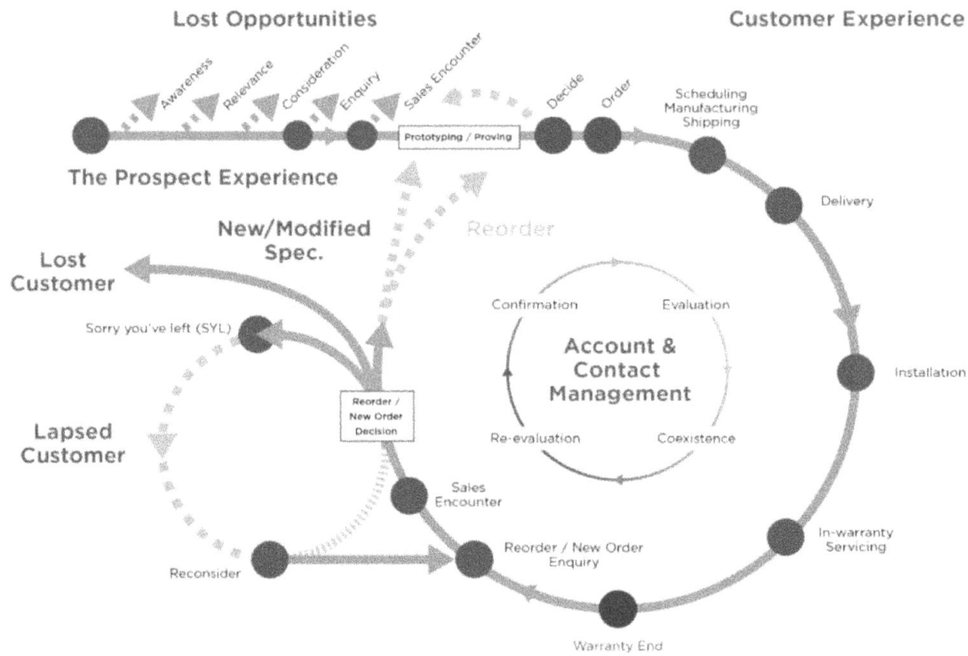

Fig. 6.9 This customer journey map example from Zendesk accounts for customer churn and reconsideration

Other types of UX maps

In addition to the five categories of customer journey maps covered above, there are two more types of UX maps worth mentioning here: empathy maps and customer experience maps.

An empathy map is a tool used to create a shared understanding around the wants, needs, thoughts, and actions of a certain type of user. While not strictly a prerequisite for creating a customer journey map, you may decide to create an empathy map as part of your journey mapping process.

Simple empathy map example from NN/g

This empathy map example from NN/g lists out the user's words, thoughts, feelings, and actions in four clear quadrants.

A **customer experience map** is used to understand human behavior as it relates to a certain topic or experience, but with no specific business or product in mind. Experience maps help visualize what the average person goes through in order to achieve a certain goal.

Like day in the life maps, customer experience maps provide contextual, anthropological insights that help you better understand your customers as people.

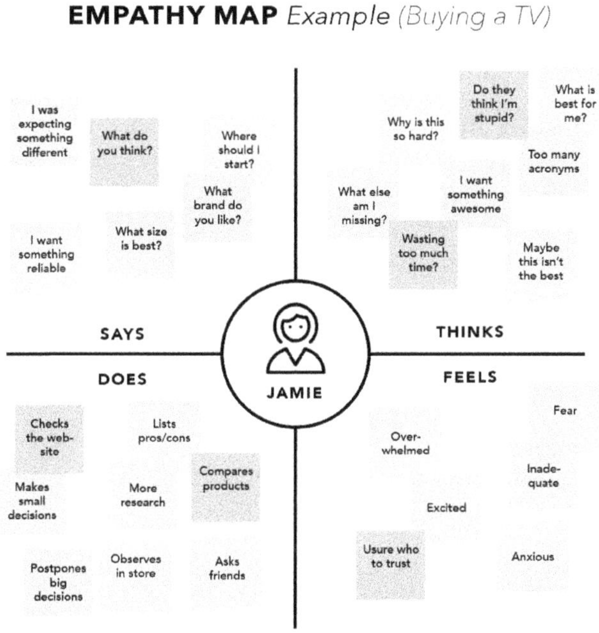

Fig. 6.10 A simple empathy map example

ANALYZING TOUCHPOINTS AND PAIN POINTS

Pain points in UX design

Pain points are problems or frustrations that users encounter when using a product or service. They can be caused by various factors, such as poor usability, lack of functionality, unmet expectations, or emotional dissatisfaction. Pain points can affect the user's satisfaction, loyalty, and retention, and can lead to negative word-of-mouth or churn. Identifying and solving pain points is a key goal of UX design, as it can enhance the user's value proposition and competitive advantage.

Customer journey touchpoints

A customer touchpoint refers to any time that a customer comes into contact with an on or offline experience, service, or showcase related to your business along their customer journey.

A common example of a customer journey with multiple touchpoints is that of an airline. While booking a flight for a holiday, a customer interacts numerous times with a business in a multitude of ways. For example, they go to the airline's website to book the ticket via their laptop, check-in via an app on their phone, liaise with ground staff at the airport, enjoy service on the flight and watch in-flight entertainment.

At each point of this journey, the customer's initial perceptions—formed from their first touchpoint with the business—are either being modified or reinforced. A customer, disinterested in a particular business, may well enjoy their experience so much that they end up becoming a loyal business ambassador. Similarly, a bad customer journey can go south.

Customer touchpoints form part of the complete end to end journey. From seeing the initial online advertisement to dealing with a sales rep, to making phone calls and complaining to a customer support team, it's the entire journey.

Importance of customer journey touchpoints

Customer journey touchpoints are important because they influence the customer's buying decision as well as any business referrals (such as through positive word of mouth).

So, when optimised correctly, customer touchpoints can be a powerful tool capable of engaging current customers, reaching new ones and influencing purchasing decisions.

Creating rewarding customer experiences with personalised touchpoints along the user journey is easier said than done.

Businesses, unfortunately, do not have access to large enough data pools and therefore much of the customers' journey along the businesses touchpoints remains unknown. The better a business can engage its customer through personalised touchpoints, the higher its ROI will become.

This is where the next generation of Customer Data Platforms (CDPs) can help. These are capable of creating customer segments that then allows businesses to hold relevant conversations with the right customers, across multiple channels. This personalised communication in turn makes the customer feel understood and valued, enhancing the experience the customer has with the business and cultivating customer loyalty.

Customer Journey Touchpoint Examples

As we defined earlier, customer touchpoints are the moments in which a customer will come into contact, interact or engage with a business. These moments of interaction can come before a purchase, during the purchasing experience, after purchasing, and when using the product or service.

Commonly they're split into three areas: Pre-purchase, purchase, and post-purchase.

Pre-purchase touchpoints

Pre-purchase touchpoints refer to the touchpoints a customer will experience before engaging with the business itself. Pre-purchase touchpoints can be harder to translate into data because some pre-purchase touchpoints will be impossible to capture, such as word-of-mouth marketing.

Pre-purchase touchpoints commonly take the form of:

- Social media marketing
- Display advertising (promoted on other websites)
- Word-of-mouth referrals
- Reviews
- User-generated content
- Forms of paid media, such as online, TV and print advertisements
- Content sponsorships
- Out-of-Home (OOH) marketing

Purchase touchpoints

Purchase touchpoints are the most crucial touchpoints in the customer journey because they define the interactions the customer has with a business while they are purchasing the product or service.

Previously, this touchpoint would have been confined to brick and mortar stores, but now these purchase touchpoints can span a number of different locations including websites, apps and social networking sites.

Common purchase touchpoints now include:

- The business website
- Social networking sites that feature shopping capabilities
- Live chat
- Sales teams
- Customer service teams
- Physical locations
- Events like pop-up shops or shows
- Distributor, retailer or supplier channels

Purchase touchpoints must be optimised to ensure that the experience a customer has at this point in the journey is positive, consistent and relevant. This increases the chance of a customer becoming a repeat customer and referring the business to their network.

Post-purchase touchpoints

Post-purchase touchpoints refer to the touchpoints a customer will come into contact with after they have made a purchase. This includes things like the product packaging, any marketing materials and the product or service itself.

Businesses can be guilty of overlooking post-purchase touchpoints, which can then have negative effects on potential returning customers or repeat purchases.

Examples of post-purchase touchpoints are:

- Customer satisfaction or experience surveys
- Referrals
- Reviews
- Social media platforms
- Email marketing and communications (i.e shipping updates)
- Newsletters
- Customer service outlets
- Loyalty programs
- Billing

Mapping Your Customer Journey Touchpoints

Customer journey mapping is a process in which marketers map out the potential journey a customer will take as they interact with various business touchpoints.

These journeys are not always linear, which is why the mapping process can be expansive, but they should still be able to display a path from the first to the final touchpoint.

It's important to consider every touch point you can think of. From digital channels, point of sale, sales team or company app. Any possible way customers interact with your business.

The following steps can help with creating a customer journey map:

Map out the journey from A to B

Creating customer personas helps to ensure that every aspect of the journey map is directed toward your ideal customer. Customer personas encompass all the demographics and psychographics which represent the average customer and are useful when deciding upon objectives for the map such as deciding the map's goals, who it is targeting, and what experiences it is being based upon.

List all of the business touchpoints

List all the touchpoints your customers and prospects are currently using, as well as any they are not using but should be. Then associate an action, emotion, or obstacle or pain point alongside these.

Actions

Actions refer to the number of actions your customers may need to take to achieve their goals, for example, buying a product but needing to click through several different menus.

Emotions and Motivations

Each action customers take is the result of an emotion, and these emotions change throughout their journey. Emotions are usually influenced by pain points or problems, so displaying solutions to these can positively impact emotions.

Obstacles and Pain Points

Obstacles or pain points stop your customers from taking action. A common example is cost. By identifying these pain points, highlighting them and then offering solutions in the customer journey, you can help to mitigate them.

Choose your maps elements

There are four types of customer journey maps that provide different insights. Depending on your specific objectives, you'll need to choose the appropriate one:

Current State

Current state maps are the most commonly used type, and they visualise actions, thoughts and emotions customers experience whilst interacting with the business.

Day in the Life

'Day in the Life' maps also visualise the actions, thoughts and emotions experienced by customers but these are extended to create a wider picture of the day-to-day life customers lead, such as their hobbies or real life pain points.

Future State

Future state maps visualise the predicted actions, thoughts and emotions of customers. These are best built with comprehensive data to ensure accuracy when setting objectives.

Service Blueprint

Service blueprints are simplified versions of one of the above styles. Their purpose is to outline the factors responsible for delivering the desired experience and are best used to identify the cause of a customer journey or outline the steps needed to attain future journeys.

Identify and make necessary changes

Bringing together the data in your analysis should give you a more insightful idea of the experience a customer has in order to take action.

This information can then be used to make the experience more refined, accurate and personalised to enable customers to have a positive experience.

How To Improve Your Customer Journey Touchpoints

Leveraging consumer data to gain better insights into their audience.

Match goals to touchpoints

Each touchpoint that your customer interacts with must serve a purpose: to propel your customer into the next stage of the buyer's journey, or to influence their purchasing decision.

With that in mind, your touchpoints need to be supporting the completion of goals that can help carry your customer through to their next step. For example, a customer's first touchpoint with your business could be through a Google search for a new kitchen appliance.

Your eCommerce site has ranked the highest because it contains the most information, and so the prospective customer clicks through onto the page where you detail the product, its uses and other relevant information.

At this moment, your customer's initial goal is to establish more information about the appliance, but their underlying goal is to ultimately end up purchasing the appliance. With this in mind, how can your touchpoint better meet your customer's underlying goal?

Instead of just displaying the information, perhaps a live chat advisor could prompt the customer and provide a selection of relevant, frequently asked questions. This meets the customers' needs as they are receiving information, and also nurtures them as potential customers for your business.

Because your company is the one being helpful and supplying more detailed information, it's subtly conveying industry expertise and credibility, which cultivates trust in your company and could influence a customer to make a purchase.

Cultivate connections

Customer experiences are always enhanced by the creation of emotional connections. Connections are what make us human and they're what change corporations from faceless entities to businesses that have swathes of loyal customers.

If customers feel that they can establish a connection, or resonate in some way with your business, product or service as they interact with a touchpoint, they will be more likely to continue their customer journey and convert. Customer journey mapping can help identify that certain touchpoint that is better suited to build relationships.

Great customer touchpoints to begin cultivating connections are those in the pre-purchase and purchase stages. Here, connections can be leveraged by directly speaking to customers by addressing their pain points, or playing to their needs and desires using techniques such as emotive language.

On social media marketing touchpoints, for example, posting content made by users (UGC) can help to establish the feel of a community, which strengthens the connections between the business and its consumers. Alternatively, if your business has a social media manager, marketing team or community manager, these employees can actively communicate with prospective customers online either through live chat features or by being active on audio chats, replying to messages or posts.

Once your customer feels in some way that they are seen as more of a person and less of a number, they may be inclined to click through to your website and continue their customer journey – especially if their experience with another business has not been as direct or personalised.

Personalise touchpoints through segmentation

Tools such as Customer Data Platforms can collate large quantities of customer data and then organise this data into such a way to form segments.

Customers can be segmented into groups according to their demographics, their hobbies or interests, or even socio-economic factors.

Having these segments then enables businesses to create personalised experiences as different customers will interact with different touchpoints in different ways.

For example, customers on a travel website interested in skiing holidays could be prompted with skiing promotions, whilst customers interested in cheap weekends away could be prompted with affordable city break offers.

Collating the data to enable segmentation would begin from as early as pre-purchase touchpoint stages where a customer may click through a social media post or other targeted advertisements.

If the business was using a CDP (Customer Data Platform) it could automatically capture data such as a cookie or tag analytic, enabling an initial customer's profile to be built and grouped by their displayed interest, i.e city breaks.

This data can then be fed into a Customer Data Platform where the customer's initial data can be enhanced to build a more comprehensive profile and segmented to enable personalised experiences to be targeted toward the customer on their return to the website.

The Benefits of Customer Journey Mapping & Identifying Customer Touchpoints

The customer experience is made up of various touchpoints occurring throughout customer journeys. These customer touchpoints define the customer experience and whether it's a positive or negative experience. How can you expect to improve the customer experience without knowing the touchpoints which make it up?

If you've created your customer journey map and are actively using it to improve the customer experience the following long term business benefits can be expected.

- **Improves customer satisfaction** - With a more tailored and responsive customer experience, you can expect customer satisfaction to be improved. Especially if you're taking customer feedback into account.
- **Increase customer retention** - With a better understanding of the end to end experience you can provide instant support and resolutions to any customer issues, this improves their satisfaction. If you're meeting, or possible exceeding customer expectations they won't be leaving any time soon.
- **Improve Sales –** If the above two points are happening, chances are you'll see an increase in sales and new customers.
- **Improve brand loyalty** - Providing a more tailored, and personalized customer journey keeps customers happy and coming back to your business. You also have the potential to identify and save negative customer experiences before the customer runs out of patience.

Part III: Design Thinking Process

CHAPTER-7

EMPATHY IN DESIGN THINKING

"Design thinking begins with skills designers have learned over many decades in their quest to match human needs with available technical resources within the practical constraints of business. By integrating what is desirable from a human point of view with what is technologically feasible and economically viable, designers have been able to create the products we enjoy today. Design thinking takes the next step, which is to put these tools into the hands of people who may have never thought of themselves as designers and apply them to a vastly greater range of problems." - *Tim Brown, Change by Design, Introduction*

Before we can understand the Design Thinking process, it's important to get to grips with the ideology behind it - that is, Design Thinking.

In simple terms, Design Thinking is a methodology that aims to tackle highly complex problems.

Complex problems - otherwise known as "wicked" problems - are those that are difficult to define and cannot be solved using standard methods and approaches. They are the opposite of "tame" problems, which can be solved by applying a tried-and-tested algorithm or logic.

Empathize

Empathize is the first stage of the design thinking process. Design teams conduct research to get personal grasps of their users' needs. They set aside assumptions to obtain insights into the users' world by observing and consulting with users. This way, they can understand users' experiences, motivations and problems.

Empathy is defined as "the action of understanding, being aware of, being sensitive to, and vicariously experiencing the feelings, thoughts, and experience of another without having the feelings, thoughts, and experience fully communicated in an objectively explicit manner."

It describes the ability to put yourself in another person's shoes; to truly see the world through their eyes in a given context or situation.

In a social context, empathy is often what drives us to take action. If we see people suffering or struggling, and we are able to empathise with their situation, we are compelled to help relieve them in some way.

Designers need to build empathy for their users in order to take the right course of action. It's important to understand how the user feels when interacting with a certain product or interface; does the layout of this website evoke feelings of frustration? What emotions does the user go through when navigating this app?

In building empathy, designers can create products which truly please the user and make their lives easier. Without this empathy, the design process lacks that all-important user-centricity which often marks the distinction between product success and failure.

Empathic design caters to real user needs, rather than supposed "averages". One of the main objectives of the empathise stage is to identify user needs and behaviours that are latent, or unarticulated. As a designer, it's important to distinguish between what people say they would do in a certain situation, and what they actually do. In reality, users may have habits or desires that they're not aware of, so it's essential for the designer to observe the user in action.

Empathic research and design is not concerned with facts about the user, such as their age or location. Rather, it focuses on their feelings towards a product and their motivations in certain situations. Why do they behave in a certain way? Why do they prefer to do this instead of that? Why do they click here rather than there when presented with a particular screen or page? These are the kinds of insights you'll uncover during the empathise phase, and they'll help you to create user experiences that cater to your audience.

BUILDING EMPATHY FOR USERS

Empathy is the ability to understand and share the feelings, needs, and perspectives of others. It is a key skill for facilitators who want to help teams solve problems creatively and collaboratively. In a design thinking session, empathy can help you define the problem, generate ideas, and test solutions with the users in mind. Here are some tips on how to build empathy with users during a design thinking session.

Identify a design challenge

A design challenge inspired by empathy for others is the starting point of every design thinking project. You can discover just such a challenge through carefully and closely observing others, and considering new perspectives.

The first step on a design thinking journey then, involves disrupting yourself, breaking your routine. Get away from screens and offices and classrooms, and venture into new spaces and places to kickstart your imagination and invigorate your creative work. Look around you, wander and explore, listen to and speak with people.

Before long, you'll notice all kinds of real-world challenges that you are inspired to create solutions for. There is no "right" design challenge to begin working on.

Fig. 7.1 Identify a design challenge

Design thinking is a deeply human approach to innovation that relies on your ability to be intuitive, to interpret what you observe and to develop ideas that are emotionally meaningful to the people you are designing for. When you listen to and develop empathy for your users, participants, clients, patients or other stakeholders, it will inspire your creative problem solving work.

Conduct Design research by observing and engaging.

Observe how users interact with their environment. Capture quotes, behaviours and other notes that reflect their experience. Watching users gives you clues as to what they think and feel - what they need. You can also learn a lot by just watching what people do, and how they lead their lives, online or offline.

As people navigate through their day, traveling, shopping, dining, working, talking, relaxing, sleeping, we rely on products and services - some of which are easy and enjoyable to use. But it's also true that we experience day-to-day complications, confusions, and problems requiring workarounds.

By noticing the "pain points" that interfere with people enjoying a seamless and satisfying experience with the products and services in our lives, design thinkers pay close attention to any frustrating moments people have, because those are red flags indicating possible product/service shortcomings. Designers then set to work creating more streamlined, smart, elegant solutions - sometimes by simplifying and eliminating extra "nice-to-have" (but not need-to-have) features. And usually by taking inspiration from the workarounds, hacks, and modifications they observed people using, and incorporating those upgrades into the final project - making it more useful, convenient, value-added, and "human" in the process.

Engage users directly - interact with and interview them, if it's feasible to do so. Engaging users reveals deeper insights into their beliefs and values. When you are seeking new understanding about other people, and why they struggle with certain experiences, you might reach out to them and gain their perspective on the issues that matter to them. Learning about users in their own words will inform and inspire you.

Asking the right kinds of open-ended questions and carefully listening to the responses (verbal and nonverbal) is the way to discover unmet needs. In the process you will gain a deeper understanding of the decisions people make and the obstacles they face. Open ended questions are questions that lead to a further discussion. They are questions that do not have a simple answer like yes or no or a number.

Examples of open-ended questions are:

- What are your favourite things about this activity?
- How did doing that activity make you feel?
- What would you change about that activity if you could change something?

These kinds of questions help researchers get to a deeper understanding of their user and the context in which the user operates.

Immerse Yourself: Embrace a beginner's mindset.

If possible, immerse yourself in your users' experience. Find (or create if necessary) ways to insert yourself in specific environments to understand first hand who you're designing for. Immersion, explains Merlijn Kouprie and Froukje Sleeswijk Visser, involves wandering around in the user's world, gathering knowledge, and staying open-minded and non-judgemental, and staying interested in absorbing a different perspective.[2]

When listening to and observing users, try to embrace a beginner's mindset. Approach situations and problems as a novice even if you already know a lot about them. When meeting with other people, ask open-ended questions, even if you think you may already have or know the answers. You might be surprised. Let yourself learn to see the world from another person's point of view.

Designers can purposefully expand their empathic horizon by regularly going off in search of new experiences, immersing themselves in the lives of others, and constantly seeking to make new personal connections. Take more photographs, ask more questions and engage in quiet contemplation, collaborate, have deeper, more meaningful and honest conversations, reserve judgements, seek genuine understanding, stay attentive to your feelings.

Notice patterns

Once you observe or speak with several people, you may see and hear some of the same things. These patterns can help you identify issues and possible solutions.

Document your findings

When you step out of an observation session, it's easy to feel overwhelmed by the amount of information you have taken in. Use the half hour immediately after the session to begin documenting your research. Take notes about what you see and/or discuss so you can reflect on what happened later. Drawings, photographs, and video can also be helpful. Before you photograph other people, be sure to get their permission so as to not violate their privacy.

How to be an Empathic Observer

1. Abandon Your Ego

Most of us have a tendency to assert ourselves, which results in an imposition upon others, as well as having more concern about our own situation rather than the needs and concerns of others. Often in our education or workplace, we are taught to adopt an egocentric view of things and be firm in our opinions and thoughts. However, in order to empathise deeply, we need to tame and put aside our egos. We need to become aware of the primary goal of empathy in Design Thinking, which is to understand and experience the feelings of others.

2. Adopt Humility

When we adopt humility, we naturally improve our ability to empathise, because through humility we elevate the value of others above ourselves. This is underscored in *Rise of the DEO*, a book by Maria Giudice, innovator and VP of Experience Design in Autodesk, and Christopher Ireland, ethnographer and CEO of design research firm Cheskin. In *Rise of the DEO*, Giudice and Ireland discuss the emerging role of design leadership and point out that humility is a characteristic of design-focused leaders who are willing to admit their own shortcomings as well as to abandon preconceived ideas for the good of the overall vision and goals.

3. Be a Good Listener

So as to empathise, we need to listen and listen attentively. We need to choose actively to block out our inner conflicting voices, and allow the other's voice to resonate. We need to train ourselves to control our natural tendency to formulate our own opinions and voice them before the other person has finished talking. Doing so would enable us to have a deeper kind of listening, which uncovers deeper meaning and experience.

4. Hone Your Observation skills

In order to develop empathy towards our users, we need to do more than listen. We need to observe others, and have a close reading of their behaviours, subtle indications, their non-verbal expressions, body language, and environments.

Only once we are able to experience the *full* range of sensations of others within context can we have a deeper and more meaningful empathic experience. Many times, what our users articulate is only a fraction of the full story. By honing our observation skills, we can fill many of the gaps, leading to a deeper understanding of someone else's experience.

5. Care

A genuine concern about the state of others, leading to the desire to act and assist, is required. This is one of the important drivers that allow us to overcome our own needs and wants and seek to understand others. We must build a sense of care, a deep concern and desire to want to help, nurture, and provide assistance. This requires a level of emotional insight.

6. Be Curious

Being genuinely curious makes engaging in empathy research not only easier but also extremely rewarding as we learn to understand what motivates people. By being curious, we are naturally inclined to dig into unexpected areas, uncover new insights, and explore all aspects of people's lives. At a glance, these details might seem unimportant, but they will expose the most important information we need for problem solving.

7. Be Sincere

Nothing kills empathy more than a lack of sincerity. When we approach people with a superficial agenda, superiority complex, or any mindset that may undermine our sincere intention to understand their experience deeply, we are placing a barrier between us and those we seek to understand. Rather than approaching people with the mindset that they are in need of our help, we should realise that we stand to benefit more out of deeply understanding them. After all, the solution exists to serve *their* needs, and your work will not be complete unless you properly understand their needs.

Learn to Understand Body Language

We should have a keen awareness of how our body language sets the scene for trust and engagement between ourselves and the people we are observing or interviewing. On top of that, we need to read and interpret the signals that our users give off via their body language. This is a skill that comes with practice, and thus practice we must. At times, body language might be *so* subtle that the messages made by our very forms (eyebrows, shoulders, hands, and virtually any other part) as well as how we sound and behave are visible only to practiced readers of body language.

If we want to connect with and engage our users on a deeper level, we need to study their body language, body signals, facial expressions, voice intonations, and the positive and negative signs that come from these. Here are some of the little things that you should pay attention to:

- Learn to read the subtle nuances in communication, change of tone, pauses and skipping back over points.
- Listen to what is *not* being said, to what's being avoided or covered up.
- Subtly know when to encourage more expression or to lead the conversation or story in a beneficial direction.
- Know *what* to ask and *how* to ask it—and when the person might be *ready* to be asked.

TECHNIQUES FOR EMPATHETIC DESIGN

Companies can engage in empathic design, or similar techniques such as contextual inquiry, in a variety of ways. However, most employ the following five-step process:

Step One: Observation

It's important to clarify who should be observed, who should do the observing, and what the observer should be watching.

Who should be observed? These individuals may be customers, noncustomers, the customers of customers, or a group of individuals who by playing different roles collectively perform a task.

Hewlett-Packard makes protocol analyzer software that enables managers of computer operations to diagnose network malfunctions. As networks became more complex, smaller companies began to offer customized software for the idiosyncratic needs of some of HP's customers. In response, HP designers conducted extensive market research, which resulted in a cacophony of requests to expand the types of data the analyzers could track and report on. Not only did that make product development flow much more difficult, it also failed to make the products any more effective. Users became inundated with data that they couldn't turn into useful information. HP developers decided to stop focusing on their traditional customers, the operations managers. Instead, they watched, among others, network maintenance technicians at work.

From those observations, the developers discovered that what their customers really needed was not, as they had been told, more data to analyze. Rather, users needed to recover swiftly from computer crashes. That change in perspective led to a shift in technological emphasis. The result was HP's highly successful Network Advisor, which de-emphasizes data collection, analysis, and reports. Instead, it identifies the network problem, recommends a solution, and suggests ways to implement the solution quickly.

Who should do the observing? Differences in training, education, and natural inclinations predispose different people to extract very different information when watching the exact same situation. A human-factors specialist may note body positions; an engineer may notice angles and mechanical interactions; a designer may see spaces and forms. Of course, many people are multiskilled observers, but the best way to capture the most important aspects of an environment is to send out a small team, each member of which has expertise in a different discipline. That's what the design firm IDEO did for Details, a subsidiary of the office-equipment supplier, Steelcase. To help Details develop a more easily repositioned computer keyboard, IDEO sent a human-factors expert, an engineer, and a designer on anthropological expeditions into office buildings. Each team member brought back a notebook full of very different data.

Because a critical objective of such an expedition is to match the unarticulated needs of users with technological possibilities, at least one member of any team should have experience in behavioral observation and another should have a deep understanding of the organizational capabilities the development team can draw upon. When the team comes from an outside consulting firm, some of the client's employees should be included to provide that deep understanding. The Doblin Group, for example, was challenged to redefine the travel experience for SAS. It convened a very large team that included not only social scientists and information designers but also pilots and flight attendants from the airline. The airline employees understood SAS's capabilities in depth and also knew how proposed service innovations might require changes not just in operations but also in corporate culture.

Few organizations have large numbers of employees capable of conducting such anthropological expeditions. When asked what characteristics members of empathic-design teams should have, managers that employ those techniques list ones rarely found on most résumés: open-mindedness, observational skills, and curiosity. Human resource departments are not set up to screen for such abilities. Some companies, such as Intel and Xerox, have hired cultural anthropologists and social psychologists for their research, marketing, or product development departments because they are trained observers who have demonstrated an interest in human behavior. Other organizations outsource this kind of work to design firms, knowing that there are employees in such specialty companies with a variety of skills: experts in human factors, in graphics and visual design, and in engineering.

What behavior should be observed? The people being observed should be carrying out normal routines—playing, eating, relaxing, or working at home or at the office. For its research on mobile communications, the Doblin Group followed a lawyer from the moment she left her children at their day care center in the morning until after the children were in bed that night, revealing a wealth of communication needs that are often overlooked. Few people, of course, are totally oblivious to a team of people hanging over their shoulders, observing them at work or play. But a real-life atmosphere—even a slightly stilted one—is still better than the highly artificial setting of a focus-group conference room or a laboratory. For some products and services, team members may conduct their observations in a highly unobtrusive way simply by planting themselves in a public setting where people are going about their normal routines and watching behaviors more systematically than the usual sidewalk observer generally does.

Step Two: Capturing Data

Because empathic-design techniques stress observation over inquiry, relatively few data are gathered through responses to questions. (See the exhibit "Inquiry Versus Observation: What's Different?") When they wish to know how to interpret people's actions, observers may ask a few very open-ended questions, such as "Why are you doing that?" They often carry a list of questions to prompt their own observations—for example, "What problems is the user encountering?" But most data are to gathered from visual, auditory, and sensory cues. Thus empathic-design teams very frequently use photography and videography as tools.

Inquiry Versus Observation: What's Different?

Video can capture subtle, fleeting body language that may convey large amounts of information and store it for future review and analysis. For more than a decade, researchers at Xerox PARC, the Xerox Palo Alto Research Center, have videotaped users when they were confronted with a product such as a new copier machine.

The researchers can see puzzled looks on the subjects' faces, they watch as people search for controls, and they can observe the kinds of automatic responses that happen when someone expects a control to be here or there and it is not. Such cues come and go within the span of mere seconds and are hard to capture in notes.

Even still photographs convey information that can be lost in verbal descriptions. Nissan Design International commissioned a photographer to travel to several cities and take pictures of people in trucks to better understand how they were being used as commuter and family cars. NDI designers were startled to discover how little their trucks (and those of competitors) were actually being used for the purposes being advertised and reported in market surveys.

NDI president Hirshberg was surprised to see how many people were eating in trucks, recalling "not just drinks, but whole spaghetti dinners!" The designers also noticed how much people resembled their vehicles and how scuffed up some of the vehicles were. They began to wonder if some vehicles should be more like denim and look better the more worn they got.

Photographs or drawings (which artists and designers can produce on the spot) show spatial arrangements and contain details that may have gone unnoticed while the team was on location. When members of one observation team displayed on a bulletin board all the candid photos they took of the people they observed in an office building, they were struck by the snake pit of wires in which everyone's feet were stuck.

That led their company to build in conduits for those wires in its next generation of dividers for modular offices. And pictures of backyard barbecues taken for the developers from the Thermos company who were working on a new charcoal grill showed women struggling with equipment designed for the generally greater height and upper body strength of men, who were (incorrectly) assumed to be the most likely outdoor family chefs.

Step Three: Reflection and Analysis

After gathering data in many forms, the team members return to reflect on what they have observed and to review their visual data with other colleagues. Those individuals—unhampered by possibly extraneous information, such as the reputations of the individuals or companies visited or the weather at the observation site—will focus on the data before them, and they, too, will see different things. They will ask questions that the team members may or may not be able to answer and that may well send them out for further observation. It is at this point that the team tries to identify all of its customers' possible problems and needs.

The IDEO team redesigning Lifeline Systems' personal-response unit for elderly people uncovered a potentially dangerous problem only after they shared their field data with colleagues. On leaving for an extended period, many users turned off their units so that Lifeline's monitoring staff would not mistake silence for an emergency.

However, because the unit lacked an obvious status indicator, users often forgot to reactivate the units when they returned. The opportunity to improve the design was recognized by engineers who were not part of the original group of IDEO observers.

Consequently, IDEO redesigned the product so that it indicated even to the vision impaired when it was turned off and automatically restarted when users tried to send their habitual "all is well" signals to the monitoring service.

Step Four: Brainstorming for Solutions

Brainstorming is a valuable part of any innovation process; within the empathic-design process, it is used specifically to transform the observations into graphic, visual representations of possible solutions. Design firms maintain that this step is often undervalued: "Our clients sometimes don't understand why brainstorming is expensive - and immensely productive - until they have sat in on a session.

Then they usually go away shaking their heads, saying, 'Wow - that was really amazing!'" Although brainstorming is generally associated with a creative process, it is not undisciplined. Managers at IDEO tell their employees to heed five rules: defer judgment, build on the ideas of others, hold one conversation at a time, stay focused on the topic, and encourage wild ideas.

Such sessions are valuable not only for the ideas that pop up during the actual brainstorming session but also for the concepts and solutions that occur to people later, at home, because the seeds to them had been planted in their minds.

Companies that routinely hold brainstorming sessions as part of the empathic-design process need supporting infrastructure. That can be as low tech as a table covered in thick paper used for doodling and taking notes; when a session is over, team members can tear off the best ideas and take them home.

It can be as high tech as the Idea Factory, a physical and virtual space being set up in San Francisco to help companies create next-generation products and business strategies. To facilitate collaborative work, the Idea Factory will boast workstations; customized groupware; and the latest white-board recording equipment, which can produce hard copies of whatever is written down or drawn on the board's surface.

Step Five: Developing Prototypes of Possible Solutions

Clearly, prototypes are not unique to empathic design. But the more radical an innovation, of course, the harder it is to understand how it should look, function, and be used. Just as researchers gather useful visual data, so too can they stimulate communication by creating some physical representation of a new concept for a product or service. Prototypes are a critical part of the empathic-design process for at least three reasons:

- Prototypes clarify the concept of the new product or service for the development team.
- They enable the team to place its concept in front of other individuals who work in functions not formally represented on the team.
- They can stimulate reaction and foster discussion with potential customers of the innovation because of their concreteness.

Sometimes, two prototypes are used, one that emulates the function but not the form, and another that illustrates the ideal physical appearance of the intended product but doesn't work. In designing the outdoor grill, Thermos's Lifestyle team produced two models, which they called the Monitor and the Merrimack (after the Civil War ships).

The Monitor was a functioning prototype, but the team considered it ugly; the Merrimack was sleek and stylish but was actually an inert object made of plastic foam. The company used both models to elicit feedback from consumers and retailers.

Simulations are also useful prototypes. And they need not be as computer-intensive and elaborate as the University of Illinois's CAVE, which simulates the three-dimensional space of a room and can be programmed to represent different environments, such as a factory.

In fact, many useful simulations are not computerized at all. When Chaparral Steel Company wanted to design metal splash guards to put along the path of the white-hot metal bars that were moving toward the rolling mill, they positioned waterlogged plywood at various angles and heights to simulate different designs.

The plywood was rapidly consumed by the hot metal, but not before the experimenters could learn what design worked best.

Role-playing is also a form of simulation. At Interval Research Corporation of Palo Alto, California, young twenty-something media-interface designers were outfitted with fogged glasses, gloves, and weights on their arms and legs so they could feel what it would be like for the very elderly to work prototype physical controls or use hand gestures in the air as a way to control the next generation of TVs, VCRs, and other electronic equipment. That simulation allowed the young researchers to apply their intensive knowledge of media possibilities within constraints that they could not otherwise personally experience (at least for some years).

CHAPTER-8

IDEATION AND BRAINSTORMING

Ideation is often closely related to the practice of brainstorming, a specific technique that is utilized to generate new ideas. A principal difference between ideation and brainstorming is that ideation is commonly more thought of as being an individual pursuit, while brainstorming is almost always a group activity. Brainstorming is usually conducted by getting a group of people together to come up with either general new ideas or ideas for solving a specific problem or dealing with a specific situation.

For example, a major corporation that recently learned it is the object of a major lawsuit may want to gather together top executives for a brainstorming session on how to publicly respond to the lawsuit being filed.

Participants in a brainstorming session are encouraged to freely toss out whatever ideas may occur to them. The thinking is that by generating a large number of ideas, the brainstorming group is likely to come up with a suitable solution for whatever issue they are addressing.

The lines between ideation and brainstorming have become a bit more blurred with the development of several brainstorming software programs, such as Brightidea and Ideawake. These software programs are designed to encourage employees of companies to generate new ideas for improving the companies' operations and, ultimately, bottom-line profitability.

The programs often combine the processes of ideation and brainstorming in that individual employees can use them, but companies may simulate brainstorming sessions by having several employees all utilize the software to generate new ideas intended to address a specific purpose.

Ideation and brainstorming are essential steps in the design thinking process, where the goal is to generate as many ideas as possible to solve a complex problem or create an innovative solution. Ideation and brainstorming are not just about coming up with *random ideas*, but rather applying *creative thinking techniques* and methods to explore different perspectives, *challenge assumptions*, and discover new possibilities. In this section, we will discuss some of the benefits and challenges of ideation and brainstorming, as well as some of the best practices and tools to facilitate *effective and productive sessions.*

Some of the benefits of ideation and brainstorming are:

- They allow the participants to express their thoughts and opinions freely, without fear of judgment or criticism.
- They foster *a collaborative and supportive environment*, where the participants can build on each other's ideas and learn from different perspectives.
- They stimulate creativity and innovation, by encouraging the participants to think outside the box and explore *unconventional solutions.*
- They increase the quantity and diversity of ideas, by generating a large pool of *potential solutions* that can be further evaluated and refined.

Some of the challenges of ideation and brainstorming are:

- They can be time-consuming and exhausting, especially if the sessions are too long or too frequent.
- They can be influenced by group dynamics and biases, such as conformity, dominance, or anchoring, which can limit the quality and variety of ideas.
- They can be affected by *external factors*, such as *the physical environment*, the facilitator, or the tools, which can either enhance or hinder *the creative low.*
- They can be difficult to document and organize, especially if the ideas are not captured or categorized properly.

Some of the best practices and tools for ideation and brainstorming are:

- Define the problem and the goal clearly, and communicate them to the participants before the session.
- Set *some ground rules* and guidelines, such as no criticism, no evaluation, and no filtering of ideas, and ensure that everyone follows them.
- Use a facilitator or a moderator, who can guide the session, encourage participation, and manage the time and the energy level.

- Use a variety of techniques and methods, such as mind mapping, sketching, SCAMPER, or *brainstorming matrix*, to stimulate different types of thinking and generate different types of ideas.
- Use *a suitable tool* or platform, such as a whiteboard, a sticky note, or *a digital app*, to capture, record, and display the ideas in *a visible and accessible way*.
- Use a simple and effective method, such as dot voting, *affinity diagram*, or impact/effort matrix, to prioritize, group, and select *the most promising ideas* for further development.

Ideation and brainstorming are not the end of the design thinking process, but rather the beginning of the journey to create innovative solutions. By applying these best practices and tools, you can make your ideation and *brainstorming sessions* more effective and productive, and generate more and better ideas for your complex problems.

GENERATING CREATIVE IDEAS IN DESIGN THINKING

Ideation phase of design thinking: a step-by-step guide

Here are the steps that you need to follow for a productive ideation process.

Step 1: Define the problem

The problem or problems that were identified during the empathize phase of your design thinking process will guide your ideation session. Your team will generate ideas that will solve these problems.

Phrase the problem using a 'How might we' prefix. For instance, if your team is solving the problem of poor user experience in an app, the question would be 'How might we create an intuitive user experience?' This phrasing focuses the ideation session while implying that there is a solution to the problem.

Step 2: Choose a space

The location of your ideation session has a huge effect on how safe and comfortable the participants will feel. Choose a large room that has whiteboards or enough wall space for you to set up your own writing materials.

It is a good idea to choose a space that is away from the environment where your team usually works in. Being in a new environment triggers creativity and alternative ways of thinking. It's also important to come up with a few icebreaker activities to help the participants loosen up.

Step 3: Set time limits

Decide beforehand how long the ideation session for each problem is going to last. Set the number of ideas that the session should generate for each problem.

These limits will give the session momentum, create energy, and an adrenaline rush which will spark even more creativity.

Step 4: Select ideation techniques

There are several ideation techniques that you can use to help your team come up with ideas. The most common ones include:

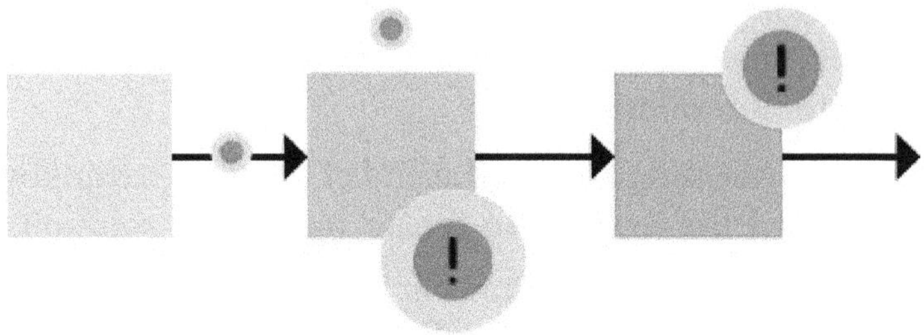

Fig. 8.1

- **Brainstorming**– verbally sharing ideas within the group.
- **Mind mapping**– visually ideating by starting with a keyword that is related to the problem and then writing all the ideas associated with it around it.
- **Storyboarding**– creating visual storylines of how users might go about solving the problem.
- **Worst possible idea**– coming up with the worst possible ideas to remove creative blocks.

Don't limit your ideation session to one technique, you are free to use more than one technique. This will ensure that your team generates the highest number of ideas.

Step 5: Rank the ideas

If your ideation session has gone according to plan, you will end up with lots of ideas. Some will be promising, others will be outrageous and others will be crazy. Together with the participants sort the ideas according to different categories such as promising, interesting, unconventional, or crazy. For each category, rank the ideas. Don't throw away any ideas as they might be useful in the future or in other design projects.

Step 6: Choose the ideas that will move to the prototyping stage

The end goal of the ideation in design thinking is to come up with ideas that can be prototyped and tested. Choose the ideas that are going to be prototyped and maintain a record of those that didn't make the final cut.

Get your team into the right mindset for ideation

The success or failure of your design thinking ideation process will depend on how you approach it and the atmosphere that you create. You need to create a safe judgment-free environment that will give all the participants the chance to express their ideas including the most outrageous or unconventional. Here's how to create the right atmosphere:

Accept all ideas

To encourage creativity and open mindedness, do not reject any ideas. If you do, you will dampen the mood of the session. Remember that the aim is to generate as many ideas as possible. On top of accepting all ideas, encourage participants to build on the ideas of others by using the 'yes and...' phrase. This will lead to interesting ideas and perspectives.

Stay on topic

During a high energy ideation session, your team can easily get derailed and start ideating on other issues that are not related to the problem. As the facilitator, it is your job to guide the session and refocus the ideation session. Should your team come up with a juicy idea that is not related to the problem, note it down for future reference and then guide the session back to the problem at hand.

Document all ideas

Ensure that you log all the ideas produced during the session. The facilitator can act as a secretary by writing the ideas down on a whiteboard. Alternatively, the participants can also document their ideas by writing them on sticky notes or on the whiteboard.

When documenting ideas, summarize them, and record the key point. For instance, if a participant suggests "we could create an interactive story-based app to improve user experience" document "create an interactive story-based app." To ensure that you don't miss any ideas, work on ideas one at a time.

Best Ideation Techniques

No "best" practice exists since their usefulness varies depending on the situation. But here are some of the most widespread and effective ones.

Mind Mapping

A mind map is like a drawing aimed at organizing thoughts. It starts with a single core idea in the middle of a page. Then, it grows when you add related ideas, pictures, or words around that central idea.

The best thing about a mind map is that it changes and evolves. It follows the flow of ideas, connecting different parts of the concept and showing the thinking process. When connecting ideas visually, people see how things relate. Therefore, you can come up with solutions that fit your problems best.

SCAMPER

SCAMPER involves creating a checklist of prompts to think about a problem from different angles and develop innovative solutions. The method guides your thinking process through seven different approaches. Each of them corresponds to one of the letters of the acronym:

- **"Substitute"** prompts you to consider parts of the problem, product, or idea you can replace or swap.
- **"Combine"** suggests merging different aspects of a product, service, or problem in new ways.
- **"Adapt"** encourages adapting or adjusting existing solutions or elements to new situations.
- **"Modify"** is about thinking of how you could change or alter the current situation or its elements.
- **"Put to another use"** involves considering how you might use an item or process other than its intended purpose.
- **"Eliminate"** is removing product, service, or process elements. It's about creating value by eliminating what's unnecessary and focusing on what's essential.
- **"Reverse"** or **"Rearrange"** suggests turning a situation or problem on its head.

Brainstorming

Brainstorming is one of the most popular UX ideation techniques. This approach uncovers various solutions that conventional thinking might miss.

The primary goal of brainstorming promotes generating multiple ideas, adhering to the principle of "quantity over quality." Participants often feel more inclined to share their thoughts and ideas when emphasizing volume.

Maintaining a non-judgmental environment during the session remains critical. All ideas, regardless of how wild or unconventional, receive a warm welcome.

Round-Robin Brainstorming

With this approach, each participant adds an idea in turns. As a result, everyone gets a chance to contribute, being helpful when some team members often dominate the conversation.

Brainwriting

This method is similar to brainstorming. But instead of sharing ideas out loud, each participant writes down their thoughts. It's a good technique for introverted team members. Also, it's helpful when you want to prevent louder voices from dominating the session.

Six Thinking Hats

This method, introduced by Edward de Bono, encourages users to approach problems "with different hats on." Each "hat" represents a different thinking type. By changing hats, participants can easily switch between different points of view:

- **White Hat** — neutrality and objectivity. Participants focus on data and information. They look at the facts, figures, and evidence.
- **Red Hat** — feelings and intuition. Participants express their emotions, gut reactions, and hunches without justification or explanation. It provides a space to explore the emotional landscape.
- **Black Hat** — judgment and caution. Team members evaluate ideas critically. They look for potential problems, risks, and adverse consequences.
- **Yellow Hat** — positivity and optimism. Participants focus on the benefits, feasibility, and positive aspects of an idea or a decision.
- **Green Hat** — creativity. Participants generate new ideas, alternative solutions, and fresh concepts.
- **Blue Hat** — control of the process. It's about organizing the thinking process, setting the agenda, and drawing conclusions. When wearing the blue hat, participants manage the other hats, summarizing and synthesizing the input gathered.

Sketching and Prototyping

Sketching and prototyping are among the most widespread product ideation techniques. They play a critical role in translating abstract ideas into something more concrete. Sketching is usually the first step in this process. It involves creating quick, simple drawings to illustrate an idea or concept.

Prototyping takes ideas visualization one step further. It varies from low-fidelity paper prototypes to high-fidelity digital interactive ones. One of the primary benefits of prototyping is identifying potential issues or improvements early in the process.

Role Play

The role-play technique involves stepping into the various stakeholders' shoes. It allows for a deeper, more empathetic understanding of the users' needs, desires, and potential frustrations. Role-playing involves simulating scenarios or tasks a user would encounter. Then, participants experience them as if they were users. For instance, you may need to navigate a website like a visually impaired user.

Journey Mapping

This technique maps out the entire user experience with a product or service. It aims to identify pain points and improvement opportunities. The primary goal of journey mapping is to gain a holistic view of the customer's interaction over time. It captures users' thoughts, feelings, expectations, and frustrations.

Journey mapping identifies the critical interaction points or "moments of truth" that shape the user's perception. These are critical touchpoints where the UX can swing from positive to negative or vice versa.

Reverse Thinking or Problem Reversal

Instead of thinking about how to solve the problem, determine what causes it. Problem Reversal might initially sound counterintuitive. But this shift in perspective often leads to a better understanding of the problem and sparks unconventional solutions.

By deliberately thinking about how to cause the problem, you must scrutinize it more closely. Explore its specifics, characteristics, and effects in detail. This approach provides a deeper comprehension of the problem's core and suggests potential solutions.

In the ideation phase of design thinking, the goal is to encourage free-thinking and foster creativity. That's why the ideation techniques design thinking employs are so diverse and adaptable.

Choose the Best Ideation Technique

Here are some tips on choosing the proper technique for your specific project.

Know Your Team

Some people may be more visually oriented, while others prefer verbal or written approaches. Consider your team members' personalities, skills, and preferences. For instance, introverted team members will likely excel in techniques like Brainwriting.

Consider the Scope

Your project's scope or challenge is crucial in determining the ideation tools and techniques. If you're working on a service design project, journey mapping is an effective way to ideate around different touchpoints. In turn, techniques like prototyping and sketching benefit a product design project more.

Timing Matters

The amount of time available also affects the technique choice. For example, Brainstorming and Round-Robin usually require less time. In contrast, ideation tools and techniques like Reverse Thinking or Role Play might take longer.

Consider these tips to ensure you select the most creative ideation techniques for your design thinking project.

FACILITATION TECHNIQUES FOR IDEATION SESSIONS

Understanding the Power of Ideation Facilitation

- Ideation facilitation is a powerful tool that can help teams unlock their creative potential and generate innovative ideas. By guiding the ideation process and creating an environment that fosters collaboration and open thinking, facilitators play a crucial role in ensuring that teams can effectively brainstorm and bring their ideas to life. Understanding the power of ideation facilitation is key to harnessing the collective intelligence of a group and driving successful innovation.
- One of the primary benefits of ideation facilitation is the ability to bring diverse perspectives together. When a facilitator creates a safe and inclusive space for team members to share their thoughts, ideas, and experiences, it opens up opportunities for cross-pollination of ideas. For example, imagine a team comprised of individuals from different departments within a company. Through effective facilitation, the team can leverage their unique perspectives to develop creative solutions that address various challenges faced by the organization.
- Effective ideation facilitation also encourages participants to think outside the box and challenge their assumptions. By introducing techniques such as brainstorming, mind mapping, or even role-playing, facilitators can help teams break free from traditional thinking patterns and explore unconventional ideas. For instance, a facilitator might ask team members to imagine themselves as customers or competitors, enabling them to view the problem from a different angle and generate fresh insights.

- Tips for successful ideation facilitation include establishing clear goals and objectives for the session, creating a structured agenda, and ensuring active participation from all team members. It is essential to set aside any personal biases and encourage an open and non-judgmental atmosphere where everyone feels comfortable sharing their ideas. Additionally, using visual aids, such as whiteboards or sticky notes, can help capture and organize the generated ideas for further exploration.
- Case studies have demonstrated the power of ideation facilitation in driving innovation. For example, in one study conducted by a leading tech company, a facilitator guided a team through an ideation session focused on improving the user experience of their mobile app. By employing various techniques and encouraging collaboration, the team generated a range of innovative ideas, resulting in significant improvements to the app's interface and functionality.
- Ideation facilitation can also be applied to problem-solving scenarios. By guiding teams through a structured ideation process, facilitators can help them identify and address the root causes of problems. This approach was successfully employed by a manufacturing company facing production inefficiencies. Through facilitated brainstorming sessions, the team identified bottlenecks in the production line and developed innovative solutions that led to increased productivity and cost savings.
- In conclusion, understanding the power of ideation facilitation is crucial for unlocking a team's creative potential. By bringing diverse perspectives together, encouraging unconventional thinking, and providing a structured framework for idea generation, facilitators can help teams generate innovative solutions to complex problems. Whether it is fostering collaboration, challenging assumptions, or driving problem-solving, effective ideation facilitation is a valuable tool for any organization seeking to harness the collective intelligence of their teams.

Ideation sessions are creative brainstorming activities that aim to generate a large number of diverse and novel ideas for solving a problem or achieving a goal. They are often used in innovation and design thinking processes, where they help to explore different possibilities and perspectives. However, ideation sessions can also be challenging to facilitate effectively, as they require careful planning, preparation, and execution. In this section, you will learn some techniques that can help you to facilitate ideation sessions that are engaging, productive, and fun.

Creating an Optimal Environment for Ideation

- **Define the objective**: Before diving into the ideation process, it is crucial to clearly define the objective or problem you are trying to solve. By setting a clear goal, you provide a focal point for your team's creative energy and ensure that everyone is on the same page. For example, if you are brainstorming ideas for a new marketing campaign, the objective could be to increase brand awareness among a specific target audience (Fig. 8.2).

- **Create a safe and inclusive space:** It is essential to create an environment where team members feel comfortable expressing their ideas without fear of judgment or criticism. Encourage an open and non-hierarchical atmosphere where everyone's input is valued. This can be achieved by establishing ground rules for respectful communication and by actively listening to each team member's contributions. By fostering a safe and inclusive space, you enable diverse perspectives and increase the likelihood of innovative ideas emerging.

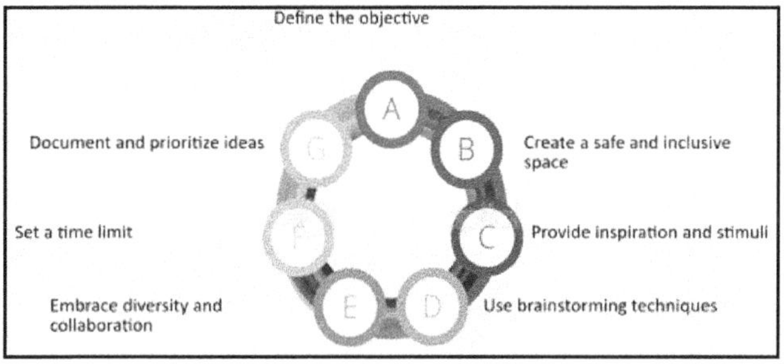

Fig. 8.2 Creating an Optimal Environment for Ideation

- **Provide inspiration and stimuli:** To fuel the ideation process, provide your team with inspiration and stimuli that are relevant to the objective. This can be in the form of case studies, industry trends, customer feedback, or even creative exercises and games. For instance, if you are brainstorming ideas for a new product, you could share success stories of similar products in the market or present a customer testimonial that highlights a pain point your team could address.
- **Use brainstorming techniques:** Brainstorming techniques can help facilitate idea generation and encourage collaboration within the team. One popular technique is "brainwriting," where team members individually write down their ideas before sharing them with the group. Another technique is "mind mapping," which involves visually organizing ideas and their connections. Experiment with different techniques to find what works best for your team and objective.
- **Embrace diversity and collaboration:** Encourage team members with different backgrounds, experiences, and perspectives to participate in the ideation process. Diversity can lead to more innovative ideas and solutions. Foster collaboration by assigning team members different roles, such as a facilitator, note-taker, or timekeeper, to ensure everyone is involved and

engaged. Additionally, consider forming cross-functional teams to leverage diverse expertise and knowledge.

- **Set a time limit:** Setting a time limit for the ideation session can help maintain focus and prevent the process from dragging on indefinitely. Time constraints can spur creativity and encourage participants to think quickly and decisively. However, it is important to strike a balance between allowing enough time for idea generation and avoiding rushing the process. Experiment with different time limits to find what works best for your team's dynamics and the complexity of the objective.
- **Document and prioritize ideas:** As ideas are generated, make sure to document them in a visible and accessible format, such as a whiteboard or digital collaboration tools. This allows the team to build upon each other's ideas and prevents duplication. Once all ideas have been shared, facilitate a discussion to prioritize and refine the most promising ones. Encourage team members to provide constructive feedback and consider the feasibility, impact, and alignment with the objective when prioritizing ideas.

Creating an optimal environment for ideation involves defining the objective, fostering a safe and inclusive space, providing inspiration and stimuli, using brainstorming techniques, embracing diversity and collaboration, setting a time limit, and documenting and prioritizing ideas. By implementing these strategies, you can guide your team to unlock their creative potential and generate innovative solutions to complex challenges.

Tools and Strategies for Sparking Creativity (Fig. 8.3)

- **Brainstorming:** One of the most well-known and widely used techniques for generating ideas is brainstorming. This technique involves a group of individuals coming together to freely share their thoughts and ideas on a particular topic. The key to successful brainstorming is to encourage a non-judgmental and open-minded atmosphere, where all ideas are welcomed and considered. By building upon each other's ideas and allowing for a free flow of creativity, brainstorming can often lead to unique and innovative solutions. For example, the famous case study of Pixar's brainstorming sessions for their movie "Toy Story" showcases how this technique can result in groundbreaking ideas that revolutionize an industry.
- **Mind mapping:** Mind mapping is a visual technique that helps in organizing and structuring thoughts and ideas. It involves creating a diagram that branches out from a central concept, with each branch representing a different idea or subtopic. Mind mapping allows for the exploration of various connections and relationships between ideas, helping to stimulate creativity. Tools like mindMeister and Xmind provide digital platforms

for creating mind maps, making it easy to collaborate with team members remotely. For instance, a marketing team can use mind mapping to generate ideas for a new advertising campaign by visually mapping out different elements such as target audience, messaging, and channels.

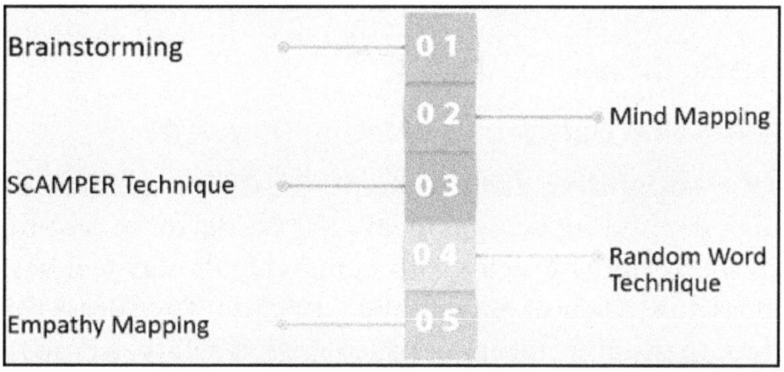

Fig. 8.3 Tools and Strategies for Sparking Creativity

- **SCAMPER Technique**: SCAMPER is an acronym that stands for Substitute, Combine, Adapt, Modify, Put to another use, Eliminate, and Reverse. This technique, developed by creativity expert Bob Eberle, provides a structured approach to generating ideas by encouraging individuals to think outside the box and explore different perspectives. Each letter of SCAMPER represents a different prompt for idea generation. For example, "Substitute" encourages individuals to think about replacing or substituting a key element, while "Combine" prompts them to consider merging or combining different ideas or concepts. By using the SCAMPER technique, teams can uncover unique solutions and come up with innovative approaches to problems.
- **Random Word Technique**: The random word technique involves selecting a random word from a dictionary or using an online random word generator and then associating that word with the problem or topic at hand. This technique helps to break free from conventional thinking patterns and encourages individuals to make unexpected connections. For example, if the random word generated is "butterfly" and the problem is to design a new packaging for a food product, the team could explore ideas inspired by the butterfly's colorful wings, delicate nature, or transformative life cycle. The random word technique can be particularly useful when teams find themselves stuck in a rut or lacking fresh perspectives.
- **Empathy mapping**: Empathy mapping is a technique that helps teams gain a deeper understanding of their target audience or users. By putting themselves in the shoes of the end-users, teams can generate ideas that directly address their needs and pain points. An empathy map typically consists of four quadrants: "Says," "Thinks," "Does," and "Feels." Each quadrant represents different aspects of the user's experience. By

empathizing with the user and filling in each quadrant with relevant information, teams can gain valuable insights that can spark creativity and innovation in product or service design.

There are various techniques and tools available to facilitate idea generation and spark creativity within teams. Whether it's through brainstorming, mind mapping, SCAMPER, the random.

Addressing Common Barriers to Ideation (Fig. 8.4)

- **Lack of a supportive environment:** Creating a conducive environment that cultivates and encourages ideation is crucial for overcoming challenges in the brainstorming process. Often, individuals may feel hesitant to share their ideas due to fear of judgment or criticism. To address this barrier, it is important to foster a culture of psychological safety, where team members feel comfortable expressing their thoughts without the fear of negative consequences. This can be achieved by promoting open communication, active listening, and valuing all perspectives.
- **Limited diversity of perspectives:** Another common barrier to ideation is the lack of diverse perspectives within a team. When team members come from similar backgrounds or have similar skill sets, it can hinder the generation of unique and innovative ideas. To overcome this challenge, it is essential to actively seek out and include individuals with diverse backgrounds, experiences, and expertise. By incorporating different viewpoints, teams can benefit from a wider range of ideas and approaches, leading to more creative solutions.
- **Fear of failure:** Fear of failure can significantly hinder the ideation process. When individuals are afraid of making mistakes or taking risks, they may hold back their ideas or opt for safer, more conventional options. Overcoming this barrier requires creating an environment that embraces experimentation and learning from failures. encouraging a growth mindset, where failures are seen as opportunities for growth and improvement, can help team members feel more confident in sharing their ideas, even if they are unconventional or uncertain.
- **Time constraints:** In today's fast-paced work environments, time constraints can often impede the ideation process. Teams may feel pressured to quickly come up with ideas, leading to rushed and less innovative outcomes. To address this challenge, it is crucial to allocate dedicated time for ideation sessions, where team members can fully focus on generating ideas without the pressure of immediate implementation. These sessions can be facilitated using various techniques such as brainstorming exercises, mind mapping, or design thinking workshops.

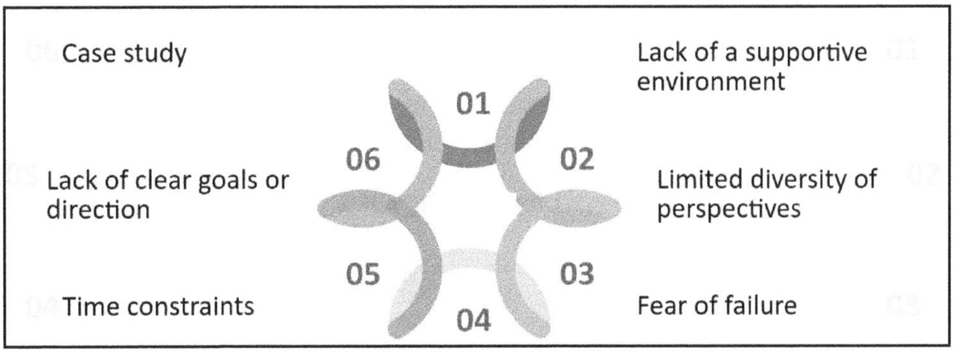

Fig. 8.4 Addressing Common Barriers to Ideation

- **Lack of clear goals or direction:** When team members lack a clear understanding of the goals or direction of the ideation process, it can be challenging to generate relevant and impactful ideas. Providing a clear brief or problem statement can help guide the ideation process and give participants a framework to work within. Additionally, setting specific objectives and desired outcomes for the ideation session can help focus the team's efforts and ensure that the generated ideas are aligned with the overall goals.
- **Case study: Pixar's "Braintrust":** An excellent example of overcoming ideation barriers is Pixar Animation Studios' "Braintrust" concept. The Braintrust is a group of experienced filmmakers and creative minds who come together to provide honest and constructive feedback on each other's projects. This approach helps address the fear of judgment and failure by creating a safe space for sharing ideas and receiving feedback. The Braintrust's collaborative and supportive environment has played a significant role in Pixar's success in producing innovative and critically acclaimed films.

Overall, overcoming challenges in the ideation process requires a combination of creating a supportive environment, embracing diversity, fostering a growth mindset, allocating dedicated time, providing clear goals, and leveraging collaborative feedback mechanisms. By addressing these common barriers, teams can unlock their creative potential and generate truly innovative ideas.

Leveraging Different Perspectives for Innovative Thinking (Fig. 8.5)

- Embracing diversity within teams has become increasingly important in today's fast-paced and interconnected world. By harnessing the power of different perspectives, organizations can unlock their creative potential and foster innovative thinking. In this section, we will explore how diversity can be leveraged to drive ideation and provide practical tips for facilitating teams to embrace diverse viewpoints.

- Diverse perspectives bring a wealth of knowledge and experiences to the table, enabling teams to approach problems from various angles. For example, imagine a team working on a marketing campaign for a new product. By including individuals from different backgrounds, such as marketing, design, and customer service, the team can leverage their unique expertise to develop a comprehensive and well-rounded strategy. Each person's perspective adds a layer of depth and insight that may have been overlooked if the team consisted of individuals with similar backgrounds.

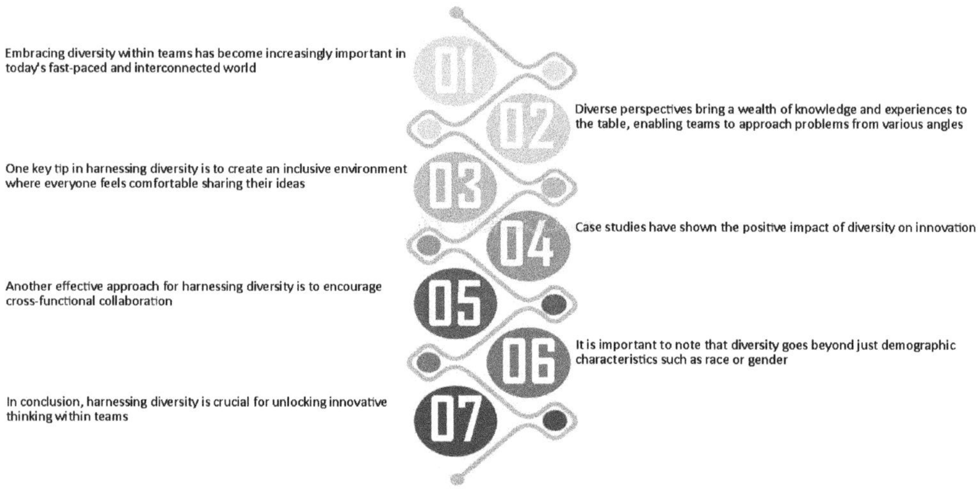

Fig. 8.5 Leveraging Different Perspectives for Innovative Thinking

- One key tip in harnessing diversity is to create an inclusive environment where everyone feels comfortable sharing their ideas. Encourage team members to voice their opinions and actively listen to each other. By valuing and respecting diverse viewpoints, teams can foster an atmosphere of trust and collaboration, which is essential for innovative thinking. Additionally, consider implementing brainstorming techniques that allow for equal participation, such as round-robin brainstorming or silent brainstorming, where ideas are shared anonymously.
- Case studies have shown the positive impact of diversity on innovation. For instance, a study conducted by McKinsey & Company found that companies with diverse executive teams were 33% more likely to outperform their industry peers in terms of profitability. This highlights the tangible benefits of embracing diversity and leveraging different perspectives within organizations.
- Another effective approach for harnessing diversity is to encourage cross-functional collaboration. By bringing together individuals with different skill sets and backgrounds, teams can tap into a broader range

of ideas and solutions. For example, a technology company may encourage collaboration between software developers, designers, and customer support representatives to create user-centered products that meet the diverse needs of their customers.

- It is important to note that diversity goes beyond just demographic characteristics such as race or gender. Diversity of thought, experiences, and skills are equally important. By actively seeking individuals with diverse backgrounds and perspectives, organizations can ensure a rich mix of ideas and approaches.
- In conclusion, harnessing diversity is crucial for unlocking innovative thinking within teams. By embracing different perspectives, organizations can tap into a wealth of knowledge and experiences that drive creativity and problem-solving. creating an inclusive environment, encouraging cross-functional collaboration, and valuing diversity of thought are key strategies for leveraging the power of diversity. Embrace the power of diversity and unlock your team's creative potential.

Designing Effective Workshops and Meetings (Fig. 8.6)

- **Define the Purpose and Goals**: When structuring ideation sessions, it is crucial to start by clearly defining the purpose and goals of the workshop or meeting. This sets the foundation for the entire session and ensures that everyone is aligned and working towards a common objective. For example, if the purpose is to generate new product ideas, the goal might be to come up with at least ten innovative concepts that address customer pain points.
- **Create a Welcoming and Inspiring Environment**: The environment plays a significant role in fostering creativity and encouraging participants to think outside the box. Consider selecting a venue that is conducive to ideation, with ample natural light, comfortable seating, and creative stimuli like whiteboards or brainstorming walls. Additionally, provide materials such as sticky notes, markers, and flip charts to facilitate idea generation and visualization.
- **Establish Ground Rules and Guidelines**: To ensure a productive and respectful ideation session, establish ground rules and guidelines at the beginning. This helps create a safe space where participants feel comfortable sharing their ideas without fear of judgment. Encourage active listening, open-mindedness, and the building upon others' ideas. For instance, the "Yes, and..." technique from improv comedy can be applied to ideation sessions, where participants are encouraged to build upon each other's ideas rather than dismissing or criticizing them.

- **Utilize Diverse Ideation Techniques:** There is a wide range of ideation techniques that can be employed to stimulate creativity and generate a variety of ideas. For instance, brainstorming, mind mapping, role-playing, storyboarding, and design thinking exercises are just a few examples. By incorporating different techniques throughout the session, you can tap into different cognitive processes and perspectives, leading to more innovative and diverse ideas.
- **Timebox Activities and Breaks:** It is essential to manage time effectively during ideation sessions to ensure that all planned activities are completed and participants remain engaged. Timeboxing involves allocating a specific amount of time for each activity or exercise. For instance, you might allocate 15 minutes for individual idea generation, followed by 30 minutes for group discussion and refinement. Additionally, schedule regular breaks to allow participants to recharge and reflect on their ideas.

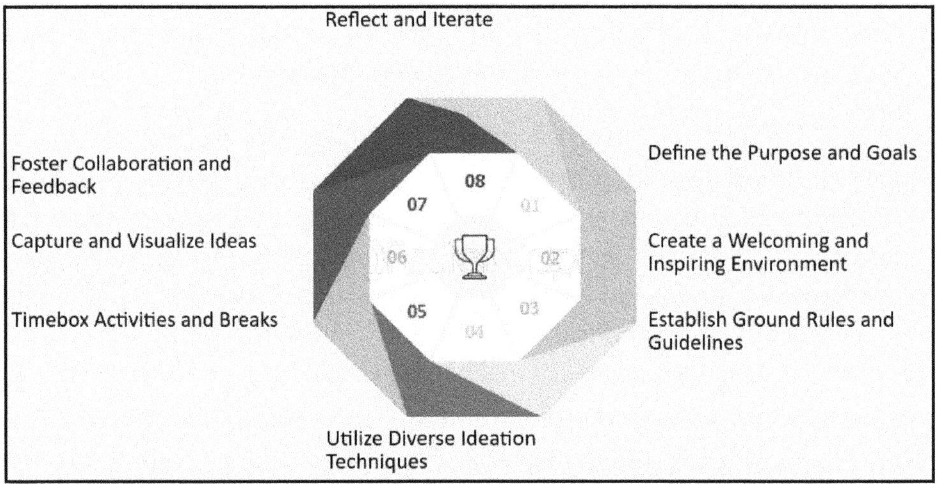

Fig. 8.6 Designing Effective Workshops and Meetings

- **Capture and Visualize Ideas:** As ideas are generated during the session, it is crucial to capture and visualize them to maintain focus and facilitate further exploration. Use tools such as digital collaboration platforms, whiteboards, or large paper sheets to record ideas. Visualizing ideas helps participants see the bigger picture and identify connections or patterns that may lead to breakthrough innovations.
- **Foster Collaboration and Feedback:** collaboration is key to successful ideation sessions. Encourage participants to collaborate and build upon each other's ideas through group activities and discussions. Additionally, provide opportunities for constructive feedback to help refine and improve ideas. Peer feedback can spark new insights and perspectives that may not have been considered initially.

- **Reflect and Iterate:** After the ideation session, take the time to reflect on the outcomes and learnings. Evaluate the effectiveness of the session by considering factors such as the number of ideas generated, the quality of ideas, and the level of participant engagement. Use this feedback to iterate and improve future ideation sessions, ensuring continuous growth and innovation.

Incorporating Visual Tools to Enhance Ideation (Fig. 8.7)

- **Visual thinking** is a powerful tool that can greatly enhance the process of ideation. By incorporating visual tools into brainstorming sessions, teams can unlock their creative potential and generate innovative ideas. In this section, we will explore the various ways in which visual thinking can be utilized to facilitate ideation, and provide tips and examples to help guide teams towards more effective and fruitful brainstorming sessions.
- **Mind maps** are a popular visual tool that can be used to organize and structure thoughts during ideation. By creating a visual representation of ideas and their relationships, mind maps help teams to see the bigger picture and identify patterns and connections that may not have been apparent before. For example, imagine a team brainstorming ideas for a new marketing campaign. By using a mind map, they can visually map out different elements such as target audience, messaging, and channels, and easily identify gaps or areas that need further exploration.

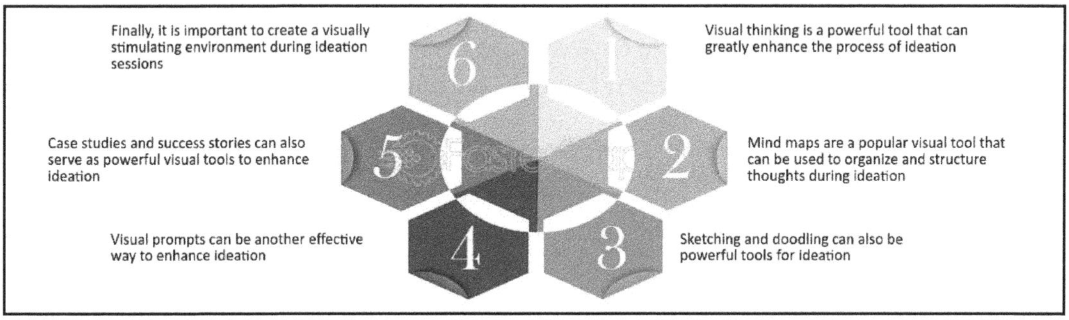

Fig. 8.7 Incorporating Visual Tools to Enhance Ideation

- **Sketching and doodling** can also be powerful tools for ideation. Encouraging team members to visually represent their ideas through simple drawings can help to stimulate creativity and generate new perspectives. For instance, during a design thinking workshop, participants may be asked to sketch their ideal user experience for a new product. This visual representation not only helps to clarify and communicate ideas, but also serves as a starting point for further discussion and refinement.

- **Visual prompts** can be another effective way to enhance ideation. By presenting teams with visual stimuli such as images, videos, or even physical objects, facilitators can spark inspiration and encourage out-of-the-box thinking. For example, a team tasked with developing a new packaging design for a product could be shown a range of visually appealing and innovative packaging designs from different industries. This exposure to diverse visual stimuli can help to trigger fresh ideas and inspire unique solutions.
- **Case studies and success stories** can also serve as powerful visual tools to enhance ideation. By sharing examples of how visual thinking has been successfully applied in different contexts, teams can gain insights and inspiration for their own ideation processes. For instance, a team working on a new website design could study **case studies of successful websites** to understand the visual elements and strategies that have proven effective in engaging users.
- Finally, it is important to create a visually stimulating environment during ideation sessions. This can be achieved through the use of visual aids such as whiteboards, sticky notes, or even digital collaboration tools. These tools not only facilitate the visualization of ideas but also encourage active participation and engagement from all team members.

Incorporating visual thinking into the ideation process can greatly enhance creativity and generate more innovative ideas. By leveraging tools such as mind maps, sketching, visual prompts, case studies, and creating a visually stimulating environment, teams can unlock their creative potential and take their brainstorming sessions to new heights.

Facilitating the Transition from Ideation to Implementation (Fig. 8.8)

- **Clearly Define the Objective**: The first step in facilitating the transition from ideation to implementation is to clearly define the objective of the project or idea. This involves understanding the desired outcome, identifying the problem or challenge that needs to be addressed, and setting specific goals. For example, if the objective is to improve customer satisfaction, the team must understand what factors contribute to customer dissatisfaction and establish measurable targets, such as reducing customer complaints by 20% within six months.
- **Break Down the Idea into Actionable Steps**: Once the objective is defined, it is essential to break down the idea into smaller, actionable steps. This helps to create a clear roadmap for implementation and enables the team to focus on specific tasks. For instance, if the idea is to develop a new product, the team can break it down into steps like conducting market

research, designing prototypes, testing, and launching. By breaking down the idea, it becomes easier to assign responsibilities and track progress.

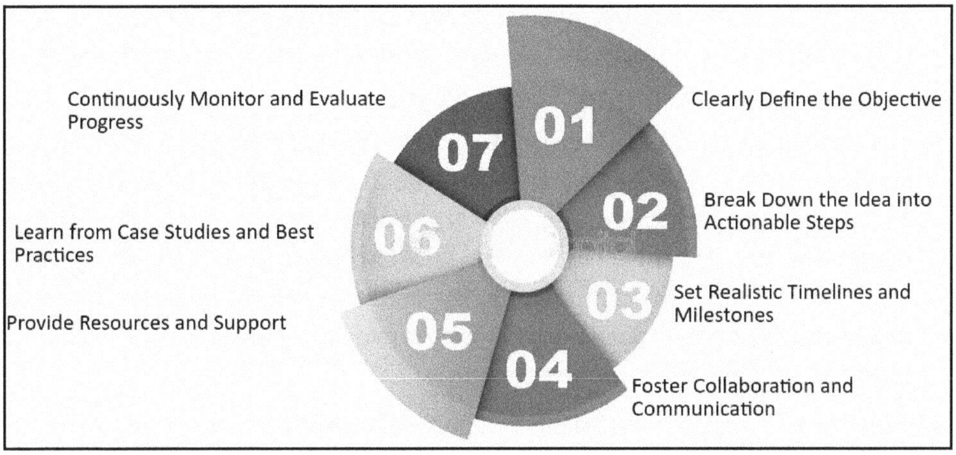

Fig. 8.8 Facilitating the Transition from Ideation to Implementation

- **Set Realistic Timelines and Milestones:** Setting realistic timelines and milestones is crucial to keep the team motivated and ensure timely progress. This involves estimating the time required for each step and considering any dependencies or constraints. For instance, if a team is working on a software development project, they may need to consider factors like coding, testing, and bug fixing. By setting milestones, such as completing the coding phase within two weeks, the team can measure their progress and make adjustments if necessary.
- **Foster Collaboration and communication:** Effective collaboration and communication play a vital role in facilitating the transition from ideation to implementation. Encourage team members to share their thoughts, ideas, and concerns openly. This can be achieved through regular team meetings, brainstorming sessions, and utilizing collaboration tools. For example, using project management software like Trello or Asana can help team members stay updated on tasks, deadlines, and progress.
- **Provide Resources and Support:** To ensure a smooth transition from ideation to implementation, it is important to provide the necessary resources and support to the team. This includes allocating budget, providing access to relevant tools and technologies, and offering training or workshops if required. For instance, if the team needs to conduct user testing for a new website, providing access to user testing software and training them on its usage can be immensely helpful.
- **Learn from Case studies and Best Practices:** learning from case studies and best practices can provide valuable insights and guidance for successful implementation. Look for examples of similar projects or ideas that have

been successfully executed and analyze the strategies and approaches used. This can help the team identify potential challenges, anticipate risks, and adopt proven methodologies. By leveraging the experiences of others, the team can avoid common pitfalls and increase their chances of success.

- **Continuously Monitor and Evaluate Progress:** Monitoring and evaluating progress is essential to ensure that the implementation process stays on track and aligns with the desired objectives. Regularly assess the team's performance, identify any bottlenecks or obstacles, and make necessary adjustments. This can be done through progress reports, feedback sessions, or periodic evaluations. By maintaining a proactive approach to monitoring, the team can address issues promptly and maintain momentum towards successful implementation.

Facilitating the transition from ideation to implementation requires careful planning, effective communication, and continuous monitoring.

Ideation techniques & strategies for your team

Consider this scenario: you're seated in a little chilly boardroom, taking notes, gazing at a whiteboard, and listening to concepts thrown around by your peers. Time passes, a few ideas are chosen to follow up on next week, and the meeting is closed. But what if there was a more practical approach to generate fresh, actionable ideas?

When the brainstorming approach was first launched in 1953, it was founded on four fundamental principles:

- Generate a considerable number of ideas
- Avoid criticism
- Encourage wild ideas
- Expand on each other's concepts

But in recent decades, technological advancements prompted innovation and creativity specialists to advocate for a more systematic approach to idea generation, refinement, and execution—all while retaining these fundamental principles. As a result, we now have organized ideation, AKA: specialized activities, methods, and models to develop ideas and accelerate corporate growth. And it's becoming increasingly popular. From building a marketing approach to revamping a product, this systematic approach to ideation helps teams across industries tackle almost any problem. Here are a few team-based brainstorming techniques that make your ideation sessions more inclusive, engaging, and effective:

1. AI for Ideation

AI can be used as an ideation technique by generating new ideas based on large amounts of data and identifying patterns and associations that humans may not recognize.

ClickUp AI can help your ideation process by leveraging machine learning algorithms to analyze your data and provide insights that can inform your decision making. Here are some specific ways that ClickUp AI can assist with ideation:

- **Idea Generation:** ClickUp AI can analyze your data to generate new ideas and concepts based on patterns and associations that humans may not recognize. By mining data from your team's projects, tasks, and activities, ClickUp AI can suggest new approaches or solutions that may have been overlooked.
- **Trend Analysis:** ClickUp AI can analyze your data to identify emerging trends and opportunities for innovation. This can help your team stay ahead of the curve and develop new products and services that meet evolving customer needs.
- **Personalization:** ClickUp AI can personalize products and services based on individual preferences and behaviors. By analyzing data on customer preferences, ClickUp AI can suggest tailored products and services that meet specific needs and preferences.
- **Optimization:** ClickUp AI can analyze your processes and systems to identify areas for improvement and suggest new approaches. This can help your team streamline operations, reduce waste, and improve efficiency.
- **Brainstorming Assistance:** ClickUp AI can assist with brainstorming sessions by providing automatic suggestions based on the input provided by your team. This can help stimulate new ideas and encourage creative thinking.

2. Mind Mapping

A mind map is a diagram tool to help you record and link together ideas to recall and generate new concepts faster. Think of it almost as a web to help you track your train of thought and help you remember how one idea evolved or connected to another.

3. Method 6-3-5

First things first: you need a team of six for this method.

This is a fully collaborative effort and you may end up with a pretty significant number of ideas with this method if you're looking for a fresh take on an issue or a list of possible solutions. Here's the breakdown:

- Each participant comes up with three recommendations to share with the group
- The team works to expand on each recommendation over the course of five iterations

So it's six people, three ideas each, five iterations: 6-3-5.

The goal is to generate as many concepts as possible for a single issue—not necessarily for each idea to be extremely detailed or well thought out. This method is more about quantity than quality, but the idea is that you'll have so many ideas, you'll be bound to find at least one good one.

4. Round Robin

This approach may sound like something you've done before, but with a little twist. This method starts by proposing the problem in the form of a question starting with "how might we ____ ?" This is also known as the HMW inquiry.

Each team member will draw (or write) a solution to the HMW inquiry, then pass their idea to the left. The person to the left will essentially iterate that new idea and present its problems and solutions going forward.

Once each HMW inquiry is passed to the left, that person will then jot down one or more reasons why that solution might fail. Then they will present the concept and its challenges, and as a group, come up with ways to keep the solution from failing.

The idea is to improve team synergy by using each other's ideas in a fast-paced environment. It's also a great method to get feedback on something you're already working on and a fresh perspective in case there are any gaps in logic or resources.

One possible obstacle here though is that round-robin is better executed in person. A way to remedy this solution though is with a powerful collaboration tool or a digital whiteboard.

Rather than passing a piece of paper between the group, share the ideas on an infinite canvas with live cursors and real-time editing to work alongside each other without overlap. Plus, virtual whiteboards have plenty of media upload, formatting, free-hand drawing, and shape features to add clarity and context to your ideas.

5. Storyboarding

Storyboarding is a brainstorming process to create a visual narrative around an issue. How would you tell the story about the problem you're having?

Bringing the tale to life allows participants to dig deeper into the issue and come up with viable solutions. Not to mention, we all digest information differently.

Our brains are built to comprehend multiple images at once and by sharing your project's story, the team can better understand and organize the sequence of events. This alone helps reveal the root of the problem and possible solutions.

6. Negative Brainstorming

Also known as reverse brainstorming, this method is the combination of brainstorming and taking the negative approach. The goal of negative brainstorming is to discover ways of aggravating a problem in order to come up with new ways to solve it.

The idea is that by flipping your focus to the opposite side of the spectrum, you can get more creative with how you arrive at a solution. Might sound a little confusing - but also kind of cool!

When it's tough to come up with straightforward answers to an issue, negative brainstorming should be your go-to. It's usually an entertaining procedure that might reveal flaws in a method or product. If your team has hit the proverbial wall, change your perspective.

This forces you to give your brain a break, and you may be surprised with how far that momentary refresh will get you! It's almost like answering that age-old question: what would you do if money was not an option?

7. Crazy 8's

One of the ideation techniques we love is Crazy 8's. First, divide a blank piece of paper into eight sections. an 8-minute stopwatch.

This activity aims for each person to draw one concept in each square - or one idea every minute - until the canvas is filled. each minute passes, you must move on to the next prompt regardless of how far you've progressed in your square. You only have a minute per square, so if you don't move on to the next one when it's time, you'll miss the flow of ideas and fall behind.

This strategy works best during the ideation stage when you already have a few basic ideas to expand on to help new, stronger takes emerge faster. The goal is to come up with a variety of new ideas in a short amount of time, so if you want to return to one after the eight minutes have passed, you will still get the chance!

8. Prototyping

Prototyping is, in fact, an ideation approach! Before proceeding to the next phase of your project process, prototypes help flesh out every final detail, issue, and concept.

Prototypes keep things visible, which is a fantastic benefit of using them in your brainstorming process. When your team can see your concept, it's much easier to support it and offer constructive feedback.

Your prototype can be as straightforward or as detailed as you like. However, having at least a rough idea of what you'll be working with can act as a springboard, and ultimately will help you nail-down specifications, design, and functionality.

9. Brainstorming

We use this term a lot, *but what does it really mean?*

Brainstorming is one of the ideation techniques that combine unofficial problem-solving with lateral thinking. Basically, the goal is to provide a safe space with no rules for team members to come up with crazy ideas. Some of these ideas are transformed into unique and innovative solutions, while others catalyze new ideas.

To use the brainstorming technique, start by outlining the problem you're trying to address and determining the goals of a potential solution. Then, before bringing the team together, come up with solutions on your own.

Participants should not be required, reprimanded, or rewarded for their contributions. This keeps the brainstorming space supportive and encourages the flow of every idea (without stifling others).

10. Sketching

Visual elements elicit more ideas and offer a wider perspective. The idea here is to develop engaging drawings that you can revisit and expand on by hanging them in your conference room or storing them on a collaborative digital whiteboard.

The sketches should be simple with just enough information to communicate your message and must be accessible for other team members to contribute to it if they wish! That's the collaborative part. This also helps people avoid becoming emotionally connected to their small art pieces.

It reminds everyone that coming up with new ideas is truly a group effort. And you can think more freely and imaginatively about your concepts by sketching them out. Then you focus on getting the thought out of your head rather than worrying about the quality of the drawing.

It may be a stick figure or a few labeled shapes, but sketches will ultimately let you capture ideas and share them with others, faster.

11. Brainwriting

Brainwriting is a slightly different take on brainstorming. Instead of yelling out concepts, the team jots them down. Each member's ideas are then forwarded to another person, who reads them and adds their own thoughts or ideas (if they have one).

CHAPTER-9

PROTOTYPING AND WIREFRAMING

Wireframing and Prototyping are two main stages of the Design Process. These two are equally important steps in a User-centered product design process. Prototypes and Wireframes are two of the most frequently produced UI and UX deliverables. These tools help design the client's needs by Illustrating Ideas and Concepts and collecting Responses from Users. These two serve different purposes during product development and both of these make product development efficient and user friendly.

Wireframing

A Wireframe is a Simplified, Static, Structural representation of any Site or Application. It is a basic two-dimensional visual layout of the design element which presents key information about the product. Wireframe allows us to simplify communication with users. It is mostly a hand-drawn sketch that helps to understand the functionality, structure, and space of the Application or Website. It's the first valid step of a project imperceptible ideas into somehow perceptible ones. Wireframes mostly depict functionality and are mostly in greyscale. It is a Low-Fidelity sketch or outline of the layout of an interface.

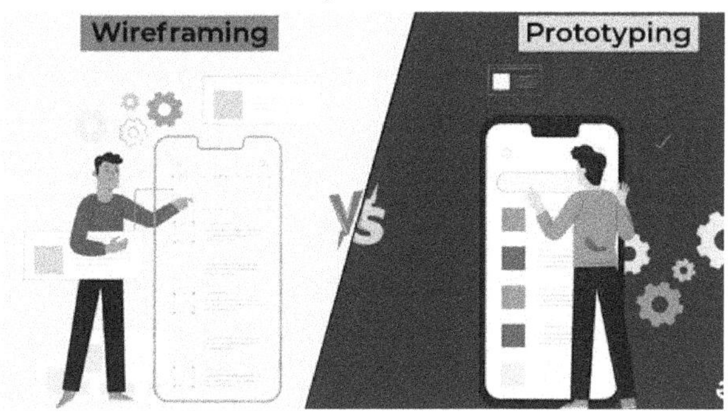

Fig. 9.1 Wireframing and Prototyping

Types of Wireframing

- **Low-fidelity Wireframes:** Low-fidelity wireframing is a technique of creating a rough visual representation of a design using simple shapes, lines, and text. It is the most basic wireframe mostly done wit pen and paper.
- **Mid-fidelity Wireframes:** Mid-fidelity wireframing refers to wireframes that are created with a moderate level of detail and design elements. This type of wireframe mostly focuses on the structure of the product and contain some basic design elements and typography.
- **High-fidelity Wireframes:** High-fidelity Wireframing are the most detailed and precised and visually-rich wireframes that somehow gives the feel of the final product.

Benefits of Using Wireframing

- Cheap and Quick to Make
- Defines and Simplify features of website and apps
- Easier to Communicate Ideas to the client
- Brings Precision to the Project
- Economical and Time Saving
- Decide website Observance

Prototyping

Prototype is a replication or sample version of a final product, which Designers use for testing before launch of any Project. Prototypes are a crucial part of the design process used in all design practice. It is a simple model or a mockup of a concept, idea, product or service.

Types of Prototyping

- **Low-fidelity prototyping:** It is mostly paper-based, which creates a quick preview of the product. They are ideal for quick brainstorming and collaboration. It is just like a skeleton of a design which is faster and cheaper as well.
- **Medium-fidelity prototyping:** These are interactive clickable prototypes. It is more detailed and realistic prototype than Low-fidelity prototyping. It has limited functionality which are built upon storyboards or user scenarios.
- **High-fidelity prototyping:** High-fidelity prototypes are highly detailed, functional and interactive. It looks like a ready application, which can be shown to get a final design approval before developing or testing.

Benefits of Using Prototyping

- Saves Money and Time
- Workflow Simplification
- Team Alignment
- Increase Conversion
- Bugs Identification
- Enhance User Involvement

RAPID PROTOTYPING FOR ITERATIVE DESIGN

Rapid prototyping is an agile strategy used throughout the product development process. With this approach, 3-dimensional prototypes of a product or feature are created and tested to optimize characteristics like shape, size, and overall usability. Rapid Prototyping involves iterating at the design and planning phase to make structural decisions that are used to steer development. The prototype is separate from the product, and developers start afresh when they begin coding the product.

Understanding the rapid prototyping process is key to appreciating its impact on the manufacturing and product development process. At its core, rapid prototyping involves turning digital designs into tangible, physical objects.

Detailed Stages of the Rapid Prototyping Process

- **Design Creation**: Using CAD software, a digital 3D model of the object is created. This stage is crucial for laying the groundwork for the prototype.
- **Data Preparation**: The CAD model is processed and converted into a format suitable for the chosen rapid prototyping technology, typically an STL file.
- **Machine Setup**: The rapid prototyping machine is prepared, calibrated, and loaded with the appropriate materials, whether plastic, resin, or metal powders.
- **Prototype Building**: The machine constructs the prototype layer by layer, adhering to the specifications of the CAD model.
- **Post-processing**: After the build process, the prototype often requires post-processing to achieve the desired surface finish or mechanical properties. This can include sanding, painting, or assembly.

In this step-by-step process, rapid prototyping demonstrates its flexibility and efficiency, accommodating an array of materials and technologies to produce everything from low-fidelity prototypes for early stage design validation to high fidelity prototypes that closely mimic the final product.

Importance of rapid prototyping

Rapid prototyping is an essential part of the user interface design process. It allows designers and product managers to test new concepts and theories with users and create a final solution that has been validated before handoff. Instead of waiting until launch to find out if a new product or feature performs well, rapid prototyping enables product teams to get the insights they need earlier in the process.

Let's now look at three benefits to making rapid prototyping part of your design process.

Benefits of rapid prototyping

1. Explore new concepts and ideas

Rapid prototyping is one of the most effective ways to quickly explore the concepts and ideas that you and your team come up with. Perhaps someone on the team noticed a trend through research, or maybe you want to refine a feature based on customer feedback. Whatever the idea is, use rapid prototyping to explore possible solutions and quickly understand if that idea is a go or not.

Rapid prototyping also helps to answer the question of whether a new product is valuable to users. For instance, when the product team at Maze started receiving requests for duplicating projects, we tested whether this solution would offer our customers any value by exploring the concept with our Customer Advisory Board.

If a product is valuable to users and provides a good user experience, they'll want to use it. Quickly prototyping potential new features and asking your customers for feedback are great ways to explore new concepts without investing too much time into developing a finished product.

2. Minimize development costs on iterations

Another benefit of rapid prototyping is that it allows product teams to minimize the need for iterations in the live product, significantly reducing development-related costs. When a feature or product has been validated with users at the design stage, the risk of building something that doesn't work or isn't valuable is minimal.

As the famous design quote from Dr. Ralf Speth says, "If you think good design is expensive, you should look at the cost of bad design." Research has found that the cost of fixing an issue after release can be four to five times as more than during product design. In that respect, prototyping a solution and testing it with users is a lot less costly than developing a fully-fledged product and blindly releasing it to the world.

3. Launch successfully

Last but not least, rapid prototyping is one of the key ingredients of successfully launching a product. There are immense benefits to including users in the product development process, from building an engaged community to identifying proponent customers.

For example, before Freetrade officially launched their mobile app to the App Store, they already had a 20,000 customer waiting list. Their community had been an integral part of the development process since the early stages, and the Freetrade team regularly contacted their users for testing and feedback. The result? A successful launch day with an already existing customer base.

Types of prototypes

Now that we went through the benefits of rapid prototyping, it's time to build a prototype and start testing. Let's look at a few types of prototypes you can create and how to get started.

In digital design, a prototype is a simulation of an interaction between the interface and the user. You can prototype almost everything in a user interface, starting with a simple interaction and up to a complete representation of the product.

Low-fidelity prototypes

The simplest way to start prototyping is to use pen and paper and create what's known as a paper prototype. This type of prototype is usually referred to as a low-fidelity prototype because of its minimal level of interactivity, visuals, and content.

Low-fidelity prototyping is a quick and easy way to turn high-level design concepts into testable artifacts. The goal is to validate the product's underlying assumptions and core value and check its functionality rather than its aesthetics.

Low-fidelity prototypes are great for ideation and ruling out multiple solutions at the earliest stage of the design process. Testing wireframes can help you identify the most effective layout of a screen, the user flow, or the best way to present information to users.

High-fidelity prototypes

As you move through the design process, start adding more components such as visuals, copy, or interactions to create a medium or high-fidelity prototype. High-fidelity prototypes are highly functional and interactive. They are best for testing during the latest stages of the design process when you want your customers to feel and interact with a prototype that feels as close to the final product as possible.

Designers usually create high-fidelity prototypes to validate the final design and uncover any usability issues before starting development. One of the main benefits of high-fidelity prototypes is that you can test specific design elements and interactions and get more accurate feedback. This type of prototype also gives your stakeholders a clear idea of how the product will look and work before it goes live.

Rapid prototyping use cases

Rapid prototyping is valuable at all stages of the product development process. Let's take a look at some common use cases:

- **Validating new product ideas or concepts:** Prototypes can be used to test ideas and concepts early on to determine which ones add real value for users. In this way, you can focus your efforts on building a solution that meets users' needs and expectations before starting development, saving precious time and resources.
- **Market validation:** Rapid prototyping can be an invaluable tool for market validation. Instead of just imagining your product, users can interact with a prototype and provide better insights into what works and what doesn't.
- **Testing new features with users:** If you want to test new features, building a prototype is the best way to go about it. You can see how users interact with your prototype, identify issues and pain points, and understand what works and what requires attention and iteration.
- **Assessing product-market fit:** Sharing your prototype with your potential users is an excellent way to gather valuable feedback and evaluate your product-market fit. It allows you to see how well your product is meeting the needs of your target audience and identify growth opportunities.
- **Getting stakeholder feedback:** Prototyping is a way to turn your idea into something tangible you can put in front of your team and stakeholders. Prototypes support communication and encourage stakeholders to provide feedback that can inform future decisions.

Tips for making rapid prototyping part of your process

There are a few best practices to keep in mind to ensure you get the most out of rapid prototyping. In this section, we explore those best practices and how you can implement them into your workflow.

- **Make it quick:** Rapid prototyping has its name for a reason. Don't try to develop the most interactive prototype and spend a lot of time making it perfect. The goal is to get your ideas out and test them with people as soon as possible.
- **Test with real users:** Selecting the right participants for your prototype test is critical. The ideal candidates are users who've requested a product or feature or participants who meet the criteria of your target personas.

- **Establish a test goal:** Before you even create a prototype, take a moment to identify what you're trying to find out by running a test. Whether that's validating a product idea, testing the usability of a design, or something else, define your end goal from the start.
- **Include stakeholders:** Rapid prototyping is helpful to different team members across the board—product designers, marketers, product managers, and so on. Results garnered from testing and user interviews can yield useful insights and allow you to get buy-in on product decisions when all stakeholders are involved.

TOOLS AND METHODS FOR CREATING WIREFRAMES

Designers have a lot of choices when deciding which wireframing tool(s) to use. New tools are continually entering the market so it can be hard to keep up. Here are a few characteristics of great wireframing tools to look for:

- The ability to produce a variety of fidelities (low to high)
- Stable software that is easy to use and frequently updated
- Built-in templates, symbols, and standard UI components with add-on capabilities

Some of the tools in this guide are focused more heavily on wireframing, while others try to strike a balance between wireframing and prototyping, and mockup functionality. Choosing to use one tool over the other (or several together) comes down to designer preference.

Balsamiq

Balsamiq is a low-fidelity, simple-to-use wireframing tool favored for its ease of use and iconic "hand drawn" look. It comes with a set of pre-built templates that can be used quickly and easily with a drag-and-drop editor. Designers can add their own assets and customize the layout.

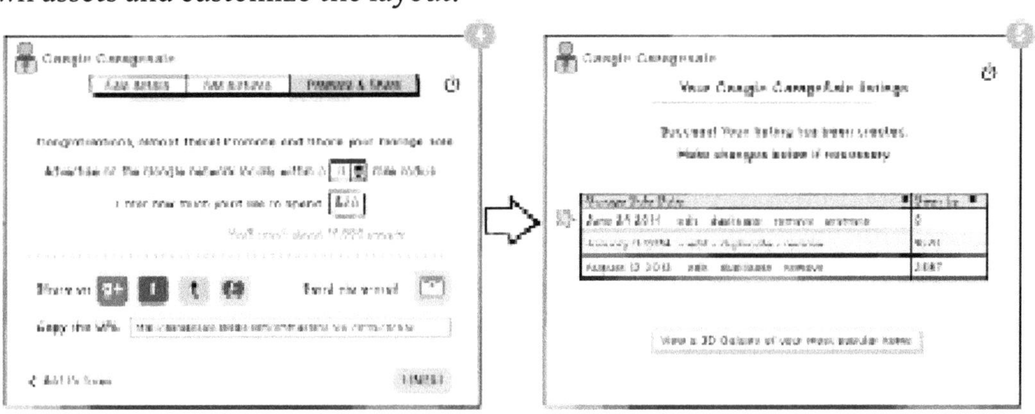

Fig. 9.2 Balsamiq

Basic prototyping can be achieved by linking mockups to create simple click-through experiences for usability testing when displaying the project in Full Screen Presentation mode or as an exported PDF.

Balsamiq is offered as a desktop version (Windows and Mac), cloud service, or as a plug-in for Google Drive, Confluence, and JIRA.

Moqups

Moqups is another creative collaboration tool that focuses on wireframing but can also be used for prototyping. Unlike Balsamiq, it is purely web-based and is meant to make wireframes for web and mobile applications.

The main difference between Moqups and Balsamiq is the fidelity of the wireframes. While Balsamiq produces a "hand drawn" look, Moqups provides full-color stencils and kits for mobile-app and web design including iOS, Android, and Bootstrap.

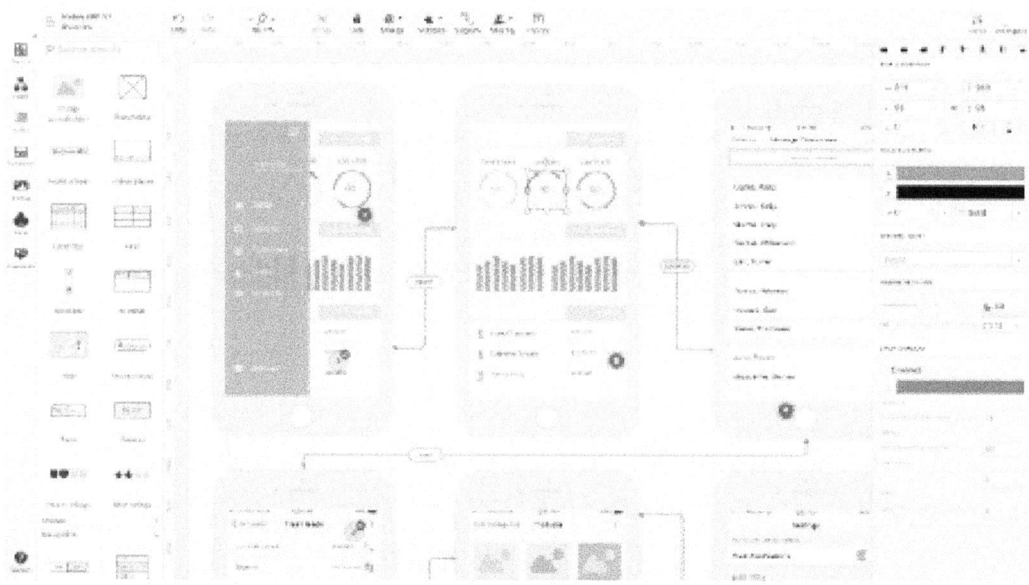

Fig. 9.3 Moqups

Moqups distinguishes from Balsamiq in a few other ways. The software allows for finite object editing and page management, giving designers the ability to define "master" objects, which can save a lot of time when making changes to the wireframes during the iteration process.

For example, a designer creates a *master* button object with a specific size, shape, and color. This button is used multiple times throughout the wireframe. Later, in the iteration process, if the designer needs to change the color of the button, instead of changing every single button object, they can change it once, and all the child button objects are immediately affected.

Pidoco

Pidoco is a top wireframing tool focused on low-fidelity deliverables with some basic interactivity. Also cloud-based, it makes use of reusable components and distinguishes from Balsamiq and Moqups with a more robust click-through wireframe experience.

Pidoco is helpful for mobile app and web design because it has built-in mobile views so designers can see how their app pages will look on various screen sizes. Another built-in feature is the *exports and specifications function*. This helps designers move from wireframe to prototype/mockup without the need for a plug-in or extension.

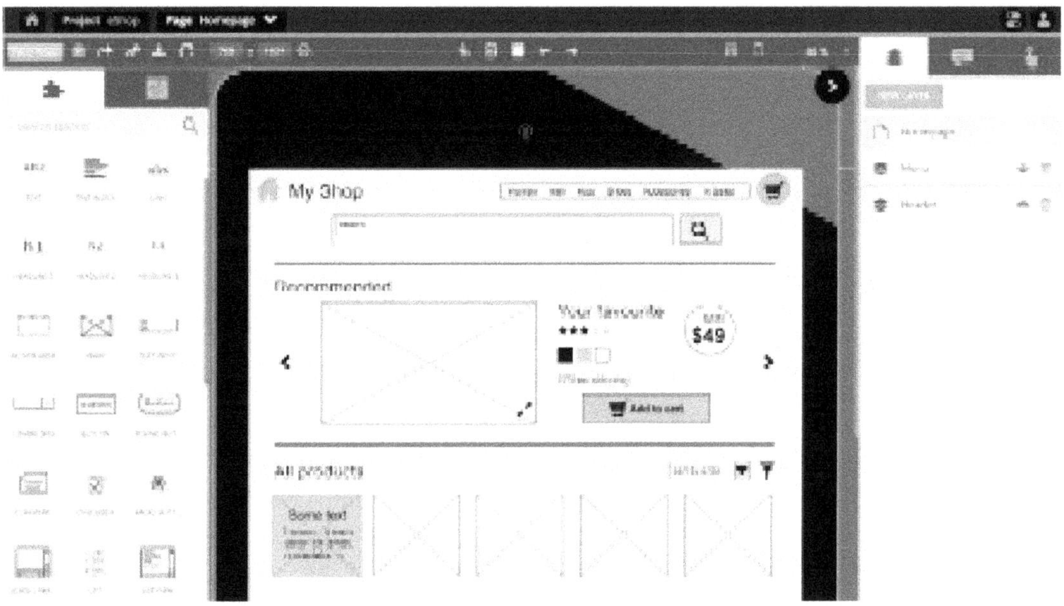

Fig. 9.4 Pidoco

Picoco looks and feels low-fidelity but includes several features that are typically found in more complex design tools. It works well for designers who are doing lean UX and need to iterate quickly with shorter feedback cycles.

Gliffy

Gliffy is a mid-fidelity wireframing tool with a few unique features that differentiate it from Balsamiq and Mockups. One unique feature is the ability to create wireflows. Gliffy has built-in flowcharting and diagramming capabilities with included stencils, mind maps, and business process modeling.

Like the other wireframing tools, Gliffy provides a library of shapes, icons, and the ability to share wireframes natively to Atlassian's Confluence, Slack, Basecamp, Trello, and WordPress.

Fig. 9.5 Gliffy

This is a relatively new UX wireframe design tool, however, it boasts a large subscriber base of professional designers who are looking for simple integrations and capabilities beyond a static wireframe.

Wireframe.cc

Wireframe.cc is a basic wireframing tool much like Balsamiq. It has a clean interface without a lot of distracting toolbars and icons. Unlike a lot of the other tools, it allows you to "sketch" wireframes with a mouse.

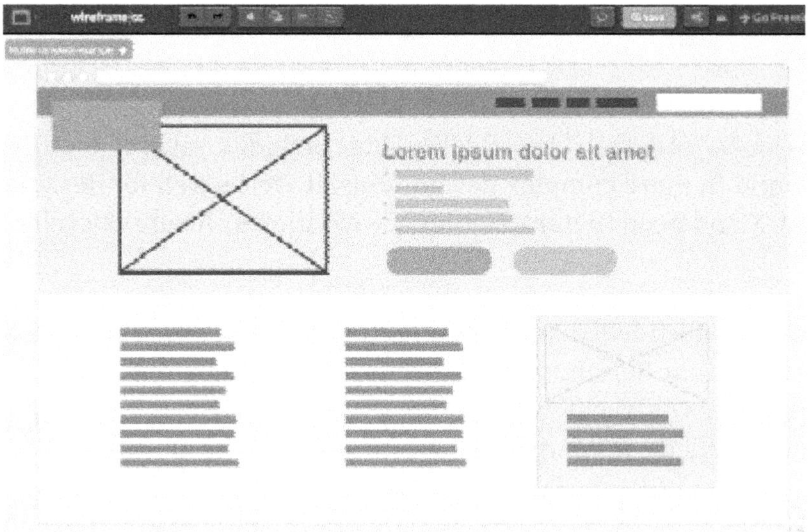

Fig. 9.6 Wireframe.cc

Wireframe.cc provides a library of stencils, and clean, uncomplicated handling of objects. A helpful element that Wireframe.cc offers when working with lean UX, is a URL for each wireframe page so it can be shared for feedback quickly and easily.

There is no prototyping or interactivity built-in as it is focused purely on low-fidelity wireframing.

Whimsical

Called the "Google Docs" for wireframes, Whimsical mimics diagramming tools such as OmniGraffle and Visio. It does not focus on prototyping/mockups, as its main focus is on wireframing and flowcharts, making it a great candidate for producing wireflows.

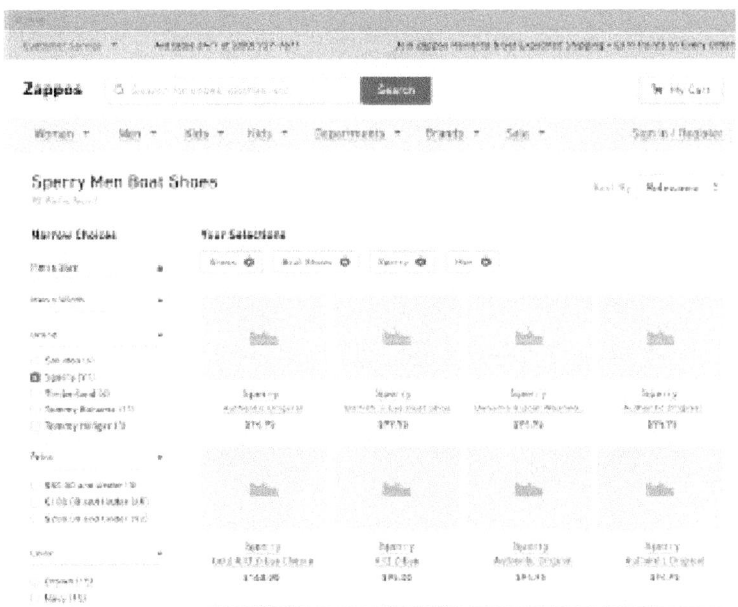

Fig. 9.7 Whimsical

Like Gliffy, Whimsical is a mid-fidelity wireframing tool and includes a large library of configurable elements (buttons, inputs, checkboxes, etc.).

Unlimited collaboration on the same wireframe document at the same time is a great built-in feature for remote design teams.

Adobe XD

Adobe XD has recently caught the attention of designers due to its simple interface, deep ties to other Adobe products, ease of use, and built-in functionality that reduces the need to rely on plugins and extensions. There are two ways to build wireframes in Adobe XD. They can be built using lines and shapes to create objects and elements, or they can be built using premade UI kits from sources like behance.net and XD resources.

One time-saving feature of Adobe XD is the ability to create "master" components (called Symbols in Sketch), which are useful when making changes since all components instantiated from the master will inherit any changes.

Another advantage to using XD as a wireframing tool is the ability to switch into prototyping mode with the click of a mouse. Prototyping mode is built into XD and works in the background so designers don't waste time when moving from wireframes to prototypes.

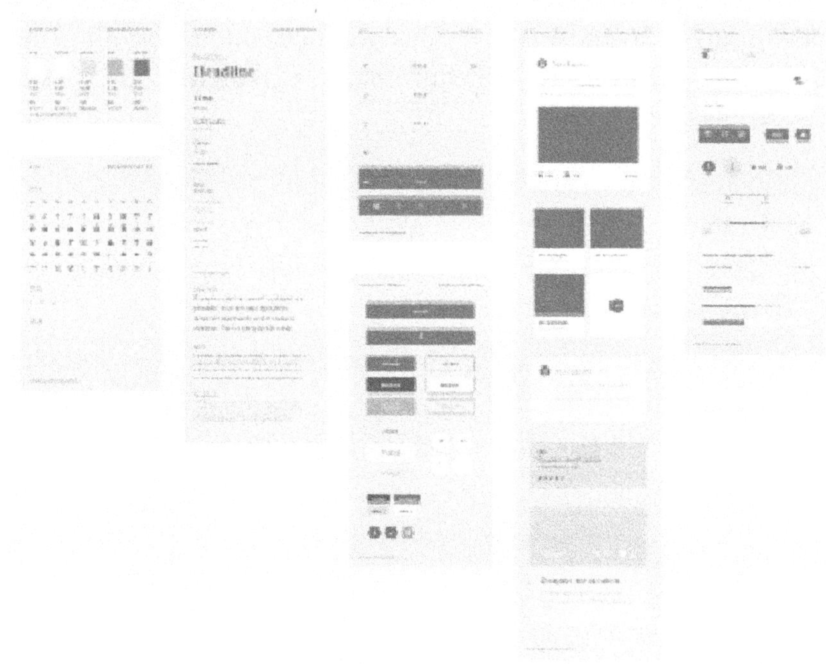

Fig. 9.8 Adobe XD

Sketch

Sketch, a popular design tool for UX/UI designers, provides a platform for vector editing, prototyping, and collaboration, and has a growing library of hundreds of plugins that extend its functionality.

Wireframing in Sketch is much like Adobe XD with its use of kits/templates and drawing tools. Sketch makes extensive use of *Symbols* which are reusable components that can be defined once and used multiple times (buttons, etc.). Instantiated Symbols also take on any changes made to the "master" Symbol. This is advantageous for designers as there are often many changes that need to be made throughout the wireframing process.

Sketch allows designers to create high-fidelity wireframes, prototypes, and mockups. It is not a cloud-based app, and one of the potential downsides is that it only works with macOS.]

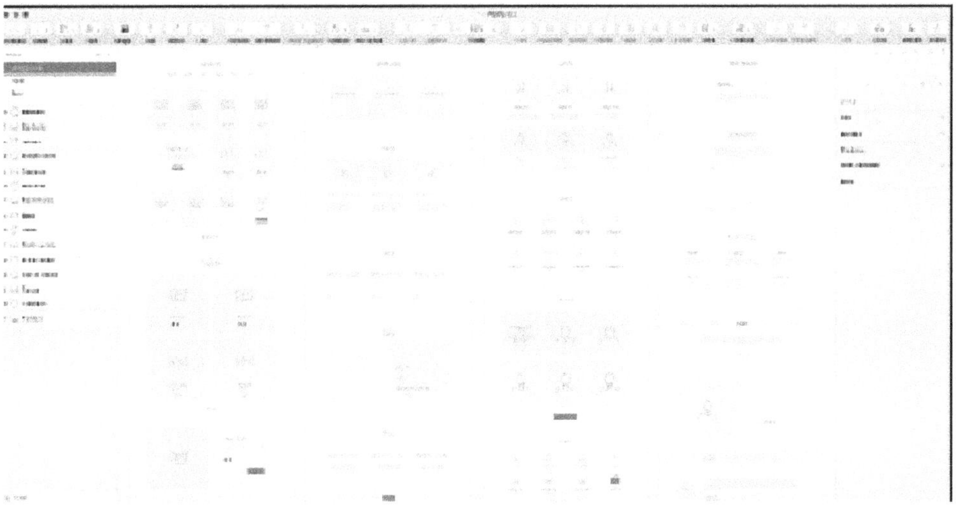

Fig. 9.9 Sketch

UXPin

UXPin is a top wireframe tool which supports interactive states, logic, and programmatic components giving designers the ability to *code* conditional interactions, variables, and expressions.

UXPin goes far beyond wireframing, focusing primarily on prototyping with UI component libraries, symbols, vector drawing tools, and co-editing.

There is a Windows, macOS, and cloud/browser version. For high-fidelity wireframing, UXPin works much like Sketch and Adobe XD. It isn't drag-and-drop like Balsamiq, but it does take prototyping and mockups to the next level for designers looking to stay within a single ecosystem.

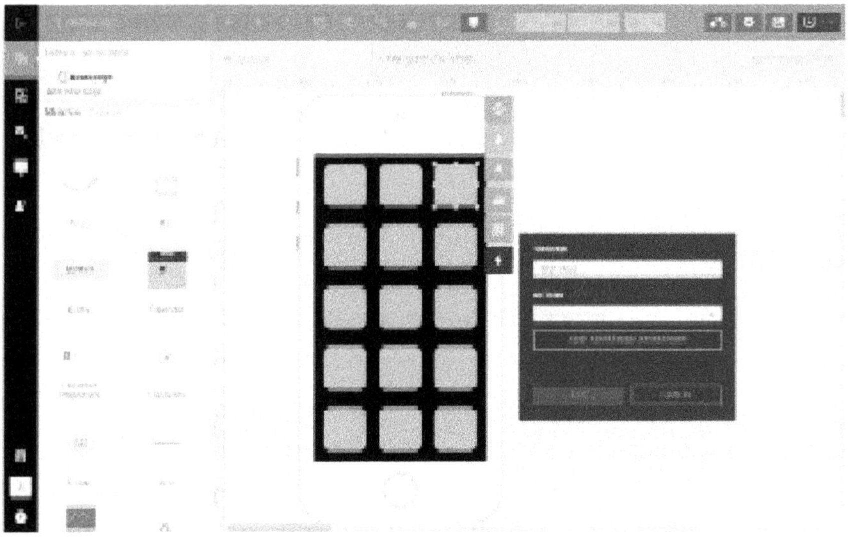

Fig. 9.10 UXPin

Marvel

Marvel, another popular design tool that facilitates wireframing and prototyping, provides designers with a familiar drag-and-drop interface for creating low to high-fidelity wireframes.

Marvel does not require any add-ons or extensions as all assets are included. The platform is fully cloud-based which makes sharing wireframes with other design team members or clients fast and easy.

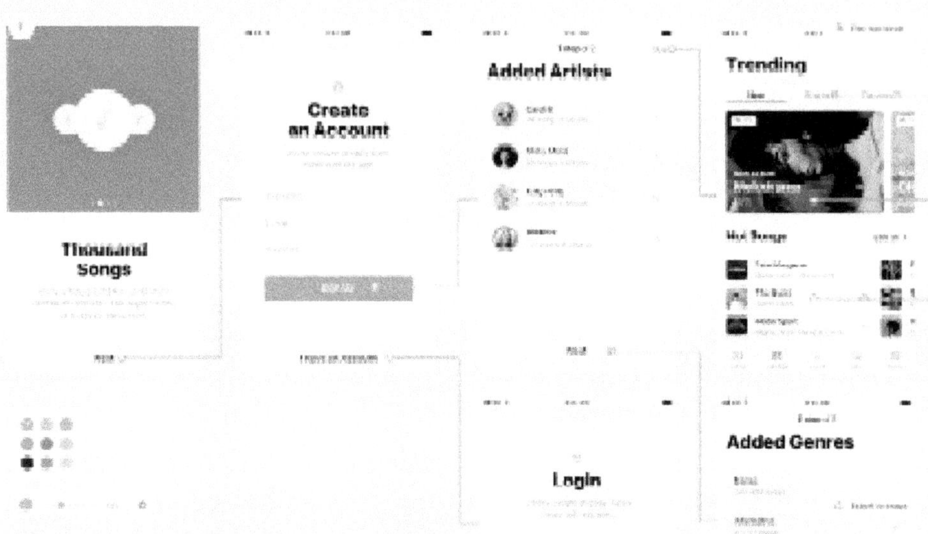

Fig. 9.11 Marvel

One of the reasons designers choose Marvel for wireframing is its integration with other platforms such as Jira, Sketch, Confluence, Dropbox, Slack, and many others. For collaboration with developers, remote design teams, and clients, this feature saves designers a lot of time.

Marvel also has a product called Pop which helps transform pen and paper wireframing sketches into interactive iPhone and Android prototypes. Pop allows designers to take a photo of their sketches and turn these into interactive wireframes.

Axure RP

Axure RP has been around for a long time and is a great tool for creating static wireframes (as well as highly interactive prototypes). It is not cloud-based though it works on both Windows and macOS.

Wireframing can be done using its massive library of drag and drop components, however, Axure RP is a complex tool that goes far beyond wireframing. Using Axure RP's programmatic features, designers can create advanced prototypes with functionality that mirrors a fully working application.

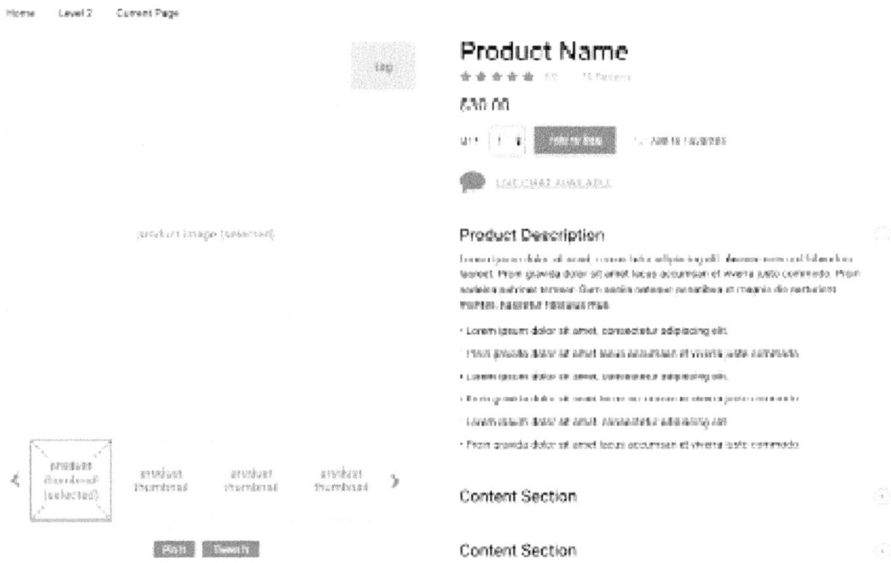

Fig. 9.12 Axure RP

Given Axure's high learning curve, it would not make sense to use it solely for static wireframes. However, if the goal is to produce prototypes that are highly polished and functional, then it would be the perfect tool for product designers.

Part IV: UX Design Principles

CHAPTER-10

VISUAL DESIGN IN UX

INTRODUCTION TO VISUAL DESIGN IN UX

Visual design aims to improve a design's/product's aesthetic appeal and usability with suitable images, typography, space, layout and color. Visual design is about more than aesthetics. Designers place elements carefully to create interfaces that optimize user experience and drive conversion.

In this video, designer and co-founder of HYPE4.com, Michal Malewicz, shares why visual skills are important and the difference between visual design for user interfaces and art.

IMPORTANCE VISUAL DESIGN

Visual Design is the first impression that you give to your customers. Studies show that it takes an average person about 50 milliseconds to make their first judgements about your product. It is in our human nature to be attracted to people or things that are good looking and studies show that adults and children both are more likely to trust someone who is attractive. The same theory applies to your application or website, people are more likely to give your product the benefit of doubt if it has an aesthetic appeal about itself.

All the time. It is an integral part of the whole design process and has to be thought of from the very first day.

Visual Design & User Experience Design

While visual design gives the end users their first impression based on the use of colours, typography and images, user experience design focuses on the complete experience of who will use the product and how they will use it. User experience design has to be done before solutions are developed by carrying out scientific research to figure out the specific needs, wants and key tasks associated with the intended end user. The results of the findings are then incorporated into the visual components of the interface to give the user a pleasurable interaction while accomplishing tasks.

A successful design is the one that maximizes its adoption to the customers by blending visual design and user experience methodologies to produce an attractive end product for the user.

BASICS OF VISUAL HIERARCHY AND AESTHETICS

Visual hierarchy is the principle of arranging elements to show their order of importance. Designers structure visual characteristics—e.g., menu icons—so users can understand information easily. By laying out elements logically and strategically, designers influence users' perceptions and guide them to desired actions.

Building Blocks of Visual Hierarchy

Hierarchy is a visual design principle which designers use to show the importance of each page/screen's contents by manipulating these characteristics:

- **Size** – Users notice larger elements more easily.
- **Color** – Bright colors typically attract more attention than muted ones.
- **Contrast** – Dramatically contrasted colors are more eye-catching.
- **Alignment** – Out-of-alignment elements stand out over aligned ones.
- **Repetition** – Repeating styles can suggest content is related.
- **Proximity** – Closely placed elements seem related.
- **Whitespace** – More space around elements draws the eye towards them.
- **Texture and Style** – Richer textures stand out over flat ones.

In user interface (UI) design, an effective visual hierarchy helps inform, impress and persuade users, who have expectations – especially about an interface's appearance. So, for a website, app or related product to succeed, it's crucial to structure its pages or screens to minimize users' uncertainty, show maximum empathy with them and give them something pleasant to view.

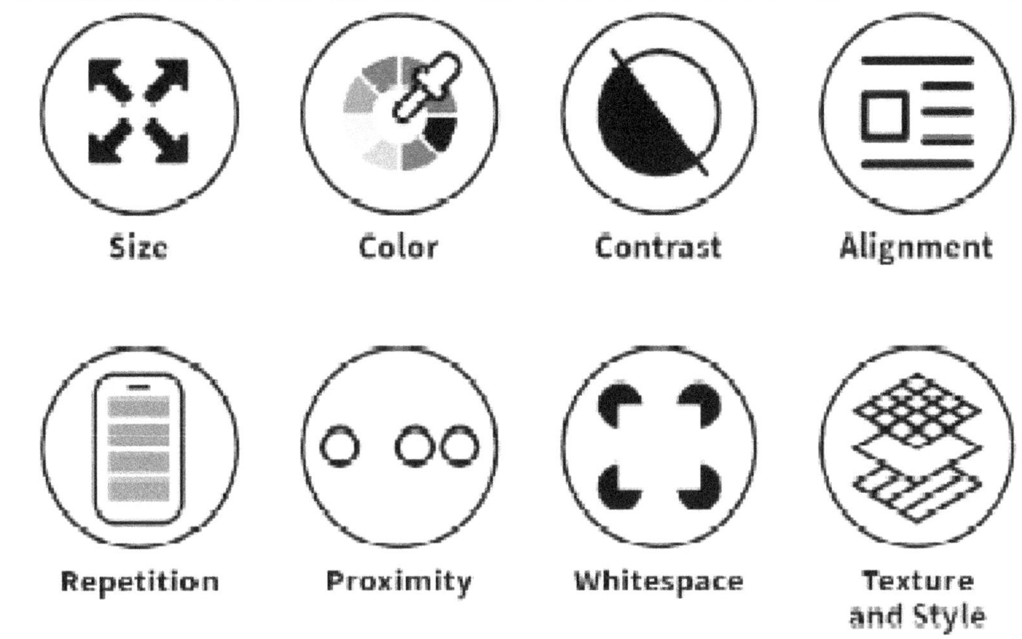

Fig. 10.1 Visual Design Principles

How to Craft a Strong Visual Hierarchy?

A strong visual hierarchy leads users to a page/screen's functionality and gives them the right visual cues. You'll need user research to learn about your users, but here are some general facts:

- **When encountering an interface, users react extremely fast** (in milliseconds), developing gut feelings about whether to stay or leave.
- **Users' eyes follow predictable reading paths, which are culturally influenced.** Left-to-right-reading Western users use an F- and a Z-pattern. So, you can design a hierarchy either to (Fig. 10.2):
  - **Reinforce** these natural patterns and lead users along a cleverly constructed path to a desired goal; or
  - **Break** these patterns to highlight a focal point for users.
  - **Users prefer recognition over recall** – hence why it's essential they can scan instead of having to work at reading and remembering things.

Considering these, you can help envision how to show users the most important things as they try to achieve goals in their individual contexts. Then, you can choose and scale elements to **make the most important information prominent—and unmissable—for users as they go from task to task.** These points are especially valuable:

- **The Gestalt principles** – These cater to the human eye. Use them to help users group visual elements, notice what's important on each page and build trust with your brand.
- **Consistency** –Familiar icons, menu hierarchy, colors, etc. are vital aids for users.
- **Center stage** – Use this UI design pattern to show users important things right up-front.
- **Whitespace** – The key to crisp, clean minimalist designs; use it to calm users' eyes and direct them to important foreground elements.
- **Typography** – Use the best font, color and contrast to present three levels of text for desktop-accessed screens, two—skipping the middle one—for mobile:

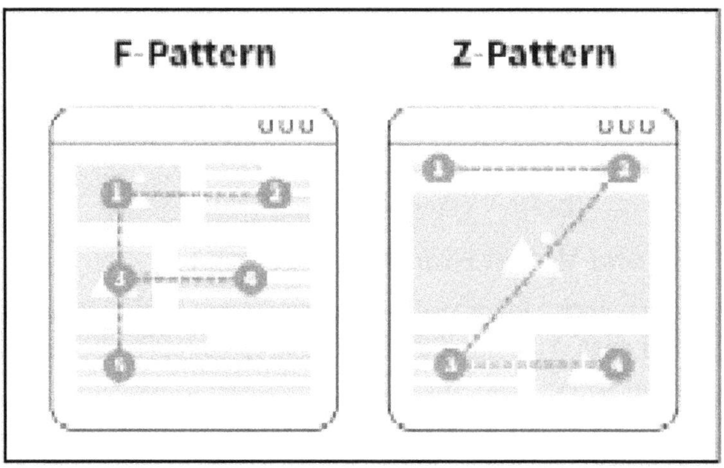

Fig. 10.2 F- and a Z-pattern

- **Mobile UX design specifics** – Users on smaller screens must be able to notice elements right away and navigate that much more easily.
- **Typography and style** – Elaborate fonts are more appropriate in some industries, but ornate text and special effects (e.g., embossed, washed-out text) might distract users, and even slight distractions reduce usability.
  - **Primary** – Use a header to attract users' attention with the page/ screen's core information, like a newspaper headline. The first two words of a header should let users understand the gist of the section below it.
  - **Secondary** – Use (e.g.) sub-headers to help users scan and navigate through content.
  - **Tertiary** – The body, smaller but still highly readable.

IMPORTANCE OF VISUAL HIERARCHY

Visual hierarchy, at the most basic level, guides a person through the content presented. It signals to them which content is the most important, how that content is organized into related sections or categories, and which content they should focus on first. This is true whether the content is text, images, video, or something else.

Information comprehension is another important function of visual hierarchy. By creating visual relationships between pieces of content, those viewing that content are given clues as to how to interpret the information.

By increasing comprehension and guiding the person consuming the information being presented, the message the design is presenting is reinforced. Without visual hierarchy, it can all come across as clutter.

But knowing the importance of visual hierarchy and knowing how to actually create it are different things. This infographic presents the basic ways to create hierarchy in a design—concepts like size and scale, typographic hierarchy, repetition, leading lines, and balance—along with examples showing them in practice.

Understanding and implementing these principles gives UX designers an advantage in creating persuasive designs that convey the necessary information while creating a delightful user experience.

Key Principles of Visual Hierarchy in UX Design

The principles of visual hierarchy are fundamental design concepts that aim to create a clear and organized visual structure to enhance the overall user experience. The main principles include:

Size and Scale

Size and scale play a crucial role in directing user attention and establishing the significance of elements within a design. The idea behind this principle is simple yet effective: larger elements naturally draw your eyes due to their visibility.

When certain elements are made larger than others, they stand out as focal points, instantly capturing your attention. You can use this technique to highlight important components such as headings, titles, or key images. By making these elements larger, they create a clear hierarchy that guides users to what matters most.

Color:

Color is a powerful tool for establishing visual hierarchy and drawing attention to specific elements. Color can be used to evoke emotions, indicate interactivity, and differentiate between various content types.

Here's how color can be effectively used for visual hierarchy:

- **Color as Signifiers:** Important elements like call-to-action buttons, alerts, or notifications can be highlighted with vibrant and contrasting colors. For example, a red "Submit" button in a form draws attention and indicates an action.
- **Color Consistency:** Consistency in color usage throughout the interface helps users associate specific colors with certain actions or meanings. For instance, using consistent colors for links and buttons creates a predictable user experience.
- **Color Gradients:** Gradients that shift from one color to another can guide the eye along a specific path or highlight the sense of depth within a design. Gradients can be applied to backgrounds or elements to create visual interest.

For example, RingCentral's brand color, the distinctive orange hue, takes center stage on its home page, showcasing a strategic and impactful approach to visual hierarchy and user engagement. In this context, color becomes more than just an aesthetic choice; it becomes a dynamic tool for conveying information and guiding interactions.

The vibrant and recognizable orange hue is deliberately applied to call-to-action buttons, the image backdrop, and other pivotal elements. Its purpose is clear: to capture attention. By employing such a vivid and contrasting shade, the design team ensures that essential interactive components, like buttons, are immediately noticeable.

RingCentral's home page exemplifies how the strategic use of its signature orange color drives visual hierarchy and user engagement.

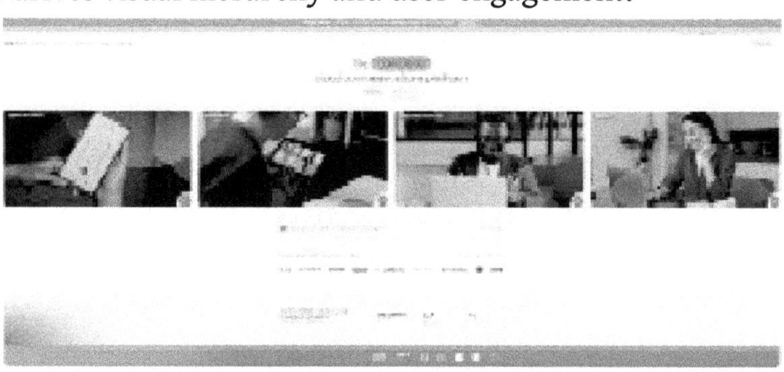

Fig. 10.3 RingCentral's home page

Contrast

Contrast refers to the difference in visual properties, such as color, size, and typography, between elements on a design surface. In a visual hierarchy, contrast plays a crucial role in guiding users' attention and creating a clear and organized visual order.

By strategically applying contrast, you can make certain elements stand out while others fade into the background. This contrast helps users quickly identify and process important information, enhancing the overall usability of the interface.

There are different shades of contracts such as:

- **Color Contrast**: Using contrasting colors for background elements ensures that content is easily readable. For example, black text on a white background provides a high level of contrast, making the text clear.
- **Size Contrast**: Varying the size of elements based on their importance or hierarchy creates a sense of importance and flow. Larger elements draw more attention and are often perceived as more significant.
- **Typography Contrast**: Combining different font sizes, weights, and styles creates contrast in typography. Headings can be bold and larger, while body text remains softer.

Typography

The principle of typography is a key component of creating an effective visual hierarchy in UX design. Typography involves the selection, arrangement, and presentation of fonts to convey information and establish a hierarchy.

The choice of fonts is crucial in UX design because different fonts convey different tones and emotions. Depending on the nature of the content and the brand's identity, you should select fonts that align with the overall design concept and the intended user experience.

For instance, a modern sans-serif font might be used for a tech-related website, while a classic serif font could be more appropriate for a news publication.

Choosing fonts that resonate with the content and target audience ensures consistency and readability throughout the interface.

Alignment and Proximity:

Alignment is the practice of positioning elements in a design in relation to each other. It's a fundamental principle that contributes to the overall organization of a user interface. By aligning elements, you can create a sense of order and harmony, allowing users to quickly grasp relationships between different elements.

For example, aligning the logo and navigation menu at the top of a webpage creates a clear connection between the branding and the main navigation, making it easier for users to understand the layout and flow of the page.

In addition, proximity is the concept of placing related elements close to each other and separating unrelated elements. This helps users naturally group and understand content based on its visual arrangement. Effective use of proximity helps users make quick decisions about where to focus their attention and which elements are connected. Alignment and proximity become even more critical when dealing with complex information or content-heavy interfaces. You can use these principles to break down complex information into small sections and guide users through the content.

Visual Consistency

Visual consistency refers to maintaining a uniform and cohesive design across all elements and screens of a user interface. It's a key principle in UX design because it creates a sense of familiarity and predictability for users. When elements are consistently styled, users can easily understand how to interact with them and navigate through the interface without confusion.

Consistency extends to various design aspects, including colors, typography, icons, spacing, and layout. For instance, if a certain color is used to indicate interactive elements (like buttons) on one screen, the same color should be used consistently throughout the entire application. Inconsistent styling can lead to user frustration and thinking pressure as users need to adapt to different visual cues.

Elements of Visual Consistency

- **Color Palette**: Consistent use of colors across the interface reinforces brand identity and helps users associate specific colors with certain actions or information types.
- **Typography**: Using a consistent set of fonts and typographic styles maintains readability and a sense of uniformity across the content.
- **Layout and Grid**: Employing a consistent grid system and layout structure throughout the interface creates a sense of order and predictability.
- **Icons and Imagery**: Using consistent icon and imagery styles ensures that visual cues remain recognizable and meaningful to users.
- **Interactions and Animations**: Keeping interactions and animations consistent across the interface provides a smooth and predictable user experience.

By applying these principles, you can create interfaces that guide users smoothly through content, make interactions intuitive, and enhance overall user satisfaction. Effective visual hierarchy contributes to better usability and engagement, ultimately leading to a more successful user experience.

Triangle of visual hierarchy

The Triangle of Visual Hierarchy, also known as the "**Golden Triangle**," is a design concept used to guide the arrangement of elements within a composition to create an effective visual hierarchy. It's based on the principles of Gestalt psychology, which focuses on how people perceive and organize visual information.

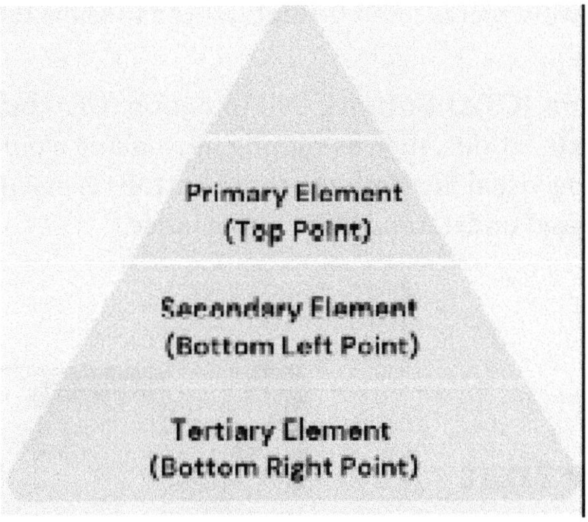

Fig. 10.4 Structure of Visual Hierarchy Triangle

Here's how the Triangle of Visual Hierarchy works:

- **Primary Element (Top Point)**: This is the most important element in your design, often the focal point or the main subject. It's placed at the top of the triangle, capturing the viewer's attention first.
- **Secondary Element (Bottom Left Point)**: This element supports the primary element and reinforces its message or purpose. It's placed at the bottom left corner of the triangle, guiding the viewer's eye in a diagonal line from the top point.
- **Tertiary Element (Bottom Right Point)**: The tertiary element complements the primary and secondary elements, completing the triangle. Placed at the bottom right corner, it helps balance the composition and provides closure to the visual journey.

Applying Visual Hierarchy in UX Design

- **Homepage Design**: When it comes to applying visual hierarchy in UX design, the homepage, and landing pages hold critical importance. These areas serve as the initial touchpoints for users, and employing visual hierarchy effectively can significantly enhance their experience. Visual hierarchy assists in arranging and presenting information on the page in a way that aligns with user priorities.

- **Navigation Menus:** Navigation menus are vital components of user interfaces, guiding users through different sections of a website or application. Applying visual hierarchy to navigation menus ensures that users can easily find and access the desired content.
- For example, If a user is on the "Home" page of a website, the "Home" link in the navigation menu could be highlighted to show that it's the currently active page.
- **Call to Action (CTA) Buttons:** Call to Action (CTA) buttons prompt users to take specific actions, such as signing up, making a purchase, or starting a trial. Applying visual hierarchy to these buttons is essential to ensure users notice them and understand their importance.

Fig. 10.5 Homepage Design

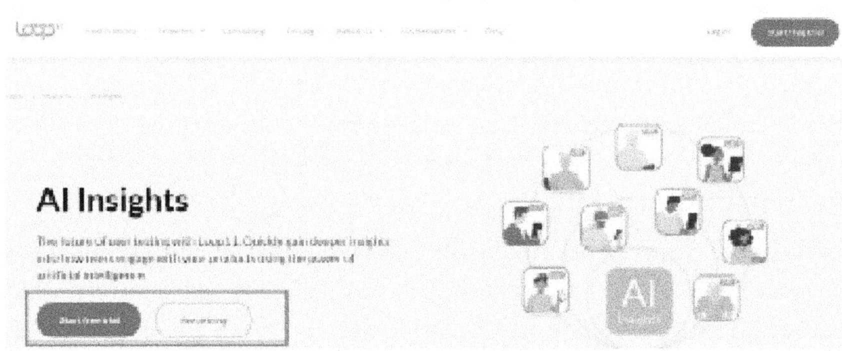

Fig. 10.6 Large free trial button on the Loop11 feature page

- For example, for a "Sign Up" CTA button on a feature page, using a contrasting color, larger size, and bold typography can make the button stand out, encouraging users to click and complete the sign-up process.
- **Content Presentation:** The effective presentation of content is crucial in UX design, as it directly influences how users consume and interact with information. Employing visual hierarchy in content presentation enhances readability, engagement, and overall user experience.

Users often scan content before committing to reading it thoroughly. Visual hierarchy assists in creating a scannable layout by using elements like bullet points, numbered lists, and bolded text to draw attention to key points.

For instance, a specialized digital portfolio page would include a variety of visual hierarchy elements.

Fig. 10.7 Digital portfolio page

These visual cues help users quickly identify the sections most relevant to their interests, improving information absorption and engagement.

- **Forms and Input Fields:** Forms are integral components of many digital experiences, serving as a means for users to provide information and interact with a platform. By applying visual hierarchy you can structure the form in a manner that guides users naturally from one field to the next.

COLOR THEORY AND ITS IMPACT ON USER PERCEPTION

Color theory is the study of how colors work together and how they affect our emotions and perceptions. It's like a toolbox for artists, designers, and creators to help them choose the right colors for their projects. Color theory enables you to pick colors that go well together and convey the right mood or message in your work.

The Psychology of Color

UX color theory and the psychological effects color can have on users is a complex and often subjective topic. But there are certain aspects that can be addressed on a more universal level.

Things like the common meanings of the main colors (primary, secondary, and tertiary), traditional color palettes, and cultural variations in color meanings are all fairly straightforward. Designers can easily learn these basics and apply them to their work. But there are finer points to be learned when it comes to using colors in UX design.

The emotional impact of interface colors shouldn't be overlooked. And while some colors are "universal" in UX design (such as black, white, and gray, at least one of which is used in virtually every good design out there), the colors they're combined with can have a huge impact on a user's perception.

Of course, the way in which color is used can also have a dramatic impact on how it's perceived. For example, blue used as a primary color in a modern, minimalist design will have a very different feel than the same blue used as an accent color in a more complex, corporate design.

The Role of Color Theory in UI/UX Designing

In the realm of UI/UX design, color isn't just a visual element—it's a powerful tool that can significantly impact user experiences, emotions, and interactions. Understanding and harnessing the principles of color theory is essential for creating visually appealing, effective, and user-friendly designs. Therefore, in this blog, we will explore the profound role that color theory plays in UI/UX design and how it can be leveraged to enhance the overall user experience.

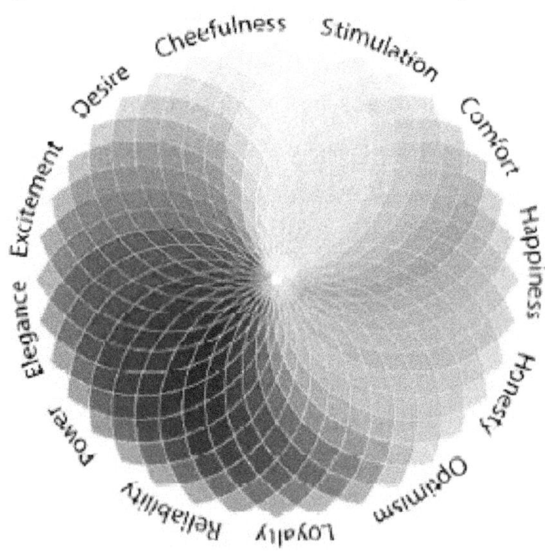

Fig. 10.8 Traditional color palettes, and cultural variations in color meanings

Enhancing Readability and Legibility

Color plays a critical role in ensuring the readability and legibility of textual content. The contrast between text and background colors is crucial for readability, especially for users with varying levels of visual acuity. Designers must choose colors that provide sufficient contrast to make text easily readable without causing strain or discomfort to the user.

Consistency and Branding

Color is a core element of brand identity. Consistency in color usage across different platforms and interfaces helps users recognize and associate a brand quickly. Integrating brand colors into UI/UX design reinforces brand recognition and creates a cohesive user experience.

Accessibility and Inclusivity

Designing with color blindness and other visual impairments in mind is an integral part of creating inclusive interfaces. Using a combination of color and other design elements, such as icons or patterns, can help convey information to users who may not perceive colors accurately. Adhering to accessible color contrast ratios ensures that designs are usable by all individuals, regardless of their visual abilities.

Cultural and Contextual Considerations

Colors carry cultural significance and associations that can vary across different regions and demographics. A color that evokes positive emotions in one culture might have different connotations in another. Designers working on global projects must be mindful of these cultural nuances to avoid unintended misunderstandings and misinterpretations. Here is the reason why a UI/UX Design Course is Worth Investing in for your Career

Creating Emotional Connections

Colors have the power to evoke emotions and establish emotional connections with users. The strategic use of colors can shape the overall mood and atmosphere of a design, influencing users' perceptions and attitudes toward a product or service. Designers can tap into color psychology to create interfaces that resonate with users on a deeper level.

Tips for Using Color Theory in UI/UX Design

Start with the Brand

- Understand the brand's color palette and integrate it thoughtfully into the design to maintain brand consistency.

Use Color Palettes Wisely

- Select a harmonious color palette that aligns with the desired emotional tone of the design. Tools like Adobe Color can help in creating balanced color schemes.

Prioritize Readability

- Ensure that text remains easily readable by choosing high-contrast color combinations. Use tools like Web Content Accessibility Guidelines (WCAG) to determine acceptable color contrast ratios.

Consider Context

- Adapt color choices based on the context of use. Different interfaces might require different color approaches, such as dark mode versus light mode.

Test and Iterate

- Conducting the user testing to gather feedback on color choices. Iteratively refine the color scheme based on user preferences and perceptions.

Balance and Contrast

- Balance vibrant and neutral colors to create visual interest and guide user focus. Contrast between elements aids in creating a clear visual hierarchy.

Stay Updated on Trends

- Keep an eye on current color trends in UI/UX design to ensure your designs remain fresh and appealing to users. With the assistance of UI/UX designing courses in Kolkata, you can easily do that!

To Wrap Upnbsp

Color theory plays a vital role in UI/UX designing, impacting user perception, emotions, and overall experience. By leveraging the psychology of color, establishing visual hierarchy, maintaining consistency, ensuring accessibility, and considering cultural and contextual factors, designers can create interfaces that engage users and communicate effectively. Learning color psychology is very important. With the assistance of UI UX designing courses in Kolkata, you can learn these things very precisely. Incorporating color theory into the design process allows for purposeful and meaningful use of color, enhancing usability, aesthetic appeal, and user satisfaction. As UI/UX designers, harnessing the potential of color theory empowers us to create interfaces that captivate and delight users, ultimately leading to successful digital experiences.

Examples of color psychology in logo design

Brands use colors thoughtfully to reinforce their identity and communicate the brand messages with the users. For instance, Google icons are designed with color psychology in mind to help users quickly identify the purpose of the different products offered by the company. It is interesting to know how each color in the Google icons conveys particular meanings.

Google

Google's core product, Search, is one of its main tools. Google uses the colors red, yellow, green, and blue colors on its logo. Red is a catchy and energetic color associated with excitement and naturally captures users' attention. Yellow evokes happiness and optimism in users, symbolizing a positive approach to the user's need of finding the answer to a query. Green conveys growth and harmony, evoking calmness and a feeling of self-development. And blue is associated with intelligence and trust, conveying that Google provides authentic information.

YouTube

The number 1 video sharing platform in the world, YouTube uses two main colors in its logo - red and white. Red represents excitement white symbolizes purity and harmony. Together, these two colors convey the brand's personality.

Amazon

E-commerce giant, Amazon, has an interesting logo – a smiling orange arc between the letters A and Z of "Amazon". The color orange is used to convey pleasure and enthusiasm and the arc's path indicates that it offers products from A to Z, meaning products of all ranges.

McDonald

McDonald's logo design is a shining example of how color psychology is used to impact users' emotions. The golden yellowish arch placed on a red background makes use of mood-elevating colors to trigger appetite.

Walt Disney

The black iconic castle from Cinderella in the logo design of Walt Disney symbolizes immersive storylines and fantasy plots. The graphic elements complement each other and show the magical face of the company.

Cultural differences in color

When dealing with colors, being mindful of cultural differences is essential. Considering cultural differences is necessary when designing products for a global audience to ensure that the intended message is rightly conveyed. For this, ethnographic UX research might help to avoid any potential misunderstandings or culturally insensitive usage of visuals.

Certain colors that have positive connotations in one culture have negative connotations in another. For example, in western nations, white color is associated with innocence and purity whereas in Asian Countries white symbolizes death and mourning.

CHAPTER-11

INFORMATION ARCHITECTURE

Information architecture may be the most effective tool in user experience design, just as blueprints are the most important document an architect can use while constructing a building. An information architecture is helpful in the process of describing the full interaction the consumer has with a product, including how they feel about the encounter, similar to a blueprint that architecture has.

It offers a representation of the entire website or app to the designers, developers, project managers, and QA experts so that they can easily plan the timeframe, choose the features to be included, and determine how the implementation will function. The information architecture makes it simple for developers to make important choices on the product to be built and determine the resources needed. It is important to note that all IAs are designed to be upgraded. With regard to products, the cycle keeps repeating itself as users modify their behavior and designs evolve. Remembering that there is always room for improvement is crucial. As a result, it is impossible to design an IA that is permanent and aims for perfection; instead, it**on** must be flexible, adaptive, and scalable.

Need forit Information Architecture

Peter Morville and Louis Rosenfeld have deeply elaborated on the different user needs in the "Information Architecture of the World Wide Web". According to them, there are 4 types of user needs.

- **Known-item seeking:** When the user visits the website with something that they know and desire.
- **Exploratory seeking:** When a user visits a website without having any knowledge about what they want but is looking for something they desire.

- **Exhaustive research:** When a user visits a website without any intention of looking for a desired product but to gather information for comparison.
- **Re-finding:** When a user needs an item again and keeps trying to find it.

Why is Information Architecture Important in UX Design?

- It all comes down to organizing and arranging data in a way that is understandable to users. Users can traverse a digital product or website more effectively and more smoothly and enjoyably when the information is well-organized and simple to find.
- The organization and labeling of identical content or functionality across the entire digital product or website is guaranteed by a consistent IA. Users can create mental models and experience less confusion with consistency.
- Collaboration between designers, developers, content producers, and stakeholders is necessary for IA. This architecture is used by different team members to ensure there is no confusion.
- IA aids managers and content producers in determining where and how to position material within a digital product. By doing this, content management is streamlined and the proper content is provided in the appropriate context.
- Growth and change can be accommodated by an efficient IA. A digital product or website may readily absorb new material or features as it develops without upsetting users or confusing them.
- The Information architecture should be designed in such a way that it aligns with the business goals. It also aims at increasing user engagement and helps in directing them in the correct direction.

Elements of an Information Architecture

The Information architecture can be divided into three major parts navigation, labels, and search.

- **Navigation:** The process by which users move inside the website to interact with the contents of the website by moving.
- **Labels:** The naming of the content material on the site.
- **Search:** Information-seeking methods (keywords, categories)

How to Design Information Architecture

- **Understand Business Aims**: Start by thoroughly understanding the goals and objectives of the business for the website or digital product. What are the main objectives? What conversions or results are wanted?

- **Define user goals:** The users' aims and objectives should be identified and defined. This stage enables the IA to better meet user wants and expectations.
- **Conduct analysis:** Make a thorough analysis that takes into account both qualitative and quantitative research. Market research, competitor analysis, and user research could all be included. assemble information about user preferences, behaviors, and pain areas.
- **Create the content:** Start developing the content for the website or digital product based on the analysis. Text, pictures, videos, papers, and any other pertinent items fall under this category.
- **Categorize them:** After the content is created it important to categorize them to ensure that content that are related are grouped together.
- **Design user navigation:** Create the menu system and access points that users will utilize to access the content. Designing menus, labels, and links falls under this category. Make sure the navigation is simple, easy to use, and consistent with the content categories.
- **Verify designs:** Now the Information Architecture created needs to be validated and made sure that they function on the basis of real world situations and to ensure that there there are no issues and rectify them.

Steps to Design

- Initially user data needs to be gathered and all the basic questions should be answered.
- User stories need to be written
- Pages, Scenarios and metadata should be added to the Information architecture
- Map the user flow for different decision flow
- Gather feedback about the architecture before moving further.

The Information Architecture of an e-commerce website is given in Fig. 11.1.

Information Architecture Principles

- **Objects:** Consider content to be a live object. It has traits, habits, and life cycles.
- **Choices:** It is vital to minimize the number of option to prevent complexity of the website.
- **Disclosure:** Display a preview of the data to let consumers understand the type of data that will be buried if they go deeper.

- **Examples:** It is important to provide examples for content so that it could be easy to understand the flow.
- **Front doors:** Always consider that users would also access the site's other pages apart from the homepage
- **Focused navigation:** Never mix diverse things together and keep navigation simple.
- **Growth:** Always assume the content would be scalable and the architecture should support that.

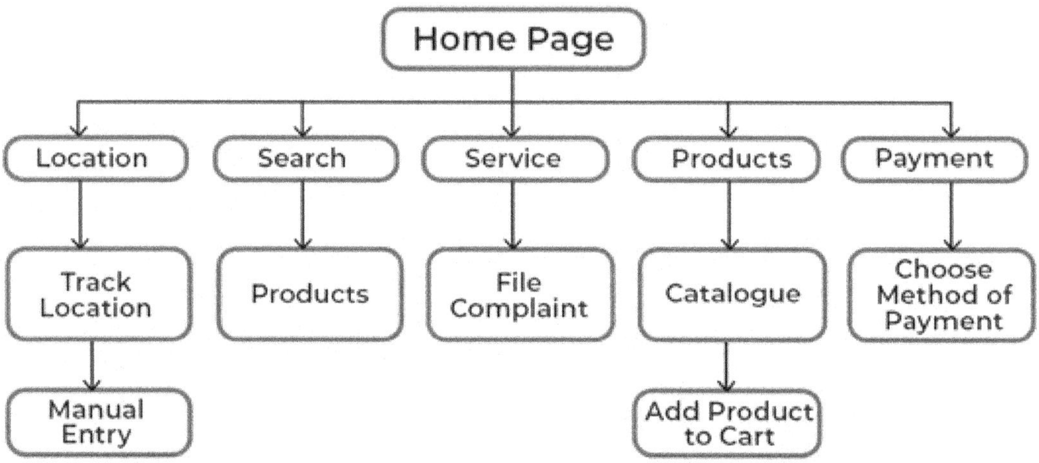

Fig. 11.1 The Information Architecture of an e-commerce website

STRUCTURING INFORMATION FOR INTUITIVE NAVIGATION

Information Architecture (IA) refers to the design and organization of digital content and functionality to meet user and business objectives. Information Architecture (IA) focuses on creating intuitive structure, labeling, and organization of elements to help users find information and complete tasks quickly. Many people often get confused about what information architecture entails and how it differs from UX design. After all, isn't UX design also about creating intuitive experiences for users?

Information Architecture is a subset of UX design that specializes in findability, usability, and accessibility of content whereas UX design considers the overall interaction of the product. We are all familiar with the processes of UX Design which involves research, wireframing, prototyping, UI Design, and continuous testing throughout the process to improve the overall user experience.

While many of these processes will be followed in information UX architecture, they also include content audits, card sorting, taxonomies, sitemaps, and navigation design.

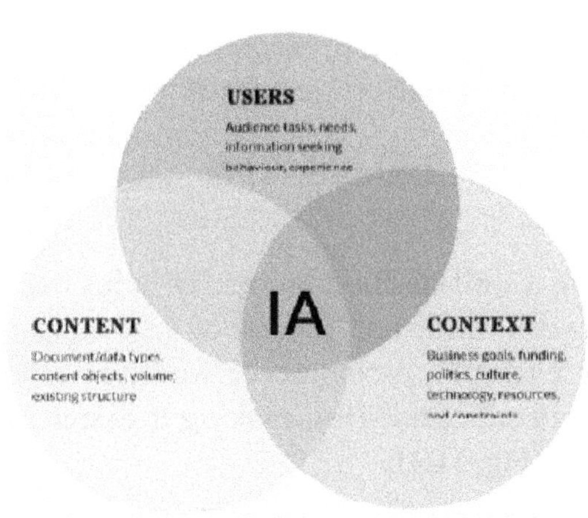

Fig. 11.2 what is IA

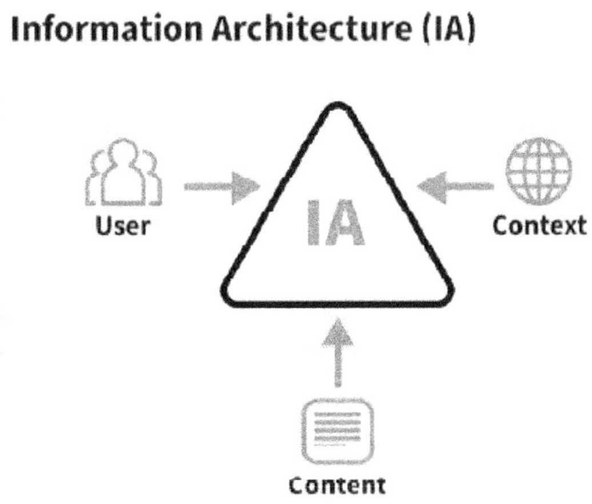

Fig. 11.3 Components of IA

Information Architecture in UX: Examples, Strategies, and Collaboration

Introduction to Information Architecture

Information Architecture (IA) refers to the design and organization of digital content and functionality to meet user and business objectives. Information Architecture (IA) focuses on creating intuitive structure, labeling, and organization of elements to help users find information and complete tasks quickly. Many people often get confused about what information architecture entails and how it differs from UX design. After all, isn't UX design also about creating intuitive experiences for users? Information Architecture is a subset of UX design that specializes in findability, usability, and accessibility of content whereas UX design considers the overall interaction of the product. We are all familiar with the processes of UX Design which involves research, wireframing, prototyping, UI Design, and continuous testing throughout the process to improve the overall user experience.

While many of these processes will be followed in information UX architecture, they also include content audits, card sorting, taxonomies, sitemaps, and navigation design.

Still confused about what is information architecture in UX?

Think of the role of UX designers like that of architects who plan the layout of the entire house, and make key decisions on the flow of the house, aesthetics, lighting, ambiance, and more. Now, think of the role of the information UX architects with that of interior designers who handle specific decisions on furniture layouts and arrangements, room labeling, etc.

The main goals of the information architecture for the website are to reduce the cognitive load that occurs when a lot of information is presented at once which can overwhelm users and enable users to find information seamlessly.

Key Aspects of Information Architecture UX with Examples

Organization

- **Hierarchical Structure:** Establishing a well-defined hierarchy helps users understand the relationships between different pieces of information and navigate more efficiently. For example, e-commerce websites often organize products into categories and subcategories, making it easier for users to find what they're looking for (Fig. 11.4).
- **Taxonomies:** Organizing and classifying related content into logical groups enhances the overall structure and findability of information. News websites often use taxonomies to categorize articles by topics, locations, or types (e.g., politics, sports, opinion pieces).
- **Metadata:** Adding descriptive metadata, such as labels or tags, to content improves searchability and discoverability. Social media platforms like Instagram and Twitter rely heavily on user-generated metadata (hashtags) to help users find relevant content.

Fig. 11.4 Structure of IA

Navigation

- **Menus and Navigation Bars:** User-friendly menus and navigation bars guide users through the information hierarchy and provide quick access to important sections or features. Popular websites like Amazon and Netflix employ intuitive navigation menus that adapt based on the user's context or preferences.
- **Bread crumbs:** Breadcrumb trails show users their current location within the information architecture, providing a sense of context and allowing

them to backtrack easily. E-commerce websites often use breadcrumbs to help users retrace their steps during the product browsing and checkout process.

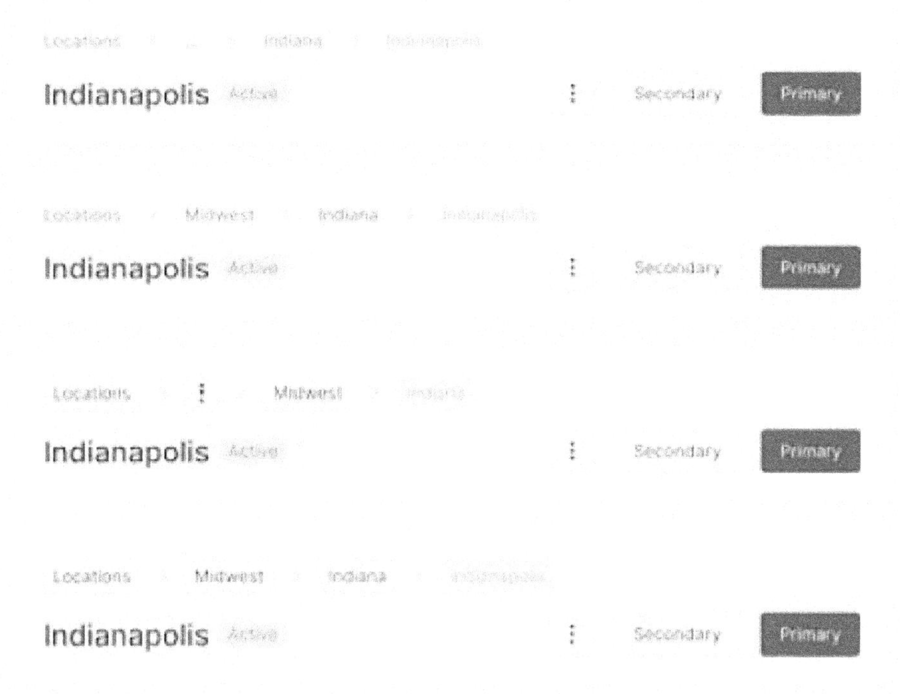

Fig. 11.5 Search functionality

- **Search functionality:** Effective search features enable users to find specific information quickly, especially in large or complex information spaces. As you mentioned, Housing.com improved feature adoption by 20% after revamping its search functionality, highlighting the importance of a well-designed search experience.

Labelling

Consistent terminology: Using consistent and clear language throughout the system prevents confusion and enhances the overall user experience. For example, popular websites like Mailchimp have established a detailed content style guide to maintain consistent terminology for their features and functionalities, making it easier for users to understand and navigate the tools.

Descriptive labels: Selecting labels that accurately describe the information they represent helps users understand the content and make informed decisions. Mobile app design often emphasizes the use of descriptive labels for icons and menu items, as screen real estate is limited, and clear communication is crucial.

Fig. 11.6 How to use label

8 Principles of Information Architecture

Dan Brown who was the founder of EightShapes has proposed eight principles of information architecture (Fig. 11.7) that serve as a framework for designing effective information architecture. These principles are:

Principle of Objects: According to this principle, data should be viewed as distinct entities or objects that may be arranged and structured to build a logical system. It is simpler to create links, hierarchies, and linkages between various kinds of information when it is treated as an object.

Principle of Choices: It is important to give users relevant alternatives and choices while browsing and accessing information. Multiple options and pathways should be provided by the information architecture so that users may search and discover content according to their preferences and mental models.

Principle of Disclosure: As users explore farther into the system, more information should be made available gradually, providing additional context or details. This idea prevents providing users with too much information upfront and helps minimize cognitive overload.

P**rinciple of Exemplars**: Exemplars, or representative examples, are what the information architecture should offer to aid users in understanding the context and meaning of information items. Users can be assisted by exemplars in understanding the organization and content of the information environment.

Principle of Front Doors: To accommodate varying user demands and needs, the information architecture should have various "front doors" or entrance points. This notion recognizes that when people access information, they can do so from many beginning points.

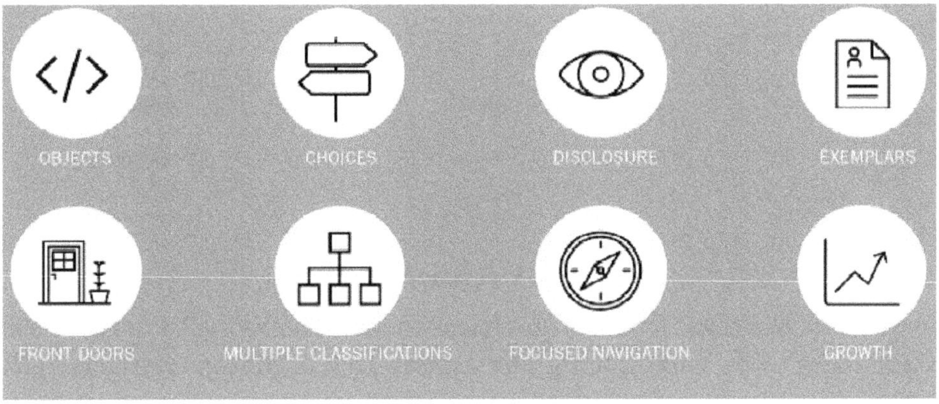

Fig. 11.7 Eight principles of IA

Principle of Multiple Classification: It is important to classify and organize information in a variety of ways to accommodate various viewpoints and classifications. This principle acknowledges that, depending on the context and the needs of the user, information can be understood and arranged differently.

Principle of Focused Navigation: To provide the user with suitable alternatives and paths depending on their present context or aim, navigation systems should be task-specific and customized. This idea lessens cognitive strain and streamlines the navigational experience.

Principle of Growth: It is important to plan the information architecture to allow for future expansion and modification. Information items and structures should be able to be added, changed, or rearranged as needed because they should be scalable and adaptable.

How to Design information architecture?

It involves several key steps such as the following:

UX Research:

No process in UX design can be devoid of UX research. In IA, researching the business goals, user profiles types of content, and functionality required are crucial.

Conducting user research is essential for understanding the needs, behaviors, and expectations of the target audience. This insight guides the creation of an IA that aligns with user mental models and supports their tasks and goals effectively. Researching business goals and objectives ensures that the IA supports the organization's strategic priorities and contributes to achieving desired outcomes. Analyzing the types of content and functionality required helps determine the appropriate structure, organization, and navigation pathways within the IA.

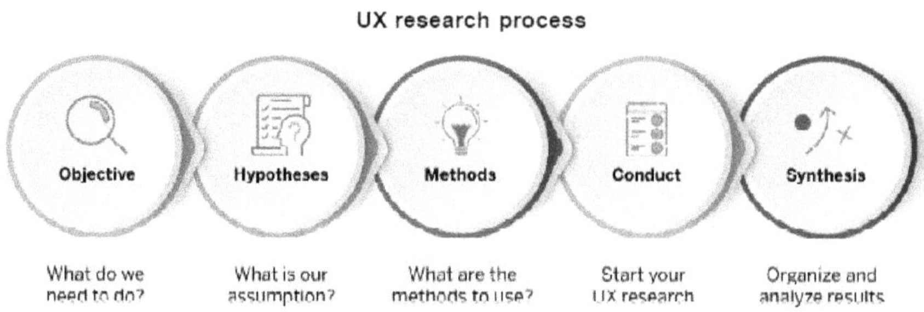

Fig. 11.8 UX research process

We will look at a topic that has much less to do with solving UI design problems and much more to do with solving *user experience* (UX) design problems—that is, navigation.

Navigation involves structuring your app in a way that promotes ease and efficiency, not merely design aesthetics. Unlike the other topics covered so far, which rely in part on personal taste as well as an awareness of changing fashions, navigation—and UX in general—tends to rely heavily on usability research.

We will explore the three key principles that both research and experience have shown underpin good navigation design:

- **Consistency** — meet user expectations
- **Simplicity** — don't do more than you need to
- **Clean interaction** — keep out of your users' way

Keeping these principles in mind as you design will help you to achieve the ideal navigational structure—that is, one that the user never notices.

Consistency

Navigation should be consistent with user expectations, leaning on standard conventions for icons, location and styling.

For example, in *Figure 1* below, you can see the spots where users will typically expect to find functionality like the menu and back buttons. The user expectation that the menu button will be at the top-left of the screen is so strong that you can even consider using a non-traditional icon to represent it, although the traditional "hamburger" icon is often the preferred choice across most platforms. For the back button, it is better to stick with Windows convention and keep it in either the leftmost spot or, if there is a Windows button, in the second-to-the-left spot (Fig. 11.9).

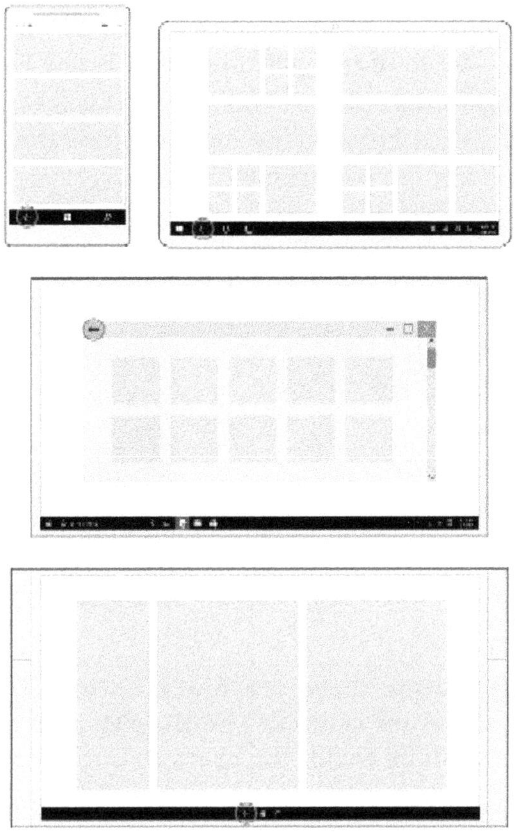

Fig. 11.9. Users expect to find certain buttons in certain places—e.g. the menu in the top left, and for UWP apps, the back button in the leftmost or second-to-the-leftmost spot. Sticking to these standard conventions helps users interpret the meaning of the buttons.

Placement of navigational elements should also change for different device families. For example, on tablets and laptops/PCs, the navigation pane is usually placed on the left side, whereas on mobile, it is on the top (Fig. 11.10).

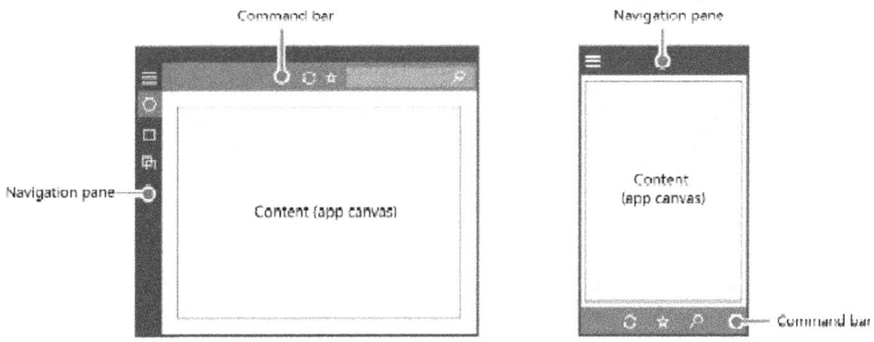

Fig.11.10. Different device families have their own conventions for navigational elements. For example, the navigation pane typically appears on the left side of the screen for tablets, but up top for mobile devices.

Simplicity

Another important factor in navigation design is the Hick-Hyman Law, often cited in relation to navigational options. This law encourages us to add fewer options to the menu (see Figure 11.11 below). The more options there are, the slower user interactions with them will be, particularly when users are exploring a new app. The same law can be applied to media content. Rather than overwhelming the user with a vast selection of media options, consider providing brief tidbits for users to explore if they choose (Fig. 11.11).

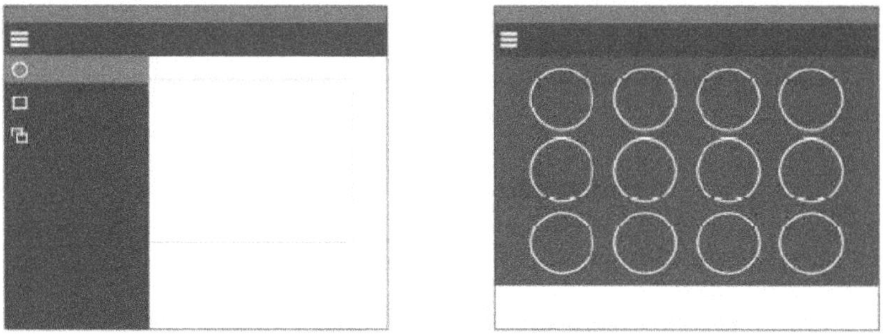

Fig. 11.11. On the left, notice there are fewer options for the user to select, whereas on the right, there are several. The Hick-Hyman Law indicates that the menu on the left will be easier for users to understand and utilize.

Clean interaction

The final key characteristic of navigation is clean interaction, which refers to the physical way that users interact with navigation across a variety of contexts.

This is one area where really putting yourself in the user's position will inform your design. Try to understand your users and their behaviors. If you're designing a cooking app, and you're expecting it to be used in the kitchen, you might want to take into account that the user will probably want to avoid using food-covered fingertips to navigate to the next cooking step. Instead, the user might use a knuckle, the back of his or her hand, or even an elbow. This should influence the size of your touch targets and the appropriate spacing between navigational elements, at the very least.

You should also keep in mind which areas of the screen are considered easy to reach. These are known as ***interaction areas***. In the mobile device illustration below (Fig. 11.12), for example, the blue area represents the optimal touch points for users (in this case, a user with the phone held in her left hand). Here, users expend the least amount of effort to interact —remember that most users hold their phones with their left hands and interact with their thumbs. Correspondingly, the dark grey region requires somewhat greater effort for interaction than the blue, and the light gray area requires the greatest amount of effort overall.

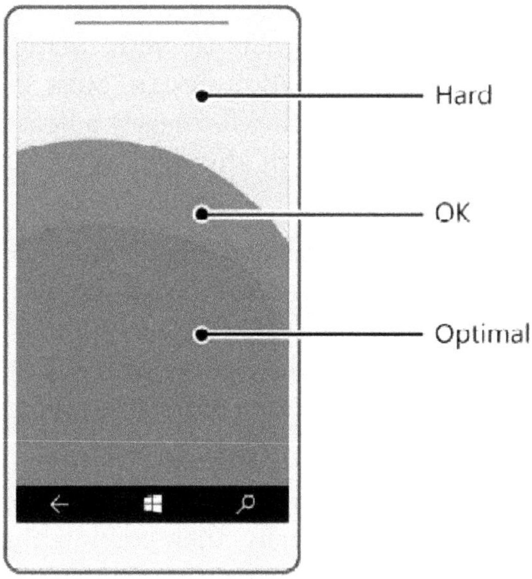

Fig. 11.12. Mobile device interaction area.

Tablet devices introduce an additional complexity because users have multiple ways of holding their device. Typically, users grip a tablet with both hands along the sides. Fig. 11.13 below shows the interaction area for the most common pose and grip of a tablet. Keep in mind as you design your navigation, however, that tablet users often switch between posing their devices in landscape and portrait orientations. Finally, note the alternative ways you yourself interact with tablets and consider whether your navigation is convenient for those scenarios, as well.

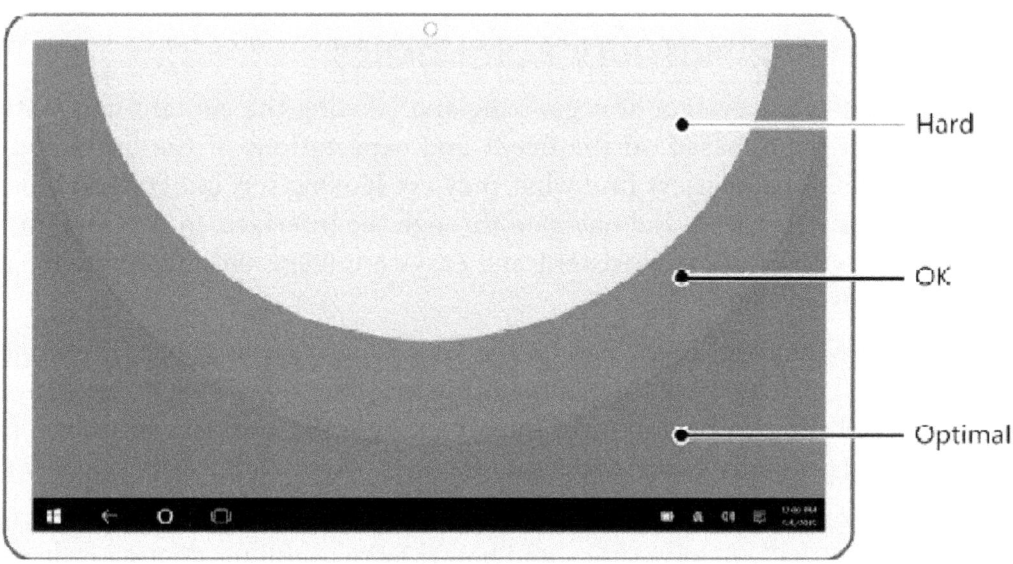

Fig. 11.13 Tablet device interaction area.

Rules of Thumb

Several rules of thumb help designers to encapsulate consistency, simplicity and clean interaction in their navigation design. Most of these come from the web design world and have been around for nearly a decade. These rules happen to work well for UWP apps, but as with any rules of thumb, use them as starting points and tweak as needed.

- ***Avoid deep navigational hierarchies.*** How many levels of navigation are best for your users? A top-level navigation and one level beneath it is usually plenty. If you go beyond three levels of navigation, then you break the principle of ***simplicity.*** Even worse, you risk stranding your user in a deep hierarchy that they will have difficulty leaving.
- ***Avoid too many navigational options.*** Three to six navigation elements per level seem about right. If your navigation needs more than this, especially at the top level of your hierarchy, then you might consider splitting your app into multiple apps, since you may be trying to do too much in one place. Too many navigation elements usually lead to inconsistent and unrelated objectives in your app.
- ***Avoid pogo-sticking.*** Pogo-sticking occurs when there is related content, but navigating to it requires the user to go up a level and then down again. Pogo-sticking violates the principle of clean interaction by requiring unnecessary clicks or interactions to achieve an obvious goal—in this case, looking at related content in a series. (The exception to this rule is in search and browse, where pogo-sticking may be the only way to provide the diversity and depth required.)

CREATING USER-FRIENDLY TAXONOMIES

Taxonomy is the system of organizing and labeling the content and features of a website or app, based on the needs and expectations of the users and the business goals. It helps users find what they are looking for, understand how the information is structured, and navigate through the interface. In this section, you will learn how to create a consistent and easy-to-understand taxonomy for user experience design (UED).

Taxonomy building might not be the first thing that aspiring UX designers think about when launching their careers, but maybe it should be! After all, a well-organized website can have a huge impact on how the audience searches, finds products, and generally experiences the site.

This section will explore what taxonomies are, how to gather the information for them and visually display them, and how they're useful for digital products.

Taxonomies are ***systems*** used to classify and organize things. So yes, when we talk about taxonomies in the animal kingdom (remember Kings Play Chess On Fine Glass Stools?), we are talking about the same type of taxonomy that gets used to organize a digital property.

A taxonomy—generally speaking—aims to understand a set of subject-specific concepts, and creates a vocabulary for those concepts, in order to ultimately organize the "physical things" related to those concepts and make them easier to find or interact with. This works well for subjects such as biology, where we organize species of plants and animals into categories based on their physical and genetic similarities/differences. House cats and lions are physically similar, and through science, we've determined that they're related enough to be grouped together in the same animal family. However, lions and housecats are still their own species—a category that is specific within the family of all cats and helps to differentiate the two.

Lions and cats are classified very similarly, but their features dictate that they be separated into different species entirely.

Taxonomies for websites and digital products function in the same way – helping to organize and classify information and features based on the similarities and differences of the concepts behind those features. This may then appear as categories within a blog or news page, or sections within a website, or metadata tags to improve search.

Of course, as UX practitioners we don't necessarily get to organize things in the way we want. Instead, we look at how users interpret and search for content on our site and sites like ours. Users of different ages, incomes, education levels, and backgrounds will use these products differently.

Scope and purpose

Before you start creating your taxonomy, you need to define the scope and purpose of your website or app. What is the main goal or function of your product? Who are your target users and what are their tasks and preferences? How do you want to communicate your brand identity and values? These questions will help you determine the level of complexity, specificity, and flexibility of your taxonomy, as well as the tone and style of your labels.

This is still quite a broad definition of taxonomy. So researcher also explains what a taxonomy is not:

- **A sitemap**: Sitemaps can be the end result of a taxonomy exercise, but sitemaps don't deal with definitions of words or how certain features are related to others. That being said, a good taxonomy can inform a good sitemap and ensure easy navigation for any digital product.

- **A content inventory:** Content inventory typically lists all the physical content that is present on a site. A taxonomy, on the other hand, organizes content, which may help determine what content is important, but taxonomies don't have to deal with every single little piece of content.
- **A list of keywords:** Taxonomies can help find keywords that actually resonate with the desired user base, but keywords and search ranking are just one part of the benefits of creating a taxonomy. Keywords alone won't help identify the relationships between different site areas and features, while a full taxonomy exercise aims to do just that.

Designers might need to do some digging to really understand what users are thinking of and looking for before creating a taxonomy. User input is one of the most informing things about a taxonomy, and it informs how we create a good taxonomy.

What do you need for a good taxonomy?

A good taxonomy is typically a collaboration between UX designers, content strategists, information architects, marketing, and development folks. Marketers might know quite a bit more about site keywords and SEO rankings, and a content strategist can help define and categorize terms and might have special insight into how users interpret content. Developers often have a different thought process and can even help with card sorting exercises, explained in the next section.

Gather Information

The first thing you need for a good taxonomy is to know what is being classified, which may take the form of a content inventory. Next, it's important to learn how users are accomplishing tasks on the site—but how do we learn what those tasks are?

- **Interviews:** User interviews are a great setting to ask users how they find products, and listen for what vocabulary and terminology they use. Users may refer to features in different ways, and have very different ways of finding those features. Pay special attention to terms that interviewees use to describe the subject matter—for example, a customer on an e-commerce site might refer to their shopping cart as a cart, a shopping bag, or "my checkout." Make a note of these variation, as it will impact the terms used in the taxonomy.
- **Sitemap:** A sitemap will help create a holistic view of the website or app. By mapping out each page in a site's navigation, you can begin to see subpages that don't belong within their sections, which is a sign of a site navigation that isn't following a clear taxonomy. If someone has already created a sitemap, they may have a taxonomy in mind, or justifications for

why sections were organized the way they were. Learning all this early on decreases the likelihood of accidentally reinventing the wheel.

- **Content inventory:** A content inventory typically appears as a spreadsheet, listing out every page on a website. Each page gets its own line—and sometimes every content element does as well, including headers, body text, articles, buttons, search, navigation bars, and interactive elements. Each type of content may then get additional notes including metadata, a "usefulness" score, alternative terms for the item, etc.
- **Competitive Analysis:** How does the competition organize or do things, and how does it work (or not work) for their given mission or end goals? Remember that someone else's successful site structure might not be directly applicable to your own, but can still offer insight.
- **Card sorts:** This is one of the best ways to learn how end-users might identify and create categories. Take up to 30 index cards and write down on each one a term, topic, phrase, or content item. Then ask end-users (or other team members, such as developers or marketers) sort these into categories that they come up with. In my experience, even just five participants will start to help identify key patterns and categories. Larger organizations might do upwards of 75 to get statistically significant results, but it will depend on the size and scope of the product. I recommend OptimalSort or Trello, or even good old pen and paper for initial card sorts.

The role of taxonomy in UX design

Taxonomy is not just about organizing information. Its role goes further, influencing how users perceive and relate to content. Effective taxonomic design facilitates flow and interaction, while poor taxonomy can create barriers, confuse users, and increase bounce rates.

How it works

UX Taxonomy involves several stages. It starts with identifying all types of content present on a platform. Then, these are grouped based on common characteristics or user behavior patterns. These groups are labeled and organized into a hierarchy that reflects the user's needs and expectations.

Benefits of good UX taxonomy

When properly implemented, UX Taxonomy can:

- Reduce the time users spend searching for information.
- Increase user satisfaction when interacting with a platform.
- Improve conversions and reduce bounce rates.
- Facilitate updating and expanding content in the future.

Importance of taxonomy in UX design

User experience (UX) design is about understanding and addressing user needs, expectations, and behaviors. An essential part of this understanding lies in how information is presented and organized in a digital environment. This is where Taxonomy plays a pivotal role.

Facilitates web navigation

The logical organization of information based on UX Taxonomy helps users quickly find what they are looking for. A well-structured taxonomy guides users through an intuitive path, reducing friction and minimizing the need to think too much or search excessively.

Improves retention and comprehension of information

When information is presented in an organized manner, users not only find what they're looking for faster but also retain and better understand that information. Properly categorized and labeled content allows users to construct a clear mental picture of where everything is and how it's related.

Ensures greater consistency

A robust taxonomy sets a standard for content organization. This means that, regardless of who adds or modifies content, there's a consistent framework to base it on. This leads to a more consistent user experience over time.

Better designs

For designers and developers, having a clear taxonomy reduces ambiguity and facilitates more informed design decisions. It also allows for quicker and more effective implementation of new features and content.

Enhances emotional connection with users

A smooth, frictionless user experience, driven by good taxonomy, can result in a positive emotional connection. Users feel valued and understood, which can lead to greater loyalty to the brand or platform.

Key Components of UX Taxonomy

UX Taxonomy is not an arbitrary process; it is based on foundational components that ensure the content organization is logical and coherent. Below, we explore the essential components that make up a robust and effective taxonomy:

- **Categories:** Categories are high-level groupings that separate content into broad thematic blocks. These should be mutually exclusive to avoid confusion and overlaps. For example, in an e-commerce website, categories might include "Clothing", "Electronics", "Home", among others.

- **Subcategories:** Subcategories further break down categories into more specific segments. Following the previous example, under the "Clothing" category, we might have subcategories like "Men", "Women", "Children", or even "T-shirts", "Pants", "Shoes".
- **Tags:** Tags provide a way to associate cross-cutting themes or features that aren't confined to a single category or subcategory. For instance, a tag like "Eco-friendly" could apply to products across several categories, from clothing to appliances.
- **Hierarchy:** Hierarchy is the order and structure used to organize categories, subcategories, and sometimes tags. It defines the relationship between different levels and how users will navigate through them. The right hierarchical structuring can ease navigation and enhance the usability of the site or app.
- **Relations:** Beyond standard hierarchy, there might be additional relations between different pieces of content. For example, "Related", "Suggested", or "Complementary" products on an e-commerce site. These relationships aid in enhancing navigability and boosting user interaction.
- **Metadata:** Metadata are additional pieces of information about content that aren't necessarily visible to end-users but are vital for internal organization and search systems. They might include details like author, publication date, keywords, among others.
- **Navigation and Menus:** Once taxonomy is defined, it translates into navigation systems and menus. These visual components allow users to explore and access content based on the established taxonomic structure.

Each component of UX Taxonomy plays a pivotal role in organizing, presenting, and accessing content. Together, these components craft a seamless and cohesive user experience, ensuring content is easily locatable and relevant to the user's needs.

Practical examples of UX Taxonomy:

Understanding the theory behind UX Taxonomy is vital, but analyzing practical examples helps us visualize its application in real-life scenarios. Let's look at some representative cases:

1. eCommerce store:

Categories: Clothing, Electronics, Toys, Home.

Subcategories (for Clothing): Men, Women, Children; or T-shirts, Pants, Dresses.

Tags: Eco-friendly, On Sale, Brand X.

Navigation: Dropdown menus by categories with subcategories listed, sidebar with filters based on tags.

Application: A user searching for an eco-friendly men's t-shirt can go to Clothing > Men > T-shirts and then filter by the "Eco-friendly" tag.

2. News Portal:

Categories: Politics, Economy, Culture, Sports.

Subcategories (for Culture): Cinema, Music, Art.

Tags: Latest News, Opinion, Interview.

Navigation: Main menus for categories, search bar with filtering options by tags and subcategories.

Application: Someone interested in the latest cinema interviews can go to Culture > Cinema and filter by the "Interview" tag.

Tips for Implementing Effective UX Taxonomy

When executed correctly, UX taxonomy can be a potent pillar in the design of any digital experience. To ensure that this structure plays in the user's favor, here are some key tips for implementing an effective taxonomy:

- **Research the user:** Before you start, it's crucial to understand your target audience. Use surveys, interviews, and usability tests to know how they search, consume, and structure information in their minds.
- **Avoid jargon:** Ensure that the categories, subcategories, and tags are understandable to all users, not just experts in the subject. Terminology should be clear and straightforward.
- **Prioritize flexibility:** The digital world changes rapidly. Your taxonomy should be flexible enough to accommodate new content or structural changes without causing confusion.
- **Consider scalability:** Think about the future. If you anticipate content growth or expansion, the taxonomy should adapt without requiring a complete overhaul.
- **Use card sorting:** This technique involves asking users to organize content into categories that make sense to them. It's a great way to gain insights into how users perceive and classify information.
- **Conduct tree testing:** After defining a structure, use tree testing to validate that users can effectively find content. This can help identify problem points in your taxonomy.
- **Don't be afraid to iterate:** If something isn't working, don't hesitate to make changes. UX taxonomy is as much an art as it is a science, and finding the perfect structure may require multiple attempts and tweaks.

By following these tips, you can guarantee a smoother and more satisfying experience for users and a more manageable structure for content creators and developers.

A Powerful Tool

Taxonomies are a potent way to build content relationships in digital products and are the hidden organizational systems backstage that fill the gaps which user-oriented navigation systems might leave.

When defined and maintained correctly, a taxonomy can support better search suggestions and subsequent search refinements, faceted navigation, and automatic linking of related content.

CHAPTER-12

INTERACTION DESIGN

INTRODUCTION TO INTERACTION DESIGN

Interaction design can be understood in simple (but not *simplified*) terms: it is the design of the interaction between users and products. Most often when people talk about interaction design, the products tend to be software products like apps or websites. The goal of interaction design is to create products that enable the user to achieve their objective(s) in the best way possible.

Interaction Design (IxD) is the design of interactive products and services in which a designer's focus goes beyond the item in development to include the *way* users will interact with it. Thus, close scrutiny of users' needs, limitations and contexts, etc. empowers designers to customize output to suit precise demands.

If this definition sounds broad, that's because the field is rather broad: the interaction between a user and a product often involves elements like aesthetics, motion, sound, space, and many more. And of course, each of these elements can involve even more specialised fields, like sound design for the crafting of sounds used in user interactions.

As you might already realise, there's a huge overlap between interaction design and UX design. After all, UX design is about shaping the experience of using a product, and most part of that experience involves some interaction between the user and the product. But UX design is more than interaction design: it also involves user research (finding out who the users are in the first place), creating user personas (why, and under what conditions, would they use the product), performing user testing and usability testing, etc.

A good use of interaction design successfully leads to positive user experiences, including:

- Greater product satisfaction
- Deeper usability comprehension

- Faster learnability
- A deeper personal connection
- Increased likelihood of repeated use

Interaction Design vs UI Design

Interaction design focuses on human-computer interaction, including animations, microinteractions, transitions, search, and other motion-based designs. They decide, for example, what happens when a user taps an element.

User interface design focuses on visual design and aesthetics, including color, fonts, iconography, layouts, etc. They decide what a user interface must look like.

- **Interaction design** is about Interactions and movement
- **UI design** is about visual design and aesthetics

In smaller companies and startups, a UI designer is often responsible for both tasks, while the roles are separate in larger organizations. Like anything in digital product design, the roles and responsibilities can synergize. It all depends on the company, product, and organizational structure.

Interaction Design vs UX Design

Interaction design is a specialized discipline within UX design. Where UX looks at the entire user experience and how everything ties together, interaction designers focus on user interactions and motion.

User experience designers apply UX fundamentals like design thinking, human-centered design, and user research to make decisions. They're specifically concerned with a user's tasks, actions, and environment, while interaction designers focus on making the digital product respond to user actions in an appropriate way. They tend to think about what happens when a user clicks a button, types a phrase into a search bar or hovers over an image.

DESIGNING ENGAGING AND RESPONSIVE INTERFACES

Introduction

In the ever-evolving digital landscape, user interfaces (UI) are the critical link between users and websites or web applications. An engaging and intuitive UI is paramount to the success of any online platform, as it directly influences user experience and overall satisfaction. As technology advances and user expectations rise, web designers must continuously adapt to ensure their interfaces remain relevant and appealing. In this academic blog article, we will delve into the best practices for creating captivating user interfaces that foster positive user interactions and drive meaningful engagement.

Responsive Design: Embracing the Multi-Device World

With the proliferation of smartphones, tablets, and various screen sizes, responsive design has become a fundamental aspect of modern web development. Designing responsively ensures that websites and applications adapt fluidly to different devices and screen sizes, providing an optimal user experience regardless of the platform. By employing flexible grids, media queries, and scalable images, responsive design enables content to flow smoothly and intuitively, enhancing usability and engagement.

Interactive Elements: Engaging Users Through Interaction

Modern web design goes beyond static pages and aims to create interactive experiences that captivate users. Incorporating interactive elements such as animations, transitions, hover effects, and microinteractions adds depth and engagement to the user interface. Interactive elements can provide visual feedback, guide users through the interface, and create a sense of interactivity and delight. However, it's important to strike a balance and ensure that interactions enhance usability rather than hinder it.

Microcopy and User-Centric Content: Crafting Meaningful Experiences

Effective web design goes hand in hand with compelling and user-centric content. Microcopy, which includes small snippets of text like error messages, tooltips, and call-to-action labels, plays a crucial role in guiding users and setting the tone of the interaction. By crafting concise, clear, and empathetic microcopy, designers can enhance usability and create a more meaningful connection with users. Thoughtful content strategy and information hierarchy also contribute to delivering content that is relevant, accessible, and engaging.

Visual Storytelling: Conveying Narratives Through Design

Visual storytelling is a powerful technique to engage users and convey narratives in a compelling way. By integrating visuals, such as images, videos, illustrations, and infographics, designers can create immersive experiences that evoke emotions and communicate messages effectively. Visual storytelling can be employed to guide users through a website, showcase products or services, or communicate complex ideas in a digestible format. It helps create a memorable and engaging user experience that resonates with the audience.

Performance Optimization: Ensuring Fast and Efficient Experiences

In today's fast-paced digital world, users expect websites and applications to load quickly and perform seamlessly. Performance optimization is critical to designing for the modern web. Techniques like lazy loading, image compression, minification of code, and caching contribute to faster load times and improved user experience. Prioritizing performance not only enhances engagement but also positively impacts search engine rankings and conversion rates.

Understand Your Target Audience

The foundation of any successful UI design lies in a thorough understanding of the target audience. Conduct comprehensive research to identify your users' needs, preferences, and pain points. Consider factors such as age, gender, location, and technical proficiency to tailor the interface to their unique requirements. Developing user personas can be particularly useful in gaining insights into user behavior, motivations, and goals. By empathizing with your audience, you can design an interface that resonates with them and addresses their specific needs.

Simplicity and Clarity

When it comes to UI design, simplicity is key. A cluttered and complex interface can overwhelm users, leading to frustration and disengagement. Opt for a clean and minimalist design approach, emphasizing clarity and ease of use. Use clear, concise language, and avoid jargon to ensure information is easily comprehensible.

Implement a consistent and logical layout with intuitive navigation. Employ visual hierarchy to prioritize essential elements and guide users to their desired actions. Intuitive icons and buttons, along with recognizable patterns, help users effortlessly interact with your interface.

Responsive Design for All Devices

With an increasing number of users accessing the web through various devices, responsiveness is no longer an option—it's a necessity. A responsive design adapts seamlessly to different screen sizes and resolutions, ensuring a consistent and engaging user experience across desktops, tablets, and smartphones.

Test your interface on various devices and browsers to ensure its functionality and aesthetics remain intact. Embrace a mobile-first design approach, considering the limitations of smaller screens first and then progressively enhancing the experience for larger devices.

Prioritize Performance and Loading Speed

A slow-loading website can deter users and lead to higher bounce rates. Speed is crucial in retaining user interest and encouraging exploration of your interface. Optimize images, leverage browser caching, and minimize HTTP requests to boost loading times.

Remember that not all users have high-speed internet connections, so focus on delivering a fast experience to all users, regardless of their location or network capabilities.

Consistent Branding and Visual Identity

A strong visual identity reinforces brand recognition and fosters a sense of trust among users. Maintain consistency in colours, typography, and design elements across all pages and interactions. Ensure your interface aligns with your brand's personality and values, creating a cohesive and memorable experience.

Intuitive Navigation and User Flow

Effective navigation is the backbone of an engaging user interface. Design navigation menus that are easy to find, intuitive to use, and clearly labelled. Users should effortlessly access various sections and content without feeling lost or confused.

Consider implementing user flow diagrams to map out the journey users will take through your interface. This will help identify potential pain points and improve the overall flow of interactions.

Embrace Microinteractions

Microinteractions are subtle and delightful animations or feedback loops that enhance user engagement. From button hover effects to form validation animations, microinteractions create a more interactive and enjoyable user experience. However, use them sparingly and purposefully, as excessive animations can lead to distraction and decreased usability.

A/B Testing and User Feedback

The key to continuous improvement in UI design lies in gathering feedback from real users. Conduct A/B testing to compare different design variations and identify which elements resonate best with your audience. Utilize analytics tools to track user behaviour and gain insights into how users interact with your interface.

Encourage user feedback through surveys, usability testing, and social media platforms. Actively address user concerns and suggestions, as they can lead to valuable improvements and innovations.

Responsive Design: Best Practices and Considerations

Responsive websites are websites that adapt to all screen sizes and resolutions, not only on desktop but also on mobile, tablet, and sometimes even TV.

According to Statista, mobile traffic was responsible for 52.64% of all global traffic in 2017, meaning that a website not well optimized for mobile devices is losing out on approximately half of its traffic. By the end of 2018, it's expected that the global traffic share for mobile devices will grow to 79%, which is an exceptional increase.

Businesses without a mobile website are falling behind at an alarming rate, because 8 in 10 visitors will stop engaging with a website that doesn't display well on their device. It's way too easy for users to hit the back button and try a rival business instead, and Google even ranks websites that don't use mobile responsive design lower in their search.

Does any of this mean that mobile is more important than desktop? No. 83% of mobile users say that they should be able to continue the experience on desktop if they wish.

Take a look (Fig. 12.1) at this mobile-optimized version of eBay vs. what it would look like if it weren't mobile-optimized. Would you even consider the non-optimized version?

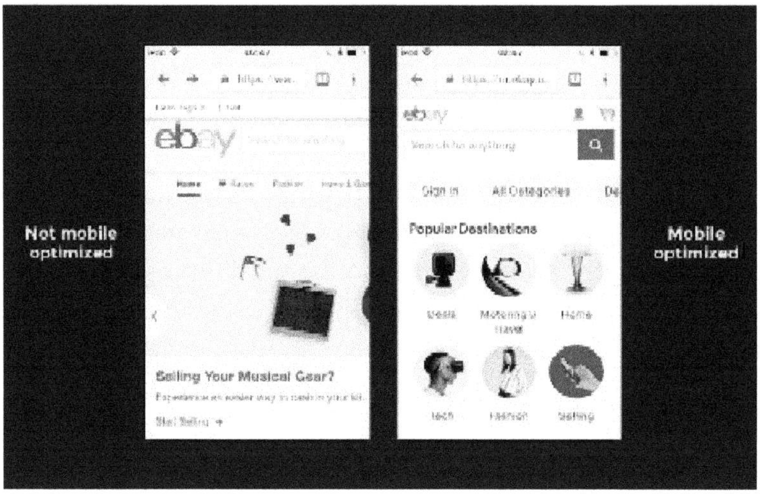

Fig. 12.1 Mobile-optimized version of eBay

In order to design websites that can compete on today's internet, web designers **must** be experts at responsive website design (RWD). Where should they start?

A Mobile-first Approach to Responsive Web Design

Mobile-first web design means designing the mobile website first and working up to the desktop version. There are a number of reasons why this approach works well.

- Mobile websites have more usability concerns (this is mostly due to the lack of screen real estate), so it's practical and more efficient for the primary focus to be on mobile design.
- It's easier to scale up the mobile version than it is to scale down the desktop version (again, because of the lack of space on mobile websites).
- Mobile-first web design helps to reevaluate what's visually and functionally necessary.

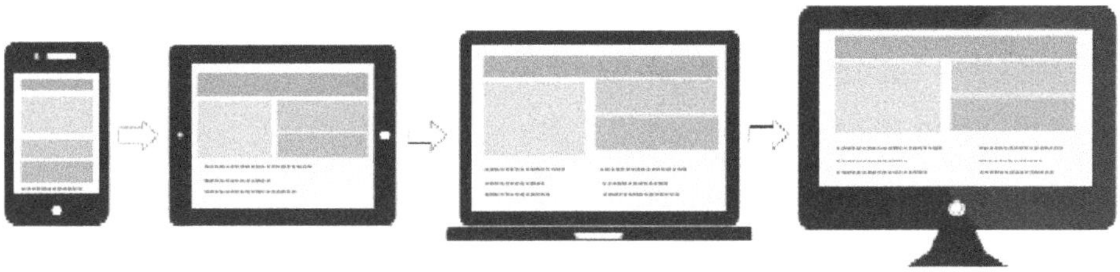

Fig. 12.2 Mobile-first web design

Designing a website as a mobile-first responsive site forces designers to ask a number of important questions because there is less screen real estate to work with. Here are the questions that need to be asked:

- Is this feature/function really necessary?
- How can we design something minimalist for mobile first that will later scale up well for desktops?
- Is this visual effect worth the time that it takes to load on mobile?
- What's the primary objective, and what visual elements help users achieve it?

We'll take a look at some responsive website examples in a moment. For now, let's talk about which devices, screen sizes, and web browsers are relevant today.

Screen Resolutions are Relevant for Responsive Web Design

Here are the most common screen resolutions across mobile, tablet, and desktop users worldwide. As you can see (Fig. 12.3), there is a wide range of resolutions, so neither mobile, tablet nor desktop is dominating the market share right now—what this tells us is that designers should consider all of them when thinking about responsive web design.

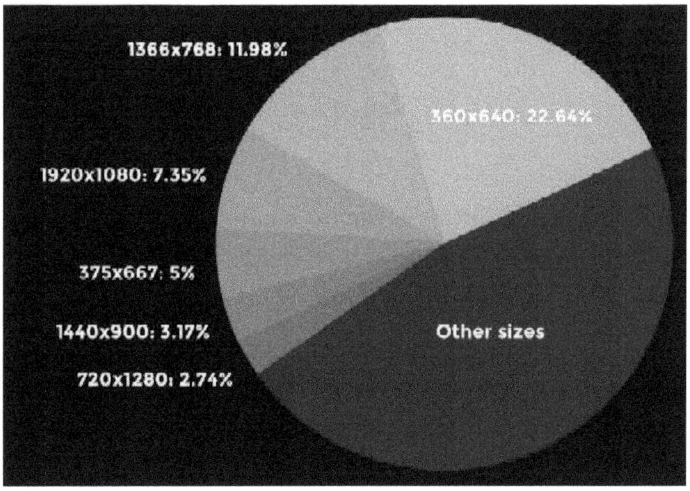

Fig. 12.3 Screen Resolutions

- **360x640 (small mobile):** 22.64%
- **1366x768 (average laptop):** 11.98%
- **1920x1080 (large desktop):** 7.35%
- **375x667 (average mobile):** 5%
- **1440x900 (average desktop):** 3.17%
- **720x1280 (large mobile):** 2.74%

Just as with device breakdown, we should segment the data by location to match the user demographics (or anticipated user demographics) of our target audience. It's also worth catering to resolutions that are gaining popularity, because while some screen sizes are currently not that common, they may be in the future. This will help responsive designers craft futureproof UX that will work even when the market share changes.

For example, 360x640 resolutions (which correspond mostly with Samsung devices using Android) have risen by 5.43% in the last year. Designers can use valuable insights like these to decide on key responsive breakpoints before starting a website design.

Fig. 12.4

Web Browsers

Responsive web design is about offering a seamless experience on any device, and since different web browsers render web pages in different ways, websites must be tested to ensure that they're compatible with a variety of mobile and desktop web browsers.

Even though making a website scale to the correct responsive breakpoints is primarily the responsibility of a web developer, it's the web designer that decides exactly how responsive UI elements will adapt to various screen sizes in order to create an optimal user experience.

Here's a worldwide breakdown of web browser market share for mobile and desktop.

- **Chrome:** 55.04%
- **Safari:** 14.86%
- **UC Browser:** 8.69%
- **Firefox:** 5.72%
- **Opera:** 4.03%
- **Internet Explorer:** 3.35%

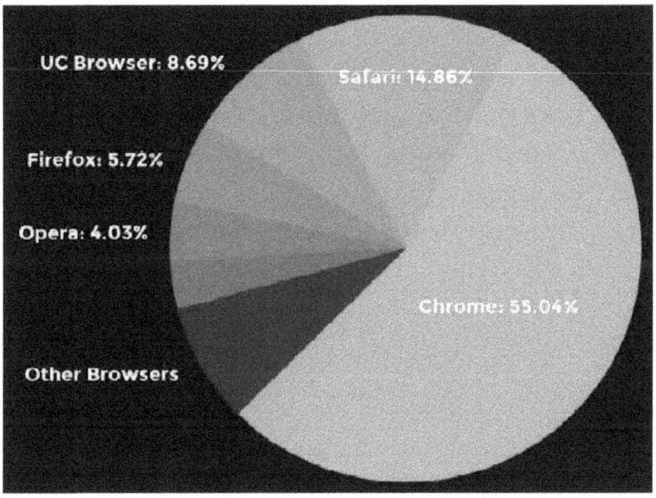

Fig. 12.5 Worldwide breakdown of web browser market

Responsive design isn't just about "making everything fit"—it's also about adapting to the capabilities of the device hardware and web browser ***as well as*** the device resolution. One example of this could be that, while Google Chrome supports the CSS property overscroll-behavior: (which defines what happens when the user scrolls too hard towards the edge of the viewport), it's not supported in any other web browser.

Responsive Design Best Practices

Eliminate Friction

As mentioned earlier, a mobile-first approach to responsive web design will help designers evaluate what's really necessary in order for the user to achieve their main objective.

As we build up to the tablet version (and later the desktop version), we can then begin to think about secondary objectives and the microinteractions, user flows, and CTAs (calls to action) that make those user objectives achievable. What's more important is that we focus on the primary objectives of the user first and eliminate any unnecessary friction that aids neither the primary nor the secondary objectives.

A primary objective could be the purchasing of a product, whereas the secondary objective could be signing up for a newsletter (which could lead to a purchase later).

Here's a terrific example of eliminating friction: Since mobile user interfaces are typically harder to navigate, it would be best to switch to a one-page checkout for mobile eCommerce stores and only enable multi-step checkout for desktop eCommerce stores.

Design for Thumbs

Responsive design UX is tricky in the sense that users will interact with the desktop website via clicks but the mobile version via taps and swipes. There are physical differences as well. Desktop users typically have their computers on a surface, whereas mobile users hold their devices in their hands. These differences significantly change the way mobile UI designers design tap targets and other important UI elements with which users interact.

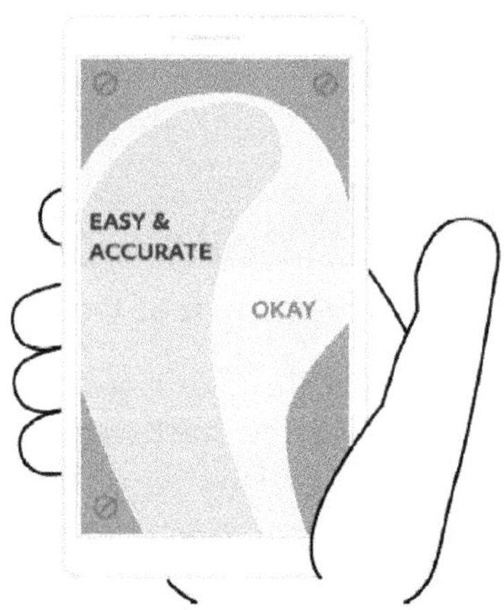

Fig. 12.6 Design for Thumbs

Let's take a look at some examples:

- People typically expect the main desktop navigation to be at the top; however, on mobile, it should be at the bottom. Thumbs don't reach the top comfortably.
- Other interactive elements should also be easy to reach. This means keeping them in the center of the screen because it's more difficult for thumbs to reach the sides and corners of device screens.
- So that they can be tapped with ease, important links and CTAs should have a height of at least 44px (smaller tap targets are bad for usability).

Advantage of Mobile Devices' Native Hardware

Mobile hardware (like the device camera, or GPS services) isn't specifically reserved for native apps, and as mentioned earlier, responsive web design isn't just about "making everything fit." It's also about adapting to the capabilities of the device. In the case of mobile web design, since mobile devices have easy to use cameras, some microinteractions—such as data input—are actually easier on smaller screens as long as websites are taking advantage of the available native hardware.

Let's take a look at some examples:

- Credit/top-up card scanning (because forms are often tricky on mobile)
- Photo-sharing on social media, because the media is already on your device
- Two-factor authentication (because you're already on your mobile device)
- Quickly checking stocks/analytics (because mobile apps simplify information)
- Performing a web search with voice (because hands-free is easier than typing)

Make Layouts Fluid/Adaptive by Default

Not every user will have their desktop browser maximized. This means that while designers need to consider the responsive breakpoints of the devices that users are using today, they also need to account for what happens in between those breakpoints.

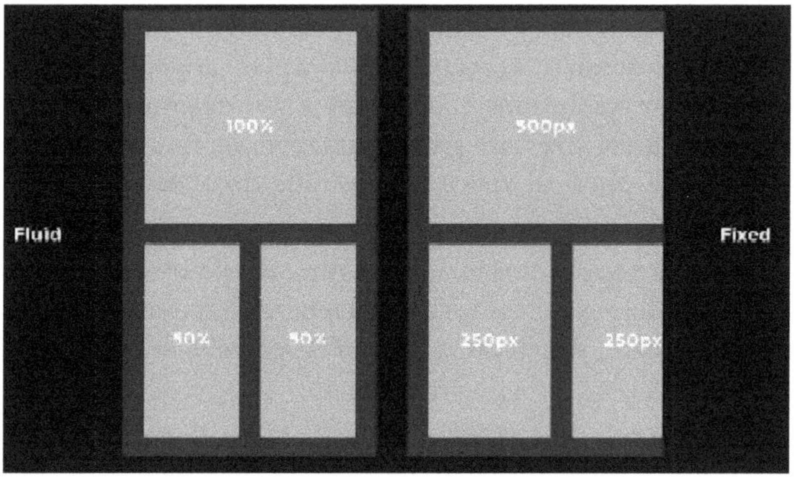

Fig. 12.7 Layouts Fluid

Responsive breakpoints should be used to "reflow" the layout and content to a new device, but to account for all the sizes in between (just in case), layouts need to be otherwise **fluid** (that is, they naturally adapt/stretch as the browser resizes).

Keep these tips in mind when designing fluid/adaptive layouts:

- Percentage units will allow elements to be fluid.
- Setting minimum and maximum widths can enable the "but don't go smaller/bigger than this" scenario.
- SVG image formats can be scaled up and down without losing quality, and are resolution-independent (as opposed to JPGs and PNGs, which are not).

Don't Forget About Landscape Orientation

We talked about specific responsive breakpoints earlier, but we also need to consider that those mobile viewports can be displayed in landscape orientation as well. While implementing a fluid layout will technically make the content adaptive, losing a fair chunk of the ***portrait*** viewport can be a hindrance to the usability and accessibility.

Navigations are usually safe (sometimes they're better, actually, since users typically navigate landscape orientation with *two* thumbs), but scrolling becomes significantly harder, which is less than optimal since the user is required to scroll more on landscape.

Designers may want to consider designing for landscape breakpoints as well; for instance, tiled elements that stack vertically on mobile could be displayed as a slider with left and right navigation buttons, meaning the user doesn't have to scroll.

Remember, Typography Can Be Responsive Too

Even though UX designers typically use pixel units to design websites, on the actual web, one point doesn't necessarily equal a pixel anymore, because different devices have different resolutions. The iPhone X, for example, has 458 PPI (Pixels Per Inch), so where pixel sizes are getting smaller, we're able to achieve crisper graphics in the same physical space (Apple calls this "Retina" technology, and Android calls it "hDPI").

This means that a 16px font size, for instance, would look bigger or smaller on some devices depending on its resolution. Web developers will typically use em units to define font sizes, which are a type of responsive unit where 1em is equal to 1 point.

Design handoff tools like Zeplin, Sympli, Marvel, and InVision can help designers collaborate with developers on matters that are a joint responsibility. While designers execute the design, and developers execute the code, as a whole the product design workflow is a team effort that requires solid communication.

Responsive Design Performance Optimization Tips and Best Practices

Responsive web design isn't just about how it looks but also about how it acts and feels. Adapting websites so that they load faster on the intended device is equally important.

Lazy Load Non-vital Images and Videos

Images and videos are what make up a large chunk of the total download size of a website, but you don't need to load them all at once. There are two scenarios where the rendering of media can be delayed: Below-the-fold content can be loaded as the user scrolls below the fold, and render-blocking media should be made to download only after the layout and content has downloaded. This practice is called lazy loading, where the loading of heavy, non-important elements is delayed to improve page performance.

Conditional Loading

Some website elements are not intended for mobile users, or at least aren't worth the extra cognitive load. We want our mobile websites to be simple, so it makes sense to hide elements in certain scenarios. That being said, we have to make sure that we aren't wasting browser resources and bandwidth by loading these elements even when they're hidden; hence, it's best practice to only include these elements in certain conditions.

Once again, a developer can achieve this with code; however, designers can improve page performance by communicating the conditions of when and where certain elements should and shouldn't exist.

Responsive Images

As mentioned earlier, some devices display more pixels per inch, which can result in images becoming blurry if they're not exported at the correct resolution. Depending on the resolution of the device, some will require images at double (@2x), triple (@3x), and even quadruple (@4x) the size. Web browsers now support the <picture> element, which chooses the correct image resolution depending on the device.

Designers crafting responsive websites can tailor images to the correct device by making sure to export at all the resolutions used on today's devices (if you're unsure, ask your developer—communication is key when it comes to responsive web design).

Fig. 12.8 Designers crafting responsive website

INCORPORATING FEEDBACK LOOPS IN INTERACTION DESIGN

Understanding Feedback Loops:

Feedback loops are processes where designers use a system's outputs as inputs to find cause-and-effect relationships within it. Some systems (e.g., the environment) have many feedback loops, and the effects of human actions can take decades to show. In complex systems, feedback loops can hide causal links and problems.

Feedback loops in UI/UX design involve a continuous cycle of gathering, analyzing, and implementing feedback from users, stakeholders, and usability testing. This iterative approach allows designers to make incremental improvements based on real-world usage and user insights. The beauty of feedback loops lies in their ability to create a dynamic and responsive design process.

User-Centric Design:

At the heart of UI/UX design is the user. Feedback loops facilitate a user-centric design approach by providing designers with valuable insights into user behavior, preferences, and pain points. By incorporating feedback at various stages of the design process, designers can align their creations more closely with user expectations, ensuring a seamless and enjoyable user experience.

Early-Stage Feedback:

Feedback loops start early in the design process, often with wireframes or prototypes. By involving users and stakeholders at this stage, designers can identify potential issues and make necessary adjustments before investing significant time and resources. This early feedback not only saves time but also contributes to a more robust foundation for the final design.

Usability Testing

Usability testing is a crucial component of feedback loops, allowing designers to observe how real users interact with the product. Through usability testing, designers can gather data on navigation patterns, user engagement, and overall satisfaction. This information becomes invaluable in fine-tuning the UI/UX to align with user expectations and preferences.

Continuous Improvement:

Feedback loops promote a culture of continuous improvement. Designers can leverage ongoing feedback to make iterative changes, addressing any issues or challenges that may arise during different stages of development. This cyclical process ensures that the UI/UX design remains adaptive and responsive to evolving user needs and technological advancements.

Collaboration and Stakeholder Involvement:

Feedback loops also foster collaboration and stakeholder involvement. By including stakeholders in the feedback process, designers can align the design with business goals and objectives. This collaborative approach ensures that the UI/UX not only meets user expectations but also aligns with broader organizational strategies.

How to design positive feedback loops?

Positive feedback loops are cycles where the system rewards the player's actions with more rewards, increasing the player's motivation and confidence. Positive feedback loops can be used to encourage the player to explore, experiment, and learn new skills, by providing them with incentives, recognition, and rewards. Examples of positive feedback loops in gamification design are points, badges, levels, leaderboards, praise, and social validation.

How to design negative feedback loops?

Negative feedback loops are cycles where the system penalizes the player's actions with more penalties, decreasing the player's motivation and confidence. Negative feedback loops can be used to discourage the player from cheating, quitting, or performing poorly, by providing them with consequences, challenges, and feedback. Examples of negative feedback loops in gamification design are time limits, lives, penalties, obstacles, criticism, and social pressure.

How to design reinforcing feedback loops?

Reinforcing feedback loops are cycles where the system amplifies the player's actions, creating a spiral of growth or decline. Reinforcing feedback loops can be used to create dynamic and complex systems, where the player's actions have long-term and cumulative effects. Examples of reinforcing feedback loops in gamification design are quests, narratives, achievements, and skill trees.

How to design balancing feedback loops?

Balancing feedback loops are cycles where the system counteracts the player's actions, creating a state of equilibrium or stability. Balancing feedback loops can be used to create balanced and fair systems, where the player's actions have short-term and proportional effects. Examples of balancing feedback loops in gamification design are difficulty adjustment, resource management, and scoring systems.

How to design immediate and delayed feedback loops?

Immediate feedback loops are cycles where the system responds to the player's actions instantly or within a short time frame. Immediate feedback loops can be used to provide the player with clear and direct feedback, enhancing their attention, retention, and correction. Examples of immediate feedback loops in gamification design are sounds, animations, pop-ups, and hints.

Delayed feedback loops are cycles where the system responds to the player's actions after a long time frame or at a specific moment. Delayed feedback loops can be used to provide the player with strategic and meaningful feedback, enhancing their anticipation, reflection, and evaluation. Examples of delayed feedback loops in gamification design are reports, reviews, summaries, and feedback sessions.

Key Stages of the Interaction Design Process

Here are the five stages that the IxD process typically involves:

- **Understand user needs and wants:** This initial phase involves researching and understanding users' needs, goals, and contexts of use. Designers gather insights through user research, which can include interviews, surveys, observations, and personas. It's essential for designers to understand the problem space in order to design solutions that meet real user needs.

Two useful research exercises include:

  - **Contextual inquiry:** This approach allows designers to immerse themselves in the user's environment. For instance, if designing a healthcare app, designers could observe how patients and doctors interact with existing systems.
  - **User interviews and surveys:** These exercises help designers gather direct insights from their target audience. For a retail app, a designer might explore shopping habits and pain points.

- **Analyze user research findings:** Designers define the interaction problem they aim to solve based on the insights they've gathered. This phase involves setting clear objectives, specifying user requirements, and establishing design principles that will guide the project. Creating user stories and scenarios and conducting task analyses can help clarify how proposed solutions fit into the users' lives.

Here are two ways designers can analyze and organize their findings:

- **Personas:** These are created based on research and should be as detailed as possible. For a project like a new educational platform, personas might include students, teachers, and administrators with distinct needs and goals.
- **Journey mapping:** Developing journey maps helps designers visualize a user's interactions with a product. This can highlight friction points in current systems, like booking a service or completing a purchase.

⦿ **Design a potential solution:** In this phase, designers brainstorm, sketch and design potential solutions. This step often involves creating low-fidelity wireframes, flow diagrams and sketches that explore different design options and how users will interact with the system. Designers also think about the look and feel of the product, as well as the logic and structure of the interaction. All of this is done according to the design guidelines and fundamental design principles established in the previous steps or within an organization's or individual's preferences.

Here are two approaches to designing at this point in the design process:

- **Sketching:** Rapid, freehand drawing helps designers quickly visualize ideas, layout arrangements, and user interfaces. This technique is excellent for initial brainstorming sessions and can be shared easily for immediate feedback.
- **Storyboarding:** This involves creating a series of drawings to depict the user journey or specific interactions with a product. Storyboards help in visualizing the context of use, user emotions, and potential pain points without detailed prototypes.

⦿ **Create prototypes from designs:** Prototyping is an extension of the design phase, where ideas are transformed into tangible artifacts that can be tested and evaluated. Prototypes range from low-fidelity sketches to high-fidelity, interactive simulations that closely mimic the final product. This stage allows designers and stakeholders to explore the viability of design concepts before full-scale development.

Here are the two main types of prototypes:

- **Low-fidelity prototyping:** Paper prototypes or basic digital mockups can demonstrate ideas and design quickly and easily. This approach is cost-effective and allows for rapid iteration based on initial feedback.

- **High-fidelity prototyping:** For a deeper test of interactions, designers can create high-fidelity prototypes using tools like Sketch or Figma. For example, an e-commerce site design would benefit from detailed prototypes that simulate the shopping experience.

- **Implement and deploy the final design:** Once the design has been refined through multiple iterations of testing and feedback, it moves into implementation, where developers build the interaction design into the product. Designers work closely with developers to ensure the design's fidelity and to adjust the interaction design as needed based on technical constraints or new insights.

Carry out these two activities at this stage of the design process:

- **Collaboration with developers:** Work closely with developers during the implementation phase to ensure the design translates well into the final product. This step is crucial for complex applications like a financial tracking tool, where functionality and user interface (UI) must align perfectly.
- **Post-launch evaluation:** After launch, designers should collect and analyze user feedback. Tools like Google Analytics or user feedback platforms can provide insights into how well the product meets user needs and where further refinements are necessary.

It's crucial for designers to have a thorough understanding of the interaction design process. This process is among several similar design methodologies, with the iterative design process of design thinking as the most popular and well-known example. In design thinking, designers work to gain and leverage essential insights that allow them to fine-tune features optimally. Only when designers know and empathize with users can they truly appreciate their real-world needs, desires, and pain points. This empathetic approach is the cornerstone of creating solutions that are not only technologically sound but also resonate with the user base and ensure that the end product effectively addresses the challenges users face in their daily lives.

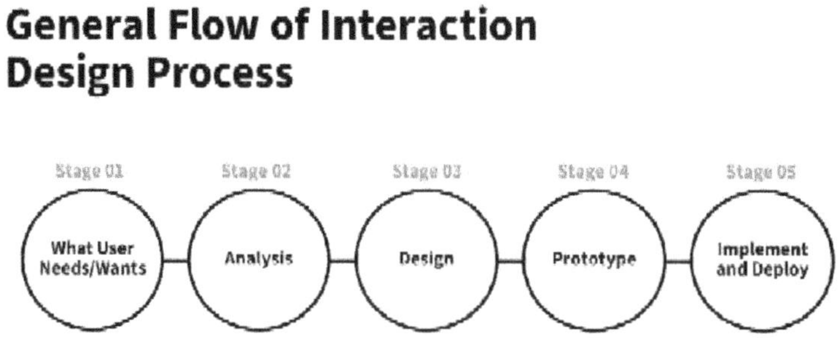

Fig. 12.9

How to Apply the IxD Process in Real-World Contexts

Applying the Interaction Design (IxD) process in real-world contexts requires navigating through its five stages, ideally without compromise. However, real-world projects often face time and financial constraints, which necessitates strategic trade-offs. Despite these challenges, it's crucial not to skimp on essential aspects like user research and testing. For instance, employing cost-effective methods such as paper prototyping can offer early insights into potential solutions, which helps to steer the design in the right direction. When designers aim for a minimum viable product (MVP)—a functional, marketable version of an app, for example—it allows for quicker iteration based on user feedback, rather than waiting for a "perfect" product.

Real-world examples demonstrate the importance of this approach. For example, the development of a running watch app. Designers focused on creating an interface that not only motivates runners but also ensures their safety by minimizing distractions. This means avoiding overly detailed text or complex navigation that could be hazardous during physical activity. Similarly, heuristic evaluations by design teams can quickly pinpoint and prioritize the correction of glaring usability flaws to enhance the user experience without significant delays.

The **moment of use** is critical; designers must scrutinize details like notification text length to prevent user frustration. Additionally, understanding how interactive elements collectively impact the user experience is vital. For example, Spotify's interface design caters to users' need for quick, effortless access to music and podcasts, without complicated navigation, recognizing the diverse contexts in which the app is used.

Part V: Implementation and Testing

CHAPTER-13

USABILITY TESTING

IMPLEMENTATION OF THE UX DESIGN PROCESS

As a UX designer, it is your responsibility to implement, and advocate for, the UX design process. With that said, the role of the UX designer can vary greatly from company to company. Let's consider where UX designers fit into the wider team in different types of companies.

The UX Designer's Place In The Team

The job of a UX designer depends heavily on the nature of the company they are working for, and the difference between one UX designer role and another can be dramatic. In this final section, we're going to discuss the role of the UX designer at both small and large companies and the UX design skills needed for each.

Keep in mind that there are pros and cons to both.

Within a start-up, a UX designer can be responsible for every part of every process, due to small budgets, small teams, and limited resources.

At a start-up, a UXer (you can call yourself that) is likely to oversee a project from beginning to end and actively take on separate processes including user research, testing, and design all by themselves.

However, within a larger corporation, a UX designer could be heading up a team of user researchers, overseeing testing, and acting in more of a managerial role. In this way, the UX designer is still overseeing the process from beginning to end, but they are much less hands-on.

When sifting through job advertisements for UX designers, it's important to read the small print. Due to the relatively new nature of the field and the ambiguity that still surrounds the term, recruiters are not always well-informed about what a UX designer is or what they actually do.

For example, a company might advertise for a UX designer when they are really looking for someone to join a team of researchers or someone to undertake testing. If this is the case, then the UX designer is not involved in the entire process, but is simply responsible for one part of the process. This is because UX has become an umbrella term for many different fields.

- If you are someone who wants to be heavily involved in every aspect of the UX design process, then a start-up could be a good fit, but remember at a start-up you will be shouldering the responsibility for each mistake you make and learning from scratch.
- If you are someone who particularly enjoys one aspect of UX design, then a job at a larger company in a particular team, for example the research team, would be more suitable and you'd likely be in a more UX-supported environment.
- If you enjoy managing teams and looking at the whole process without being too hands-on, a more managerial role in a UX team at a larger corporation could be more up your street.

Holger Egger, UX designer at Levelgreen gave us this advice about the overall process:

> "A good design process can be your secret weapon. The tasks you do will change and the devices you do this on will definitively change. But if you can do a user-centered design process, adapted to your project's context, and get everybody on board, then you're golden!"

UX Designer at a Startup

There are a number of benefits to getting your first experience as a UX designer at a startup. We've broken them down into a list for you below.

Pros of working at a startup:

- You are more likely to see the whole picture
- You'll get to experience decision-making firsthand
- You'll have a significant influence on the end product
- Your work environment will likely to be more experimental. If the startup succeeds, you'll likely receive not only financial remuneration but also recognition for your part in its success.

Cons of working at a startup:

- Less time to spend getting a feel for what you're doing
- Many fast changes in a short period of time
- Pressure to deliver results quickly

- Job security isn't always guaranteed
- Wages will not be as high as at a big corporation
- Many startups fail in the first year

UX Designer at a Big Corporation

Don't see yourself working at a startup? Let's take a look at the advantages and disadvantages of working for a big corporation

Pros of working at a big corporation

- Job security, competitive salary, benefits, and other perks
- You get to see long-range plans realized
- Regular access to latest technology and a broad range of resources and experts
- Knowledge that your work directly affects a large number of people
- Clearer expectations

Cons of working at a big corporation

- Less personal working environment
- Larger teams and more bureaucracy to contend with
- Seeing the results of your labor can be a long and frustrating process
- Generally less flexible to try new strategies or ideas

The important thing to bear in mind is that how you view these pros and cons depends on your work style, your personality, needs, and goals. As a UX designer, you're working with management, other designers, developers, testers, marketing, support, and more besides. You're the interface and the glue between all these stakeholders and sometimes you're the only one who focuses on the user (other stakeholders sometimes have other motivations).

While you cannot get everybody to agree on everything, the best thing you can do is to get everybody to agree on a user-centered design process. Whether at a startup or a big corporation, as long as everybody follows this, then you're in a great position to succeed!

UX Designer's Role Within The Team

The UX designer's role within the team is to steer the team through the process we have outlined in this post and generally in this order, too (with plenty more testing):

- Research
- Design

- Testing
- Implementation

You'll start with the research, then try things out with wireframes and prototypes, and test everything as you go along—much to the chagrin of your team. You'll be the creator, the advocate, the moderator, and the cheerleader. If you do your job well, you will not get any recognition for your work because it will have been a seamless process for all involved.

Fig. 13.1 UX designer's role within the team

Despite the lack of recognition, you will still get the rewarding feeling of having created such a useful, usable, and delightful product for your users while meeting the goals of your business.

UI/UX Testing

The user's feedback helps the design team make important improvements to the user interface and user experience. Usability studies can take place at various points in the design process, here are thee important stages in design process where we can perform UI/UX testing:

- **Stage I:** You can conduct a usability study when you have an early idea, this would be like a basic prototype that is just little interactive. this is called Conceptual testing.
- **Stage II:** You can also conduct a usability study when you have an interactive prototype. This is where most of the designers conduct a study because it gives the design team insight on what needs to be revised or added before the product launches.
- **Stage III:** You can even conduct a usability study with a product when it is complete. This is done when you may want to change a feature of the product or test if the product is usable with a specific group of people.

Need of Testing in UI/UX

In this fast-happening world, every business and every team wants to release the next update or the next application as soon as possible, because of this teams or UI/UX designers often miss out on a very important thing – properly testing the design. But why does this even matter? who focuses on testing anyways? can the users not give us feedback after release rather than taking feedback through testing? These are the questions designers ask and in this section, we will answer these questions.

In this section, we will discuss the need for testing in UI/UX, why it is so important, and why you must add it to your UI/UX workflow if you haven't. But before that, we will start from the basics about what Usability testing or UI/UX testing is.

Fig. 13.2 Need of Testing in UI/UX

Usability Testing or UI/UX Testing

A Usability study usability testing or UI/UX testing is a research method for assessing how easy it is for participants to complete the important tasks in a design. During a usability study, participants are provided the designs/products and researchers follow participants when they interact with the product/design. All the feedback from the users is then collected and worked upon.

The user's feedback helps the design team make important improvements to the user interface and user experience. During the design process, usability studies can take place at different stages:

- **Stage I (Conceptual testing):** If you've got an initial idea you can conduct a usability study, this would be like a basic prototype that is just a little interactive. this is called concept testing.
- **Stage II:** You can also conduct a usability study when you have an interactive prototype. This is where most of the designers conduct a study because it gives the design team insight on what needs to be revised or added before the product launches.

- **Stage III:** You can even conduct a usability study with a product when it is complete. This is done when you may want to change a feature of the product or test if the product is usable with a specific group of people.

Reasons on why do we Need of Testing in UI/UX

Following are the reasons on why do we need Testing in UI/UX designing process:

- **Iterative Design:** Not even the best of the best designers gets it right in the first go. even they can't design a good user experience without iterative design driven by observations of real users. This make usability design an essential step in any good designer's workflow.
- **Finding Design Issues:** Imagine this scenario. Your team designed a website, and they asked you to create a new feature that will allow customers to place orders on the website. You have created a prototype of the website that includes this new feature to place an online order. But how would you know the imperfections and mistakes you made in you design, for that you will have to conduct a usability study, gather feedback and improve those aspects of your design. The earlier you realize your mistakes as a designer, the better the design comes out. And you can only know those mistakes by getting a review from another designer, which may be costly, or simply getting it tested by the people who will thereafter also use your final product.
- **Knowing the User:** Usability testing is a great way to get to know the people you're designing for. You can get a better sense of how your specific users see the world and what they want from your designs. These insights only help your website but also you to grow as a designer.
- **Gathering user Observations:** Usability testing is a great way to collect observations from users about your application or website. Observations about where do people get stuck? what confuses them? What errors do they run into? These insights are helpful before we release the application or website or rollout a new version. Always remember, user centricity is the key to a great design.
- **Giving Users What Users Want:** During creating new features, you as a designer might have your best intensions for the customers but only they know what they want. No matter how great the concept or the design is, customers will only use stuff that they actually need. UI/UX testing allows us to find a balance between what the business want, what you can deliver as a designer and what the user wants.

- **Saves Resources and Time:** UI/UX testing is very useful for saving the capital and human resources for a company. A feature that is anyways not effective and not going to be used by the customers can be discontinued rather than wasting time and resources on it. Another way in which UI/UX testing saves resources and time is that designers get to know their mistakes early, and those are immediately worked upon rather than realizing it during rollout and losing valuable customers.

Tools used for UI/UX Testing

There are many tools in the market for UI/UX testing, here is the list of the more useful tools widely accepted and used by the industry:

UserTesting

UserTesting is one of the most popular tool for Testing the design, specially for mobile testing. UserTesting is widely used in the industry even by companies like Canva, GoDaddy, Microsoft, HP, etc. The most recent feature that they have added it their catalog is AI based analysis for better UI/UX. UserTesting provides us flexible pricing and you can choose to pay as per the three plans introduced by them:

- Essentials
- Advanced
- Ultimate

Features of UserTesting includes:

- Test builder and template gallery.
- You can even filter the users by Demographic.
- A dedicated Dashboard and metrics for how the design is performing.
- You can also get the Transcripts of the user Interviews.
- Integrations with applications like Slack, Jira, and Trello.
- Sentiment analysis to check if the product appeals to the user's emotion or not.
- Card sorting and tree testing methods of UI/UX testing.
- Safe and Secured prototype testing.
- AI-powered analysis and insights.

Optimal Workshop

Optimal Workshop is one of the best tool for working on User navigation and User Experience. If you are actually building information architecture, then this tool will be a great choice. Optimal Workshop is widely used in the industry even by companies like IBM, Uber, yelp, etc.

Features offered by Optimal Workshop are:

- UX research methods like card sorting.
- Tree testing: a method for testing the structure or architecture of any product's design.
- Qualitative research.
- First-click testing.
- Online surveys for feedbacks from the users.

Lookback:

Lookback is widely used in the industry even by companies like Google, Nike, Spotify, Facebook, Netflix etc. There are two types of interviews you can do while UI/UX testing – Moderated interviews and Unmoderated interviews. And Lookback helps us with both type of user interviews.

Features offered by Lookback are:

- Usability testing for testing your application and website in mobile a well as larger devices.
- User Interviews for getting feedback.

PLANNING AND CONDUCTING USABILITY TESTS

Usability testing is a method used to evaluate how easy a website is to use. The tests take place with real users to measure how 'usable' or 'intuitive' a website is and how easy it is for users to reach their goals.

Usability testing is the practice of testing how easy a design is to use with a group of representative users. It usually involves observing users as they attempt to complete tasks and can be done for different types of designs. It is often conducted repeatedly, from early development until a product's release.

Usability Testing Leads to the Right Products

Through usability testing, you can find design flaws you might otherwise overlook. When you watch how test users behave while they try to execute tasks, you'll get vital insights into how well your design/product works. Then, you can leverage these insights to make improvements. Whenever you run a usability test, your chief objectives are to:

- Determine whether testers can complete tasks successfully and independently.

- Assess their performance and mental state as they try to complete tasks, to see how well your design works.
- See how much users enjoy using it.
- Identify problems and their severity.
- Find solutions.

While usability tests (Fig. 13.3) can help you create the right products, they shouldn't be the only tool in your UX research toolbox. If you just focus on the evaluation activity, you won't improve the usability overall.

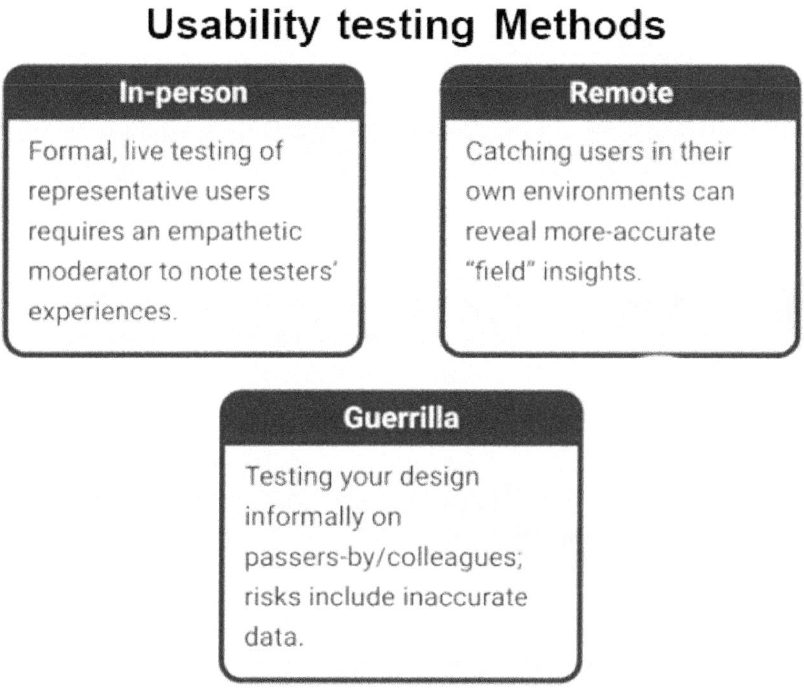

Fig. 13.3 There are different methods for usability testing. Which one you choose depends on your product and where you are in your design process.

Usability Testing is an Iterative Process

To make usability testing work best, you should:

- **Plan** –
  - **Define what you want to test**. Ask yourself questions about your design/product. What aspect/s of it do you want to test? You can make a hypothesis from each answer. With a clear hypothesis, you'll have the exact aspect you want to test.
  - **Decide how to conduct your test** – e.g., remotely. Define the *scope* of what to test (e.g., navigation) and stick to it throughout the test. When

you test aspects individually, you'll eventually build a broader view of how well your design works overall.

- **Set user tasks** –
  - **Prioritize the most important tasks to meet objectives** (e.g., complete checkout), no more than 5 per participant. Allow a 60-minute timeframe.
  - **Clearly define tasks with realistic goals.**
  - **Create scenarios where users can try to use the design naturally.** That means you let them get to grips with it on their own rather than direct them with instructions.
- **Recruit testers** – Know who your users are as a target group. Use screening questionnaires (e.g., Google Forms) to find suitable candidates. You can advertise and offer incentives. You can also find contacts through community groups, etc. If you test with only 5 users, you can still reveal 85% of core issues.
- **Facilitate/Moderate testing** –Set up testing in a suitable environment. Observe and interview users. Notice issues. See if users fail to see things, go in the wrong direction or misinterpret rules. When you record usability sessions, you can more easily count the number of times users become confused. Ask users to think aloud and tell you how they feel as they go through the test. From this, you can check whether your designer's mental model is accurate: Does what you think users can do with your design match what these test users show?

If you choose **remote testing,** you can moderate via Google Hangouts, etc., or use unmoderated testing. You can use this software to carry out remote moderated and unmoderated testing and have the benefit of tools such as heatmaps (Fig. 13.4).

Tips for Moderating Usability Tests

How to Keep Tests Smooth

- Let users struggle, don't over moderate
- Use pauses and silence if you need to
- Do not leave too much silence during task – say okay often
- Say "Okay" and "uh-huh" to fill in gaps
- Use a monotone tonality with users
- Ask "reverse questions": Is this what you expect to find there?

Fig. 13.4 Keep usability tests smooth by following these guidelines.

- **Assess user behavior** – Use these metrics:
  - **Quantitative** – time users take on a task, success and failure rates, effort (how many clicks users take, instances of confusion, etc.)
  - **Qualitative** – users' stress responses (facial reactions, body-language changes, squinting, etc.), subjective satisfaction (which they give through a post-test questionnaire) and ***perceived*** level of effort/difficulty
- **Create a test report** – Review video footage and analyzed data. Clearly define design issues and best practices. Involve the entire team.
  - Overall, you should test not your design's functionality, but users' ***experience of it***. Some users may be too polite to be entirely honest about problems. So, always examine ***all*** data carefully.

Step-by-Step Guide for UX Designers

Step 1: Define Your Goals

Before you start designing your usability test, you need to define your goals. What do you want to achieve? What questions do you want to answer? This will help you create a test that is focused and effective.

For example, in our recent usability test for a risk advice feature, our goals were to test if users understood how the risk analysis chart worked, if they could navigate the carousel of product categories, and if they understood how the broker consultation worked.

Step 2: Create a Test Plan

Once you have defined your goals, it's time to create a test plan. This includes outlining the questions you will ask, the tasks you will ask users to perform, and the prototypes or designs you will test.

We created a maze project that integrated the questions and prototypes. We did a dry run of the test maze within the design and product team and received feedback on the structure of the test, which we refined accordingly.

Step 3: Recruit Test Participants

Now that you have a plan in place, it's time to recruit test participants. Think about your target audience and where you can find them. In our case, we recruited English-speaking employees of our organisation.

Step 4: Conduct the Test

When it's time to conduct the test, make sure you have all the materials you need, such as a computer or device for the user to interact with, and a recording tool to capture their responses. In our own case, we shared the Maze link in a public channel in our domain and this meant the test could be done remotely.

During the test, ask participants to complete the tasks you have outlined, and ask them questions along the way to get feedback on their experience.

Step 5: Analyse Results

Once you have completed the test, it's time to analyse the results. Look for patterns in the feedback and identify areas where users had difficulty or confusion. We had a total of around 130 participants in total so the results were quite huge.

What we did was look for patterns and areas where there was difficulty in understanding the screens. We devised a system of using red stickies for users who were confused about the screens and Green stickies for users who did not have any trouble going through the process.

We also had an open question section and this helped us in gathering insights on the exact areas users struggled with in the general experience.

Step 6: Iterate and Improve

Use the insights gained from the test to make improvements to your design. The usability test provides valuable insights for improving your app experience. We identified areas where users may face challenges and received suggestions for enhancing the user experience. With these results in mind, we can then make targeted design improvements that will lead to a more user-friendly and effective feature.

Key Component of UX Design

Usability Testing is a crucial aspect of user experience (UX) design in web development. It involves evaluating a website or web application by observing real users as they interact with it. This process provides valuable insights into how well a digital product meets user needs and expectations. Usability testing helps identify and address usability issues, ensuring a user-friendly and effective design.

Types of Usability Testing

There are several types of usability testing, each serving specific purposes:

- **Moderated Usability Testing:** In this method, a moderator guides users through a series of tasks while observing and recording their interactions.
- **Unmoderated Usability Testing:** Participants complete tasks independently, often using remote testing software. This method is useful for larger sample sizes and remote user testing.
- **Guerrilla Usability Testing:** Quick and informal tests conducted with a small number of users to uncover immediate issues.

- **Comparative Usability Testing:** This involves comparing two or more designs or iterations to determine which performs better in terms of usability.

Use of Usability Testing?

Usability testing is essential for the following reasons:

- **User-Centered Design:** It ensures that the design is centered around the needs and preferences of the target audience.
- **Issue Identification:** Usability testing helps uncover design flaws, navigation problems, and content issues that might otherwise go unnoticed.
- **Validation:** It validates design decisions and provides data-driven insights to make informed improvements.
- **Cost-Efficiency:** Early detection and correction of usability issues save time and resources compared to addressing them after launch.

Benefits of Usability Testing

- **Improved User Satisfaction:** Usability testing leads to a more user-friendly product, enhancing user satisfaction and **loyalty.**
- **Higher Conversion Rates:** Better usability often translates to higher conversion rates, whether it's sales, sign-ups, or other desired actions.
- **Reduced Bounce Rates:** Users are more likely to stay and explore a website or app if it's easy to use, reducing bounce rates.
- **Enhanced Brand Reputation:** A user-friendly design reflects positively on the brand, increasing trust and credibility.

Key Elements of Usability Testing

Usability testing typically includes the following key elements:

- **Test Participants:** Select a diverse group of participants who represent the target audience.
- **Test Scenarios:** Create realistic tasks or scenarios that users need to complete on the website or app.
- **Testing Environment:** Choose a controlled environment with recording tools and equipment to capture user interactions.
- **Moderator (if applicable):** A moderator guides users through the test and records their feedback.
- **Data Analysis:** Analyze user interactions, feedback, and metrics to identify usability issues.

How to Do Usability Testing?

Usability testing typically follows these steps:

Planning

- **Define Clear Objectives:** Start by outlining the specific goals you want to achieve through usability testing. What are you trying to learn or validate? These objectives will guide the entire testing process.
- **Recruit Participants:** Carefully select participants who represent your target audience. Define demographic criteria and recruit a diverse group of users to ensure a comprehensive perspective.
- **Create Test Scenarios:** Develop realistic and relevant test scenarios or tasks. These tasks should mimic common user goals and interactions with your website or application. Ensure that they align with the objectives you've defined.

Preparation

- **Set Up a Controlled Environment:** Choose a suitable location for the usability tests. It could be a usability lab, a conference room, or a remote testing environment, depending on your resources and needs.
- **Equipment and Tools:** Ensure you have the necessary equipment, such as computers, mobile devices, screen recording software, cameras, and microphones, to capture user interactions and feedback effectively.
- **Consent Forms:** Prepare consent forms for participants, explaining the purpose of the test and any data usage. Make sure participants understand and agree to your terms.

Testing

- **Participant Briefing:** Begin by providing participants with an overview of the usability test, explaining its purpose and the tasks they'll perform. Emphasize that you're evaluating the product, not the participants.
- **Think-Aloud Protocol:** Encourage participants to think aloud as they navigate the website or app and complete the predefined tasks. This verbalization of thoughts helps capture their decision-making processes and any difficulties they encounter.
- **Task Execution:** Have participants perform the tasks one by one, recording their actions and verbal feedback. Observe their interactions closely, noting any signs of frustration, confusion, or success.
- **Note-Taking:** Take detailed notes during the test, documenting user actions, comments, and facial expressions. These notes will be valuable during the analysis phase.

Data Analysis

- **Review Test Recordings:** Carefully review the recorded sessions, paying attention to the participants' interactions, task completion rates, and their spoken thoughts. Identify patterns, issues, and areas of concern.
- **User Feedback:** Consider the feedback provided by participants during the think-aloud process. This qualitative data is valuable for understanding user perceptions and pain points.
- **Performance Metrics:** If applicable, analyze quantitative metrics, such as task completion time, error rates, and success rates. These metrics provide additional insights into usability.

Reporting

- **Compile Findings:** Summarize your findings in a comprehensive report. Organize your report with clear headings, including an executive summary, methodology, key findings, and recommendations.
- **Prioritize Usability Issues:** Rank identified issues based on severity and potential impact on user experience. Prioritize critical issues that require immediate attention.
- **Suggest Actionable Recommendations:** Provide concrete and actionable recommendations for improving usability. Include specific design changes or enhancements to address identified issues.
- **Visual Aids:** Incorporate visual aids, such as screenshots or video clips from the tests, to illustrate usability issues and successes.

Iterate

- **Implement Design Changes:** Based on the findings and recommendations from the usability test, make necessary design changes or improvements to your website or application.
- **Repeat Usability Testing:** After implementing changes, consider conducting another round of usability testing to validate the effectiveness of your design improvements. This iterative process ensures continuous refinement of the user experience.

By following these steps with precision and thoroughness, usability testing becomes a powerful tool for optimizing your digital products, enhancing user satisfaction, and achieving your UX goals.

Practices to Avoid

To ensure the effectiveness of usability testing, avoid the following practices:

- **Biased Moderation:** Moderators should remain neutral and avoid leading participants, as their role is to observe and record, not influence.

- **Ignoring Negative Feedback:** Negative feedback should be embraced as an opportunity for improvement rather than dismissed.
- **Testing with Team Members:** Team members may have biases and preconceptions about the design. It's essential to use actual users or participants who closely match the target audience.
- **Overcomplicating Tasks:** Keep test tasks straightforward and realistic to avoid confusing participants. Overly complex tasks may not reflect real user behavior.

ANALYZING AND ACTING ON USABILITY TEST RESULTS

Usability Test Analysis and Reporting

This section explains six major steps to Usability Test Analysis and Reporting that will assist researchers in gathering, organizing, and prioritizing usability data to produce actionable redesign suggestions that can dramatically improve the user experience as a whole. The ability to master these stages will enable you to make data-driven decisions and produce better user-friendly and efficient products, whether you are a UX specialist, product manager, or developer.

Tabulate Data

In usability testing, tabulating data is putting the gathered information into a structured table format and summarizing it. Tabulation is a critical phase in the analysis process because it enables researchers to find trends in the usability test data, compare outcomes, and derive insights.

Data tabulation is a detailed process, which is carried out using the following steps:

- **Identify Data Categories:** As a designer/researcher, you must choose the categories or variables you wish to analyze before you can create the table. The goals of your usability test and the metrics you're tracking will determine which of these categories you choose. Participant ID, task name or number, completion status, time on task, mistakes, satisfaction ratings, and qualitative comments or observations are examples of typical categories.
- **Create the Table Structure:** After you've determined the types of data, use spreadsheet programs like Microsoft Excel or Google Sheets to build the table structure. The rows of the table will correspond to each participant or test session, and the columns will reflect the data categories. Below is an example of a table structure you can refer to while tabulating data.
- **Fill and Populate Data in Table:** Fill in the appropriate data in the table cells for each participant and task. This could involve language, categorized labels, or numerical numbers, depending on the kind of data you gathered.

- **Columns under which you can populate the data:**
- **Task/Activity Completion:** To indicate whether or not the participant finished the activity successfully, use "Completed" or "Not Completed."
- **Time Spent on Task:** Note the amount of time it took to finish the assignment or enter "N/A" for assignments that were not finished.
- **Error count:** Count the number of mistakes that each participant made while completing each activity.
- **User Ratings:** Record the participant's numerical evaluation of satisfaction (for instance, on a scale of 1 to 5).
- **Additional Comments or Quotes:** Don't forget to mention any in-depth criticism or observations the test subject offered.

Analysing Data and Listing Down Findings

In usability testing, data analysis and listing findings include carefully going over the data that has been gathered, spotting patterns and trends, and then summarizing the findings in a clear and understandable way.

Here's a step-by-step guide on how to analyze data and list findings in usability testing:

- **Review the data:** Start by going over all the information gathered during the usability testing procedure. This may comprise task sheets that have been completed, audio or video recordings, observation notes, user feedback forms, and any other pertinent data.
- **Identify Key Metrics:** Choose the important metrics and data points that support the goals of your usability testing. Task completion rates, time on task, error rates, user satisfaction scores, and qualitative comments are examples of common metrics. By outlining these indicators beforehand, you may concentrate your investigation on the information that matters most.
- **Summarise "Quantitative" Data:** Quantitative data (numeric data), calculate summary statistics and metrics. This includes data like:
- Task Completion Rate
- Time on Task
- Error Count:
- User Satisfaction Ratings
- **Analyze "Qualitative" Data:** Conduct a thematic analysis of qualitative data (text data), such as user comments and observations. Analyze the input for recurrent themes, problems, and patterns. Pay attention to

all comments, favorable and bad, since they might reveal important information about user experiences and problems.

- **Group and Categorize Findings:** Based on the tasks or features of the product being evaluated, arrange the findings into categories or themes. Consider separating usability problems including navigation, layout, language, and visual design. This aids in providing a report that is well-structured and coordinated.

Findings Prioritisation

Prioritizing test results can help you concentrate on solving the most important problems that have an impact on the user experience. You can effectively allocate resources and decide which usability issues to address first by using prioritization. Depending on how serious they are and how they affect the user experience, give the identified usability concerns a priority. High-priority problems are those that seriously impede work completion or aggravate users, whereas low-priority problems might only be niggling inconveniences.

To start with prioritization, start with the following steps:

- **Collect Analyzed and Grouped conclusions:** From the previous step, collect and review all of the results of your usability testing first. Quantitative information (such as completion rates, time spent on work, and error rates), as well as qualitative feedback (such as user comments and observations), may be included in these findings. Organize related concerns into groups to spot recurring themes and patterns. You can better organize the findings for prioritization with the help of this initial grouping.
- **Establish Clear Prioritisation Criterion:** Clearly define the criteria for prioritization. Your standards ought to be in line with the aims and purposes of the usability test. Take into account elements like the degree of the usability issue, how frequently it occurs, how it affects the user experience, and how many users are impacted. Additionally, think about how simple it would be to implement and how much it may cost to resolve each issue.
- **Assign Severity Ratings:** Using the predetermined criteria, assign a severity level to each usability issue. Standard severity scales include:
- **Critical:** Problems that seriously hinder task completion or make a product practically useless. These problems require immediate attention.
- **High:** Issues that greatly impair the user experience and generate aggravation for users. They require quick attention.
- **Medium:** Problems that affect usability noticeably yet may not be critical. In the medium term, they can be dealt with.

- **Low:** Minor problems or ideas for enhancement that hardly influence usability. Later on or in a subsequent version, these can be addressed.
- **Rank all Findings:** After you have given the results severity ratings, order them according to importance. To organize the issues, you can use a simple rating system (such as high, medium, and low) or a number scale (such as 1 to 5).
- **Find Quick Wins:** Look for usability problems that, although they can be resolved quickly and with little work, have a significant negative influence on the user experience. Setting quick wins as a top priority can produce noticeable results right away and generate momentum for more usability improvements.

Recommendation based on Findings

Utilizing the knowledge gained from the testing process to provide specific suggestions for adjustments to improve the usability of a system or product is known as creating redesign recommendations. The objective is to pinpoint usability problems and offer practical and workable strategies to fix them. Here's a detailed guide on how to create redesign recommendations in usability testing:

- **Understand Root Causes:** Investigate further to discover the underlying reasons for the cited usability problems. Examine user comments and behavior to ascertain the causes of these problems. Designing efficient solutions requires determining the underlying issues.
- **Produce Redesign Recommendations:** Produce detailed redesign recommendations based on the prioritized usability concerns and their underlying causes. Each suggestion ought to be specifically related to resolving a specific usability problem. For each piece of advice, follow a clear and succinct format and take into account the following factors:
- **Description of the Issue:** Clearly state the usability problem that the recommendation seeks to fix in the issue description. To demonstrate the issue, utilize real-world instances or quotes from users.
- **Proposed Repair:** Specify the precise modifications or enhancements required to deal with the problem. Give as many specific instructions for the makeover as you can.
- **Justification:** Justify why you believe the suggested solution would be successful in enhancing the user experience. To support your justification, refer to the usability findings and any pertinent research.
- **Technical Feasibility:** Consider the viability of putting the suggested modifications into action. Examine elements including time limits, development resources, and technical limitations.

- **Provide Visuals:** Use wireframes, mockups, or sketches, as necessary, to demonstrate the redesign suggestions. Visuals can aid stakeholders in comprehending your suggested modifications and imagining how they can affect the user interface.
- **Describe the suggestions for a redesign:** To communicate the redesign recommendations to the appropriate stakeholders, such as product managers, designers, and developers, and create a well-structured report or presentation. Explain each recommendation's importance and any potential positive effects on the user experience.
- **Work together with developers and designers:** Make sure the redesign proposals are clearly understood and feasible by working closely with designers and developers. Collaborative conversations can result in innovative solutions that solve problems and go beyond any obstacles.
- **Test and Validate Redesigns:** After the suggested modifications have been made, carry out more usability testing to confirm the viability of the redesign suggestions. This will assist you in ensuring that the changes actually address the noted usability problems and enhance the user experience.

Create a Report

Usability testing management presentations or reports must clearly and succinctly convey the main conclusions, insights, and suggestions to stakeholders. The objective is to provide the usability test results in a way that supports informed decision-making for product changes and aids decision-makers in understanding the user experience concerns.

Here's a detailed guide on how to create a management presentation or report in usability testing:

- **Introduce Usability Test Objective:** Describe the backdrop of the usability testing, including its goals and the system or product being assessed. Briefly describe the usability testing approach, including the number of participants, testing environment, tasks assigned, and data collection techniques.
- **Include Usability metrics:** Give examples of quantitative usability measures, including task completion times, mistake rates, and user satisfaction ratings. For simpler understanding, visualize these metrics using charts or graphs. To give context and insights into performance, compare the measurements with industry benchmarks or prior usability testing (where available).

- **Show Relevant Findings:** Sort the usability results into areas that are obvious and distinct (such as navigation, layout, terminology, etc.). List the exact usability problems and testing difficulties that occurred for each category. To provide stakeholders with a clear sense of user feedback, back up each conclusion with pertinent data and user quotes.
- **Talk about Prioritization:** Emphasize the usability issues that have been given the highest priority based on their importance, frequency, and effect on the user experience. Explain the prioritization process in detail, stressing the need of resolving high-priority concerns.
- **Add Redesign Recommendations:** Offer precise and practical redesign advice for each of the issues with usability that you have prioritized. Explain in detail how each suggestion improves the user experience and responds to the highlighted usability issue. Include illustrations of the suggested redesigns using visuals, such as wireframes or mockups, if at all possible.
- **Cost Benefits Analysis:** Include a cost-benefit analysis for each suggestion for redesigning, if applicable. In comparison to the possible benefits to the user experience and business objectives, weigh the resources (time, effort, and costs) needed to accomplish the improvements.
- **Conclude Study:** List the main conclusions, issues in order of importance, and suggestions for redesign. In order to increase the success of the product and user pleasure, it is crucial to fix the identified usability concerns.
- **Next Steps:** Describe the next steps for resolving the usability problems and putting the redesign suggestions into practice. Give parties participating in the usability enhancements more clarity regarding their roles and obligations.
- **Appendix:** Include any more statistics, thorough usability test results, or other evidence that helps to substantiate the conclusions in the appendix.

Plan follow-up sessions

Planning follow-up sessions include the actions that are taken after the usability test has been completed. This part of the usability testing process is vital since it entails data analysis, refining the conclusions, and taking the necessary steps to address the found usability concerns.

Here's a detailed explanation of what happens during the follow-up post-usability session:

- **Data transcription and summarization:** Following the conclusion of the usability testing sessions, it is necessary to summarize and transcribe the recorded data (audio/video recordings, observation notes, etc.). This stage entails the transcription of any user interactions and test-related observations that were captured. The important findings and usability concerns that surfaced during the testing process can be identified with the use of a data summary.

- **Refining Findings:** The first results of the usability test are organized and refined based on the data analysis. Depending on how serious they are and how they affect the user experience, usability issues are categorized and given priority. This process aids in ensuring that the final conclusions are precise and useful.
- **Presentation to Stakeholders:** After completion, the usability test report is distributed to the appropriate parties, including product managers, designers, developers, and other decision-makers. The presentation is an opportunity to discuss the results and redesign suggestions while also responding to any stakeholders' queries or worries.
- **Implementation:** Following the presentation, the stakeholders choose how to put the redesign suggestions into practice. The product or system's needed updates and upgrades are put into place by the development and design teams working collaboratively.
- **Follow-Up Usability Testings (If required):** Follow-up usability testing may occasionally be carried out to confirm the efficacy of the applied improvements. This stage assists in ensuring that the user experience has been improved and the identified issues have been successfully handled by the usability improvements.

Analyze your Usability Test Results

There are several different ways to analyze your usability test results. Here are some tips:

- **Identify areas of improvement**: Look at your results and identify areas where users struggled or had difficulty completing tasks. These are areas that you will want to focus on improving.
- **Compare results to previous tests**: If you have conducted multiple usability tests, compare the results of the latest test to those of previous tests. This will help you see if any progress is made in terms of user experience.
- **Determine which metrics are most important:** Several different metrics can be used to measure usability, such as task completion rate, time on task, error rate, and satisfaction rating. Determine which metrics are most important for your organization and focus on those when analyzing your results.

- **Analyze individual results:** In addition to looking at overall trends, it can also be helpful to analyze the results of individual users. This can help you identify common problems and areas of confusion.
- **Take action based on your findings:** Once you have analyzed your usability test results, taking action based on your findings is vital. Make changes to your product or website based on the user feedback you received. This will help improve the user experience and make your product or website more user-friendly.

CHAPTER-14

ITERATIVE DESIGN PROCESS

Design iteration is the repeatable process of improving a product (or part of a product) in relatively short but regular bursts, otherwise known as 'design iterations'. These design iterations can consist of high-fidelity prototypes, mid-fidelity wireframes, low-fidelity sketches, or even simple diagrams such as sitemaps.

Design iteration drives the overall design process forward.

Iterative design is a design methodology based on a cyclical approach of prototyping, testing, analyzing, and refining a product at any stage of the design process. You can think of iterative design as a rapid and repetitive trial-and-error process intended to deliver a product that meets user goals and expectations. How users say they behave with a digital product versus how they behave is rarely the same. The iterative design recognizes this by laying a framework for product teams to develop a prototype quickly and then test it with real-world users to determine what they do with the product.

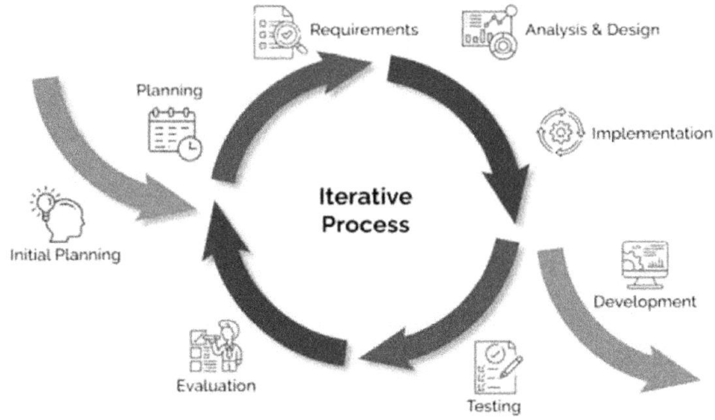

Fig. 14. Iterative Process Model

Use of the iterative design

Designers can apply an iterative approach at any stage of the product development process. Organizations can even introduce or adopt iterative design even if a product has already been shipped to market, especially if they're looking to make improvements. However, the earlier iterative design is implemented in the product lifecycle, the more likely the product can meet user objectives and expectations. Further, it's also more likely that the design process can be more cost-effective and achieve faster time to market.

Non-iterative approach

The Waterfall model is the most common non-iterative process wherein each project phase (e.g., discovery, conceptualization, design, development, testing, launch) must be completed in its entirety before moving on to the next one. In a non-iterative approach, as in the waterfall model, teams emphasized the planning phase more than the execution process — documenting everything in advance, such as the user interface, user stories, and features and variations. Non-iterative methods require more time during the conceptualization and creation phase, aiming for the product to work as intended during testing.

Requirements and resources are typically locked after project planning, and teams avoid project modifications as much as possible. Typically, teams design and develop a final product with the minimal exploration of new ideas along the way. Non-iterative design processes can be challenging because it doesn't allow time and space for unknowns and surprises and the necessary adjustments to address them.

Benefits of iterative design

Companies and organizations of all shapes and sizes have lauded adopting an iterative approach to their design and development processes. Here are the key benefits of iterative design:

- **Efficiency:** By working on products in quick sprints, teams can adjust their products in each iteration rather than rework an entire design as new insights or feedback emerge. Further, workload among team members can be spread out more evenly throughout the development lifecycle.
- **Progress visibility:** Iterative design gives product stakeholders visibility of a project's progress at the end of each iteration.
- **Collaboration:** Designers can generate feedback from clients and stakeholders based on the results from each iteration. An iterative process draws better engagement from them as they can see the evolution of the project and that the design team is meeting their requirements rather than "dumping" a finished product on them.

- **Eliminates confusion:** The repetitive or cyclical nature of iterative design enables rapid resolution of misunderstandings or disorders within the project team as early as possible. Further, teams can detect flaws in the design, architecture, code, and other implementations with each iteration, severely impacting the product if left undetected.
- **Ability to work in parallel:** Unlike non-iterative methodologies such as the waterfall method, the iterative process decreases dependence on the work that comes in previous phases. Team members can work on several parts of a project in parallel, leading to faster time to market.
- **Usability:** Iterative design keeps users at the heart of the process, with each iteration ideally based on user research, behavior, and feedback. For instance, testing and debugging in smaller or faster iterations can identify defects or flaws early in the design process, with target users providing insight in each iteration.
- **Continuous improvement:** Each iteration enables design teams to incorporate lessons learned from previous runs giving the final product the best chance to meet customer expectations.
- **Cost-effective:** Changes arising from an iterative approach are likely to be less costly than in a Waterfall approach. Since modifications are common in product development, discovering them at the earliest possible stage makes it easier for organizations to adjust their resources.

Here are some familiar examples of iterative design:

- **Iteration during product development:** Engineering teams apply an iterative approach in developing new features, implementing bug fixes, and A/B testing new strategies. It's not uncommon for engineering teams to create a few promising versions, then test them out with users. They'll note good and bad user experiences and then continue building the iteration that tested the best.
- **Wikis:** With user-generated content, anyone can write new entries or improve existing ones. Reviewers or editors then decide whether new content passes specific standards or whether the changes made improve the content. Users expect this iteration system in sites like Wikipedia to present the best available information on any given topic over time.
- **Urban design:** Urban designers see 10-year plans made by local governments as strategies and principles. Urban designers execute new ideas at a small scale and gather feedback before expanding their programs for implementation. For instance, they may try a living street design for one year before scaling them either at the exact location or in another area.

THE ROLE OF ITERATION IN UX AND DESIGN THINKING

Iteration is the process of repeating a set of operations or steps. It is like doing something over and over again to make it better. The essence of iteration is cyclical in nature, where each successive repetition (or iteration) is intended to bring one step closer to the final goal or to enhance the outcome of ongoing process.

Synonyms of iteration

Repetition, Recurrence, Reiteration, Redo, Replication, Cycle, Loop, Reprise, Renewal, Repeat

Use of iteration in a Sentence – Examples

- The software's third iteration fixed all the previous bugs.
- What is the use of this constant iteration of the same things?
- In the latest iteration of the app, they added voice control features.
- After many iterations, the cake recipe finally tasted perfect.
- Every iteration of the marketing plan was more focused and targeted.
- The game's fifth iteration included better graphics and new levels.

Design Thinking is Helpful in Many Areas

- It is used in project management, it is used to define the scope and architecture of the project.
- It is used for business management. It used to focus on the features which have more value in the actual world.
- It helps to allocate the goal so that we can go towards the exact direction with more clear views. In this way, it is helpful in the development field.
- For most of the team works, It allows us to work in a more effective manner and according to users' requirements.

Design Thinking is also known as Out of the Box thinking. Designers trying to find more and more ways for solving the most common problems. Design Thinking is a way to develop the products by the complete study of how customers interact with products and the conditions in which they implement. Design thinking helps us to research the right topic and create exact prototype according to the customer's needs. It helps to go in-depth for better understanding and powerful research. It discovers new ways to upgrade the product with its design. Design Thinking is an iterative process. It is non-linear too. It means that the previous results are continuously examined and reviewed by the development team for better understanding. It also helps to add an alternative solution that replaces the previous model or design.

Principles of Design Thinking

- **Empathy:** This principle is depends on empathize phase of design thinking. User requirement is the first priority of design thinking. There is no need to focus on the optional features for users. But the smartness to develop a design that fulfills the customer's requirements.
- **Expansive Thinking:** It is the principle of finding many ways to solve the problem of finding the solution. This principle is also known as ***BrainStorming***. The main motive for this is to think big.
- **Experimentation:** After finding many solutions, you have to find that optimized solution from the list. Experiments are necessary for building a more effective prototype. For the selection of the correct prototype, it must be tested before releasing it for the public. It is a method that is accessible form almost everyone.

Design Thinking methodology is applied in many of the industries like Airbnb, IBM, Stanford Hospitals, Uber eats, Bank of America, and many more. Instead of using more traditional approaches and producing things in sequential steps, we have chosen to iterate through the six design thinking stages. Empathize. Define, Ideate, Prototype, Test, Implement. This allowed us to produce a very well-received product.

Iteration in Team Project

Iteration in team projects is a repeat process where team members work together to improve their project step by step. It is a way to make things better by trying again and again, using feedback to guide changes.

- Repeating steps to improve work.
- Allows for feedback and changes.
- Team members collaborate and refine.
- Useful in software and design projects
- Adapts to changing project needs.
- Step-by-step improvement process

Iteration in Business Intelligence

Iteration in Business Intelligence involves repeatedly analyzing data, refining strategies and adjusting business practices based on insights. This cyclical process helps businesses adapt to market changes, improve decision-making, and enhance overall performance.

- Continuously analyzing and interpreting data
- Refining business strategies based on insights.

- Adjusting practices for better outcomes
- Helps in adapting to market trends.
- Improves decision-making processes.
- Enhances business performance and growth.

Iteration in Software Development

Iteration in software development enables developers to create and improve software in repeated cycles. It involves gradually building and refining the software, allowing for regular feedback and adjustments based on testing and user input.

- Developing software in repeated cycles
- Gradual building and refining of features.
- Regular feedback integration
- Adjustments based on testing and user feedback.
- Allows for continuous improvement.
- Adapts to changing requirements and technology.

Iteration in Programming

Iteration in programming is a fundamental concept where a set of instructions is executed repeatedly. It's used to perform tasks multiple times, often with slight variations or until a certain condition is met.

- Repeating code blocks for tasks
- Used in loops like for, while do-while.
- Executes tasks multiple times.
- Can vary each cycle slightly.
- Continues until a condition is met.
- Essential for tasks like traversing data structures

Iteration planning

Iteration planning is generally a process of adapting as the project unfolds by making alterations to plans. Plans are changed simply based on feedback from the monitoring process, some changes on project assumptions, risks, and changes in scope, budget, or schedule. It is essential to include the team in the planning process. Planning is generally concerned with explaining and defining the actual sequence of intermediate results. It is an event where each team member identifies how much of the team backlog, they can commit to delivering during an upcoming iteration. Iteration planning is generally the process of discussing and planning the next cycle, phase, or iteration of a software application that is in the process of development. An evolutionary developed plan is very essential because there are always adjustments in developed content and schedule as an early conjecture that simply evolves into highly and well-understood project circumstances (Fig. 14.2).

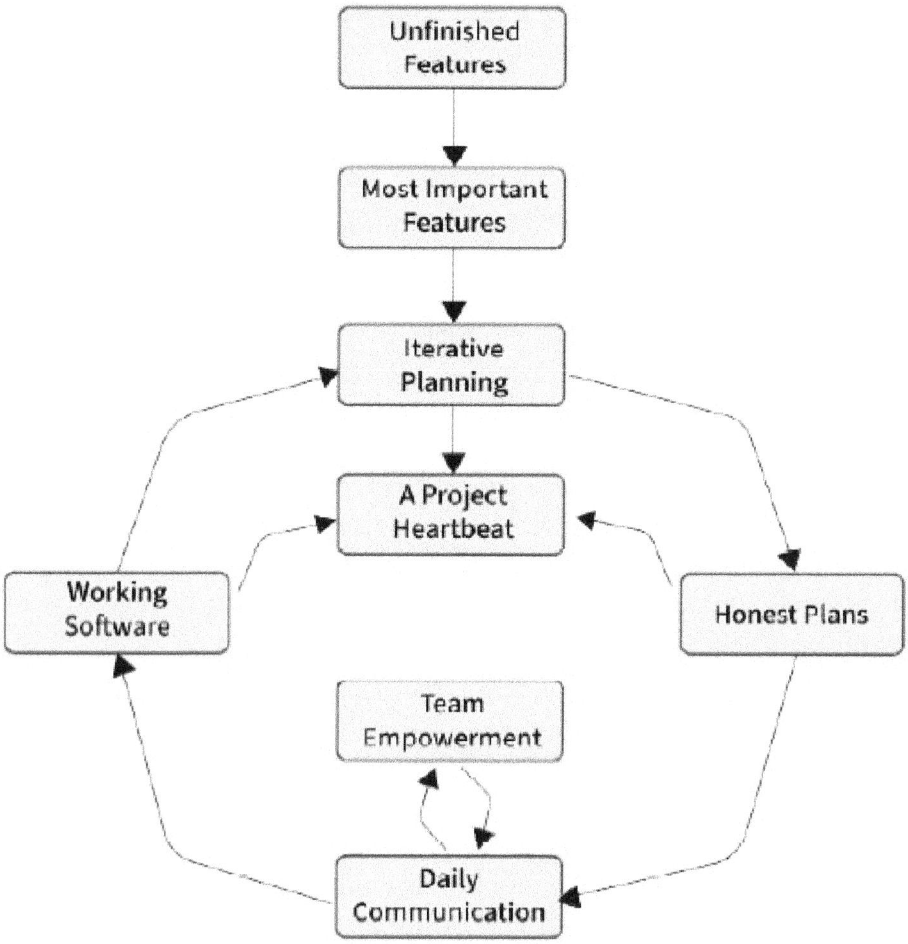

Fig. 14.2 Iteration Planning

- **Inception Iterations:** In some of cases where the project includes a new product roll-out or simply the creation of new technology, iterations might be essential to further explain the scope of the project, risks, and all benefits. It might also involve a further increase in the quality of the use-case model, business case, risk list, architectural proof-of-concept, or even project and iteration plans. Extension of this inception phase can also be advised in some cases where both risk and required investment are high. It can also be advised where the problem domain is new or the team is not experienced. The early prototyping technique also integrates the foundation components of the architecture of the candidate and also provides an executable framework for explaining and simply elaborating the use cases of the system. To achieve an acceptable prototype, Large-scale, and custom developments are two iterations. But various projects should be able to get by use of only one. Inception iteration is generally responsible for establishing scope and vision and explaining and defining the business case.

- **Elaboration Iterations:** In each of iteration, supporting environment is refined further. If the initial elaboration is only focused on the preparation of the environment for analysis design and implementation then the second iteration might focus on the preparation of the test environment. The preparation of the test environment includes configuring test processes, writing the development case part, and preparing or generating templates and guidelines that need to be followed for test and setting up test tools. Elaboration iteration also results in architecture with a complete framework and infrastructure for execution. To achieve an acceptable architecture baseline, some of the projects require two iterations. Some additional and extra iterations may be required by unprecedented architectures. On the other hand, projects that are developed on highly well-established architecture frameworks can be achieved by the use of a single iteration. During elaboration iteration, requirements are defined fully and architectures are well-established.
- **Construction Iterations:** The essential result of late iteration in the construction phase is that more functionality is added, which yields an increasingly complete system. During construction iteration, use cases are generally realized and architectures are fleshed out. Some projects need and require two construction iterations. First is an alpha release that includes executable capability for each of the critical use cases. Second, is a beta release that provides 95 % of the total product capability breadth and also achieves some of the essential quality attributes that are needed and important.
- **Transition Iterations for migrating:** Transition iteration is generally responsible for migrating products into the user community. Several projects use only one iteration to transition the beta release into the end product or final product. Even these projects learn to live with only one iteration between the beta release and the end product or final product release.

Iteration in Scratch Programming

Scratch is a high-level visual programming language tool that interacts with users through diagrams and blocks that have the basics of a program inbuilt in it. Scratch is used to make interactive programs especially for kids using the block kind of interfaces so that they can easily learn languages and it is free to use.

Scratch iteration block

Iteration is the concept that allows the repetition of commands or a set of lines. It is also known as a loop in the computer programming language. When the code executes(repeated) one time then this repetition is known as one iteration. The Iteration control block basically reduces the number of similar tasks to be performed by grouping the similar tasks in one block. In Scratch, the control block contains iteration tools as shown in the below image (Fig. 14.3):

Fig. 14.3 Scratch control block

Now, let's understand each iteration block in detail:

1. repeat (number n) block

It is a control block. This iteration block iterates the given set of commands 'n' number of times. The number n can be any positive integer. Here, n is the stopping condition of the iteration block. If the value of n is infinite then the loop runs forever, if the value n is a non-positive number then this loop will not run, and if the value of n is a decimal number then the number is round up. Let us understand the working of the repeat block with the help of a simple project:

Procedure:

Step 1: Click on event block and choose 1st control block denoting the start of the program(drag it to center).

Step 2: Click on add extension and choose pen block for drawing square.

Step 3: Place pen down block below the event block.

Step 4: Now drag the repeat block from the control block and place it down of pen down block. Change the number from 10 to 4.

Step 5: Click on motion block and drag move block and place it inside repeat block. Change the number from 10 to 50.

Step 6: Click on the turn block and place it below the move block inside the repeat block. Change the number from 15 to 90.

Step 7: Now run the program.

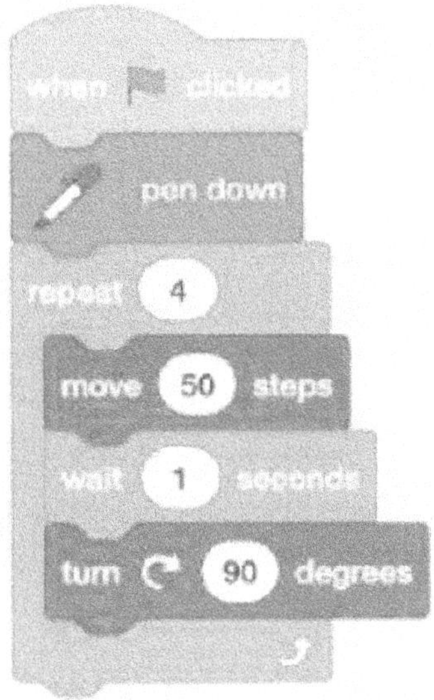

Fig. 14.4

Below is the implementation of the procedure (Fig. 14.5):

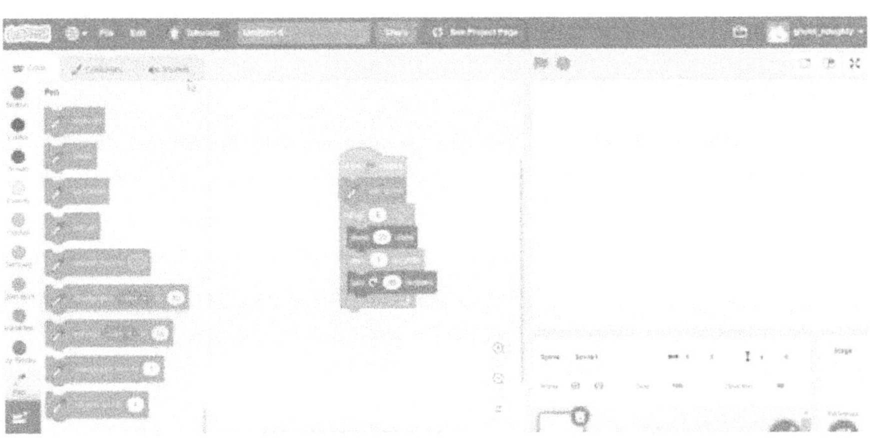

Fig. 14.5 Implementation of the procedure

2. nested repeat block

A nested repeat block is created by placing a repeat block inside another repeat block. Here, two integer numbers will be used for the stopping condition. Let's understand this by making a small project:

Procedure:

Step 1: Click on the event block and choose the 1st control block denoting the start of the program(drag it to center).

Step 2: Click on add extension and choose pen block for drawing a square.

Step 3: Place pen down block below the event block.

Step 4: Now drag repeat block from control block and place it down to the pen down block. Now change the number from 10 to 2.

Step 5: Now, again drag the repeat block from the control block and place it inside the first repeat block. Now, change the number from 10 to 2.

Step 6: Click on the motion block and drag the move block and place it inside the repeat block. Now, change the number from 10 to 50.

Step 7: Click on the turn block and place it below the move block inside the nested repeat block. Now, change the number from 15 to 90.

Step 8: Now run the program.

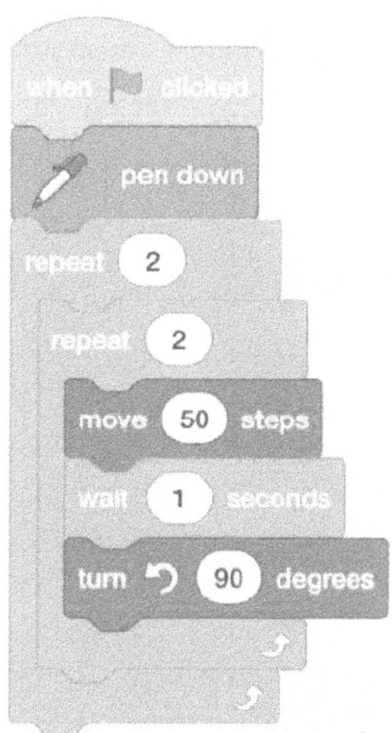

Fig. 14.6

Figure 14.7 below is the implementation of the procedure:

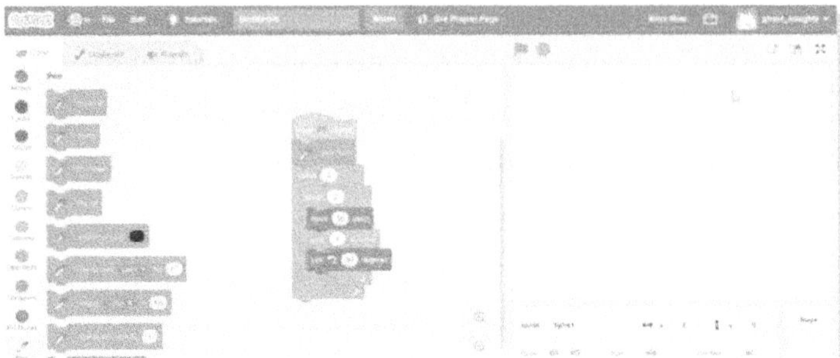

Fig 14.7 The implementation of the procedure

3. forever block

It is a control block. This iteration block executes a particular set of commands infinitely. There is no stopping condition present in forever block. This kind of block is used to make patterns that are infinite in nature. For example, the square spiral. Let us understand the working of the forever block with the help of a simple project(i.e. square spiral):

Procedure:

Step 1: Click on event block and choose 1st control block denoting the start of the program(drag it to center).

Step 2: Click on add extension and choose pen block for drawing square spiral.

Step 3: Place pen down the block below the event block.

Step 4: Go to variable block and drag "set my variable to 80".

Step 5: Drag the forever block from the

Step 8: Go to variable block and drag "change my variable by 5".

Step 9: Now run the program.

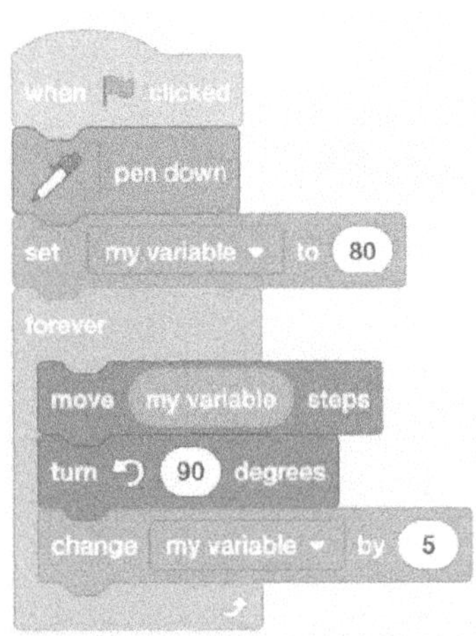

Fig. 14.8

Below (Fig. 14.9) is the implementation of the procedure:

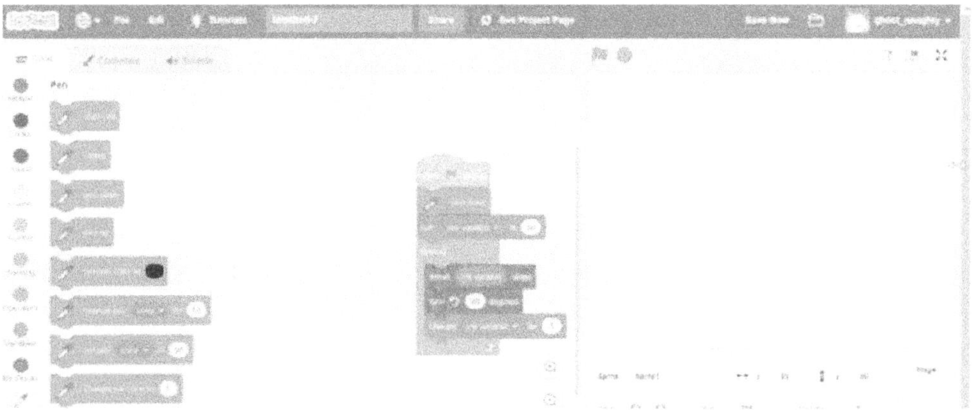

Fig. 14.9 The implementation of the procedure

4. repeat until block

It is a control block. This iteration block executes a particular set of commands until a particular condition is not satisfied. The condition inserted in until is the stopping condition of the loop. This block is used when the stopping condition is known beforehand. Let us understand the working of the forever block with the help of a simple project. In this project, we draw a hexagon and the stopping condition of the hexagon would be 6.

Procedure:

Step 1: Click on the event block and choose the 1st control block denoting the start of the program(drag it to center).

Step 2: Click on add extension and choose pen block for drawing a square spiral.

Step 3: Place pen down block below the event block.

Step 4: Go to variable block and drag "set my variable to 0".

Step 5: Drag repeat until block from control block and place it down of pen down the block.

Step 6: Go to operator block and drag 0 = 0 block and fill in the left blank with "my variable" and right blank with 6. Fix this in until blank.

Step 7: Click on motion block and drag move block and place it inside repeat until block. Now change the number to 50

Step 8: Click on turn block(inside motion block) and place it below the move block inside repeat until block. Now change the number from 15 to 60.

Step 9: Go to variable block and drag "change my variable by 1".

Step 10: Now run the program.

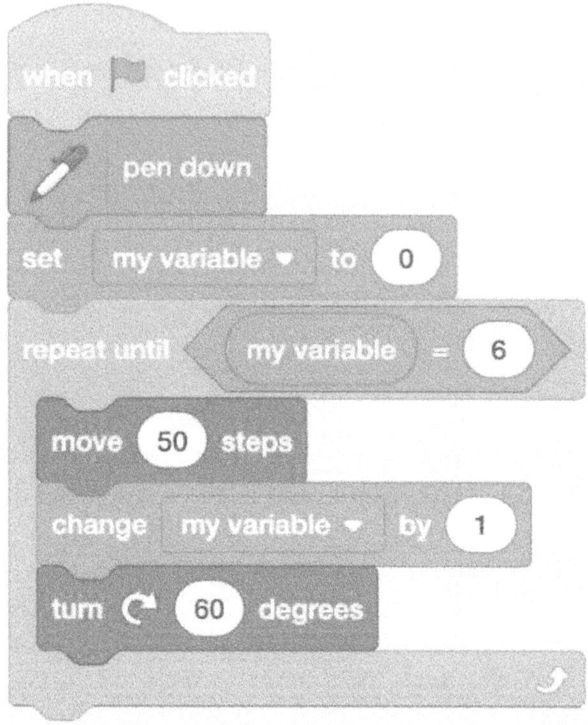

Fig. 14.10

Below (Fig. 14.11) is the implementation of the procedure:

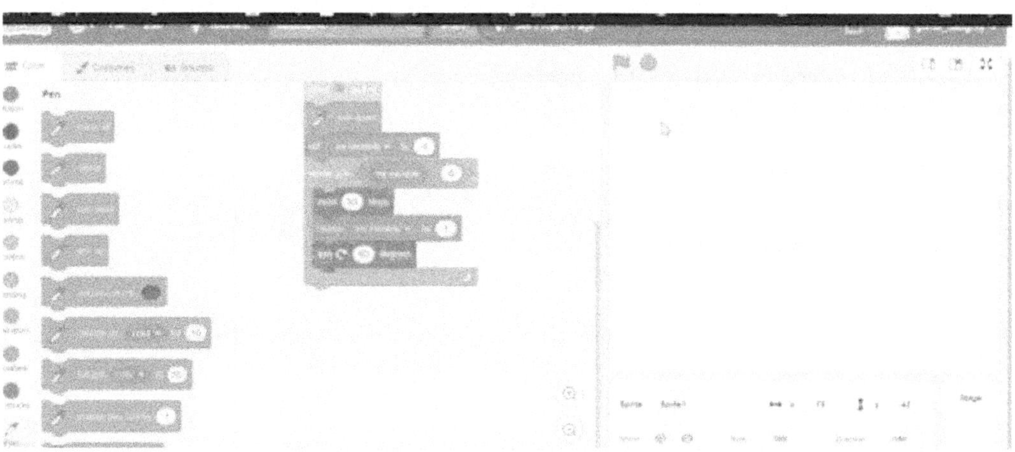

Fig. 14.11 The implementation of the procedure

5. nested repeat until block

A nested repeat until block is created by placing a repeat until block is placed inside another repeat until block. Here, two conditions will be used for stopping conditions. Let's understand this by making a small project.

Procedure:

Step 1: Click on event block and choose 1st control block denoting start of the program(drag it to center).

Step 2: Click on add extension and choose pen block for drawing square.

Step 3: Place pen down block below the event block.

Step 4: Go to variable block and click on "make a variable", name it a, drag "set a to 0".

Step 5: Drag repeat until block from control block and insert it in another repeat until block.

Step 6: Go to operator block and drag 0=0 block and fill the left blank with "a" and right blank with 3. Fix this in until blank.

Step 7: Go to the variable block and drag "set my variable to 0" and place it inside repeat until block.

Step 8: Go to operator block and drag 0=0 block and fill left blank with "my variable" and right blank with 3. Fix this in the second repeat until blank.

Step 9: Click on motion block and drag move block and place it inside repeat block. Now, change the number from 10 to 50.

Step 10: Go to variable block and drag "change my variable by 1".

Step 11: Click on the turn block and place it below the move block inside the repeat block. Now, change the number from 15 to 60.

Step 12: Outside the inner repeat block, go to the variable block and drag "change a by 1".

Step 13: Now run the program.

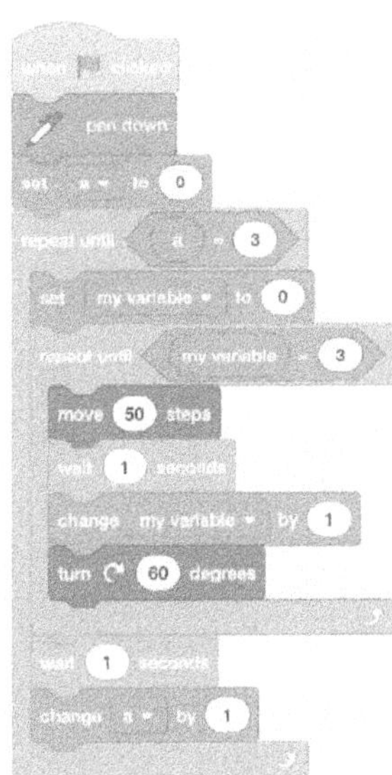

Fig. 14.12

INCORPORATING USER FEEDBACK FOR CONTINUOUS IMPROVEMENT

When building or iterating a product, understanding the user's perspective is paramount. User feedback serves as a compass, guiding entrepreneurs towards a product that not only meets market needs but also resonates with its intended audience. Incorporating this feedback through iterative design ensures that a product evolves in tandem with user expectations, leading to continuous improvement and heightened user satisfaction.

The Value of User Feedback

User feedback is the voice of your market. It provides direct insights into what users like, dislike, need, or find redundant. By actively seeking and analyzing this feedback, entrepreneurs can identify gaps in their product, making necessary adjustments before these gaps become critical issues. Moreover, it fosters a sense of community, where users feel valued and heard, leading to increased brand loyalty and trust.

IKEA is an example of a company that understands their users. Alex Soliman, Customer Care Centre Manager for Malaysia, Philippines, Singapore, Thailand and Mexico said "consumers are now more pressed for time and would have like to have more support in their journey of furnishing a home". IKEA is now very focused on the digital customer experience. "Mobile self-support, order tracking, conversational support through social media and remote design support are just a few examples that we are looking at today. And that requires us to have the right digital foundation so we can meet customer expectations".

Iterative Design: A Cycle of Refinement

Paul Rand, American designer best known for creating the IBM and ABC logos once said, "The designer does not, as a rule, begin with some preconceived idea. Rather the idea is the result of careful study and observation, and the design is the product of that idea."

Tools and Techniques for Gathering Feedback

In today's digital age, there are numerous tools available for gathering user feedback. From simple surveys and feedback forms to more advanced user testing platforms, entrepreneurs have a plethora of options. Techniques like A/B testing can also provide quantitative data on user preferences. It's essential to choose methods that align with your product stage and audience size, ensuring that the feedback gathered is both relevant and actionable.

The Balance: Feedback vs. Vision

Incorporating user feedback through iterative design is a powerful strategy for continuous product improvement. It places the user at the heart of the development process, ensuring that their needs and preferences shape the product's evolution.

While user feedback is invaluable, it's crucial to strike a balance between incorporating feedback and staying true to the product's core vision. Not all feedback will align with the product's long-term goals or the entrepreneur's vision. It's essential to discern which feedback to act upon and which to set aside, ensuring that the product remains coherent and purpose-driven.

CHAPTER-15

ACCESSIBILITY IN UX

INTRODUCTION TO ACCESSIBILITY

The practice of ensuring that products, content, and applications are useful and accessible to individuals with disabilities is known as Accessibility, in the context of technology and design. In UI/UX Design, Accessibility aims to give people with disabilities the same opportunities, a similar user experience, and the ability to fully participate in society as people without disabilities. There are many different facets of accessibility, such as digital material, physical spaces, transportation, and more.

A11Y - Accessibility's Other Name

A11Y is the abbreviation—a numeronym, to be exact—for accessibility, where "11" represents the number of letters between the letters A and Y. Often, people in the design field use the shorthand on social media or in blogs when they refer to accessibility-related topics and have a limited word or character count.

We can pronounce A11Y as "A-one-one-Y," "A-eleven-Y" or even as "ally," but it's best just to say "accessibility." (Fig. 15.1) As with most abbreviations, A11Y is a form of jargon, so be sure to clarify its meaning upfront with any audience that might not understand it, whether in writing or verbally.

Fig. 15.1 Accessibility's Other Name

Accessibility and its type

Accessibility and its type in detail:

Digital Accessibility

- **Web Accessibility:** It is concerned with facilitating the use of websites and web applications by individuals with disabilities. Assistive technology compatibility is improved by using semantic **HTML**, providing captions for movies, assuring keyboard navigation, and building websites that can be navigated by screen readers.
- **Software and Mobile Apps:** Designing user interfaces that can be handled using a variety of input methods, such as touch, voice, or keyboard, is an important component of accessibility in software and mobile apps. It also entails supporting accessibility features on multiple operating systems and providing text equivalents for non-text information.
- **Document Accessibility:** Creating accessible documents means ensuring that text documents (e.g., PDFs) are readable by screen readers, and multimedia presentations (e.g., PowerPoint slides) are designed to accommodate individuals with hearing or visual impairments.

Physical Accessibility

- **Architectural Design:** Including amenities like ramps, larger entrances, and accessible restrooms in the design of public buildings and places makes them wheelchair-friendly. Parking areas and entrances are also accessible.
- **Accessible Transportation:** Alternatives include ramps or lifts on buses, trains, and airplanes, special seating sections for people with disabilities, and audible stop announcements.

Communication Accessibility

- **Sign Language Interpretation:** Having sign language interpreters available for those who are hard of hearing or deaf is essential for productive interaction in a variety of contexts, including conferences, open forums, and professional consultations.
- **Captioning and Subtitling:** People who are deaf or have hearing difficulties, as well as those who might not understand the spoken language, benefit from adding captions and subtitles to videos and live presentations.

Disability, Design & Society

In order to develop inclusive and accessible digital goods and services for people with disabilities, the field of design known as UX (User Experience) design has made disability, design, and society a crucial area of attention. It takes into account the various requirements and capacities of users and aims to remove obstacles that can impede people with disabilities from fully interacting with the digital environment.

Disability

Any physical, cognitive, sensory, or mental impairment that may significantly reduce a person's capacity to engage in daily activities or interact with their environment is referred to as a disability. Disabilities can range considerably from person to person and might be permanent, transitory, or situational. Examples of widespread disabilities include those related to vision, hearing, motor skills, cognition, and neurodiversity (such as autism spectrum disorders).

Accessibility Web Design

Accessibility in web design is when we make websites that everyone, including people with disabilities, can easily use. It means we make sure that people who have trouble seeing, hearing, moving, or understanding can still use and understand the website. We do things like adding descriptions for images so that special software can read them aloud, making it easy to navigate with a keyboard, providing captions or written versions for videos, and making sure the colors on the site are clear for everyone. This kind of design follows rules like the Web Content Accessibility Guidelines to ensure that the website is friendly and useful for all kinds of people.

Importance of Accessibility in Web Design

It is very important for websites to be accessible to all users. As for general people, they can access almost all websites but people with certain disabilities face problems while accessing a website. Designing and making websites that can be accessed by everybody especially people with disability is a necessity in today's world. It allows them the same features and functionalities that others can access. Services like online shopping, online banking, health services, government schemes and programs, etc should be accessible to everybody regardless of their condition. Ensuring that everyone has the same access to online content is necessary.

Points to include in Accessibility in Web Design

- **Including Contrast:** Reading for some people can become hard if a proper contrast between background and the content is not present.
- **Responsiveness:** Responsiveness helps in people to view websites on different viewports which increases the website's accessibility.
- **Including Media Elements:** Including Images and Videos can helps people to visualize and understand stuff that they normally can't understand.
- **Using Symbols:** Some people can not see every color so using symbols with colors to highlight important parts helps people with disability to understand better.

- **Better Identification of Interactive Elements:** Interactive Elements like buttons, links, etc should be easily identifiable so that people can access them easily.
- **Using good Typography and Spacing:** Including different types of texts with different sizes and fonts and using proper spacing to distinguish them helps maintaining the readability.

Benefits of Accessibility in Web Design

- **Higher Web Traffic:** Since the Website becomes accessbile to a higher number of users, the web traffic increases.
- **Better User Experience:** Website being accessible to users with disability helps them gain access to information like everyone else which enhances their Experience with the website.
- **Higher User Engagement:** Higher accessibility of a website leads to users spending more time on the website engaging with its features increasing User Engagement.
- **Improves Website SEO:** Higher User Engagement and Higher web traffic helps the website to get high SERP ranking.
- **Improves Brand Identity:** Making the Brand Website accessible to more people helps improving the brand's reputation and increases awareness about the Brand in the market.
- **Reduces Bounce Rate:** Website being more accessible and Interactive helps in reducing the bounce rate by making users engage with the website more.

Accessibility vs Usability

Since they have similarities, accessibility is sometimes confused with usability. Both overlap and are vital parts of user experience (UX) (Fig. 15.2) design, but there are also key distinctions between them. Usability is concerned with whether designs are effective, efficient and satisfying to use.

Theoretically, this means that usability includes accessibility, since a product that is inaccessible is also unusable to someone with a disability; practically, however, usability tends not to specifically focus on the user experience of people with disabilities. Accessibility, on the other hand, is concerned with whether all users are able to access an equivalent user experience, however they encounter a product or service (e.g., using assistive devices). Unlike usability, accessibility focuses on people with disabilities.

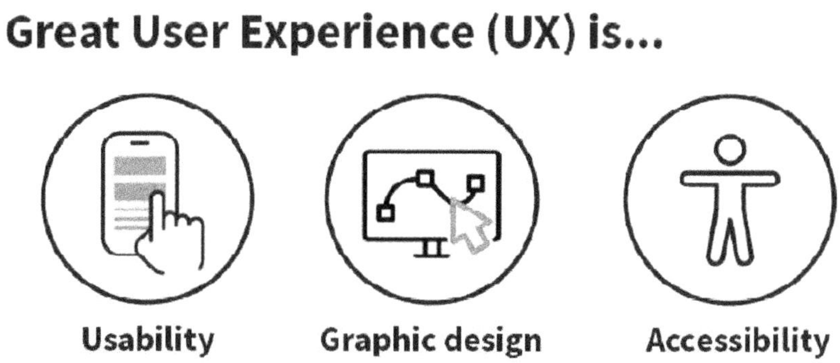

Fig. 15.2 User experience (UX) design

DESIGNING INCLUSIVE USER EXPERIENCES

In short, inclusive design is the practice of intentionally including the needs of users who likely experience exclusion in many aspects of their daily lives due to being part of an oppressed group or a statistical minority. If we don't intentionally include the risk is to unintentionally exclude.

As a UX professional (aspiring, new, or seasoned), you hold the power to shape things—to alter the nature and direction of a project. That is a tremendous responsibility, and it means that you have the ability to influence design decisions in ways that benefit people who are often overlooked or ignored.

In fact, everyone contributing to the design of a digital product—the UXers, of course, but also software developers, product managers, and even talent acquisition professionals - is responsible for the social impact of the solutions they deliver, for the decisions they make and for those they choose not (or forget) to make. This is why understanding the scope and complexity of inclusive design is essential for aspiring tech professionals.

If we don't intentionally include the risk is to unintentionally exclude.

People with disabilities, oppressed minorities, and potentially any user (ourselves included) can and do experience exclusion when interacting with a digital product. Negative, exclusionary, and discriminatory user experiences come in many forms, including:

- Denied access
- Identity demeaning experiences
- Unwanted exposure of sensitive information (real or perceived)
- Frustrating experiences

Taking this into consideration, one way we can define an inclusive design approach is to say that it should enable the delivery of solutions that are not just easy to access, but also make people feel welcomed, safe, and valued.

Fundamental Principles and Practices for Inclusive UX Design

- **Empathy-Driven Design:** Empathy-driven design involves creating interfaces that cater to diverse user needs. For instance, an e-commerce platform offering various font sizes, color schemes, and screen reader compatibility ensures accessibility for users with visual impairments. This approach acknowledges and addresses different abilities and preferences.
- **Collaboration and Co-creation:** Involving diverse stakeholders, such as designers, developers, accessibility experts, and end-users, in the design process ensures a holistic perspective. For instance, when designing a mobile app, involving users from different age groups and backgrounds in usability testing ensures that the interface is intuitive and usable for a broad range of users.
- **Iterative Improvement:** Implementing iterative improvement involves collecting and integrating feedback at various stages of the design process. For instance, after launching a website, conducting regular user testing sessions and analyzing user behavior through heatmaps can highlight areas needing improvement. This continuous feedback loop aids in refining the user experience iteratively.

Implementing Inclusivity in UX Design

- **Color and Visual Accessibility:** Design with sufficient color contrast and consider alternative ways of conveying information for users with visual impairments.
- **Navigation and Screen Reader Compatibility:** Ensure clear and intuitive navigation, coupled with compatibility with screen readers and assistive technologies.
- **Content Adaptation for Different User Needs:** Craft content that is easy to understand and adaptable for users with varying literacy levels, languages, or cognitive abilities.
- **Inclusivity Testing and User Feedback:** Integrate inclusive usability testing throughout the design process. Seek feedback from diverse users to identify potential barriers and improve inclusivity.

Advancing Inclusive UX Design

- **Inclusive Design Systems:** Develop design systems that inherently incorporate inclusivity and accessibility features.
- **Continuous Learning and Adaptation:** Stay updated with evolving inclusivity trends, guidelines, and technologies to adapt your designs for diverse user needs.

- **Advocacy and Awareness:** Advocate for inclusive design practices within your organization and spread awareness about the importance of inclusivity in UX design.

Inclusive Design Takes Accessibility a Step Further

Accessibility is about people with disabilities being able to use a design. Inclusive design takes the process a step further to ensure the website or app in question serves everyone who visits that website. Inclusive design is a mindset. Accessibility is one outcome of that mindset.

People around the world visit websites for a variety of reasons: for information, to shop, and to be entertained. Those people come from a variety of backgrounds and can't always interact with a site in the same ways. What happens when someone visits a website for information but has limited literacy skills? If audio or video content is available, they can access information that would be off-limits if it were purely text-based.

The inclusive design process aims to create websites that are welcoming to all. It's common sense to think about that process in terms of ***including*** different groups, but it pays for designers also to consider what groups are typically ***excluded.***

When approaching a new design project, designers should think about the groups that typically ***haven't*** had easy access to existing products. The example with limited literacy skills mentioned above is one such situation. But what other groups may be excluded?

Consider socioeconomic factors. Information or situations that a middle-class person from North America or Europe might be familiar with as part of their daily lives might be entirely foreign to a poor person in Southeast Asia, for example. The opposite is also true.

Creating of inclusive designs

Creating inclusive designs is a fairly straightforward process. The first step is setting up a team with a variety of perspectives. While it's unlikely a design team will include the perspectives of every potential visitor to a website, the more diverse the team, the more comprehensive the results will be.

When talking about diverse design teams, there are several factors to consider: people from different socioeconomic backgrounds, people from different cultures, people with differing abilities, people of different genders, people from different parts of the country (and world), and different ages.

When a team can incorporate different perspectives from the outset, the designs they create will be leagues ahead of designers that come from a design team that all share similar backgrounds and abilities.

However, a diverse team only goes so far. After the first iterations of a design are created, designers need to incorporate user testing with a heterogeneous group of people. Look for people who represent the broadest range of potential end users of a product.

Accessibility guidelines sometimes serve more like a band-aid than a real solution. Real solutions exist in removing barriers altogether, rather than just giving people tools to adapt to them. Every website and digital product will likely need to approach these solutions differently, but thinking about them critically will help the inclusive design process.

Microsoft has proposed inclusive design principles that are worth studying and incorporating. They focus on recognizing exclusion as the first step toward inclusive UX. They encourage designers to learn from diversity.

But the most interesting and useful takeaway from Microsoft's inclusive design principles is the idea of solving for one but extending to many. This idea proposes that the constraints of designing for people with disabilities benefits all users in the end. All people share common experiences—they all have motivations and build relationships—and those commonalities can serve as the foundation for creating universally beneficial designs.

Take an example from Microsoft's Inclusive Design Toolkit. A product might be designed for a person who only has one hand (a permanent disability), for example. The obvious extension of that would be that the same design could be helpful to anyone who has a temporary hand injury. And there are extensions beyond that. A new parent who often has their newborn in one arm and only uses one hand for most interactions could also benefit. There are multiple use cases where an interface that only requires one hand to use is useful beyond only helping the person it was adapted for initially.

Benefits of inclusive UX design for businesses.

1. Expand customer reach

Inclusive UX design caters to a broader range of potential users. For example, an e-commerce site that accommodates different languages, age groups, and abilities can attract a diverse customer base globally.

2. Improve customer satisfaction and loyalty

Your business can enhance user experience and customer satisfaction by catering to diverse needs. For instance, a language learning app for tech-savvy millennials and less tech-savvy older adults can foster brand loyalty across multiple demographics.

3. Enhance brand reputation

Inclusive design signals your company's commitment to social responsibility. For instance, a streaming service that offers robust closed captioning and audio description options demonstrates a commitment to accessibility, improving public perception.

4. Gain a competitive advantage

Inclusive design can help your organization stand out from its competitors. As an example, a fitness app that includes workout modifications for individuals with physical limitations stands out in a crowded market of apps primarily targeting non-disabled individuals.

5. Reduce long-term costs

Designing with inclusion in mind from the start avoids costly adaptations later. Consider a restaurant review platform. Designing it with features like image descriptions for the visually impaired and easy navigation for those with motor skill issues could save costly post-launch redesign expenses.

6. Boost revenue and profit

With the above-mentioned points, inclusive design can ultimately drive higher profits. A travel website that's not only accessible to people with disabilities but also caters to a variety of language preferences and cultural nuances could tap into new markets and increase potential revenue.

Building inclusivity in your UX design process

1. Tie inclusive design into your business objectives

Integrating inclusive design into your business objectives isn't just a nice-to-have – it's a strategic advantage. It goes hand-in-hand with reaching a wider audience, fostering brand loyalty, and driving innovation.

Let's say your business goal is to take your brand global. As the team's designer, you must consider language options, regional date formats, and culturally appropriate visuals. You also need to be aware of cultural differences in symbols, colors, and web regulations for each country.

2. Define your organization's inclusive UX design principles

Inclusive design principles should be foundational to your UX approach, like Airbnb's comprehensive guidelines emphasizing universal accessibility. The key is to define your inclusive principles, mirroring your organization's ethos and the diversity of your user base.

For instance, these principles could focus on enhancing accessibility – such as ensuring good color contrast for users with visual impairments or incorporating alternative text for images. Or they could underline the need for gender-neutral language and diverse representation in your visuals. These principles will serve as your team's roadmap, guiding design decisions toward creating a user experience that respects and addresses the needs of all users.

3. Look out for exclusion in your products or services

Every user should feel that your product is built for them, not for someone else. Look out for exclusion or for those parts of your design that, though unintentional, might inadvertently create boundaries for some users.

Consider a fitness app as an example. If it only showcases young, fit individuals, it could inadvertently send a message that it's designed only for a certain group. This could potentially alienate older users, or those who are less fit or just starting their fitness journey. The key is to develop a keen eye for these exclusions, whether in your imagery, your copy, or even how you structure your user interface.

4. Build a diverse design team

When it comes to building a great design team, it's important to think beyond just skills. Diversity is key. This means having a mix of different age groups, cultures, gender identities, abilities, and a variety of professional backgrounds and specialties in UX design.

A diverse team can better anticipate and address potential design issues because of their wide range of experiences and viewpoints. For example, a team member with a background in healthcare could bring invaluable insights about making a product more usable for busy healthcare professionals.

5. Get started with user research and usability testing

If you want to be more inclusive as a design team, there's no better guide than your users. Get to know the people you're designing through research and user testing.

These approaches help you understand not just what they want but what they need, enabling you and your team to cater to them more effectively.

New to user research? Read User research questions: Questions I explore the most as a user researcher.

Not sure how to get started with testing? Check out our library of usability testing guides.

6. Use inclusive imagery and diverse illustrations

Inclusivity in design isn't limited to functionality; it also extends to visuals. Just like a good storyteller, your design should reflect the diverse identities of your audience. This is where inclusive imagery and diverse illustrations come into play.

Take Microsoft, for example. They've developed a library of inclusive stock imagery representing a wide spectrum of people. By doing this, they tell their users, "We see you, we value you, and we've designed with you in mind."

Applying this mindset to your designs means incorporating visuals representing people of different races, ages, abilities, genders, and other facets of identity. It might be an illustration featuring people with different skin tones or an image showing someone using a wheelchair.

These inclusive visuals serve two important purposes:

- They help every user see themselves in your design, promoting a sense of belonging.
- They show your commitment to inclusivity, not just in design but also in the broader sense of your organization's values.

7. Write inclusive copy

Words, just like visuals, carry weight and can shape how users perceive your product and whether they feel included. Writing inclusive copy and content is using gender-neutral and non-discriminatory language, avoiding stereotypes, and making every reader feel acknowledged and respected.

Consider a simple greeting on a website. Instead of "Hey, guys!" you might use a more inclusive phrase like "Hello, everyone!". Similarly, when asking for personal details, offer a range of gender options or consider whether that information is even necessary.

8. Be mindful of the reading experience

Want to make sure everyone can easily read and enjoy your content? Consider font size, line spacing, color contrast, and typeface. These may seem like small details, but they can make a big difference for users with visual impairments or who prefer different viewing settings.

Dark mode can also be a good option for reducing eye strain, especially when using screens in low-light conditions.

Check out Apple's Human Interface Guidelines for more tips on creating an inclusive and comfortable user experience.

9. Provide a wide range of demographic identifiers

Allowing users to self-identify through a comprehensive set of demographic options demonstrates respect for their identities and acknowledges the diverse makeup of your user base.

In practice, this involves providing a broad range of options in forms where users are asked to provide demographic information. For example, in the gender field, instead of providing just 'male' and 'female' options, consider including 'non-binary', 'prefer not to say', or an 'other' field where users can write in their identification.

You can also use this approach for other demographic characteristics like race, ethnicity, and age. For instance, when asking about age, rather than having specific age brackets, consider having a fill-in-the-blank field to avoid potential age discrimination.

Offering these choices also helps create a database that more accurately reflects the diversity of your users, which can further inform and improve your design decisions.

10. Design clear affordances

Affordance refers to the properties of an object that indicate how it can be used. In UX design, affordances are cues that tell users how they can interact with the interface. For example, a raised button suggests it can be clicked or tapped, and a slider might have visual cues indicating that the user can drag it.

Designing clear affordances in your designs means making these interactive cues obvious so users don't have to guess or experiment to figure out how to use your interface. Good affordance design enhances accessibility, aiding users with cognitive, visual, or motor impairments to interact more easily with your product.

ENSURING ACCESSIBILITY COMPLIANCE

It is often thought that accessibility deals only with people who have special needs. For example, screen readers are used by individuals with visual impairments. This is not true for UX designers. When it comes to the design of a product or service, accessibility refers to all the ways in which a design can be made more useful. This can include special physical needs and also the context in which a product is being used. For example, when you're using a navigation application while driving, the situation changes depending on whether you have any physical disabilities or not.

It is important to consider the needs of individuals with certain disabilities and to create assistive technologies so that their needs can be fulfilled in a comprehensive manner. To meet the needs of all the users, a UX designer needs a set of principles that are beneficial to all. This is what a UX team is really after when referring to accessibility in UX design.

Fig. 15.3 Accessibility Problems in UX Design (Toptal)

Accessibility is not just usability

Accessibility is often confused with usability, and this can set very low standards for a design to be labeled as accessible. A design is regarded as usable if it is effective, responsive, and interactive, thus giving an overall satisfying experience to the audience. Accessibility, on the other hand, ensures that the design takes care of the users' special needs and provides an equitable experience to all the individuals in the audience group. It is one of the UX design principles that all designers need to be considerate of.

This means that all the users are given equal importance, and the needs of all the target customers are prioritized irrespective of their physical and/or cognitive disabilities. Individuals in the target audience may have different ability levels when it comes to interacting with technology, but this should not impact the level of satisfaction a design provides.

Common accessibility concerns

It is important to take a look at common accessibility concerns when designing a new product or service. Most of these are linked to the physical abilities and disabilities of the users.

- The experiences of individuals who are visually impaired can be negatively impacted by the lack of sufficient contrast.
- The media content with audio may not be useful for hearing impaired users.
- For forms with predefined input methods, multiple modes may be required when targeting a diverse audience.
- When a product or service is being used on smaller, hand-held devices, it may require specific features to be responsive.

- When the users interact with a design in different environments, such as driving a car, the mobility concerns need due consideration.
- If a product or service has new and unique features, it may require a tutorial so the users can learn how to interact with the design.
- To provide all this information, an accessibility statement and/or disabilities form needs to be created and made available to the audience.

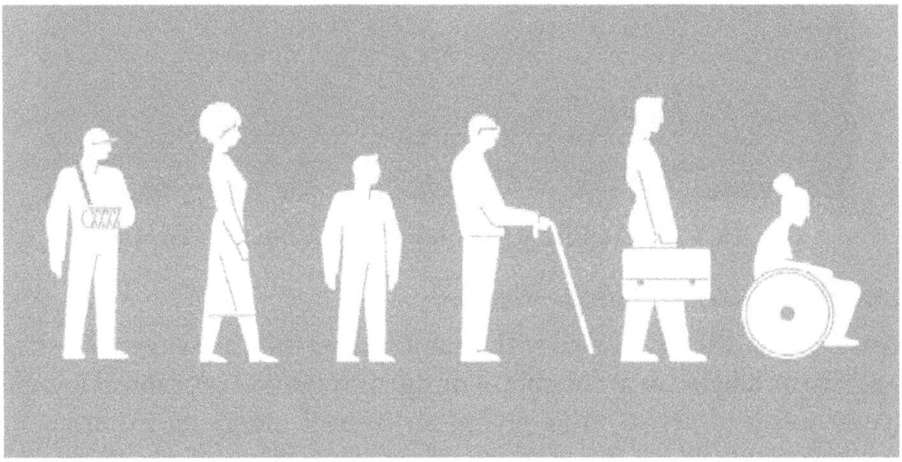

Fig. 15.4 Common Accessibility Issues in UX Design (Toptal)

Accessibility UX design principles

Given that there is a diverse range of concerns when it comes to designing for accessibility. It is important to ask how can UI/UX designers take care of all these aspects, ensuring that their products and services are representative, inclusive, usable, and useful.

Accessibility guidelines for UX designers

1. Create user personas

One of the most important guidelines for accessibility in UX design is to create user personas that are representative of a diverse audience. The creation of personas may vary based on the nature of the product, but designers need to be careful while selecting the final personas. Thinking about individuals with special needs in all audience groups is always helpful.

2. Design for all platforms and devices

Along with different audiences, it is also essential to design for different devices and platforms. In today's digital world, the users interacting with a design may use devices with various operating systems, screen sizes, and functionalities. It is important to consider the responsiveness of a design on such devices and platforms.

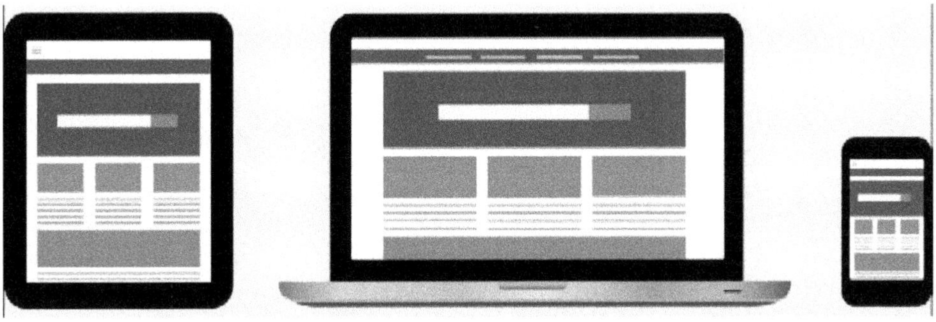

Fig. 15.5 Accessible Designs for All Platforms (Pixabay)

3. Organize the content logically

The accessibility of your content, whether in the form of a mobile application, a website, or a physical product, is directly related to the extent of understandability. This is why it is important to organize the content in a logical manner is essential for accessibility. One way to achieve this is by creating an information architecture that can comprehensively illustrate the organization of the content, thus making it easier to address the needs of the target audience.

4. Ensure consistency in design

To make a design useful and accessible, there should be some level of consistency in the product or service. This means that the users should be able to navigate through the design with ease without coming across any unexpected and frustrating surprises. Consistent designs are also helpful to individuals with disabilities that require less effort in understanding and are more compatible with assistive devices and tools.

5. Use accessible fonts

The way your written content appears can have a huge impact on the overall accessibility of the design. It is, therefore, important to choose fonts that are easy to read and do not cause any trouble for individuals with special needs. You should always use simple, sans serif fonts for most of the content. If you have to use decorative fonts, only do so for headings and title texts, restricting their use to a minimum.

6. Choose appropriate color contrast

Choosing the right colors is one of the most important and challenging tasks when it comes to accessibility. There are certain limitations, such as branding and aesthetics, that dictate the choice of colors. Here, designers must not forget that it is not easy for everyone to distinguish between all the colors. Therefore, color contrast should be selected appropriately such that it does not hinder the readability of the content.

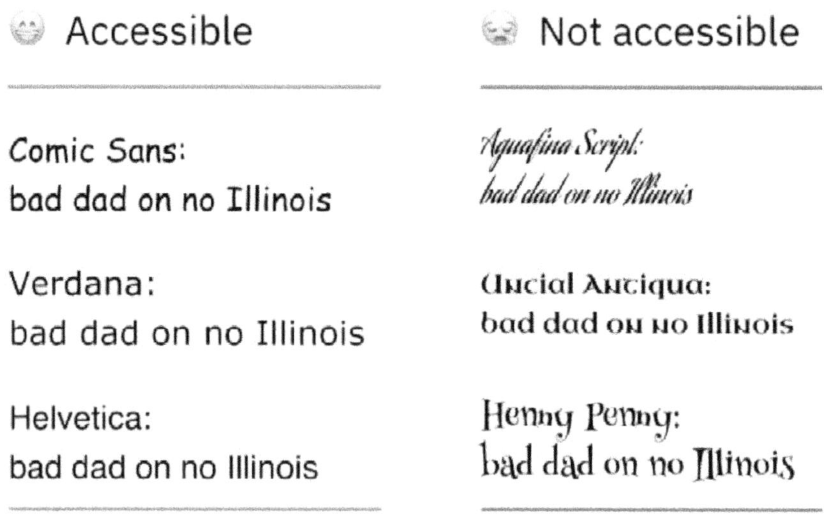

Fig. 15.6 Fonts to Create Accessible Websites (Alex Chen on Medium)

7. Include alt-text for media content

One of the simple and highly effective ways to improve the accessibility of online content is to include alt-text with all the media content. This means that all the images, videos, and animations should be accompanied by a brief descriptive text that can be picked up by screen readers. This way, individuals with visual impairments can also understand what the image is about and what its purpose is in the design.

8. Provide transcriptions and subtitles

In addition to alt-text, transcriptions and subtitles are also strong tools for creating accessible designs. These not only help individuals with hearing and visual impairments but also cater to the needs of a global audience. This is where designers can also include the transcriptions in multiple languages so that a diverse audience can interact with the product or service.

9. Avoid excessive animation

It can be tempting to include a lot of moving images in the design. This choice demands some careful consideration. It is advisable to include a mix of text and visual elements in the content so that all the users can interact with it in an equitable manner. Additionally, moving images - particularly flashing images - can be of concern to some individuals and should, therefore, be avoided.

10. Ensure meaningful anchor text

When inserting links in the content, make sure that the anchor text is meaningful. Inserting long URLs in the content can be frustrating for individuals using screen readers. Meaningful links not only improve the readability and accessibility of the content but also add to your credibility, making the content useful at the same time.

11. Use proper headings and HTML tags

Almost all the assistive technology seeks help from headings and other HTML tags to make sense of the content. Therefore, to ensure accessibility of a design, it is essential that these standards are taken into consideration when creating content, particularly when it comes to websites and mobile applications.

12. Make the design screen-reader friendly

When designing for a diverse audience with varying physical and cognitive needs, screen readers are a common tool to consider. According to accessiBe, around 7.3 million people in the US rely on screen readers to navigate the web. It will be wrong to neglect this tool when designing a product or service with any online presence. All of your online content should be accessible and readable using a screen reader (Fig. 15.7).

Fig. 15.7 Audio Resources for Visually Impaired Users (EBSCO)

13. Include keyboard shortcuts

Keyboard shortcuts are an excellent way to provide alternative navigation for any online content. When designing a product for the online world, make sure that your content can be accessed with the help of only the keyboard. The converse should also be true: if a user interacts only with a mouse or trackpad, the design should be equally responsive.

14. Use accessibility tools

There are a number of standards and tools to test the accessibility of your digital designs. The World Wide Web Consortium (W3C) has a rich database which the designers can seek help from. The standards set by W3C are extremely helpful in creating accessible online content. Similarly, accessibility testing tools such as WAVE can identify major issues on a website in no time. UI/UX designers can then address these issues and make the design more responsive and accessible.

Fig. 15.8 Tools for Web Content Accessibility Guidelines (WAVE)

15. Test with different users

In any UX design project, user research and usability testing are of prime importance. This also holds true when it comes to the creation of accessible designs. At different stages in the design process, UI/UX professionals must test the product or service with different users. The users selected should have varying physical and cognitive needs, thus making sure that the input of a diverse range of users is being incorporated into the design.

Part VI: UX in Different Contexts

CHAPTER-16

MOBILE UX DESIGN

UX IN DIFFERENT CONTEXTS

One of the key focal points of user-centered design is the contexts in which the designs will be used. For technology products and services, contexts of use include a potentially broad array of factors – physical and social environments, human abilities and disabilities, cultural issues and similar.

Contexts describe the actual circumstances of use. While not all of the aspects mentioned above apply in each case, it is important to consider what is and isn't relevant. For example, almost all products and services operate within a legal context that requires them to be operable by people with disabilities. Other legal contexts govern the use of personal data – the GDPR in Europe, for instance – the ages for which certain content may be shown, along with strict laws in some locations around gambling and betting.

Environmental and physical contexts may not be particularly relevant to most websites, but this can change dramatically for systems used outside the typical home or office. Examples include external Automated Teller Machines (Fig. 16.1) ("cash machines" or "cash dispensers"), computing systems used in farming – some of which must be steam cleaned – and systems used for stock control in unheated warehouses or, more challenging still, cold stores (Fig. 16.2).

Fig. 16.1 Cash dispensers are a common example of an unusual context of use.

Fig. 16.2 Desktop computers are not always an appropriate solution. Here a warehouse worker scans stock using a portable reader and tablet.

Contexts of Use in HCI

In user-centered and user experience design, one of our main concerns is usability. The international standard on the ergonomics of human-system interaction (see Learn More About Contexts of Use) defines usability as "...the extent to which a system, product or service can be used by specified users to achieve specified goals with effectiveness, efficiency and satisfaction in a specified context of use."

Notice that the very definition of usability depends on the context of use. This isn't hard to understand outside of software systems. But because contexts of use are outside of the normal considerations in most software development methods, contexts are usually overlooked.

The standard goes on to describe the components:

- "The context of use comprises a combination of users, goals, tasks, resources, and the technical, physical and social, cultural and organizational environments in which a system, product or service is used."

This is a much broader definition of contexts than is used in practice, but it is complete. Less formal definitions tend to group users, goals, tasks and resources separately from the environments as described above. However, the benefit of grouping all of these elements together becomes obvious when considering how the standard describes achieving usability in design and development. The steps are:

- Understand and specify the context of use.
- Specify the user requirements including usability considerations.

- Produce design solutions making use of the above.
- Evaluate the design solutions.

When referring to a complete system, the context of use would include all users along with their respective goals, tasks and the required resources as well as the environmental contexts across all of those factors. These include

- **Technical environment** – equipment and applications, including hardware, furniture; information (data the users have access to) relevant to the tasks; support services, either human- or system-based (such as assistive technology).
- **Physical environment** – where the system will be used and what the environmental factors would be (consider the warehouse, farm or cold storage examples earlier).
- **Social, cultural and organizational environment** – other people involved (such as stakeholders) and the relationships between them, the organizational structure, language, legislation, cultural norms and values, work practices, group working and privacy.

Contexts of Use in Mobile

The context of mobile use is very different from that of desktops. In this video, the founder of Experience Dynamics Frank Spillers shares practical tips on how to understand context of use and how to take it into account when designing for mobile devices.

Mobile user's context that included:

- Personal goals (such as identity, status, and social interaction).
- Attention levels (complete or partial, intermittent or continuous).
- Tasks (for example, make calls, send a video, or get directions).
- Device constraints (including, among other things, software, sensors, battery and network).
- Secondary activities (such as walking, eating, etc.).
- Environment (sound, light, space, etc.).
- Culture (economics, religion, law, etc.).

INTRODUCTION TO MOBILE UX DESIGN

It is the responsibility of UX designers to create a product that is enjoyable to use and provides a relevant and meaningful experience for the user. In mobile UX design, it is crucial to consider the entire customer journey, including interactions, content, and sound design.

The difference between UX and UI (user interface) is important, as UX design encompasses much more than just the graphical elements of the UI. Mobile User Experience design goes beyond the graphical representation and thinks about the emotions, goals, and challenges of users.

Importance of mobile UX Design

The goal of mobile UX designers is to design the experience that users have before, during, and after using the app. Good mobile UX design should be useful, usable, desirable, findable, accessible, and credible, as outlined below:

- **Useful:** The system must fulfill the users' wishes and needs.
- **Usable:** The system must be as easy and self-descriptive as possible.
- **Desirable:** The style of the system must evoke positive emotions and appreciation. Users must want to use your system.
- **Findable:** Navigating through the system must be easy and self-descriptive. Moreover, users must find important information quickly.
- **Accessible:** Disabled users, e.g., users with very poor eyesight, must have the chance to use your system and get the same user experience as non-disabled users.
- **Credible:** Users must trust you and your product.

Differences between desktop and mobile app UX Design

To give your users the best experience possible, you must know the differences between desktop and mobile app UX design. You shouldn't follow the same design principles for both.

1. Size

Desktop: Computers are big, so you can put a lot of information on one page and it will still look great and organized.

Smartphone: If you were to shrink your website to the regular size of a 4–5 ½ inch mobile device without changing anything, it would look awful and confuse your users.

Pay attention: You have to decide which information is important enough to make it to a smartphone design. If something doesn't need to be there, skip it, or place it under a menu or on another page.

Moreover, because of the bigger screen size of desktops, you can arrange your content in several columns next to each other. For a great mobile UX design, you have to structure your content in just one column. Users scroll down to see all the content.

Session replay is a valuable tool that allows you to see how your mobile app performs on different device sizes and configurations. By watching recordings of user sessions, you can get a better understanding of how users interact with your app and identify any pain points or areas for improvement.

This can be particularly useful for identifying issues specific to mobile devices, such as content that is too small to read or buttons that are too close together to use accurately on a touchscreen. With UXCam's session replay, you can fine-tune your mobile UX design to ensure that users have a seamless and enjoyable experience no matter what device they are using.

2. Screen orientation

Desktop: They are horizontally oriented. Users can't change this orientation.

Smartphone: On mobile devices, users have the option to change the screen orientation if they want. 94% of users use their smartphone vertically, while 6% do so horizontally.

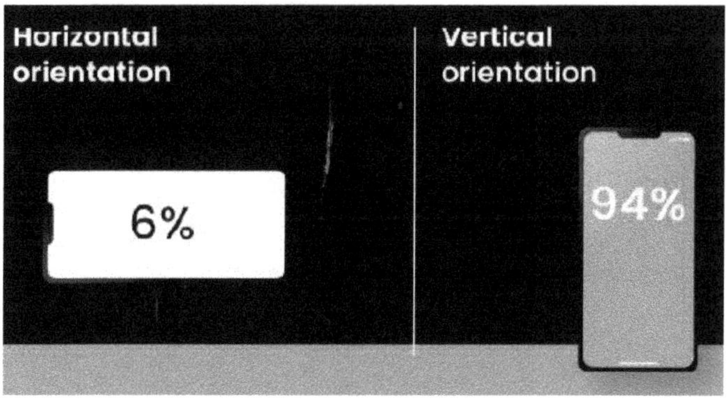

Fig. 16.3 Screen orientation

Designers should take this into consideration when creating mobile interfaces. Portrait mode is typically better suited for tasks that involve reading and scrolling, while landscape mode is better suited for tasks that involve watching videos or playing games.

To accommodate for this, designers should ensure that the layout and design of the interface adapt seamlessly to different screen orientations. This means that the layout should be designed to work well in both portrait and landscape mode and that the design elements should be optimized for both orientations.

You can track changes in behavior based on screen orientation with heatmaps. For example, a heatmap may show that a button placed at the bottom of the screen is not getting enough attention in portrait mode, but is getting more attention in landscape mode. This information can help designers make informed decisions about how to optimize the layout and design for different orientations.

UXCam's **heatmaps** can also be used to track user behavior over time, which can be especially useful when comparing usage between different screen orientations. This can help designers understand how users engage with the interface over time, and can help identify any changes in behavior that may be related to changes in screen orientation.

3. Screen size

UX designers must take into account the fact that many users prefer to use their mobile phones with one thumb. 49% of users prefer to use their mobile phones with just one thumb (Fig. 16.4).

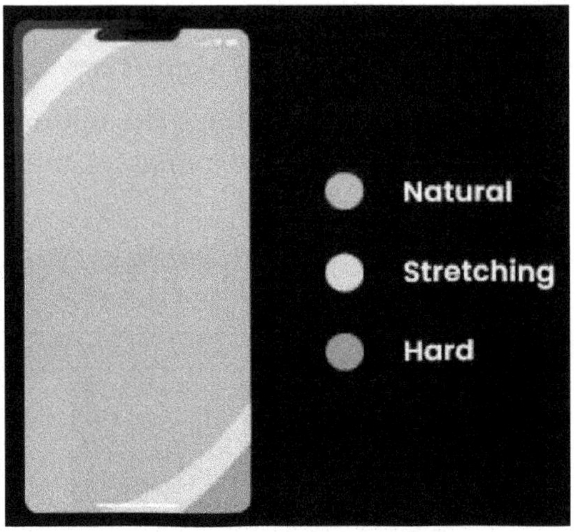

Fig. 16.4 Screen size

The bigger the screen size, the fewer points that can be reached comfortably with one thumb. This means that the layout and design of the interface should be optimized for one-handed use, with important elements and buttons placed within easy reach of the thumb.

Furthermore, this also means that designers should be mindful of the screen size when designing for mobile devices. The larger the screen size, the fewer points on the screen can be comfortably reached with one thumb. This means that designers must carefully consider the placement of elements and buttons on larger screens to ensure that they are easily accessible for one-handed use.

Pay attention: To make sure that the mobile app or website is easily accessible for one-handed use, designers can use techniques like:

- Placing important elements and buttons within thumb's reach.
- Utilizing gesture-based navigation to minimize the need to reach for buttons.
- Making sure that the layout is consistent across different screen sizes.

- Avoiding placing important elements or buttons at the top or bottom of the screen, as these areas are harder to reach with one thumb.

By taking these factors into account, designers can create mobile interfaces that are comfortable and easy to use for the majority of users, regardless of screen size.

Again, heatmaps can be a valuable tool for analyzing user behavior on different screen sizes. For example, heatmaps can show how users engage with the interface on small screens, such as those of smartphones, versus larger screens, such as tablets.

A heatmap may show that a button placed at the bottom of the screen is getting a lot of attention on a smartphone, but is not getting enough attention on a tablet.

This information can help designers make informed decisions about how to optimize the layout and design for different screen sizes.

4. Navigation and input

Desktop: A keyboard and a mouse are the most common input devices for desktops. Sometimes you will find desktops with a touchscreen but, even then, those tend to have an additional mouse and keyboard of their own.

Smartphone: On a mobile device, users don't have a mouse or a physical keyboard to rely on. To type or select elements, mobile device users have to use their touchscreens.

Pay attention: If your users have to type anything — for example, during the sign-in process — you should offer them a keyboard. Help your users and make the input much more comfortable by offering them different keyboards depending on what they have to enter.

If the information requested by you is a phone number or a ZIP code, a normal keyboard won't do; offer them a numeric keyboard instead (Fig. 16.5).

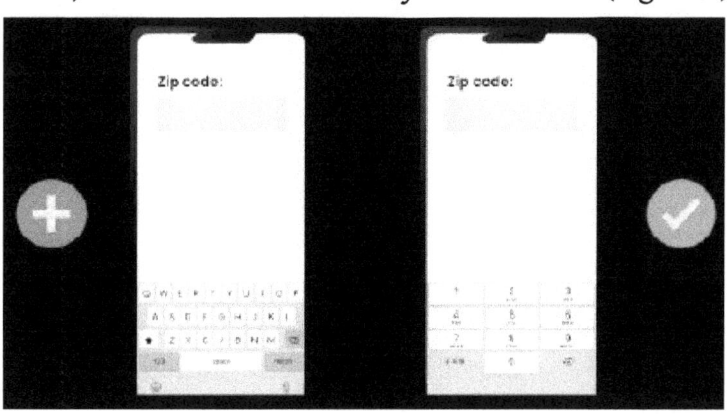

Fig. 16.5

The size of the action icons is also important. Too many action icons too close to each other, and the chance of missteps is high. Make sure that the buttons are big enough to be tapped with a finger.

Mobile devices go beyond allowing users to touch buttons; there are other gestures that users can perform. The most common ones are scrolling, sliding, pulling down, and tapping (long, short, or double taps). Pulling down, for example, is a common gesture for refreshing a page.

By analyzing user gestures, such as taps, swipes, and scrolls, you can gain a deeper understanding of how users navigate your mobile app and identify areas for improvement. **UXCam** is a mobile app analytics tool that enables you to track user gestures in real time, providing valuable insights into how users interact with your app.

For example, you may discover that certain buttons or links are difficult for users to tap accurately, or that certain screens are causing users to become frustrated or confused. With this information, you can make changes to your app's user interface and design to improve the overall user experience. Overall, tracking user gestures with UXCam can help you to optimize your app's UX and ensure that it is as intuitive and enjoyable as possible for your users.

5. Environment

Desktop: Users often use desktops for more serious or important tasks e.g., working in the office or shopping.

Smartphone: Mobile phones provide more personalization than desktops. That is why they are used everywhere; at the restaurant, at home, in the bathroom... anywhere. Sure, you can install a desktop PC in your bathroom or take it with you on the subway to read the news. But most users will go for their smartphone in this kind of situation.

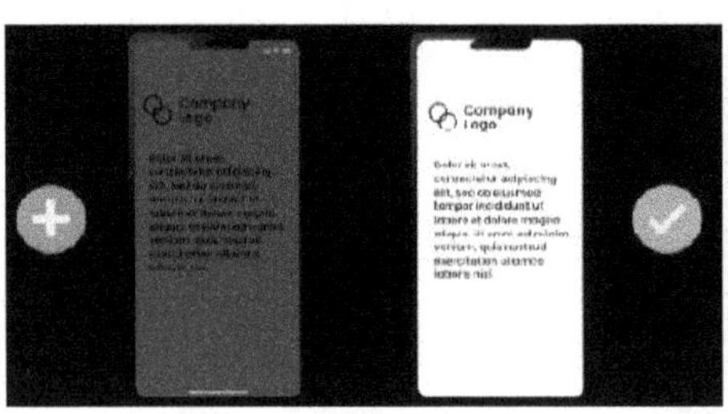

Fig. 16.6

Fig. 16.7

Pay attention: Realizing that users will access your app anywhere leads you to understand that your app should be easy-to-use outdoors. Design your app with high-contrast colors to ensure that your users can read everything, even if the sun is shining on their smartphones.

Sometimes, users don't trust mobile apps. They may second guess giving their private data away to a mobile app. To not overstrain your users, only ask for what is really important for using the app. Minimize the need for input for a perfect mobile design. This doesn't mean that you should add unnecessary questions to a desktop app. Even on desktops, users will drop off if they feel like you're asking for too much information.

6. Split screen

Desktop: Users sometimes open several apps and websites simultaneously. For example, your app and a calculator. They can have them both open at the same time side by side.

Smartphone: Newer smartphones support split screens too, but it still isn't a commonly used feature, definitely not as much as on a desktop.

You should care about most of your users, who probably have smartphones without the split-screen function. If users need to compare exchange rates or check the location of a town to fully use your app and you don't offer this functionality, they may have to leave your app to open a calculator or Google Maps.

The issue here is that with this comes the temptation to completely close the app, whether consciously or subconsciously. Sometimes users forget that they were on a different app to begin with because they get distracted by another one. Other times they get annoyed at apps that don't come with everything they need to properly use them. Try to keep users on your app by offering them everything they need. Moreover, don't take users to a browser to complete actions like registration or login.

7. Symbols

Symbols are relevant for both desktop and mobile devices. When users go on different apps, they learn the meaning of common symbols and icons.

Ensure that you use typical symbols how they're usually used. The unexpected use of symbols confuses users and they may not want to continue using your app.

8. Seamless design

If you want to offer your app for both mobile and desktop devices, you need to consider creating a seamless design.

CHALLENGES AND BEST PRACTICES IN MOBILE UX

Challenges

Screen size and resolution

Mobile devices come in various shapes and sizes, with different screen dimensions and pixel densities. This means that mobile UX designers have to design for multiple screen sizes and resolutions, and ensure that their layouts, fonts, icons, images, and interactions are responsive and adaptable to different devices. They also have to consider the readability, visibility, and accessibility of their content and elements, and avoid cluttering the screen with too much information or functionality.

Touch input and gestures

Mobile devices rely on touch input and gestures as the primary mode of interaction, unlike desktop computers that use mouse and keyboard. This means that mobile UX designers have to design for touch-friendly and intuitive interfaces, and use gestures that are familiar and consistent with the mobile platform and the user's expectations. They also have to account for the size and position of the user's fingers, and avoid accidental taps, swipes, or pinches that could disrupt the user experience.

Connectivity and performance

Mobile devices depend on wireless networks and cellular data for connectivity, which can vary in speed, reliability, and availability depending on the location and situation of the user. This means that mobile UX designers have to design for offline scenarios, and ensure that their applications can handle network interruptions, errors, or delays gracefully. They also have to optimize the performance and efficiency of their applications, and reduce the loading time, bandwidth consumption, and battery drain of their features and functions.

Context and environment

Mobile devices are used in different contexts and environments, such as at home, at work, on the go, or in public places. This means that mobile UX designers have to design for different user scenarios, needs, and goals, and provide relevant and personalized content and services to the user. They also have to consider the environmental factors that could affect the user experience, such as noise, lighting, temperature, or privacy, and adapt their interfaces and interactions accordingly.

Diversity and inclusivity

Mobile devices are used by a diverse and inclusive range of users, with different backgrounds, cultures, languages, abilities, preferences, and expectations. This means that mobile UX designers have to design for diversity and inclusivity, and ensure that their applications are accessible, usable, and enjoyable for all users. They also have to respect the user's identity, values, and choices, and avoid stereotypes, biases, or discrimination in their content and design.

Mobile UX design is a challenging but rewarding field that requires creativity, empathy, and problem-solving skills. By overcoming these challenges, mobile

UX designers can create meaningful and memorable user experiences for mobile devices.

Best Practices for Mobile UX Design

Mobile UX design is tricky. As stated previously, there are so many things we have to consider, including the growing list of mobile devices, the ways people interact with them, and the fact that people want consistent and pleasurable experiences across all device types.

Google's 25 Mobile UX Design Tips

In 2015, Google published 25 mobile UX design best practices based on internal research. These tips were recently updated to bring them more up-to-date. The author also includes a downloadable PDF of all 25 tips that is nice to keep handy for any mobile UX project.

Apple's Human Interface Guidelines

Another great resource to keep handy is Apple's Human Interface Guidelines for mobile design (Fig. 16.8). They are easy to read with a beautiful layout and peppered with best practices, tips, and Apple's own take on design principles. For mobile UX designers these guidelines are a great resource for delivering high quality user experiences.

Additional Mobile UX Best Practices

Here are a few more mobile UX design best practices that might not be as well known as Google's, but are just as important for mobile designers to take into account.

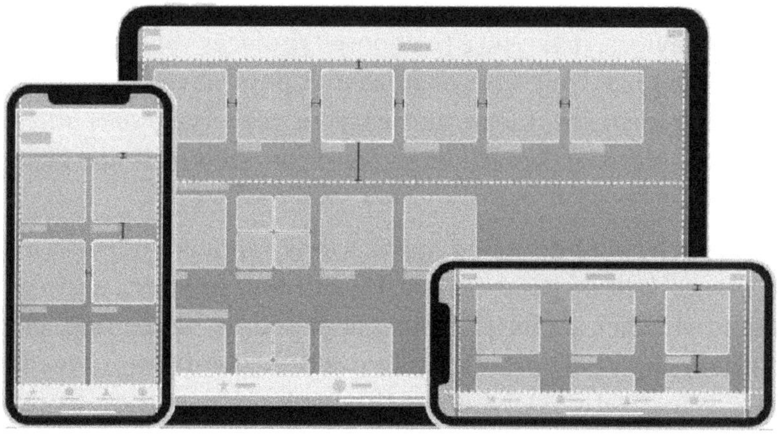

Fig. 16.8 Apple's Human Interface Guidelines for mobile design

- **UX Research.** At a certain point, we may feel inclined to get right into mockups or prototypes, however, doing proper UX research first is something that cannot be understated. Always remember that "you are not your user," and a positive user experience relies on thorough UX research in every case. Here is Adobe's comprehensive guide to UX research methods for further reference.

- **Clutter.** We have all experienced the anxiety of a cluttered desktop—imagine it on a mobile device! Every added button, image, piece of content, etc., makes things that much more complicated. It's a good idea to get rid of anything in a mobile UI that isn't absolutely necessary. A great tip is to strive for minimalism, but not at the peril of good usability. This can often be achieved by prioritizing one main action on each screen.
- **Prioritize.** There is a tendency to try and add as many features as possible. We feel that leaving something out will somehow create less of an experience for users. To the contrary, keep features highly focused based on core objectives, and refine the design by analyzing which features are used the most then put the effort into making those features both intuitive and pleasurable.
- **Touch Targets.** Users can get physically angry and start hitting their mobile devices when they tap on something and it doesn't respond. A study done at MIT found that they were tapping on something that had too small of a touch target. A best practice is to create controls, buttons, links, etc. (anything that's a touch target) at least 7-10 mm which is the average fingertip width. It's also a good idea to ensure that there is ample spacing between these UI elements.
- **Legible Text.** Since so much of what users do is based on content consumption, in order to provide a consistent experience across all types of mobile devices, make sure to choose typefaces that work well in multiple sizes and weights. Font sizes of at least 11 points are recommended in order to reduce eye strain. Clean and easy to read typefaces such as Google's Roboto and Noto or Apple's new San Francisco font are great choices to explore.
- **UI Feedback.** Well designed applications keep us informed as we interact with them. Lack of good feedback can confuse users and cause them to question whether something has happened, is happening, or why it did/didn't happen. A best practice is to use different forms of feedback (sound, haptics, visualizations), based on the UI element or the current state of the app.
- **Accessibility.** This is probably one of the most overlooked aspects of user experience design and especially mobile UX design. 15% of the world's population experiences some form of disability. The Web Content

Accessibility Guidelines is a freely available resource, and for digital designers, is a "must have" as part of their toolbox.

Fig. 16.9

One Screen, One Task

Reduce the effort users have to put in to get what the want

Every screen you design for the app should support ***a single action of real value*** to the person using it. To make things easier for users, design every screen for one thing and one thing only. Prioritize one call-to-action per screen. It will reduce the time required to learn the app and simplify overall user interaction with a product.

Take Uber, for instance. Uber knows that the goal of the user who uses the app is to order a ride. App does not overwhelm the user with too much of information: it automatically detects users location based on GEO data and the only thing users have to do is to select a pickup location.

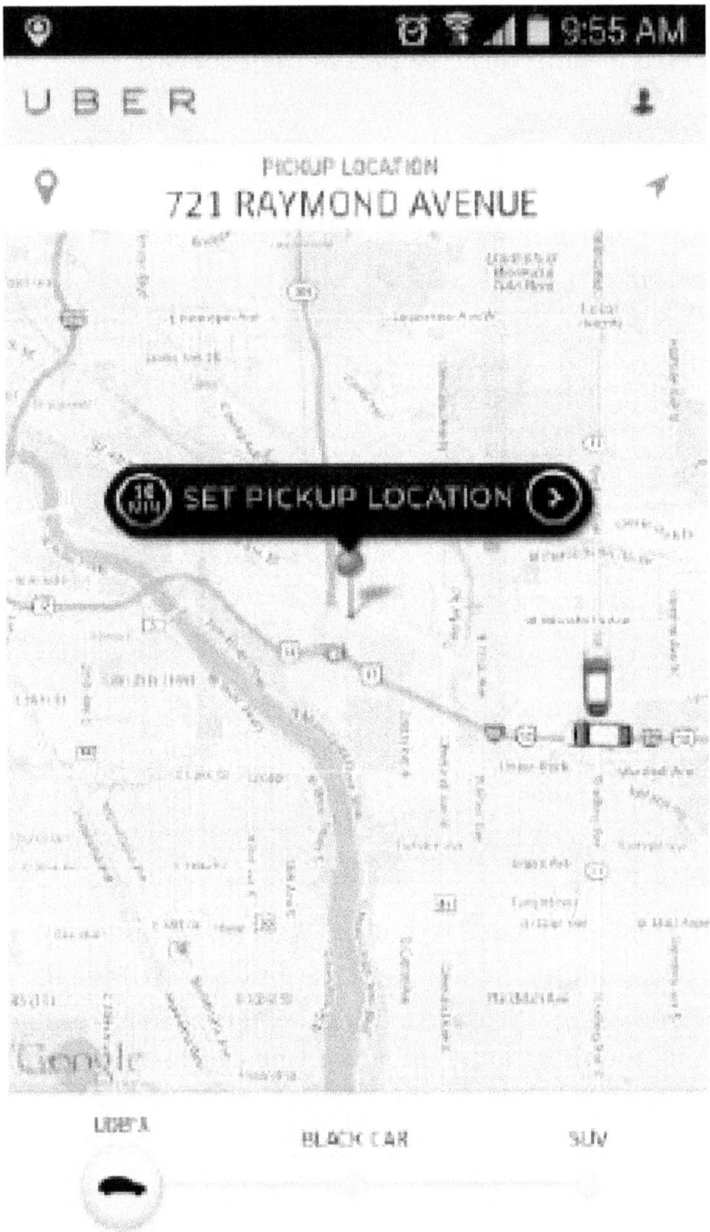

Fig. 16.10 One Screen, One Task

Invisible User Interface

Content becomes an interface

Put content in the spotlight by removing all unnecessary elements that do not support user tasks. Content should become the interface. Google Maps is a great example of this rule — during a redesign phase Google removed all the unnecessary panels and buttons and Google said that the map is the interface (Fig. 16.11).

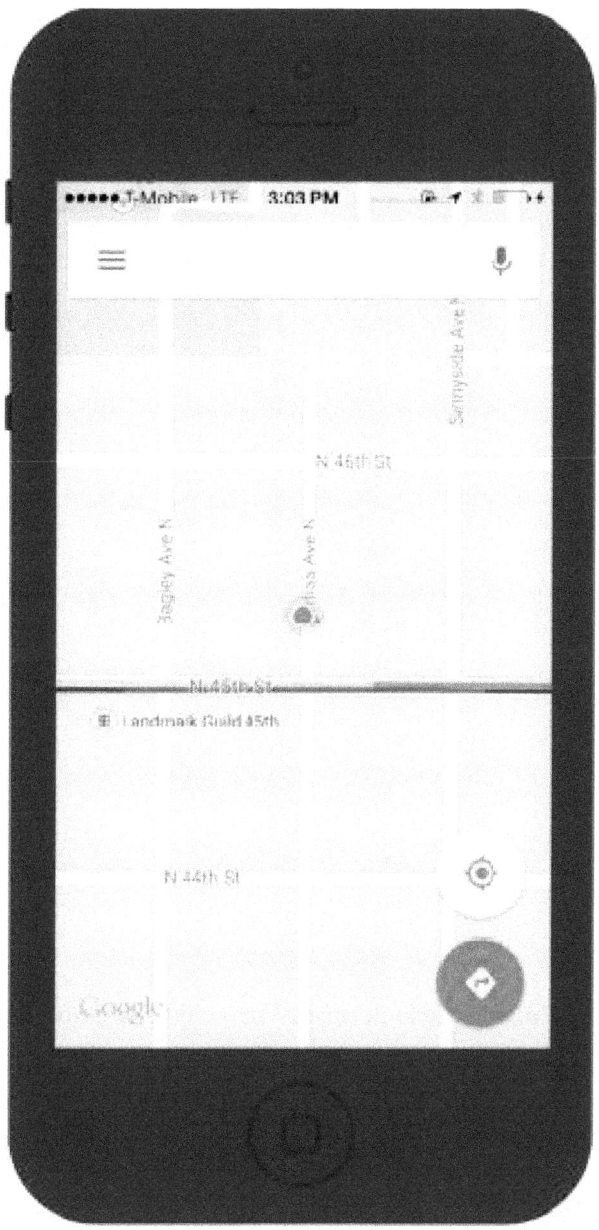

Fig. 16.11

Breathing Space

Use negative space to draw attention to important content

White space or "negative space", referring to the empty space between and around elements of a design or page layout, is often overlooked and neglected. Although many designers may consider it a waste of valuable screen estate, white space is an *essential* element in mobile design (Fig. 16.12).

Fig. 16.12 Follow "less is more" principle in your designs

Not only is white space responsible for readability and content prioritization, it also plays an important role in the visual layout. Thus, it can simplify UI and improve UX.

4. Navigation Made Simple

Make navigation self-evident

Helping users navigate should be a high priority for every app. Mobile navigation must be discoverable, accessible, and take little screen space. However, making navigation accessible is a challenge on mobile due to the limitations of the small screen and the need of prioritizing the content over decorative elements.

Tab bars and navigation bars are well suited for apps with relatively few navigation options. They are great because they display all major navigation options and with one simple tap user can instantly go from one page to another.

Fig. 16.13 Tab bar navigation in Apple AppStore

5. One Hand Operation

Adapt your design to the bigger screens

Mobile phones are getting bigger and bigger in size. The primary reason for that is to create devices with bigger screens (Fig. 1614).

Fig. 16.14

Here are three basic ways of how people are holding their phones (Fig. 16.15):

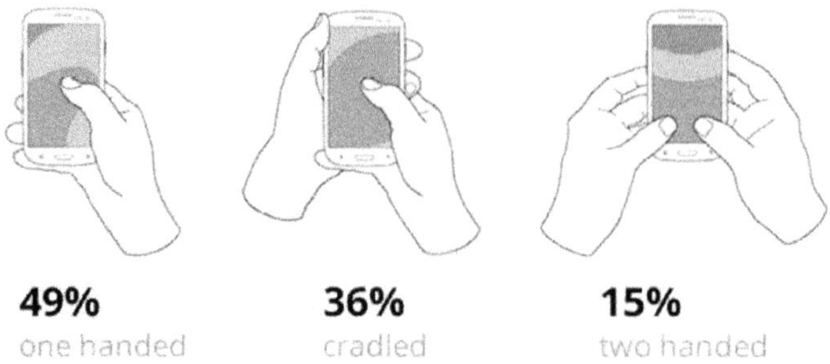

Fig. 16.15 Basic ways of how people are holding their phones. Research by Steven Hoober

85% of observed users working with their phones using one hand. The following heat map shows sorts of the thumb zones applied to every iPhone display size since 2007. You can see that the bigger the display is, the less easily-accessible zone is (Fig. 16.16).

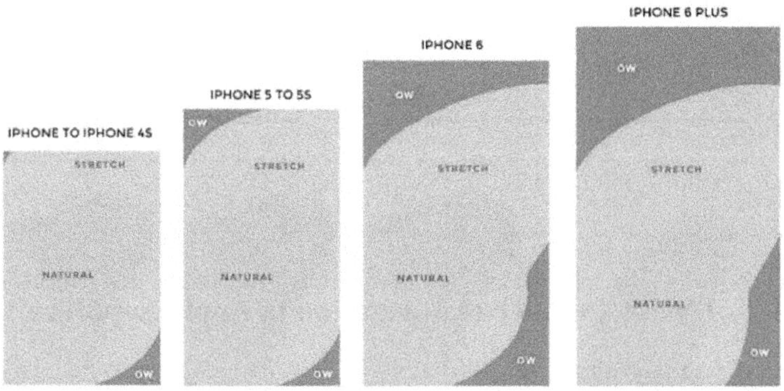

Fig. 16.16 Thumb zones. According to the observation by Scott Hurff

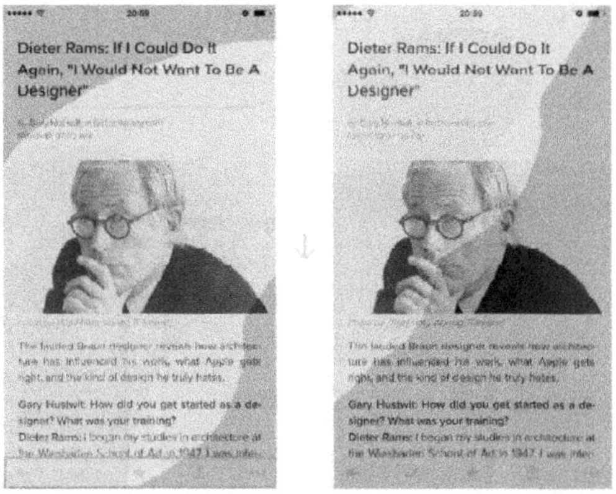

Fig. 16.17 Pocket app for iOS. All the navigation controls are in the footer. They can be easily reached in case you hold your phone normally.

It's necessary to adapt a design to improve the user experience. Ensure that your app can be easily used on a large screen with one hand. Place navigation options within the thumb's reach.

6. Make App Appear Fast

Don't make users wait for content

Try as much as possible to make the app fast and responsive. Do things in the background to make the all as fast as possible. A good example of this technique can be found in Instagram (uploading pictures on Instagram). As soon as the user chooses a picture to share, it starts uploading. The user is invited to select tags and as soon as they finish this step and tap Share the picture will be posted almost instantly (Fig. 16.18).

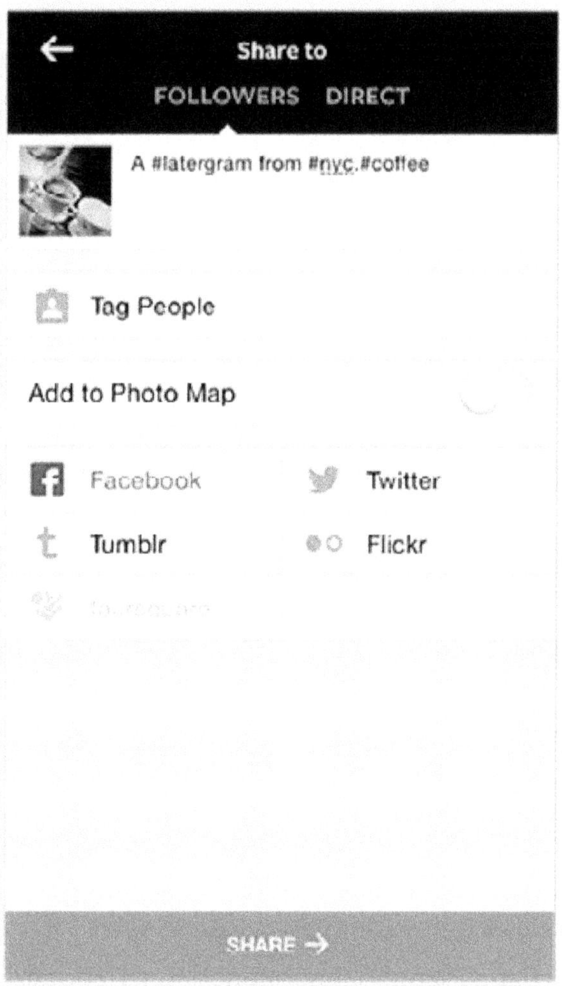

Fig. 16.18 Instagram invites the user to add tags as the picture uploads in the background.

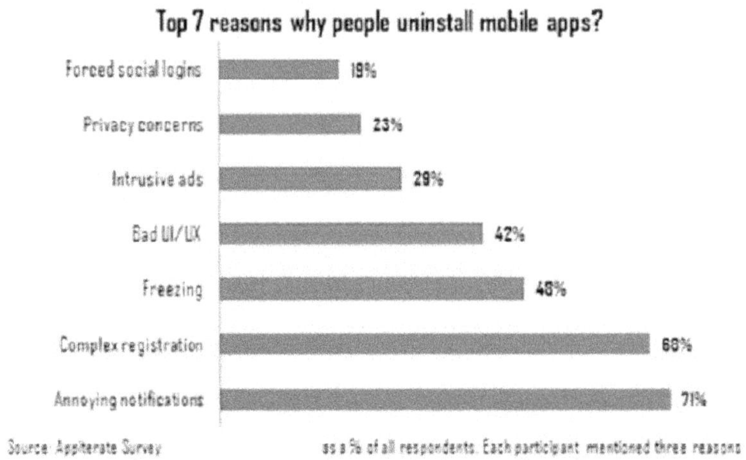

Fig. 16.19 Push Notifications

7. Use Push Notifications Wisely

Think twice before sending a message

Everyday, users are bombarded with useless notifications that distract them from their activities. Annoying notifications is the #1 reason people uninstall mobile apps (71% of respondents).

RESPONSIVE DESIGN FOR CROSS-PLATFORM EXPERIENCES

Introduction

UX designers play a pivotal role in this process. They must consider the unique nuances of each platform while ensuring that the core design remains consistent. This involves making responsive design choices that adapt seamlessly to different screen sizes, from mobile phones to laptop computers.

At Varseno Solutions, we understand the pivotal role that user experience plays in the success of digital products. In this section, let's explore the importance of adapting UI/UX design for cross-platform consistency and how it can elevate your brand's digital presence.

The Challenge of Cross-Platform Design: Gone are the days when users interacted with digital products on a single device. Today, your audience might access your website or application from a desktop, laptop, tablet, or smartphone. Each platform comes with its unique challenges, screen sizes, and user behaviors, making cross-platform design a complex puzzle to solve.

The Essence of Consistency: Consistency in UI/UX design is not just about aesthetics; it's about creating a cohesive and familiar experience for users across all platforms. Whether a user switches from a desktop to a mobile device, they should feel a sense of continuity in design elements, navigation patterns, and overall interaction.

Strategies for Achieving Cross-Platform Consistency:

Responsive Design: Embrace responsive design principles to ensure that your interface adapts fluidly to different screen sizes. This not only enhances user experience but also contributes to better SEO performance.

- **Unified Design Language**: Establish a unified design language that includes consistent color schemes, typography, and iconography. This creates a visual identity that remains constant regardless of the platform.
- **Adaptive Navigation**: Tailor navigation patterns to suit each platform's conventions. While maintaining consistency, adapt navigation elements to align with the natural flow expected on specific devices.
- **Performance Optimization**: Optimize performance for each platform to ensure swift loading times and seamless interactions. Slow-loading interfaces can negatively impact user experience, leading to frustration and bounce rates.
- **The Impact on User Satisfaction and Brand Image**: Consistent cross-platform design contributes significantly to user satisfaction. When users can effortlessly navigate and interact with your product across various devices, it builds trust and loyalty. Moreover, a cohesive design language reinforces your brand identity, making it instantly recognizable and memorable.

Cross-Platform Design

At Varseno Solutions, our UI/UX design experts follow a meticulous approach to ensure cross-platform consistency. We combine creativity with technical precision, employing responsive design techniques, and adhering to a unified design language to deliver seamless experiences that transcend devices.

In a world where user expectations are constantly evolving, adapting UI/UX design for cross-platform consistency is not just a best practice; it's a necessity. It's about crafting experiences that are not bound by devices but are fluid, intuitive, and consistently reflect your brand's essence.

CHAPTER-17

ENTERPRISE UX

Enterprise UX refers to the design of enterprise products, that is, the products for people at work. The users are employees of enterprises and not the general customers. Hence, these solutions are tailor-made for different business domains, job roles, or organizations. Examples include HR management systems, intranets, ERP systems, and CRM systems.

Enterprise user experience is vital for businesses as it directly affects the business outcome. When employees are given tools that let them work more efficiently, it reflects in the productivity of organizations. Good enterprise UX lays the groundwork for good business.

IMPORTANCE OF ENTERPRISE UX

Often, enterprise software focuses on functionality more and the usability aspects are not given much thought. Quality enterprise UX design provides several advantages to organizations as they consider end-user behavior and design the solutions to be more usable. Enterprise UX is important because it leads to:

- **Increased productivity:** Enterprise software is used by employees 8-10 hours a day. When such systems are redesigned to make them easy and swift to use, employees perform better. Moreover, optimized user journeys and intuitive navigation help them save time. Thus, it contributes to increased productivity.
- **Easier understanding:** With data visualization and dashboards, enterprise UX design makes information rich interfaces easier to understand. Users can gather key insights quickly and make better informed decisions.
- **Improved internal interactions:** Internal interaction is critical for efficient teamwork. In the present day hybrid work culture, it is unavoidable to build a cooperative team. Enterprise UX design can improve internal interactions with messaging features that are on par with customer-oriented software.

- **Faster results:** When a design system is developed, the team doesn't have to start from scratch. Moreover, they can save time where repetitive design occurs by reusing components from the design library. Thus, it takes reduced time to move from ideation to prototyping.
- **Consistent design:** An inconsistent interface is not only annoying, it also brings down the credibility and trustworthiness of the design team. With a design system, consistency can be achieved easily as templates, patterns, and other components are predesigned.
- **Smoother handoff:** The handoff process between designers and developers can be simplified with a design system. The collaboration between both sides also can be improved.
- **Easier iteration:**Iterations can be done faster, which influences the testing and feedback processes, reducing the entire cycle time and improving the project development timeline.
- **Fast updation:** In enterprise software, updating a single element can be time-consuming. Ensuring that the update is reflected throughout the design wherever that element occurs, takes time and effort. With a design system, updates can be done effortlessly as change must be made only in the design system and it be updated throughout.

Challenges of Enterprise User Experience Design

Consumer-facing UX design receives more appreciation, attention, and investment when compared to enterprise design. While there are many factors that contribute to this, the challenges that designing for enterprises pose to UX designers must be addressed. In this section, we will focus on the unique challenges of enterprise design.

Difficulty in conducting UX research: Since for enterprise solutions, the customers who purchase the solutions and users who use them are different, it creates a barrier for designers. Conducting UX research to better understand enterprise users is a hurdle as designers will be dealing with the executives (buyers) and not the actual users. And most times, the buyers aren't very clear about the user needs, which leaves designers in a bind.

A shift in user context: The context in which enterprise solutions are used varies entirely from that of consumer solutions. Enterprise apps must be designed for better focus and more time commitment. Further, creating MVP is not beneficial for enterprise apps as achieving goals with half-implemented functionalities is not practical.

The right information density: Enterprise apps are rich in information. As a result, the screen designs may be packed and lead to cognitive load for users. But hiding information to simplify the user interface may create risks and confusion. It may lead to employees not being able to find important information quickly and cause disastrous results. So it's very challenging for designers to find the optimum information density.

Tough testing conditions: Since enterprise solutions are often uniquely designed for specific organizations or domains, it is difficult to find dummy users to conduct testing. And when it comes to real users, they may be willing to perform usability tests and provide feedback, but reaching out to them and finding a free slot in their busy schedule is tough. And as mentioned before, most times, your customers won't be the users, so it is a far-fetched possibility.

Conflict in opinion: Since stakeholders of different power levels are involved in creating an enterprise app, there are chances of conflicts in opinion. In such cases, the powerhouse stakeholders "win" even if their suggested features don't suit the solution well. As a result, most users will have to deal with solutions that are irrelevant to them and do not meet their needs.

Consolidating legacy systems: Often, enterprise systems may be a merger of legacy systems. It isn't easy to consolidate old systems into a new single system as the process is time consuming and complex. Starting fresh with a new system is impossible in concept as old systems cannot be completely ignored. Rather, they must be reconciled, mapped, and incorporated, which is a humongous task.

UX CONSIDERATIONS IN ENTERPRISE SOFTWARE

Key considerations for conducting enterprise software UXR

UX research can make a big impact when it comes to building better enterprise software tools. But the special challenges require a particular skill set and approach. Some considerations UX researchers should account for include:

Enterprise Software requires a heavier lift

In many cases, changes to enterprise software take more work than comparable customer-facing tools due to the longer time between iterations and re-designs. A key factor in this disparity is the idea that the internal tools are "good enough" for workers to accomplish JTBDs and that it is better to spend more money, time, and energy on profit-generating customer-facing products. This mentality is certainly understandable in a competitive marketplace but it often leads to tools reaching a breaking point before being updated or replaced. What that means for UX teams is that research and design need more iterations to get to a toolkit that really boosts productivity and reduces team-member stress. It takes patience and good persuasion to assure users and stakeholders that the project is on track.

Participant dynamics can be a challenge

With many enterprise software UXR projects, the company may not offer its employees or contractors any incentive to participate in research. Participants may have been "voluntold" by a supervisor or other high-ranking stakeholder to participate in research for the good of the company. Participants may be unclear on the reason for the study, and could even resent the requirement to participate. It is important for UXRs to discern at the beginning of an interview if a participant needs an explanation of the purpose of the study and to provide it where necessary. Research ethics also dictate that the UXR state that participation is voluntary and the participant may opt out if he, she, or they choose to do so. In that vein it is also important to be flexible in scheduling sessions and respectful of a participant's time; chances are that participant is on the clock during session times.

Navigating stakeholder buy-in

Conducting a study and presenting findings does not guarantee those recommendations will be implemented, or even well-received. Sometimes it is important to do some detective work to ensure all relevant stakeholders have had a say in the research plan, objectives, or even the decision to improve the tool. An important group may have been omitted from the kickoff by mistake. Factors that detract from stakeholder buy-in include:

- Scope and complexity of the workflow processes the tool(s) supports; how many steps and workflows are involved?
- Internal politics you may not be aware of
- Technical experts feeling like they should have been included in the process earlier
- Users being resistant to change after years of using current features

Navigating these challenges takes not only fundamental UXR knowledge and skills but also the ability to navigate complex social landscapes, the instinct to be in conversation with a range of stakeholders, and a great deal of equanimity and patience.

Understanding information density and specificity

Enterprise software users may tolerate a higher information density than typical customer-facing software users because they often have a need for more details and specificity to get the job done. A successful localization project or cell tower build takes a great deal more information and expertise to accomplish than a search for a good restaurant nearby. In enterprise software, clean and pretty are good, but functionality is key.

Key considerations for enterprise software UXR project deliverables

A successful enterprise software UXR project report needs to balance concision with sufficient detail to address questions and concerns of a highly technical nature. It also may take more than one share out with a design or product team to successfully implement.

Balance detail with concision

The optimal balance of detail and concision in reports and share outs varies by work stream and stakeholder, more so than in customer-facing software. Stakeholders often want more detailed information about functions and features than with customer-facing apps and platforms due to the technical needs of the user-base and the fact that team members with different roles have at times divergent needs. A UXR can hone reports to the right level of density by being flexible and attuned to communication with stakeholders about what level of detail they need.

Go the extra mile to get buy-in

Getting buy-in and action on recommendations may involve work beyond the report, e.g., detective work to discover key stakeholders, research on the solution architects and business decision makers as well as end users, etc. It is important to remember that users are an important stakeholder but that their needs may have to be balanced with technical constraints or larger business needs. A UXR can tackle these challenges by going the extra mile to see what impacts the process beyond the current software tools.

Support end-users with contextual documentation and in-app guidance

Speaking of enterprise-specific assistance, there are several avenues you can use to impart the skill new users need and simplify your product's learning curve, such as:

- Self-guided experiences and certification programs
- Guided on boarding experiences, e.g. interactive walkthroughs and step-by-step product tours.
- A self-help support library with wikis, product docs, and pre-recorded demos users can access at their convenience.

And, if you're on the lookout for an all-in-one solution, the What fix digital adoption platform enables enterprise organizations to take a user-centric approach by empowering end-users with real-time, contextual, guided experiences.

IT teams can embed a self-help widget with universal search where users can search through every piece of relevant content on the topic they need help with. End-users can leverage in-app guided Flows, Task Lists, Field Validation, Smart Tips, and more to help navigate complex processes and receive real-time support.

Use analytics to analyze and optimize enterprise UX

Product analytics tools offer an unfiltered, front-end view of how users interact with your product's UX, issues end-users face, and bits of insights that can help you build a better experience that enables end-users and drive business outcomes. Common user behavior and analytic capabilities product analytics tools can empower enterprise IT and UX teams with include:

- Custom event tracking to monitor any user behavior.
- User flow analysis to map common user paths and identify areas of user friction across different cohorts of users.
- Monitor overall adoption levels across types of end-users and analyze software license usage.
- Heatmaps that offer a distilled footprint of user activity on your landing pages and digital assets (applications, etc.)
- Session recordings that replay your users' on-screen interactions, including mouse movements, page visits, taps, scrolling, etc. as one cohesive step-by-step narrative you can follow from start to finish.
- Cohort analysis, which groups users into buckets based on the characteristics they share in order to understand how to improve your product for them.
- Funnel analysis, which shows conversion trends from the first landing page users visit until they take it to your desired CTA.

Whatfix provides enterprises with a no-code tool to monitor, analyze, and optimize enterprise workflows to overcome user friction and create the most efficient processes.

Maintain consistency across your enterprise applications

Enterprises often invest in dozens of applications that enable employees across business functions and internal use cases. This leads to fractured, inconsistent end-user experiences, which hurts productivity – especially for enterprise workflows that span multiple applications.

Here are some tips that can help you bring consistency to your enterprise UX across your software stack:

- Standardize UI elements (e.g., buttons, menus, and search bars) and ensure a consistent layout to minimize confusion across you enterprise apps (ie. your CRM, ERP, HCM, etc.). To assist standardization, consider QMS implementation from a tool like Veeva QMS.
- Maintain a consistent testing environment to simulate real-world user conditions and verify that design elements and functionality perform consistently.

- Develop comprehensive design guidelines that outline visual elements, typography, color schemes, and UI components to be used consistently across all applications.
- Train your development and design teams on design guidelines and the proper usage of design components to enforce consistency.
- Conduct regular audits and quality assurance checks to identify and rectify inconsistencies, both in terms of design and functionality.
- Define and adhere to brand guidelines and identity standards, including logos, color palettes, and iconography to reinforce brand recognition.

Whatfix's no-code DAP enables organizations with a simple content editor to create, launch, and test in-app content and UX tips that adhere to your branding.

Consider intended business outcomes when designing enterprise UX

Design teams tend to overemphasize form over function, building out beautiful bells and whistles to the detriment of core features their major users rely on.

The only way to balance your desire for beauty and your customers' desire for a product that just works is to:

- Start by thoroughly understanding the specific business goals and objectives that the enterprise software is intended to support. This may involve working closely with stakeholders to define key performance indicators (KPIs) and success criteria.
- Design your product(s) to be customizable by default to accommodate different industries, use cases, and edge cases.
- Prioritize productivity and real use cases vs. design for its own sake.
- Use behavioral analytics data to prioritize features, tools, and design decisions.
- Invest in user training and on-boarding to ensure your end-users have what it takes to use your product to the maximum.

Or, in summary, don't sacrifice usability for aesthetics—and talk to your customers a lot to learn what they want.

DESIGNING FOR COMPLEX WORKFLOWS AND USER ROLES

Understand the workflow

The first step in designing user interfaces for complex workflows is to understand the workflow itself. You need to map out the goals, tasks, roles, inputs, outputs, and dependencies of each step in the workflow. You also need to identify the pain points, problems, and opportunities for improvement. You can use tools like flowcharts, diagrams, or user journey maps to visualize the workflow and communicate it with your team and stakeholders.

Simplify the workflow

The next step is to simplify the workflow as much as possible. You want to reduce the cognitive load, errors, and frustration for the users. You can do this by eliminating unnecessary steps, consolidating related tasks, automating repetitive actions, providing clear feedback, and offering help and guidance. You can also use design patterns and principles like progressive disclosure, chunking, hierarchy, and consistency to organize and present the information and controls in a logical and coherent way.

The Role of UX in Making Complexity Simple

The true test of UX design's effectiveness lies in its ability to make complex processes feel simple and intuitive to users. In a world where technology is advancing at a rapid pace, users are often confronted with intricate tasks and vast amounts of information. This complexity can be overwhelming, but it's the role of UX designers to bridge the gap between the user's goals and the digital interface, making the experience as straightforward as possible.

1. Clear Information Architecture

One of the fundamental principles of UX design is the creation of a clear and logical information architecture. This involves structuring content and features in a way that is easy for users to understand and navigate. By organising information into a hierarchy, users can quickly locate what they need, even within a complex system.

2. Intuitive Navigation

Effective navigation is key to simplifying complex processes. The navigation menu should be intuitive, with easily recognisable labels and logical groupings. Users should be able to move between different sections of a website or application effortlessly, without needing to think about how to get there.

3. Streamlined Workflows

Complex processes often involve a series of steps. UX designers aim to streamline these workflows by eliminating unnecessary steps and simplifying the user's journey. This reduces friction and makes the process feel more intuitive.

4. Visual Hierarchy

Visual hierarchy plays a significant role in UX design. By using typography, colour, and layout effectively, designers can guide the user's attention to the most important elements on a page. This helps users focus on the essential information and tasks, making complex processes seem more manageable.

5. User-Centered Design

A user-centered approach is at the core of UX design. Designers must understand their target audience, their goals, and their pain points. By conducting user research, designers can tailor the interface to meet the needs of the users, thus making complex tasks feel more intuitive and user-friendly.

Case Study: Online Banking

A prime example of how UX design simplifies complex processes is in the realm of online banking. In the UK, online banking has witnessed remarkable growth, with an increasing number of individuals opting for digital banking services. According to a report by The Guardian, over 70% of UK adults use online banking services regularly, emphasising the importance of an impeccable user experience.

Clear Information Architecture

Online banking platforms, like the ones offered by leading UK banks, exemplify the importance of clear information architecture. When users log in, they are presented with a straightforward menu, separating features such as account balance, transaction history, and fund transfers. The information is structured logically, allowing users to quickly find what they need.

Intuitive Navigation

The navigation within online banking platforms is highly intuitive. Users can easily switch between their accounts, access statements, and perform transactions with minimal effort. The menu items are labelled clearly and the path to various actions is streamlined.

Streamlined Workflows

Online banking thrives on streamlined workflows. For example, transferring money to another account is often a complex process involving multiple steps. However, UX designers ensure that this process is as simple as possible, guiding users through each step and providing clear instructions.

Visual Hierarchy

The visual hierarchy in online banking applications is designed to focus the user's attention on important information. Account balances, transaction alerts, and payment due dates are displayed prominently, ensuring that users don't miss critical financial details.

User-Centered Design

UK banks frequently invest in user research to understand their customer's needs better. This results in tailored experiences for different user segments, making the platform more intuitive for all users, from tech-savvy individuals to those less familiar with online banking.

To make the design process manageable and create a robust feature with great UX, we leaned on this set of five ideas to drive the project:

Identify patterns

During user interviews, we saw that users did steps in different order, spent varying amounts of time on sections, and had distinct vocabularies when talking about their process. Although each had a unique workflow for building a custom data set, there was also a lot of overlap in the types of actions they took. We found that they had general data themes in common which we then surfaced in the first step of the building process (see below). It was critical to zoom out and focus on the patterns across users instead of getting overwhelmed by the complexity of an enterprise analytics workflow.

Fig. 17.1 The top four reporting areas were surfaced as quick selections in the Report Builder UI

Be aware of the context

We observed that users had varying start and end points for their workflows. For some, the report creation process began with an ad hoc request from their manager, versus others who started the process on their own as a part of a daily morning routine. After extracting the data from SmartRecruiters, most of our users continued their building workflow in another software (eg. Excel, Tableau) before the report was ready to be used. From seeing this, we realized that we had to accommodate for different starting mindsets and maintain a smooth experience with other software that came before the final report.

To better understand the mindset of your users as they enter the product, be aware that the true starting point of their workflow may be in a different application entirely. You can better design the steps of your experience once you have an understanding of the common entry points. If you can identify a common partner software used as well, you could use similar navigation to that software and workflow patterns to create a more cohesive experience overall despite the shifts. For example, we knew that most users also worked in Excel so we incorporated a spreadsheet style visual preview into our feature.

Fig. 17.2 Users reporting workflow often started and ended externally

Full customization 1 Good UX

Building a report is a fundamentally exploratory process. However, it can be difficult for users to conceptualize all the intricate relationships between different objects within our software. We had initially considered opening up all the pathways to give users full report control, but realized this would not be the best approach. They would be at risk of encountering dead ends, errors, or empty reports when selecting data because the underlying data structure may not support a specific data pairing. To dig deeper into this, we worked with our engineering team to solidify which pathways worked and which would fail. In order to prevent frustration, we only surfaced the successful pairing options by default.

Users can still select most custom data points with this approach, but they are prevented from selection patterns that would result in a complicated error message. We also designed a toggle that allowed users to see the data points that may not be available for a specific type of report. This helped users to transparently access how they might reconfigure the report to get certain data. Just because users can or want to customize everything does not mean they should. Over-customization can be overwhelming. Apply restrictions in a friendly way to guide users to successful outcomes.

Fig. 17.3 Available columns were restricted to only those that would produce a valid report

Bring automation to workflows

We accounted for both ad hoc and recurring reports while designing Report Builder, but knew that the majority of users would utilize recurring reports more often. We did not want users to be unnecessarily repeating the task of creating the same report and manually running it again and again. After a user sets up a report, the template is saved, accessible, and editable whenever needed. We also introduced scheduling in an effort to further automate the process. Users can schedule a report so it comes directly to them every day, week, etc. Together, these features ensured our users would have a smooth, automated process for reporting.

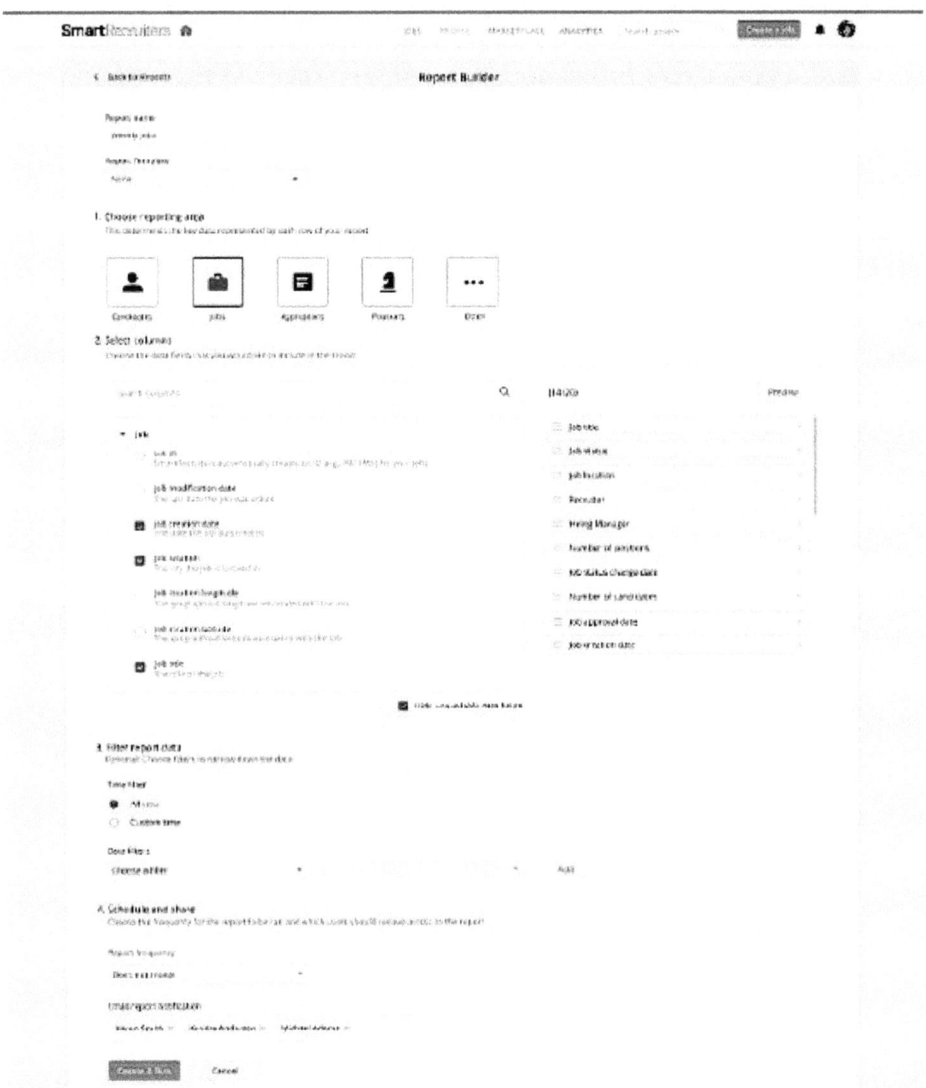

Fig. 17.4 Entire Report Builder form

Give yourself time to iterate

Report Builder was not designed in one go, it was the result of many iterations and a strong partnership with Product & Engineering. The design process started with user interviews, storyboarding, competitor analysis, and several low-fidelity wireframes. I mocked up many different layouts and interaction patterns before getting to a design. Once fully developed, we ran a beta program as well to collect feedback and made further design adjustments to the feature. The combination of extensive ideation, teamwork, and user feedback were critical to the success of Report Builder.

Fig. 17.5 A few of the design iterations for Report Builder

Part VII: Case Studies and Best Practices

CHAPTER-18

UX AND DESIGN THINKING CASE STUDIES

Design Thinking Case Studies demonstrate the value of the Design Thinking methodology. They show how this Design Thinking methodology helps creatively solve problems and improve the success rate of innovation and increase collaboration in corporations, education, social impact work and the public sector by focusing on the needs of humans.

There are many Design Thinking Case Study examples on the web, but few meet the criteria for a robust case study: a clear description of the methodology, steps undertaken, experimentation through rapid prototypes and testing with people and finally documented results from the process. In this section, we have been selective about the design thinking case study examples that we highlight. We look for Design Thinking Case Studies that demonstrate how a problem was tackled and wherever possible the results or effect that the project produced. Our goal in curating this section of Design Thinking Case Study examples is quality over quantity.

REAL-WORLD EXAMPLES OF SUCCESSFUL UX AND DESIGN THINKING PROJECTS

Now that you understand the theory and process of design thinking, let's look at some examples in action where design thinking had a real-world impact.

Case Study 1: American Family Insurance's Moonrise App

American Family Insurance, a company that offers life, business, auto, and home insurance, came to design company IDEO with the goal of innovating in a way that would help working families.

Stages 1 & 2: Empathise and Define

While American Family thought their customers might benefit from budgeting tools, IDEO found from their research in the Empathise phase that, actually, people needed a way to build up their savings against unforeseen needs.

They noticed a lot of people had meticulously planned budgets, which made budgeting tools a moot point. But they were living just within their means and an extra expense, like a doctor's visit or kid's basketball uniform, could throw their budget off. These people didn't want to take on debt though, they wanted extra work so they could have a cushion.

Stages 3 & 4: Ideate and Prototype

IDEO took that idea and ran with it, creating Moonrise, an app that matches people looking for work with extra hours and income. Today's businesses depend on on-demand work but the temp agencies they work with tend to want permanent placements. Moonrise does things differently. It enables companies to find people who are already employed elsewhere for short-term work through a simple text message interface. The employers can list shifts on the platform and workers are paid as soon as they finish their shifts.

Stage 5: Test

To test the app, 11 Moonrisers, six employers, and a team of designers and programmers were assembled for a one week period to work out the kinks in the platform.

Based on the test's success, American Family Insurance now owns the startup Moonrise, which launched in Chicago in 2018 and has since expanded to additional states. In 2018, over 7,000 shifts have been fulfilled and over $500,000 has been earned by people on the app.

Case Study 2: GE Healthcare's Scanning Tools

GE Healthcare has cutting-edge diagnostic imaging tools at its disposal, but for kids they're an unpleasant experience.

"The room itself is kind of dark and has those flickering fluorescent lights.... That machine that I had designed basically looked like a brick with a hole in it," explained Doug Dietz, a designer who worked for GE. How could they make the experience better for kids?

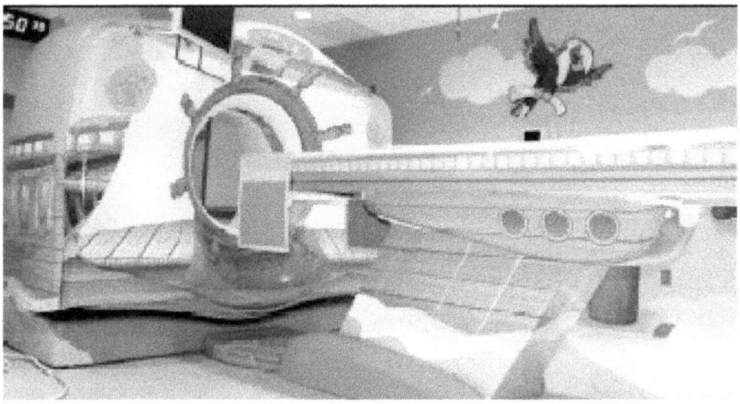

Stages 1 & 2: Empathise and Define

The team at GE began by observing and gaining empathy for children at a daycare centre and talking to specialists who knew what paediatric patients went through. The team then recruited experts from a children's museum and doctors from two hospitals. This gave them a lot of insight into what children went through when they had to sit for these procedures and what could be done to lessen the children's stress.

Stages 3, 4 & 5: Ideate, Prototype, and Test

The first prototype of the new and improved "Adventure Series" scanner was invented. Through research and pilot programs, the redesign made imaging machines more child-friendly, making sure they have other things to focus on than the scary looks and sounds of the machine. For example, the Coral City Adventure in the emergency room gives children an underwater experience where they get into a yellow submarine and listen to the sound of harps while their procedure takes place.

Patient satisfaction scores increased to 90% and children no longer suffer such anxiety about their scans. The children hold still for their procedures more easily, making repeats of the scans unnecessary. There's also less need for anesthesiologists, which improved the bottom line for those hospitals that used the scanning machines because more patients could get scanned each day.

Case Study 3: Oral B

Design thinking not only succeeds at finding effective solutions for companies but also at putting initiatives to the test before implementation.

When Oral B wanted to upgrade its electric toothbrush, it enlisted designers Kim Colin and Sam Hecht to help. The company's request was to add more functions for electric toothbrush users, such as tracking brushing frequency, observing gum sensitivity, and playing music.

While clarifying the problem, however, Colin and Hecht pointed out that brushing teeth was a neurotic act for many people. Users didn't want additional functionality and, in many cases, thought it could potentially cause more stress. Instead, they recommended two solutions that could improve user experience without adding gimmicks.

Their first recommendation was to make the toothbrush easier to charge, especially while users were on the road. Another was making it more convenient for users to order replacement heads by allowing toothbrushes to connect to phones and send reminder notifications. Both proposals were successful because they focused on what users wanted rather than what the company wanted to roll out.

Case Study 4: Netflix

Although many companies have successfully used design thinking, Netflix has repeatedly leveraged it to become an industry giant. During the company's inception, its main competitor, Blockbuster, required customers to drive to brick-and-mortar stores to rent DVDs. The process was the same for returns, which was a major pain point for many. Netflix eliminated that inconvenience by delivering DVDs directly to customers' homes with a subscription model.

While this revolutionized the movie industry, Netflix's real success has been in its innovation over the years. For example, when the company realized DVDs were becoming outdated, it created an on-demand streaming service to stay ahead of the curve. This also inadvertently eliminated the inconvenience of having to wait for DVDs.

Subsequently, in 2011, Netflix took its design thinking one step further and responded to customers' need for original, provocative content that wasn't airing on traditional networks. Later, in 2016, it improved its user experience by adding short trailers to its interface. Each of Netflix's major updates was in response to customers' needs and driven by an effective design thinking process.

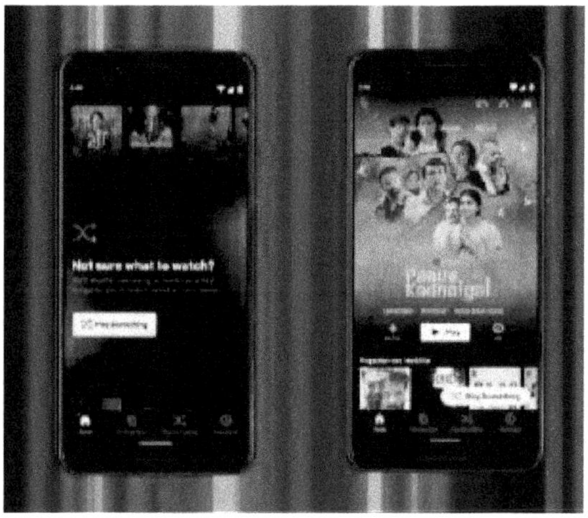

Case Study 5: Airbnb

Another household name, Airbnb, started by only making around $200 a week. After some observation, its founders recognized that the advertising pictures hosts were posting online weren't of a high enough quality, which often deterred customers from renting rooms.

To empathize with customers, the founders spent time traveling to each location, imagining what users look for in a temporary place to stay. Their solution? Invest in a high-quality camera and take pictures of what customers want to see, based on their travel observations. For example, showing every room rather than a select few, listing special features like a hot tub or pool in the description, and highlighting the neighborhood or areas in close proximity to the residence. The result? A week later, Airbnb's revenue doubled.

Instead of focusing on reaching a bigger audience, Airbnb's founders used design thinking to determine why their existing audience wasn't utilizing their services. They realized that rather than focusing on traditional business values, like scalability, they needed to simply put themselves in users' shoes to solve business problems.

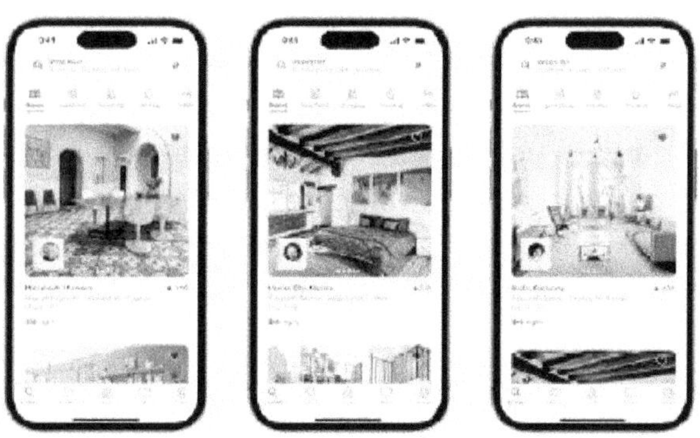

Case Study 6: UberEats

The go-to food delivery service app UberEats attributes its success to its ability to reiterate quickly and empathize with customers.

A prime example of this is UberEats's Walkabout Program, where designers observe cities in which the company operates. Some elements they inspect are food culture, cuisine, infrastructure, delivery processes, and transportation. One of the innovations that came from their immersive research is the driver app, which focuses on delivery partners' pain points around parking in highly populated urban areas. To address this, the driver app provides step-by-step directions from restaurant to customer to ensure smoother delivery processes.

LESSONS LEARNED AND KEY TAKEAWAYS

When we explore successful UX design projects, we can identify several key characteristics that distinguish them from others. Analyzing these projects provides valuable insights into the factors contributing to their success, which we can apply to our own work.

At the core of successful design projects lies a strong emphasis on user-centered design. This approach underlines the importance of understanding users' needs, preferences, and pain points, allowing designers to create tailored solutions that address specific requirements. Ensuring our solutions are both effective and delightful involves prioritizing the user experience and placing them at the heart of the design process.

Examining successful UX projects reveals how these principles have been put into practice. For instance, Airbnb's user-friendly platform has revolutionized the vacation rental industry with its intuitive design. By focusing on user needs and incorporating a clean, visually appealing interface, Airbnb has facilitated the process of finding and booking unique accommodations for millions of travelers worldwide.

Similarly, Apple's success can be largely attributed to its dedication to user-centered design. The seamless integration of hardware, software, and services within the Apple ecosystem leads to a cohesive and intuitive user experience that customers have come to appreciate and expect.

To ensure that our designs resonate with users and deliver outstanding experiences, we can incorporate the insights from successful design projects that identify key ingredients for triumph.

Lessons from failed design projects

While we can learn a great deal from successful design projects, there are also valuable insights to be gained from those that did not meet their goals. Examining failed design projects helps us recognize common pitfalls and obstacles, enabling us to sidestep these mistakes in our own work.

One crucial lesson from projects that fell short is the importance of iteration and adaptation. Designers must be ready to continuously refine their solutions based on user feedback and changing circumstances. A failure to adapt and evolve often results in a suboptimal user experience.

For example, Google Glass, an ambitious attempt by Google to enter the wearable technology market, ultimately fell short due to various factors such as privacy concerns, limited functionality, and an unappealing design. Despite the initial excitement surrounding the product, Google Glass failed to connect with users and was discontinued.

Another notable example is Microsoft's Clippy, the infamous assistant introduced in Microsoft Office 97. Clippy was intended to make the software more user-friendly; however, users found it intrusive and unhelpful. As a result, Clippy was eventually removed from the Office suite.

A deeper understanding of potential pitfalls that could hinder our efforts can be gained by studying failed design projects and others. This knowledge enables us to proactively address potential issues, leading to more successful outcomes in our own projects.

Applying lessons to your own projects

With the insights gleaned from analyzing both successful and failed design projects, we can apply these lessons to our own work, fueling continuous improvement and growth. To incorporate these learnings into your design process, consider the following strategies:

Embrace a user-centered mindset by prioritizing the understanding of your users' needs, preferences, and pain points. Use this information to inform your design decisions and create solutions tailored to their specific requirements.

Adopt an iterative and adaptive approach, refining your designs based on user feedback and changing circumstances. Continuously test and improve your solutions to ensure they remain relevant and effective.

Collaboration and communication are essential, so foster open dialogue with your team and stakeholders. Share your findings and insights while being receptive to feedback from others. This collaborative approach helps develop more comprehensive solutions.

Balancing user needs and business goals is crucial. While focusing on user needs is vital, considering your organization's objectives is equally important. Strive to create designs that satisfy both user requirements and business goals, delivering value to all parties involved.

Weaving these strategies into your design process enables you to utilize the insights gained from UX case studies, thereby improving your skills, developing more efficient solutions, and achieving superior outcomes for your projects. Remember that the key to success in UX design lies in continuous learning, adaptation, and growth.

Steering clear of common UX design mistakes

Steering clear of common UX design mistakes can significantly improve your projects and create better experiences for your users. Let's explore some top UX design mistakes, their impact on users and projects, and tips for avoiding them:

- **Neglecting user research:** Failing to conduct proper user research can lead to designs that don't meet user needs or expectations. To avoid this, invest time in thorough user research, including interviews, surveys, and usability tests, to better understand your users.
- **Overloading users with information:** Providing too much information can cause confusion and negatively affect the user experience. To counter this, practice content hierarchy and keep interfaces clean and focused on essential elements.
- **Inconsistent design elements:** Inconsistency in design elements can disorient users and diminish brand recognition. To ensure a cohesive experience, develop a robust design system and adhere to it throughout your project.
- **Poor navigation:** Difficult navigation frustrates users and hinders their ability to find information or complete tasks. To enhance usability, design

intuitive and straightforward navigation that allows users to easily access the desired content.

- **Ignoring accessibility:** Neglecting accessibility can exclude users with disabilities, limiting the reach of your design. To create an inclusive experience, follow accessibility guidelines and ensure your design is usable for all users.

To create more effective and inclusive designs that cater to the needs of a diverse user base, and ultimately lead to more successful projects, it is important to be aware of these common UX design mistakes and take proactive steps to avoid them.

The role of collaboration and feedback

Collaboration and feedback play a crucial role in the UX design process, significantly contributing to the success of a project. The importance of teamwork in UX design cannot be overstated, as it allows for the pooling of diverse skills, perspectives, and ideas, leading to more innovative and well-rounded solutions.

In addition to collaboration among design team members, gathering input from various stakeholders, such as product managers, developers, and even users, is essential. This input provides valuable insights that can be incorporated into the design process, ensuring that solutions align with user needs and expectations, as well as business objectives.

An essential aspect of the collaborative process is iterating and refining design solutions based on feedback. Designers must be open to critique and willing to make adjustments as needed. This iterative approach ensures that the design evolves and improves over time, ultimately resulting in a more effective and satisfying user experience.

Both collaboration and feedback are integral components of the UX design process. Designers can leverage the insights and expertise of a diverse group of stakeholders to create user-centered solutions that meet both user needs and business goals, by fostering a culture of open communication and teamwork. Embracing this collaborative mindset is key to achieving success in UX design.

CHAPTER-19

BEST PRACTICES IN UX AND DESIGN THINKING

Good UX design doesn't come from following UX design best practices. You need to test your product to tell if it offers great UX and fulfills user needs. That's where prototyping tools come in. With a tool like UXPin, design teams can prototype their product, and then optimize their design through series of iterations and usability testing with real users.

ESSENTIAL STRATEGIES FOR EFFECTIVE UX DESIGN

Start with research

Nothing is more important for a consistent experience than quality research.

This should not be underestimated or hurried. Time and budget are always a necessary consideration in product design. Without either of these, a product would never ship. Although they are important to the process, we can't lose sight of who actually uses the product, what their customer journey looks like, whether they are desktop or mobile users.

Keep your users top of mind and don't overlook UX research in the beginning stages of product design planning.

Define user goals

Get into the mindset of a new user. What do they want to accomplish? How will the application help them? List our goals and refer back to these throughout the UI or UX design process.

For example, let's assume we're building a travel app. This travel application allows users to select a vacation timeframe and find deals on flights and hotels within their budget. But it's not just the standard travel site. It connects to your Facebook account, works its magic, and plans the top five vacations based on the content that you've shared. The user selects the vacation plan that they like best and all the details are taken care of.

Here are some of the user goals:

- View vacation options within a specified timeframe
- Compare different vacation options
- Select a vacation based on users interests
- Keep within vacation budget

Now that we know the breakdown of goals, we can design to meet user expectations.

Familiarize yourself with common UI patterns

Don't reinvent the wheel when it comes to established UI patterns. Recurring patterns solve common UX and UI design problems.

Of course, UX designers shouldn't just "copy" the entire layout of another similar web or mobile app. They need to filter and modify the patterns based on specific user goals.

Establish design patterns for product UI and UX design consistency

One of the keys to a successful — and consistent — UI is the user performing tasks with the minimum number of actions is. If a task that takes four steps can easily be completed in two, the UI should always be modified for the shorter task flow. UI patterns can help with this... after all, this efficiency is why they became patterns in the first place.

Design hierarchy

Along with design patterns, having an established visual hierarchy of UI design elements does wonders for UI consistency. Whether users are aware of it or not, they instinctively pay attention to the order and priority of the elements they interact with.

When it comes to visuals and the human eye, some elements take precedence over others (bigger sizes, bright colors, etc.), depending on how "noticeable" they are. Think about your screen visuals in terms of what people will see first, second, third, and so on.

This allows UX designers to ensure users find primary functions faster than others, but they can also present secondary and tertiary functions with the appropriate amount of attention.

UI elements

There is a multitude of design elements that go into an application's UI, and each makes up the building blocks that form UI patterns. Keep an organized inventory and check that elements are used properly to maintain a consistent experience.

Branding elements

Stay consistent with the overall brand. Typography, logo, correct image styles, brand color schemes, etc. should be reflected in the application, just like the rest of the brand's properties.

Is the correct logo used? Are branding colors consistent? Does the typeface match the others? Brand consistency helps new projects feel like part of the brand's family, rather than a black sheep. Style guides usually provide all the information you'll need.

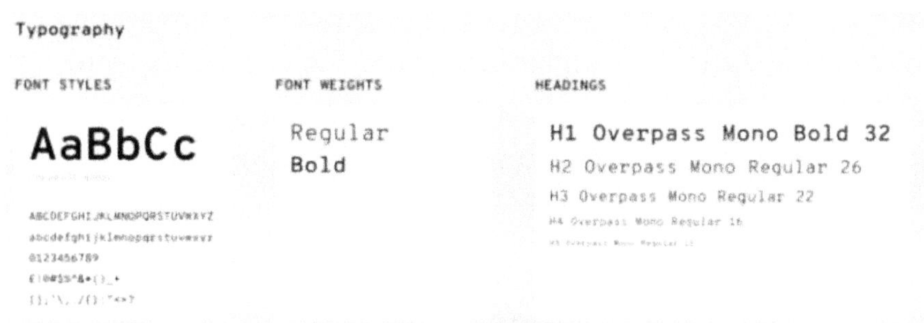

Fig. 19.1 Making sure colors and typography are on brand gives each of the company's products a consistent look and feel.

Typography

Elements with the most visual impact like typography should always be "on brand."

This visual element is especially important, not just for hierarchy, but for the entire UX as well. Changing the sizes, fonts, and arrangement of the text can improve scanability, legibility, readability, and even navigation.

UI components

During user research, become familiar with UI patterns and their components. Knowing how each component behaves, within the pattern and outside it, lets UX designers properly prioritize all elements on the screen without anything slipping through the cracks.

"Components" can refer to any number of elements that make up a pattern, such as:

- Buttons

- Cards
- Forms
- Lists
- Panels
- Progress bars

Let's say you're considering adding pagination to long lists so the user doesn't have to scroll far with long lists.

As you examine the wireframes, you notice that one list has pagination with 20 or more items, while in another part of the application, a list only has pagination with 40 or more items. Which is correct? This example illustrates how making definitive decisions about guidelines is the backbone of UI and UX design consistency.

Templates

If you're having difficulty standardizing your site or app, try using templates.

Most applications allow them, and because the layout and elements look the same, they streamline UI features across the products. Plus, you can reuse the same UI templates over and over, even years down the line.

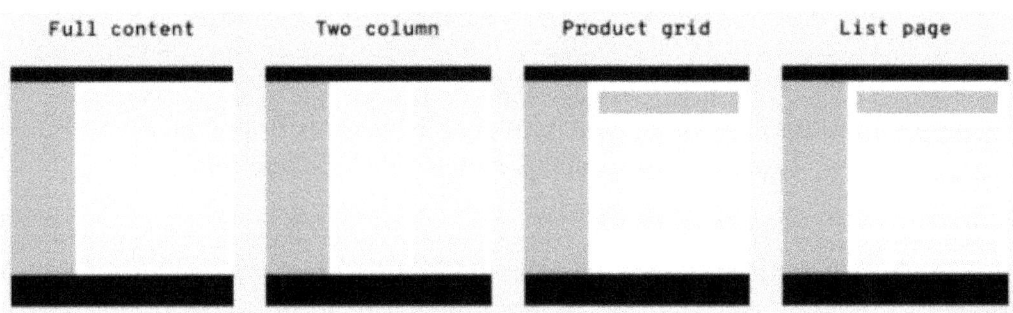

Fig. 19.2

Pattern library and design system

It may not be user-facing, but it is one of the keys to consistency. Today, many teams have a pattern library or design system as a point of reference to keep everyone on the same page. Pattern libraries and design systems are the rulebooks that anyone on the team can reference at any time. For team-wide consistency, they are essential.

A pattern library may not be as robust as a design system since it's limited to design patterns specifically. A design system has more information all around, including helpful documentation about all the UI patterns and various components. A pattern library can also be a subsection of a design system.

Make actions consistent

Everyone loves when an application is user-friendly. It saves time, avoids headaches, and helps users accomplish their goals by eliminating confusion — all requirements for creating satisfied customers.

Consistent actions remove the need for user discovery and therefore make their task flow run more smoothly. If a user knows how to use the functionality in one section, they know how to use it in all sections (as long as it's consistent).

Users inherently transfer past knowledge to new contexts as they explore new parts of the application. Consistent actions become second nature and eventually, the user can use the application without even thinking. Furthermore, users bring these expectations into new features or aspects of the product that they haven't explored yet, minimizing the learning curve.

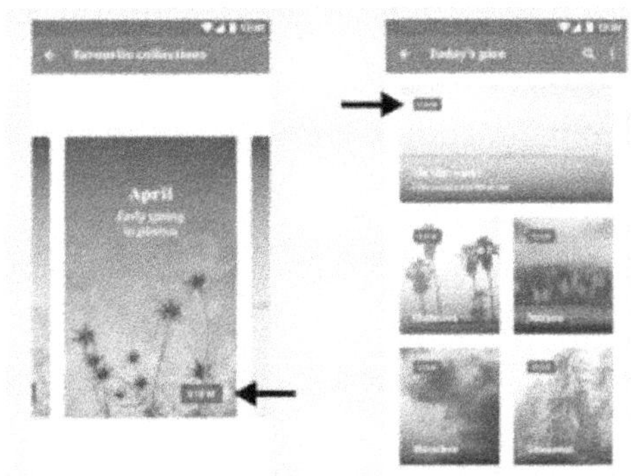

Fig. 19.3 "View" placement is not consistent. On most of the cards, it's toward the top, but on the collection card, it's at the bottom. This inconsistency might cause the user to pause for a moment to search for the "View" option, not to mention it undermines their own natural habit-forming processes.

So what, specifically, should you consider when designing your interface? Ask yourself these questions during the entire process:

- Do all parts of the application behave the same way?
- How do interactions work? Are they predictable and consistent?
- How much discovery is needed for a user to understand this interaction?

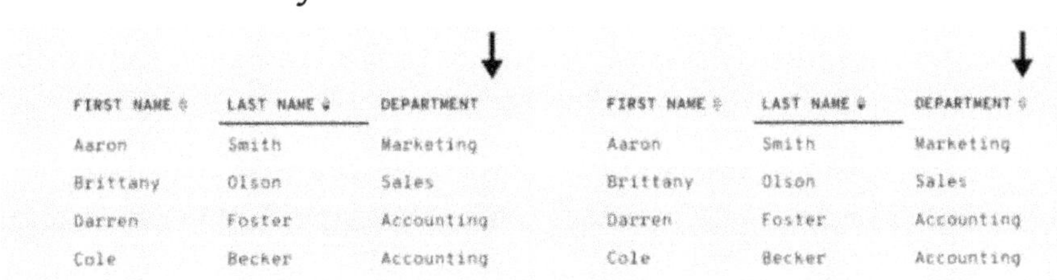

Fig. 19.4 The example on the left has inconsistent sorting; not all columns have the option to sort. Users may want to sort data in other columns. The example on the right has consistent sorting on all columns.

Review your content

It's not just about the visual elements, but also the text throughout the application.

Consistent copy — especially consistent terminology — in each place in the application is another key. Using two different words for the same function makes them seem like different functions, causing a momentary pause in the workflow while the user sorts out the discrepancy.

Consistent copy avoids this confusion.

Content structure

Content plays a crucial role in UI elements, whether something as simple as navigation listings or as complex as product documentation. It's not just the words themselves, but how to copy text is presented visually, such as body copy, list items, table content, etc.

In particular, pay attention to how content is handled in these areas:

- Navigation
- Dropdowns
- Form fields
- Validation messages
- Tooltips
- Charts
- Image captions
- Error messages
- Loading screens
- Confirmation pages
- Product support documentation

Brand consistency in content

You know that feeling when a certain part of an application feels "off." A lot of times the reason is an inconsistency in the content's language, for example, if one button says "Logout" and another says "Sign out."

Even less noticeable inconsistencies can create that "off" feeling.

For the Oxford comma fans out there, something as "minor" as comma usage is picked up subconsciously. After enough of these subconscious flags, the user's *conscious* brain starts to notice.

Other writing guidelines such as title case and voice/tone also influence the user's experience. While title typography is more empirical, voice and tone are a little harder to pin down. The trouble escalates if most content uses a casual style that clashes with a more formal "brand language."

Appropriate user defaults

By considering user goals upfront, you can set realistic defaults to reduce the burden on the user.

If the defaults are set to the most popular preferences, the user may not have to make any adjustments at all. Take the date picker on an airline or car rental site. Often the starting default date is sometime in the near future, the most likely choice according to past statistics.

Pay close attention to forms, too; they're a great opportunity for defaults to reduce the amount of user effort.

CONSISTENT COMMUNICATION

Search results, form submit messages, error windows — every interaction with your user is communication. For an app to be successful, it must speak to the user and keep them informed on what's happening. And, as with everything else, the way you communicate should be consistent.

Changes in state and helpful information

Users appreciate feedback: a toggle that changes color to indicate "on" or "off," for example, or a sound effect to verify a completed action.

Your user should never waste time wondering whether an action took place or not. Form field submissions are notorious for this, but it happens in other areas as well. In situations where it may not be clear, a quick success (or error) message is all you need.

Play it safe. Even when it's apparent that the action was successful, a lot of users still prefer a quick confirmation.

Reduce user frustration

The most common cause of user frustration happens when it's not clear what to do next. Some tasks are not so self-explanatory, but UI and UX designers are often too close to it to notice. Luckily, some instructional text — even just a line or two — can solve the problem.

For the same reason, error messages are useful too. While users may not like seeing them, they still need to know what happened and how it can be corrected.

Level Up Design Consistency with UXPin

Consistency in UI is a huge undertaking, and it's easy for some parts to slip through the cracks. The end goal is, of course, a perfectly consistent and in-sync interface, but that's not always possible right out of the gate.

For startups, you can try an MVP (minimum viable product). Even if the product starts out with some inconsistencies, your team can iron them out one by one over time once you start receiving feedback.

OVERCOMING COMMON CHALLENGES

Keep a balance between user needs and business goals.

The first challenge is prevalent; you will experience it in almost all projects. Users have different desires and needs, and businesses have goals and requirements.

You have to balance them to find the right solution. You have to design a product that perfectly strikes a balance between user needs and business goals. Most business goals are profitability, user engagement, customer retention, etc. Ensuring the delicate balance is what the finest UX designers do.

Solution:

- Research user persona, target audience, competitor analysis, and know what your customers expect from the product.
- Discuss business goals thoroughly with the client.
- Use various data analytics to measure user engagement and meet business requirements.
- Involve stakeholders in the design process to meet user needs.
- Go for a user-centric design to meet user needs.

Compatibility for different devices and platforms

In today's tech-driven era, users access apps or websites on various devices and platforms. You must ensure the app offers a uniform user experience across all devices. If the app does not work flawlessly across all devices and platforms, users will not appreciate it.

Ensure the app works seamlessly on tablets, computers, mobile browsers, and Android iOS platforms. Hire a web development company with talented, experienced UX designers to ensure high-end compatibility across all devices.

Solutions:

You can follow these approaches to offer a seamless user experience across all devices and platforms.

- You should use a system that perfectly defines consistent design patterns and components.
- Conduct thorough testing across all devices and platforms to find usability issues and inconsistencies.
- Follow platform-specific design guidelines to ensure a flawless performance.
- Offer a personalised experience to users by considering the user's needs, location, devices, preferences, and interests.

Highly intuitive and impressive User Interfaces

Users interact with the app through a user interface. It is the first section they come across with. Users might feel disappointed if you have a cluttered, unimpressive, dull user interface. You must design an intuitive, impressive, visually appealing user interface to score high in the first match.

An ideal user interface allows users to easily navigate, use, and understand the app. Designers must design a user interface with the right mix of colours, typography, layouts, and visual hierarchy. Also, the user interface must offer high-end functionality to users.

Solutions:

Here are guidelines to ensure highly creative and intuitive user interfaces.

- Work on the user's attention and focus by creating a visual hierarchy.
- Use the right mix of colour, typography, and visual design.
- Give users a sense of delight with micro-interactions and animations.
- Test the app's user interface regularly to identify and fix usability issues disturbing users' journeys.
- Go for a user-centric design approach to meet the needs and preferences of users.

Accessibility and inclusivity

Does your web or app design allow people with disabilities to access it? If not, you need to think about it. Accessibility and inclusivity are the primary traits to consider while designing an app or a website. Also, your website design must follow accessibility standards like Web Content Accessibility Guidelines (WACG).

Furthermore, you must design an app considering various needs and backgrounds like age, race, culture, language, and gender identity. Users should be able to access and use the app or website regardless of their abilities, backgrounds, and physical disabilities.

Solutions:

Here is a list of tips to ensure accessibility and inclusivity in design.

- Receive feedback from people with disabilities to design the app appropriately.
- Follow user accessibility standards while designing the app.
- Go for an inclusive design approach that perfectly caters to users of all backgrounds.
- Avoid jargon and technical terms that might be difficult for people to understand.
- Come up with various web app ideas and representations to ensure the diversity of users.

Budget and Time Restrictions

Your client wants the app to be designed and developed by this week. However, you have lots of work to do. Such deadlines might kill creativity. Also, you have budget restrictions to think of. In such scenarios, designers face challenges developing high-end, impressive, and unique designs. It might compromise your creativity.

Solutions:

Here is what you do in case of budget and time constraints.

- Prioritise your tasks in a manner that you finish all the tasks before the deadline ends.
- The best way to do this is to break the project into various small, manageable tasks.
- Set realistic deadlines that can be met without compromising quality.
- Hire a professional UI UX design services provider with a team of talented UI UX designers who are good at planning the design process.

Confused and Complex Chatbots

Chatbots are great at guiding users in a dilemma or want answers. However, sometimes, these chatbots confuse customers by offering irrelevant solutions. It might impact user engagement and abandonments. These chatbots are generally AI chatbots, and they sometimes miss what customers are looking for. In such scenarios, designers might face challenges in how to overcome such confusion.

Solutions:

Here is what you can do to overcome this challenge:

- The best way is to keep the language of the chatbots simple for questions and answers.
- Connect users with support agents immediately if the question is complex.
- Iterate on design to improve the performance of chatbots.

Lack of Understanding of Your Role

The most common challenge among freshly recruited designers is not knowing their roles and needing to know their responsibilities. It might create confusion and chaos. Sometimes, it could result in over-commitment and under-delivery. Also, it might jeopardize your company, reputation, and delivery schedule.

Solution

Here is a list of things you can do to avoid it.

- The designer must be well-versed in their role and responsibilities. Take a proper training session with them to educate them about their role.
- They should know what exactly is expected from them.
- Keep a communication channel open with them to avoid communication gaps.

Keeping up to date with design trends

Another challenge for designers is to keep up with the latest design trends. The UX design is a broad spectrum, and new design trends rule it globally. Designers must be familiar with the latest trends and design aspects to offer the best design solutions to their clients. They should be well-versed in the latest design tools and other resources.

Solution:

- Keep a design journal to note essential design aspects and trends.
- Steal daily or weekly to learn and upskill yourself with different design trends.
- Keep reading web and app design resources to keep updated with the latest designs.

A/B Testing Errors

Sometimes, A/B testing leads to inaccuracies and might affect design consistency. Designers might develop better design choices that can improve the overall visual impact of the user interface. Such A/B testing errors occur due to unclear hypotheses, false or misleading metrics, or insufficient sample sizes.

Solution:

- Ensure clear hypotheses to avoid such misinterpreting results.
- Ensure to start the test when all the components are in the right place.
- Choose the right audience and use an excellent sizable sample to get accurate results.

Design-Development Gap

This is the last but the most critical challenge to understand and conquer. When designers fail to balance the design and development phases, it might lead to inaccuracies. Some design features must be implemented appropriately, leading to a UX design that does not meet users' needs.

The design-development gap occurs when developers face issues while implementing the design features. The leading cause of this issue is the need for more communication between designers and developers. This gap might lead to delayed deliveries, inconsis-tencies, increased costs, and poor outcomes.

Solution:

- Involve developers in the design process to ensure transparency.
- Ensure that developers understand technical constraints and feasibility.
- Developers should also offer valuable feedback and suggestions to improve the product's overall design.
- Use a design system, a collection of various design components, styles, guidelines, and other valuable resources that clearly define the functional and visual aspects of the product.

Part VIII: Future Trends and Innovations

CHAPTER-20

EMERGING TRENDS IN UX AND DESIGN THINKING

AL AND MACHINE LEARNING IN UX

Artificial intelligence (AI) has been making waves for years now, impacting major industries as varied as retail, healthcare, and security. With each passing year, the rapidly advancing technology reshapes our world in ways that were once just fantasy.

For some, "the rise of the robots" is something to fear. Many people view it as a threat to their jobs, a relentless machine that can do everything they do, only faster, better, and without pay or sleep.

But here's the thing: AI won't just take jobs, it will create them too. In fact, by the year 2022, AI and machine learning will have displaced 75 million jobs but will have created 133 million as well.

One area that is being revolutionized by improvements in AI is user experience (UX).

The impact of AI and ML on UX design is significant and will continue to grow in the future. These technologies are already being used to create more personalized, engaging, and efficient user experiences. As AI and ML continue to develop, they will have an even greater impact on the way we design products and services.

Here are some of the ways that AI and ML are impacting UX design:

- **Personalization:** AI can be used to personalize the user experience by tailoring content and features to each individual user. This can be done by using data about the user's interests, demographics, and behavior. The rise of AI and ML has made it possible to create highly personalized user experiences. Machine learning algorithms can analyze user data, including demographics, behavior, and preferences, to deliver personalized content and recommendations. This approach, known as User-Centered Design, can help designers create interfaces tailored to each user's individual needs. For example, a travel website can use ML algorithms to suggest destinations based on the user's search history, location, and preferences. This level of personalization can lead to higher engagement, satisfaction, and loyalty.
- **Engagement:** AI can be used to create more engaging user experiences by using natural language processing to generate text that is tailored to the user's interests. This can be done by using chatbots, virtual assistants, and other AI-powered tools.
- **Efficiency:** AI can be used to improve the efficiency of the user experience by automating tasks that are typically performed by humans. This can be done by using machine learning to identify patterns in user behavior and then automating tasks based on those patterns.

The multiple benefits of ML-driven UX design include:

- **Increased user satisfaction**: At the forefront of ML-driven UX design is its unparalleled ability to increase user satisfaction. ML algorithms analyze massive datasets of user interactions to uncover patterns, preferences, and pain points; armed with this deep insight, designers can make data-driven decisions to enrich the user journey. For example, ML can predict the type of content users are most likely to engage with, leading to hyper-targeted recommendations and increased user satisfaction.
- **Real-time adaptability**: In the relentless pace of the digital world, static designs are no longer sustainable. Users increasingly demand interfaces that dynamically adapt to their evolving needs. Machine learning delivers this adaptability by constantly examining user interactions and recalibrating

the interface accordingly; this ensures that users receive a dynamic and personalized experience, driving greater engagement and loyalty.

- **Data-driven design decisions**: Machine learning empowers designers with actionable insights derived from data. Decisions are no longer based on intuition alone, but are informed by tangible user behavior patterns; this data-driven approach significantly reduces the need for design guesswork, resulting in more effective UX improvements.

Machine learning applications in UX design include:

Personalized content recommendations

ML algorithms underpin the personalized content recommendations that are ubiquitous on platforms like Netflix and Spotify. By analyzing user behavior, machine learning deftly suggests content tailored to individual tastes, resulting in greater user engagement and longer sessions.

Chatbots and virtual assistants

Machine learning is responsible for the proliferation of chatbots and virtual assistants in digital interfaces. ML equips these bots with the ability to understand user queries, provide relevant responses, and even anticipate user needs, resulting in more efficient and user-friendly interactions.

A/B Testing optimization

A/B testing is a staple of UX design, but machine learning takes it to another level. Machine Learning can autonomously analyze A/B test results and make real-time adjustments to optimize the user experience based on what resonates most with users.

The future of Machine Learning in UX design

Hyper-personalization

As machine learning algorithms become more sophisticated, hyper-personalization will dominate the UX design landscape. Interfaces will not only cater to users' preferences, but also take into account their emotions, context, and even physiological responses, fostering an unprecedented level of personalization.

Cross-platform consistency

Machine learning will usher in a new era of seamless consistency across different digital platforms and devices. Users will enjoy a harmonious experience, whether they're on a website, mobile app, or IoT device, thanks to ML's ability to adapt interfaces to different contexts.

THE IMPACT OF VIRTUAL AND AUGMENTED REALITY

As technology continues to evolve, the landscape for UX and UI designers is transforming. New ways of designing spaces, experiences, and interactions are rapidly emerging, and nowhere is this more evident than in the worlds of augmented reality (AR) and virtual reality (VR). These technologies are revolutionizing the very essence of UX/UI design, demanding innovative responses to high levels of user immersion and interaction.

Traditional design models focus on 2D or 3D graphical interfaces displayed on flat screens. However, AR and VR technologies move beyond these flat, static experiences. They immerse users in digitally-rendered environments or overlay digital elements onto the physical world, thereby creating surreal experiences. These experiences challenge UX/UI designers to navigate uncharted territories of spatial, multi-sensory, and movement-based interaction.

One significant shift that AR and VR technologies have brought to UX/UI design pertains to spatial design. In contrast with traditional interfaces, these experience-rich technologies require designers to think in terms of physical space, volume, and dimensionality. An optimal AR or VR experience is not just about how it looks, but also about how it feels to navigate the designed environment.

One practical example of this new design thinking is exhibited in the game "Beat Saber." To hit blocks in time with the rhythm, players have to physically move their bodies. This design effectively utilizes the physical and spatial elements of the interface, creating a more engaging and immersive user experience.

Another crucial aspect that VR/AR is adding to UX/UI design is the challenge of information display. In traditional screen-based interfaces, all information is typically laid out on the screen. With AR/VR, designers need to think about presenting information in ways that users can interact with and that won't interfere with their immersive experiences. For instance, "Google Lens" uses AR to overlay digital information over real-world objects as users point their smartphones at them. By doing this, relevant information becomes readily available without disrupting the user's experience.

Furthermore, sound design is becoming an increasingly important facet of the user interface within these technologies. Alongside the visual design, sound provides users with important feedback and can significantly influence their interaction with the virtual environment. A practical example includes VR applications such as "Tilt Brush" where sound effects are utilized to enhance user interaction and feedback.

Augmented Reality (AR): Blurring the Lines Between the Physical and Digital Worlds

AR seamlessly overlays digital information onto the real world, creating a hybrid experience that seamlessly blends the physical and digital realms. This innovative technology has ignited a wave of creativity and innovation in UI/UX design, enabling designers to craft experiences that were once considered unimaginable.

Revolutionizing Product Demos and Experiences

AR empowers users to visualize and interact with virtual products in their own physical environments. For instance, furniture retailers can leverage AR technology to allow customers to virtually place furniture in their homes, enabling them to make informed purchasing decisions.

Enhancing Navigation and Guidance

AR provides real-time information and guidance, seamlessly integrating digital directions into the user's physical surroundings. This technology has revolutionized navigation, offering users a more intuitive and immersive way to find their way around unfamiliar places.

Gamification and Interactive Experiences

AR unlocks a world of possibilities for interactive games and experiences. Users can engage with virtual objects and environments, blurring the lines between play and reality.

Virtual Reality (VR): Creating Immersive and Captivating Digital Environments.

VR transports users into entirely immersive virtual environments, offering a level of engagement and realism that was previously unattainable. This technology has opened up a new frontier in UI/UX design, enabling designers to create experiences that are both captivating and transformative.

Training and Simulation

VR has emerged as a powerful tool for training and simulation, providing realistic and engaging scenarios that replicate real-world situations. This technology is revolutionizing training across a wide range of industries, from aviation to healthcare.

Entertainment and Storytelling:

VR is redefining entertainment, offering users immersive experiences that transport them to new worlds and stories. VR movies, concerts, and games are captivating audiences worldwide.

TRENDS SHAPING THE FUTURE OF AR AND VR UI/UX DESIGN

As AR and VR continue to evolve, several key trends are shaping the future of UI/UX design in these domains:

- **Natural Interactions:** AR and VR applications are becoming increasingly intuitive and user-friendly, adopting natural interactions such as gestures and voice commands.
- **Personalized Experiences:** AR and VR applications are harnessing data and analytics to provide personalized and relevant experiences, tailoring content and interactions to individual users.
- **Cross-Platform Development:**AR and VR applications are being designed to work seamlessly across a variety of devices, from smartphones and tablets to dedicated headsets, ensuring a consistent user experience.

THE FUTURE OF AR AND VR UI/UX DESIGN:A REALM OF POSSIBILITIES

The future of AR and VR is incredibly bright, with the potential to revolutionize the way we interact with the world around us. Here are some of the key trends that are shaping the future of AR and VR:

Increased Accessibility and Affordability

AR and VR devices are becoming more affordable and accessible, making them available to a wider range of users. This will lead to more innovative applications and experiences being developed for these technologies.

Improved Hardware and Software

The hardware and software for AR and VR are constantly improving, which will enable even more immersive and realistic experiences. This will make it possible to create experiences that are more engaging and interactive than ever before.

Convergence with Other Technologies

AR and VR are already converging with other technologies, such as artificial intelligence (AI) and machine learning (ML). This will lead to even more powerful and sophisticated applications that can adapt to the user's needs and preferences.

Integration into Everyday Life

AR and VR will become more integrated into our everyday lives, from shopping to education to entertainment. This will make it possible to experience the world in new and exciting ways.

Personalized and Adaptive Experiences

AR and VR will become more personalized and adaptive, tailoring content and interactions to individual users. This will create more engaging and meaningful experiences.

Seamless Multi-Device Interactivity

AR and VR will seamlessly interact with other devices, such as smartphones, tablets, and computers, creating a more connected and integrated user experience.

Emotional Connection and Storytelling

AR and VR will be used to create more emotional and immersive storytelling experiences, transporting users to new worlds and perspectives.

Gamification and Interactive Experiences

AR and VR will continue to be used to create gamified and interactive experiences, blurring the lines between play and reality.

Advanced Analytics and User Insights

AR and VR will generate rich data and user insights, allowing designers to create more effective and personalized experiences.

Ethical Considerations and Responsible Design

AR and VR developers will need to consider the ethical implications of their work, ensuring that these technologies are used responsibly and with respect to user privacy and well-being.

GLOSSARY OF UX AND DESIGN THINKING TERMS

A/B testing: A/B testing (also known as split testing), is the comparison of two designs against each other to determine which performs better.

Accessibility: The practice of designing experiences for people who experience disabilities. This means considering and designing for people who are color blind, blind, deaf, and people with cognitive disabilities, etc.

Active Listening: Active listening is a communication technique that requires the listener to demonstrate the act of alert, intentional hearing in order to extract the meaning from what the speaker is saying.

Affinity Diagramming: An exercise used to organise a large number of data and ideas, sorting them into groups based on their natural relationships and into more meaningful categories. Affinity Diagramming is frequently used following brainstorming sessions.

Affordance: In usability terms, Affordance refers to an objects characteristics in relation to its function. Affordances are clues that tell us how an element should behave. For example, a door handle is an affordance designed to tell us it can be pulled or pushed.

Agile: Agile is an incremental approach to software development. The methodology incorporates iteration, continuous delivery, and feedback cycles called "Sprints". Instead of building the entire product at once, Agile breaks it down into smaller bits of user functionality.

Analytics: A broad term that encompasses a variety of tools, techniques, and processes used to better understand and interpret patterns of behaviour on the products we use. Analytics in UX often measures user behaviour.

Anticipatory Design: Anticipatory Design is an approach to design where decisions are anticipated and made on behalf of customers, thus removing the need for choice and reducing cognitive load.

API: Application Programming Interfaces, or APIs, are pieces of software that help different applications communicate with each other. Products develop APIs to let you access and read information on their server easily.

Artificial Intelligence (AI) : Artificial Intelligence is the theory and development of computer systems able to perform tasks normally requiring human intelligence, such as visual perception, speech recognition, and decision-making.

Augmented Reality (AR) : A technology that adds a computer-generated, visual layer on top of the real world. For example, generating graphics, sound, or video into a live view of the user's physical environment in real-time.

Avatar: Avatar is an object that represents the user's identity on screen. Avatars are one of the most common UI elements usually within a circle or square. We have avatars in business apps, social networks, games.

Back-End Development: Back-end Development refers to the server-side of development where you are primarily focused on how the app or website works. T

Backlog: The backlog is a list of tasks to be completed. The list is prioritized and ideally, the tasks will be completed in the order listed.

Beacon: Beacons are small Bluetooth radio transmitters. They communicate with the user's smartphone and are used to share information.

Beta: A version of the product that is not final. A beta launch has limited functionality and is used to find bugs to improve the final product.

Benchmarking: Evaluate something, such as a user interface, against a standard or external comparator such as when comparing a website with a competitor.

Blind Voting: Blind voting is where the votes from each person included in the poll remain hidden or secret until all votes are cast. This prevents bias and vote influencing.

Brainstorming: Brainstorming is the process of generating ideas and solutions in a short amount of time. This main technique is divided into two sub-techniques: Brainwriting and Brainwalking.

Branding: The process of creating and marketing a consistent idea or image of a product, so that it is recognisable by the public.

Breadcrumb: Breadcrumb is a type of navigation to help users understand their location in a website or app. They'll show a sequence of steps users have to take to get where they are.

Bug: Bugs are mistakes in software that can cause a product to glitch, behave in unintended ways, or even crash.

Business Analyst (BA) : In software development, business analysts often act as the bridge between product development and business stakeholders to craft and document product requirements and help ensure that product decisions make business sense.

Call-To-Action (CTA) : A call to action (CTA) is a message that invites a reader, user, or consumer to take an action such as download, buy, read.

Card Sorting: Card Sorting is a user-centered research method used to inform the design of the information architecture. Card sorting involves users 'sorting' cards into groups that make the most sense to them. There are two different types: an open or close card sort.

Cascading Style Sheets (CSS) : A language that describes how HTML should be displayed. HTML is the barebones of the content, whereas CSS is applied to HTML to give elements styling options like layout, color, typography, and more.

Case Study: A UX case study (usually making up a UX portfolio) showcases the process of solving design problems. An emphasis is placed on how design thinking, methods, and deliverables were used to solve user experience problems.

Chatbot: Chatbots let you ask the system questions via a chat interface. They are a popular customer service tool and resemble the experience of texting a friend.

Closed Questions: Closed questions are those that require only a yes or no response when answered.

Co-creation: Co-creation is the method by which products, services, and processes are created with the involvement of the organisation plus customers or users and other third parties, such as agencies. The process can often be led by a design agency on behalf of a client. Often referred to as Collaborative Design.

Cognitive Biases: Cognitive biases are errors in reasoning, memory, or other cognitive processes that result from holding onto existing beliefs regardless of contrary information. There are more than 100 documented cognitive biases, commonly categorized into four categories: biases that arise from too much information, not enough meaning, the need to act quickly, and the limits of memory. Cognitive biases are particularly important to be aware of while conducting research, as a way of arriving at truer findings instead of relying on personal preferences.

Cognitive Load: Cognitive load refers to the amount of effort that is exerted or required while reasoning and thinking. Any mental process, from memory to perception to language, creates a cognitive load because it requires energy and effort. When cognitive load is high, thought processes are potentially interfered with. To the UX designer, a common goal when designing interfaces would be to keep users' cognitive load to a minimum.

Cognitive Walkthrough: Cognitive walkthrough is a usability method carried out by a trained professional who attempts to identify usability issues by mimicking the actions of a user.

Competitor Analysis: Competitor analysis in strategic terms is a technique used to evaluate and identify the marketing and business strategy of competitive brands, businesses, and products. In user experience terms it is applied to identifying and analysing competitor's web, mobile or digital strategies.

Content Management System (CMS): Software that allows publishing, editing, and maintaining content from a central interface.

Content Strategist: Content strategists help maximize the usability and profitability of content, throughout the full content lifecycle: analyzing, planning, writing, editing, distributing, managing, and monitoring content. Due to the wide breadth of this field, the work that content strategists do often affect and involve information architecture and the user experience.

Content Strategy: The strategy, organization, and management of content that aligns between the user and business goals.

Contextual Inquiry: Contextual inquiry is a type of ethnographic field study that involves in-depth observation and interviews to gain an understanding of work practices and behaviors. The research takes place in the users' natural environment as they conduct their activities the way they normally would. The context could be in their home, office, or somewhere else entirely. The researcher watches the user as she performs her task and asks for information to understand how and why users do what they do.

Conversion Rate: The Conversion Rate of a product or site is the percentage of users who complete a desired action. For example, an e-commerce website's desired action is a successful purchase. The Conversion Rate would tell us how many users bought an item.

Conversational Interface: A Conversational Interface (or Conversation User Interface) emulates a conversation with a real human. It uses voice recognition and natural language processing to mimic human conversation. For example, Amazon's Alexa, Apple's Siri, Microsoft's Cortana. and the Google assistant.

Customer-Centric: Customer centricity refers to companies that select a strategy focussed or built upon a specific orientation toward its customers and prospective customers. For example, Amazon's #1 Leadership Principle is Customer Obsession. Their leaders start with the customer and work backwards. Although leaders pay attention to competitors, they obsess over customers.

Customer Experience (CX) : Customer Experience or CX refers to all the different interactions a user has with a brand through its different channels and products, and how a user feels about them.

Customer Journey Map: A holistic, visual representation of your users' interactions with your organisation, products, or services. It helps you tell the story of your customers' experiences with your brand across all touchpoints. Also called the Buyer Journey or User Journey).

Customer Relationship Management (CRM) : Customer Relationship Management software systems help manage business processes, like sales, data, and customer interactions.

Dashboard: A Dashboard is a simple visual representation of often complex data sets designed to make understanding and decision making easier.

Dark Patterns: Tricks used in websites and apps that cause unintended user action, like buying or signing up for things that you didn't mean to. For example, a checkbox beneath a password field when signing up in, but instead of "Keep me logged in", it says, "I agree to subscribe to this newsletter." That's a dark pattern — when a product tricks you into buying or signing up for things that you actually don't want.

Data Science: Data science is an interdisciplinary field that uses scientific methods, processes, algorithms, and systems to extract knowledge and insights from data. The goal is to uncover valuable insights that help us make better product decisions.

Demographic: Demographics relates to how a population is structured and is used in user experience when defining participant profiles.

Design Debt: Design debt represents the full spectrum of design work that has been deprioritized in the backlog. It includes everything from lack of design thinking processes to specific UI bugs that need fixing. For example, a newly launched web form is not consistent with the rest of the website, because a whole page template would need to be recoded.

Design Exercise: Often a take-home "quiz" of sorts to determine a design process. Sometimes a part of UX interviews.

Design Facilitation: The skill of facilitating design process and efforts, such as presenting to stakeholders or conducting design workshops.

Design Patterns: Repeatable design elements and components, often leveraging widespread user recognition to aid in the design process. For example, a hamburger menu is now a design pattern that most users know how to interact with.

Design Sprint: The Design Sprint is a 5-day (sometimes shorter) process for answering critical business questions through design, prototyping, and testing ideas with customers.

Design System: A design system is a collection of reusable components, guided by clear standards, that can be assembled together to build any number of applications.

Design Thinking: Design thinking is a 5-stage method for creative problem-solving. The 5 stages are: 1. Empathize: Understand the challenge, 2.Ideate: Brainstorm potential solutions, 3. Prototype: Build your solutions and 4. Test: Test your solutions.

Diary Study: A qualitative research method asking users to record their experiences and thoughts about a product or task in a journal over a set period of time.

Edge Case: An edge case is a rare occurrence in the product or service. Edge cases deal with the extreme maximums and minimums of parameters. Sometimes edge cases threaten to break a system and lead to poor user experience. For example, if an application allows for "unlimited" photo uploads knowing that users rarely upload more than 1000, how does the system deal with the edge case of the user who uploads millions of photos? Are there boundaries at this maximum end? That is an edge case, an unlikely-yet-potentially disastrous situation.

Empathy Map: Empathy maps are collaborative tools that help us visualize user behavior, attitudes, and feelings. This is split into 4 equal quadrants containing information about what the user is saying, thinking, doing, and feeling. At the center, is our user persona. Each quadrant is filled with information gathered from user research.

End-User: The person we are designing the product for.

Engagement: A typical success metric defined by an organisation. For example, time spent on a web page, number of interactions on a piece of content (likes, shares, comments), etc.

Ergonomics: Ergonomics is the study or science of understanding the interactions between humans and systems, products, or equipment. The goal is to design in order to optimize human well-being and overall system performance.

Ethnography: Ethnography is a qualitative research method used to capture information about behaviour in the context of people's real-world environments. Through observations, It can be used to obtain unarticulated needs, motivations, and drivers to develop innovative designs.

Experience Design: Experience design is the approach for designing systems, products, processes, services, interfaces, and more with emphasis on the experience the user will have at the forefront of the design process.

Eye-Tracking: Eye-tracking measures the users eye activity whilst they are engaged in a particular task. Where a person looks, what they ignore, and when they blink. Eye-tracking provides quantitative measures of attention. These can be correlated with task completion time, error rate, success rate, backtracking rate, and other indicators of an interface's efficiency and used together as results from usability testing or as a standalone tool to tackle specific issues.

Facilitator: A facilitator, in the context of UX, is a practitioner who leads workshops, meetings, focus groups, or one-to-one sessions. The objective is to lead the group to achieve a common goal and/or be the main driver of the session.

Fitt's Law: Fitt's Law is a model that helps designers place and position the size and location of user interface elements for their optimal utility. Fitt's Law states "the time to acquire a target is a function of the distance to and size of the target".

Flat Design: Flat design is a style of interface design emphasising minimum use of stylistic elements that give the illusion of three dimensions and is focused on a minimalist use of simple elements, typography, and colours.

Flowchart: A flow chart or flow diagram is a visual representation of a series of steps in a process that explains how the process works. Often used to illustrate the steps a user can take to complete a task on a product.

Focus groups: A Focus group is a session held with a group of representative users or consumers facilitated by a researcher who guides the discussion about a specific product, service, system, brand, or interface.

Front-End Development: Front-end development is the practice of implementing designs in code to be displayed on the web. Front-end developers primarily use HTML, CSS, and JavaScript to code designs. "Front-end" refers to the "client-side" - for example, a user's browser window.

Gamification: Gamification is the process of integrating game-design mechanics and principles in non-game contexts such as websites and mobile applications in an effort to drive increase user adoption, engagement, and retention.

Gestalt Principles: Gestalt principle is also known as the law of simplicity and concerns the principle that the whole is greater than the sum of the parts and that people tend to perceive things in their simplest form.

GitHub: GitHub is a collaborative development platform used by developers.

Graphic Design: Graphic design is one of the best-known practices within the world of design and technology. It includes fundamentals of design like typography, colour theory, illustration, and even photography. Sometimes also referred to as communication design, the practice of developing and communicating media to target audiences.

Grid System: A grid system works as a framework that helps product teams to arrange UI elements in a way that allows maintaining good visual balance from page to page. Text, images, and functions are aligned on the column-based structure. It allows designers and developers to create more consistent and appealing UI.

Guerrilla Usability Testing: Guerrilla usability testing is a quick and inexpensive way of testing a prototype or website with real users. Instead of recruiting a specific targeted audience to take part in sessions, participants are approached in public places and asked to take part in the research. These sessions normally last for only 10-15 minutes with little or no incentive.

Heat Map: A heat map is a graphical representation of the areas on your product that receive the most user attention. It uses a warm-to-cool colour spectrum to show you where exactly your users are going. Red indicates a high frequency of attention with degrees to white representing lower levels of attention.

Heuristic Evaluation: Heuristic evaluation is the documentation of a website or app's usability flaws and other areas for improvement against the 10 best practice guidelines published by Jakob Nielsen to help guide usability assessments.

Hick's Law: Hick's law, sometimes referred to as Hick-Hyman law, is a model for measuring human reaction time based on the number of choices presented to them. Hick's Law states "the time it takes to make a decision increases with the number and complexity of choices".

High Fidelity Prototype: A prototype that is polished and similar to a final design, with lots of detail and a good indication of the final proposed aesthetics and functionality. It is sufficiently well formed to allow for rigorous testing with users.

HTML: Hypertext Markup Language, or HTML, is the standard programming language used to create websites and web applications. Unlike CSS, it is concerned with the structure of a website, similar to a blueprint of a building.

Human-Computer Interaction (HCI) : Human-computer interaction (HCI) is a multidisciplinary field of study focusing on the design of computer technology and, in particular, the interaction between humans (the users) and computers. While initially concerned with computers, HCI has since expanded to cover almost all forms of information technology design.

Ideation: Ideation refers to a process or method for forming ideas or concepts.

Inclusive Design: Inclusive Design is a methodology, born out of digital environments, that enables and draws on the full range of human diversity. Most importantly, this means including and learning from people with a range of perspectives.

Industrial Design: Industrial design uses both applied art and science to improve the aesthetics, functionality, ergonomics, and or usability of a physical product.

Infographic: Infographics or information graphics are visual representations of information or data designed to communicate complex or detailed information simply and contextually.

Information Architecture: Information architecture (IA) is the practice organizing and arranging information to make it understandable. This includes defining hierarchies, parent-child relationships and in general making sense out of an (informational) mess.

Innovation: Innovation is the process of developing or introducing something new.

Iteration: Iterating is the act of repeating a process with the aim of approaching a desired goal, target, or result. Each repetition of the process is also called an iteration.

Interface: An interface is the point at which a person or user comes in to contact with an organisations systems, processes, products, or services.

Interaction Design (IxD): Interaction Design, or IxD, is the practice of designing interactive digital products and considering the way in which users will interact with them. A discipline that focuses specifically on how users interact with products (both digital and analog). This could be buttons on a page, swipes on an app, or how to use a can opener that only has one handle.

JavaScript: A call to action (CTA) is a message that invites a reader, user, or consumer to take an action such as download, buy, read.

Job-To-Be-Done: Jobs-to-be-done is a theory of consumer action. It describes the mechanisms that cause a consumer to adopt an innovation. The theory states that markets grow, evolve, and renew whenever customers have a Job to be Done, and then buy a product to complete it (get the Job Done).

Job Stories: Job stories (from jobs-to-be-done) help define user tasks in product design. Different from user stories, it attempts to avoid leading a design with persona-first phrasing. Format: When [name situation], I want to [list motivations and forces], so I can [expected outcome]. Example: When I go shopping for groceries, I want to find the cheapest available produce, so I can save money shopping.

Kerning: Kerning is the spacing between individual letters or characters. Unlike tracking, which adjusts the amount of space between the letters of an entire word in equal increments, kerning is focused on how type looks – creating readable text that's visually pleasing.

KPI: KPIs, or Key Performance Indicators, are measurable values that help us understand and track how well a product is doing. As a UX designer, you'll often work with KPIs like task success rate, user error rate, and time on task.

Landing Page: Any page a user lands on is considered a landing page. However, landing pages are often tied to ads and search results and are designed to meet specific conversion goals. Not only are they the page a user lands on, but they are also a crucial part of marketing campaigns. It's common for landing pages that are part of a marketing campaign to be designed slightly differently than normal websites. Often, you'll find that they do not feature a navigation and tend to push a single action, like a download, purchase, or registration.

Law of Common Region: Law of Common Region states "Elements tend to be perceived into groups if they are sharing an area with a clearly defined boundary." Adding a border around an element or group of elements is an easy way to create common region. Common region can be created by defining a background behind an element or group of elements.

Law of Proximity: Law of Proximity states "Objects that are near, or proximate to each other, tend to be grouped together." Proximity helps to establish a relationship with nearby objects. Proximity helps users understand and organize information faster and more efficiently.

Law of Prägnanz: Law of Prägnanz states "People will perceive and interpret ambiguous or complex images as the simplest form possible because it is the interpretation that requires the least cognitive effort of us." The human eye likes to find simplicity and order in complex shapes because it prevents us from becoming overwhelmed with information. Research confirms that people are better able to visually process and remember simple figures than complex figures.

Law of Similarity: Law of Similarity states "The human eye tends to perceive similar elements in a design as a complete picture, shape, or group, even if those elements are separated." Elements that are visually similar will be perceived as related. Color, shape, and size, orientation and movement can signal that elements belong to the same group and likely share a common meaning or functionality. Ensure that links and navigation systems are visually differentiated from normal text elements.

Law of Uniform Connectedness: Law of Uniform Connectedness states "Elements that are visually connected are perceived as more related than elements with no connection. Group functions of a similar nature so they are visually connected via colors, lines, frames, or other shapes. Alternately, you can use a tangible connecting reference (line, arrow, etc) from one element to the next to also create a visual connection. Use uniform connectedness to show context or to emphasize the relationship between similar items.

Lean UX: Lean UX, based on Agile, is a collaborative user-centric approach that prioritizes "learning loops" (building, learning, and measuring through iterations) over design documentation. Whereas traditional UX may include rounds of wireframes and design reviews, Lean UX would prioritize the development of an MVP to gather user feedback.

Learnability: Learnability is 1 of the 5 quality components of usability (the others being efficiency, memorability, errors, and satisfaction). Learnability considers how easy it is for users to accomplish a task the first time they encounter the interface and how many repetitions it takes for them to become efficient at that task. Testing learnability is especially valuable for complex applications and systems that users access frequently, though knowing how quickly users can acclimate to your interface is valuable for even objectively simple systems.

Likert Scale: A Likert scale is a scale commonly used in surveys and market research questionnaires. A typical Likert scale contains 5 possible answers to a question. A Likert scale assumes that the strength/intensity of an attitude is linear, i.e. on a continuum from strongly agree to strongly disagree, and makes the assumption that attitudes can be measured. For example, each of the 5 responses would have a numerical value which would be used to measure the attitude under investigation.

Load Time: The load time is the amount of time taken to download and display the entire content of a web page or application.

Localisation: Localisation, used in field of UX, means the degree to which design, language, terminology, features, and functionality are adapted for a specific market.

Long tail: A long tail is a statistical term that refers to a probability distribution where a larger share of the population rests within the tail than normally would. A product strategy that allows companies to realize significant profits by selling low volumes of hard-to-find items to many customers, instead of only selling large volumes of a reduced number of popular items.

Look & Feel: Look and Feel is a term used in respect of a graphical user interface, including elements such as colours, shapes, layout, and typefaces (the "look"), as well as the behaviour of dynamic elements such as buttons, boxes, and menus (the "feel").

Low Fidelity Prototype: Low-fidelity prototypes are simple and low-tech concepts. All you need to get started is a pen and paper. The goal is to turn your ideas into testable artifacts that you can then use to collect and analyze feedback in the early stages.

Machine Learning: Machine learning is an application of artificial intelligence (AI) that provides systems the ability to automatically learn and improve from experience without being explicitly programmed. Machine learning focuses on the development of computer programs that can access data and use it to learn for themselves. The process of learning begins with observations or data.

Market research: Market research refers to the industry and profession that gathers and analyses information about how consumers use, interact with, perceive and consume goods and services.

Material Design: Material Design, often called just Material, is a design system developed by Google and native to Android devices.

Memorability: The degree to which users can remember how to use an interface. It poses the question, "when users return to the design after a period of not using it, how easily can they reestablish proficiency?"

Mental Model: A mental model represents what the user believes to be true about a product's functionality. The more a user's mental model aligns with a product's functionality, the easier it will be for them to use it. There is a hypothesis that this plays a major role in decision-making and how they approach a problem. For example, to navigate further down a page, some users have the mental model of "swiping up" on a screen, whereas other users are accustomed to "scrolling down."

Microcopy: Microcopy is everywhere on interfaces. It's the small bits of text you see on apps or websites that help you navigate it. Think labels on buttons, error messages, placeholder text in input fields, and text on tooltips. Small bits of text, big impact on your product's UX.

Microinteractions: Micro-interactions are events which have one main task and they're found all over your device and within apps. Microinteractions happen pairs in which (1) the trigger can be a user action or an alteration in the system's state; (2) the feedback is a narrowly targeted response to the trigger and is communicated through small, highly contextual (usually visual) changes in the user interface.

Miller's Law: Miller's Law "states "The average person can only keep 7 (plus or minus 2) items in their working memory." Organize content into smaller chunks to help users process, understand, and memorize easily.

Mind Map: A mind map is a visual representation through a spider diagram used to represent the thoughts, words, and ideas linked to or arranged around a keyword or theme.

Minimum Viable Product (MVP): A Minimum Viable Product, or MVP, refers to a product with core features to launch. The goal of the MVP is to save time & resources by incorporating early customer feedback before committing resources to build features users may not care about or even use. It also serves as a good tangible tool to test the value proposition.

Mobile Web: The mobile web refers to the use of the internet through handheld mobile devices. Designers create solutions to meet mobile users' unique requirements and restrictions. The focus is typically on accessibility, discoverability, and efficiency to optimize on-the-go interactive experiences.

Mockup: Mockups are representations of the final design. product. Unlike a prototype, a mockup is static and doesn't include any interactions. This is usually shared with clients and stakeholders between the phases of wireframes and prototypes.

Modal: A modal window is a pop-up window within an application. It creates a mode that disables the main application but keeps it visible. Users must interact with the modal before they can proceed or return to the application. Modals are commonly used during onboarding, confirmations, etc.

Mood Board: A mood board is a collage of images, fonts, interactions, features, icons, and UI elements to communicate the artistic direction of a project.

Multivariate testing (MVT): If A/B testing concerns two "variables," then multivariate testing concerns 3 or more options. The goal of multivariate testing is to determine which combination of variations performs the best out of all possible combinations.

Natural Language Processing (NLP): Natural language processing (NLP) is the ability of a computer program to understand human speech as it is spoken. They do this by processing and analysing large amounts of language data. NLP is a subfield of linguistics, computer science, and artificial intelligence.

Needfinding: Needfinding is the research process of identifying a user's need for a solution. The process of needfinding is based on the observation and study of people. This involves a blend of techniques including interviews carried out by researchers as well as close observations in real-world scenarios.

Net Promoter Score: A Net Promoter Score is used to measure brand loyalty. It is an index ranging from -100 to 100 that measures the willingness of customers to recommend a company's products or services to others.

Norman Door: A Norman door is a poorly designed door that confuses or fails to give you an idea whether to push or pull. It was named after Don Norman, the author of The Design of Everyday Things which explored the phenomenon.

Occam's Razor: Occam's Razor states "Among competing hypotheses that predict equally well, the one with the fewest assumptions should be selected." The best method for reducing complexity is to avoid it in the first place. Analyze each element and remove as many as possible, without compromising the overall function. Consider completion only when no additional items can be removed.

Omnichannel: Omnichannel is a cross-channel content strategy for retailers. A fully-integrated approach to commerce, providing consumers a unified experience across all channels or touchpoints. Omnichannel merges the worlds of websites, emails, retargeted ads, social media marketing, and physical locations to show personalized offers, products, and messages.

Open Card Sort: In open card sorts, there are no pre-determined categories (hence "open"). Participants sort cards into categories that make the most sense to them, then create their own labels for these groups.

Open Questions: Open questions are those that typically include a what, how, why, when and where component and cannot be answered with a yes or no response.

Open Source: Anything you stumble upon that is open source is available for public use and free. You can use it, modify it, and build with it without running into trouble. For example, Android is an open source operating system.

Operating System (OS) : An Operating System (OS) is a software that acts as an interface between computer hardware components and the user.

Pairing Designing: The practice of putting two designers together to solve design problems. The benefits of pair design include: separating of strategic and tactical thinking, producing higher-quality designs faster by providing continuous testing of ideas before they reach stakeholders, and develop a deeper design practice and stronger design culture.

Paper prototype: A rough, often hand-sketched, drawing of a user interface, used in a usability test to gather feedback. : Participants point to locations on the page that they would click, and screens are manually presented to the user based on the interactions they indicate.

Paradox of Choice: The paradox of choice describes paralysis and dissatisfaction one feels when presented with too many choices.

Pareto Principle: The Pareto principle states that "for many events, roughly 80% of the effects come from 20% of the causes." Focus the majority of effort on the areas that will bring the largest benefits to the most users.

Parkinson's Law: Parkinson's Law states "Any task will inflate until all of the available time is spent."

Peak-End Rule: Peak-end rule states "People judge an experience largely based on how they felt at its peak and at its end, rather than the total sum or average of every moment of the experience." Identify the moments when your product is most helpful, valuable, or entertaining and design to delight the end user. Pay close attention to the most intense points and the final moments (the "end") of the user journey. Remember that people recall negative experiences more vividly than positive ones.

Persona: A persona is a representation of the target user you're designing for. They aren't necessarily a real individual but are constructed using real information and data based on real users. Personas are often is created early in the design process so you know who you're designing for.

Pixel: Pixels are tiny squares used to construct the images we see on our device displays.

Pluralistic walkthrough: Pluralistic walkthrough is a usability method that revolves around a group of users, designers or developers together with usability practitioners stepping through tasks and scenarios in an attempt to identify usability issues and establish solutions.

Product Design: The entire process of creating usable products and experiences, starting by defining real-world problems and thinking about possible solutions. Highly synonymous with the broad nature of user experience design.

Product Designer: A product designer is responsible for the user experience of a product, usually helping to define the direction of the feature goals and objectives with product management. Synonymous with user experience designer, often with the added expectation of implementing designs end-to-end.

Production Environment: A production environment is where the latest versions of software, products, or updates are pushed live to the intended users. Think of it as the final phase of launching a digital product. This is the environment where the end-user can see, experience, and interact with the new product.

Product Management: Product management is the practice of strategically driving the development, market launch, and continual support and improvement of a company's products.

Product Managers: Professionals who navigate and manage the product cycle, from researching users and managing a roadmap to overseeing the development of the product. Depending on the business, a product manager may be responsible for one major feature, line of business or other project. Often considered "mini-CEOs" of a product because PMs have a direct impact on business revenue, cost, and growth.

Project Kickoff: A project kickoff is the start of any product and/or feature where UX designers needs to validate early assumptions, gather information from clients and/or team and set expectations of deliverables.

Progressive Disclosure: An interactive design technique that helps maintain the focus of a user's attention by reducing clutter, confusion, and cognitive workload. It improves usability by presenting only the minimum data required for the task at hand. The principle is also used in journalism's 'inverted pyramid' style, learning's 'spiral approach', and the game 'twenty questions'.

Progressive Web Application (PWA) : A progressive web application takes advantage of the latest technologies to combine the best of web and mobile apps. Think of it as a website built using web technologies but that acts and feels like an app. PWAs take advantage of the much larger web ecosystem, plugins, and community and the relative ease of deploying and maintaining a website when compared to a native application in the respective app stores.

Proto-Persona: Proto-personas helps you represent different user types of your product or service through fictional characters. Each of them represents the desires, motivations, and needs of a group of real users based on assumptions and the team's current knowledge and experience.

Prototype: Prototypes are interactive mockups of websites and mobile applications designed to look and feel like the real thing. They're much quicker to make, and although they aren't full-featured, they allow us to spot mistakes before we build the real thing.

Qualitative: Qualitative research is expressed in words. It is used to understand concepts, thoughts or experiences. This type of research enables you to gather in-depth insights on topics that are not well understood. Common qualitative methods include interviews with open-ended questions, observations described in words, and literature reviews that explore concepts and theories.

Quality Assurance (QA) : Quality assurance (QA) is a way of preventing mistakes in products and avoiding problems when delivering services to users. In the manufacturing world, the role of QA helps identify and reduce defects in products. In the software world, quality assurance and testers work hand-in-hand with product teams to test edge cases. In essence, their job is to intentionally find breaking points in products so that users don't have to.

Quantitative: Quantitative research is expressed in numbers and graphs. It is used to test or confirm hypotheses and assumptions. This type of research can be used to establish generalizable facts about a topic. Common quantitative methods include experiments, observations recorded as numbers, and surveys with closed-ended questions.

Questionnaires: A research instrument consisting of a series of questions and other prompts for the purpose of gathering information from respondents. Questionnaires provide a relatively cheap, quick, and efficient way of obtaining large amounts of information from a large sample of people.

Rapid Prototyping: Rapid prototyping is a design workflow that consists of ideation, creating a workable prototype, and testing to discover and validate their ideas quickly.

Readability: Readability measures the complexity of the words and sentence structure in a piece of content. The assumption behind this metric is that complex sentences are harder to parse and read than simpler ones.

Refactoring: Refactoring is the process of cleaning up and tidying code without affecting functionality, essentially increasing its quality. It isn't done all at once but rather in small, incremental steps.

Requirements Gathering: Requirements gathering is the process by which the scope and detail of a requirement is elicited from customers, users and stakeholders.

Responsive Design: A design approach that responds to the user's behavior and environment based on screen size, platform, and orientation. The practice consists of a mix of flexible grids and layouts, images, and an intelligent use of CSS media queries.

Retention: Retention is a matter of keeping your existing users for X amount of time. That might be an indefinite amount of time for products with long-term utility.

Return On Investment (ROI) : A measure for evaluating business performance. In traditional finance, ROI is the most common "profitability ratio" most often calculated by dividing net profit by total assets. The general idea of ROI helps product teams evaluate whether certain efforts are worth pursuing.

SaaS: Software as a Service, or SaaS, is a software distribution model in which software is licensed on a subscription basis and hosted on external servers. Subscribing users are able to access it through the web. For example, Netflix, Google Suite, Spotify, etc.

Scannability: The ease with which a body of text can be digested by the user.

Scrum: Scrum is an agile software development framework. The framework is used to manage product development and other knowledge work. Scrum is empirical in that it provides a means for teams to establish a hypothesis of how they think something works, try it out, reflect on the experience, and make the appropriate adjustments.

SDK: A software development kit, or SDK, is a software package that contains the tools required to develop products for a specific platform or operating system. They help expedite the development process by providing "parts" developers can use instead of having to write the code for them from scratch.

SEO: Search engine optimization (SEO) is the process of increasing a website's visibility in free, or organic, search results. It often involves writing useful content on a website around words and phrases users use in searches related to the brand's product or service.

Service Design: Service design is the process by which services are designed and developed from a user-centered, both from the employee's and user's perspective. A service design experience often involves multiple channels, contexts, and products. The goal is to optimize an organization's operations to better support customer journeys.

Serial Position Effect: Serial Position Effect states "Users have a propensity to best remember the first and last items in a series." Placing the least important items in the middle of lists can be helpful because these items tend to be stored less frequently in long-term and working memory. Positioning key actions on the far left and right within elements such as navigation can increase memorization.

Sitemap: A sitemap provides the overall structure, hierarchy, and organisation of a website or application. During the design process, sitemaps help define the informational structure of an experience, for example which categories fall under what page.

Sketching: Sketching is a distinctive form of drawing which UX designers use, typically, as a first wave of attack to tackle a design problem. Sketches are a useful part of the UX design process to explore, propose, refine and communicate design decisions.

Sprints: In agile software development, we call defined periods of time assigned to complete certain tasks "sprints." Their length can vary but is usually around 1-3 weeks. This name inspired GV's Design Sprints.

Stakeholder Interviews: Conversations with the key contacts (often internally within the organisation) regarding the project. Stakeholder interviews help you gain context and knowledge about the product, service, clients, customers, and overall project.

Storyboard: A tool inspired by the filmmaking industry, where a visual sequence of events is used to capture a user's interactions with a product. Storyboards look a lot like comic strips and include dialogue, instructions, and represent a user journey, scenario, or process.

Styleguide: A document containing the styling options that are repeated throughout a design, for the purpose of maintaining visual consistency throughout an experience. Styleguides are basically a set of rules of when to apply certain fonts, sizes, and more.

Survey: An online form designed to solicit feedback from current or potential users. A UX research survey is a set of questions, sent to a targeted group of users, that probes their attitudes and preferences. Surveys can be a quick, easy, and inexpensive way to obtain data questions you ask. A survey is a research method for capturing answers to structured questions from users or consumers. These can be qualitative and quantiative.

SVG: A popular image format, Scalable Vector Graphics, or SVGs, are scalable two-dimensional graphics that can be manipulated and animated with code.

T-Shaped Designer: T-shaped designers are strong generalists who know how to do all aspects of design sufficiently but excels especially in one discipline. The horizontal part of the letter "T" refers to the breadth of design skills, while the vertical part of "T" refers to the depth in one design specialty. Some teams are built by selecting T-shaped designers whose strengths work well together.

Task Analysis: Task analysis is the process of listing tasks or the steps a user takes to complete any given goal from the user's perspective. It is typically done during early stages of product development to help us identify and communicate problems in the user experience.

Taxonomy: The practice of classifying things and concepts. For example, how a website is separated into categories and sub-categories so that they are simple, easy to use, and learnable.

Tesler's Law: Tesler's Law, also known as The Law of Conservation of Complexity, states that "for any system, there is a certain amount of complexity which cannot be reduced." All processes have a core of complexity that cannot be designed away and therefore must be assumed by either the system or the user. Ensure as much as possible of the burden is lifted from users by dealing with inherent complexity during design and development. Take care not to simplify interfaces to the point of abstraction.

Think-Aloud Protocol: Think-Aloud Protocol (TAP) is a method used to gather information in usability testing. The participant, test subject, or user is asked to verbalise their thoughts as they progress through the test.

Tree Testing: A UX research method designed to understand and evaluate the findability, labels, and structure of a website's navigation menu. A tree test evaluates a hierarchical category structure, or tree, by having users find the locations in the tree where specific tasks can be completed. This is commonly used to test the findability, labeling, and structure of a navigation menu.

True Intent Study: A research method designed to collect data to understand user's objectives as they visit a website.

UI Kit: UI kits, or user interface kits, help you improve your design workflow. They also encourage recycling components instead of creating new ones from scratch. Commonly used for mobile design or prototyping, largely because two of the biggest operating systems—iOS and Android—both have robust, well-documented, and heavily supported design systems.

Unit Testing: The process of testing parts of an application to ensure they're working properly. It can be done manually or can be an automated process.

Usability: Usability is how easy and intuitive an experience is for users. How easy is a product to use? How intuitive is a feature? Does it get the job done, and if so, how much effort does a user have to exert before getting there?

Usability Testing: Usability testing is the practice of testing how easy a design is to use with a group of representative users. During usability tests, researchers observe participants who attempt to complete tasks. The goal is to identify usability problems, collect qualitative and quantitative data and determine participants' reactions to an experience.

User Experience (UX) : The User Experience refers to a user's emotions, attitude, and perceptions about a product, system, or service. In other words, it is how you feel while interacting with an app or website. Good UX makes a product useful, usable, desirable, findable, accessible, and credible.

User Groups: User Groups are similar to focus groups but tend to be used in usability research and involve a higher level of interaction between group participants and digital interfaces being evaluated or discussed.

User Flow: A user flow, or UX flow, is the path created by a user on a website or app to complete the task at hand. User flows are similar to a traditional flow chart, but they include visual interfaces or gestures. The flow maps out the user's entry point, exit point, and every step they take along the way. User flows focus on a specific user task, and eventually include all possible alternative paths. Designing for the "happy path"—the best way to complete a task without errors or exceptions—allows the designer to focus on exactly what the user needs, and nothing else.

User Interface (UI) : The medium through which users interact with an experience, product or device. Your mobile screen, the automated checkout kiosks at grocery stories, the keyboard on your laptop and the way Alexa responds to your voice are all examples of user interfaces.

User Interface (UI) Design: User interface design (UI design) refers to the visual elements of a product or digital experience. In essence, it's the translation of a brand's vision into a product or piece of software. The look and feel of a product. The most common UIs are on the phone, computer, or tablet you're using right now; at the ATM where you take out cash; and in your car.

User Journey: The step-by-step journey that a user takes to reach their goal.

User Research: User Research focuses on understanding users' behaviors, needs, worldviews, and motivations through a variety of analytical and observational techniques. While market research looks at broader demographic factors and trends, user research focuses on individual goals and behaviors.

User Stories: A method of translating research into actionable user goals and tasks. User stories are built from the perspective of target personas. Format: As a [persona], I want to [action], so that [expected outcome]. For example, as a busy designer, I want to learn a low barrier to entry to learning UX, so that I can get a promotion.

UX Portfolio: A showcase of a designer's best work. UX portfolios usually include in-depth case studies focusing on the design process and problem-solving. Most commonly presented as a website or presentation.

UX Researcher: A user research professional conducts research and helps translate those insights into actionable goals for product teams. User researchers apply both quantitative and qualitative focus to their work.

UX/UI Developer: Primarily a front-end developer with a knack for usability and a sensibility for coding products with the user in mind. Sometimes companies use this as a catchall unicorn role for someone who designs and codes.

UX Writer: UX writers develop written copy for user interfaces, with the aim of helping customers interact and use a product. The writing that's produced - whether it's the label on a button or help text under a form field, is often referred to as microcopy.

Virtual Reality (VR) : A simulation of 3d environments that users can interact with, often using special electronics like VR helmets, goggles, gloves, and sensors. Just like AR, VR is a new platform that will demand more UX & UI expertise from designers.

Visual Hierarchy: Commonly referred to as hierarchy in the Principles of Design, visual hierarchy is a way to visually rank your design elements. It's based on the order of visual importance, rather than aesthetics or design styles. A good design leads the eye through each area in a specific order that influences how objects are perceived by using contrast, balance, emphasis, and/or scale within the objects in a design. A good rule of thumb is that your most important elements should be the most prominent.

Visual Design: Also called communication design. A discipline that combines design and information development in order to develop and communicate a media message to a target audience.

Voice User Interface (VUI) : Interfaces that enable users to use voice input to control computers and devices. Functional VUIs depend on speech recognition in order to translate voice iput into commands a machine can understand.

Von Restorff Effect: The Von Restorff effect, also known as The Isolation Effect, predicts "that when multiple similar objects are present, the one that differs from the rest is most likely to be remembered." Make important information or key actions visually distinctive. Don't exclude those with a colour vision deficiency or low vision by relying exclusively on colour to communicate contrast.

Waterfall: Compared to agile or lean, waterfall is a software development method with a relatively linear, sequential process. Originating from heavy manufacturing and automotive industries, waterfall is now seen as a less flexible and iterative way of design. For proven, repeatable projects, waterfall may still have a place.

Wayfinding: Wayfinding refers to information systems that guide people through a physical environment and enhance their understanding and experience of the space. Wayfinding is particularly important in complex built environments such as urban centers, healthcare, and educational campuses, and transportation facilities.

Wearables: Wearables are electronics that can be worn on the body, either as an accessory or as part of material used in clothing. For example, Apple Watch, Fitbit Fitness Tracker, etc.

Web Apps: Web Apps or web applications, which is a computer program that users run in their web browser, also referred to as "client-side." A website can contain a mix of informational content (webpages) or functional applications (webapps).

Website: A website is a collection of web pages and related content that is identified by a common domain name and published on at least one web server.

Whiteboard Exercise: Whiteboards are used for collaborative design and brainstorming, so whiteboard exercises are often used to test applicants on their design problem-solving abilities. Whiteboard exercises ask: are you able to visualize a process, show your work and arrive at a set of recommendations? Here's a common exercise: Design a [interface] for an [audience], e.g. "Design an ATM for children."

White Space: White or negative space refers to the unoccupied or blank space on a page.

Wireframe: A wireframe is a simple visual guide that represents the skeletal framework of a website or digital product. Think of it as the blueprint for your final design. Wireframing is the process of designing a product or feature (desktop or mobile) at a structure level to gain design insight early and identify any major usability issues.

Wizard of Oz: Wizard of Oz describes a research method where a person carries out an experiment (the wizard) enacting the role of the computer. The participant may or may not know that the system they are interacting with is being manually manipulated behind the scenes.

Zeigarnik Effect: People remember uncompleted or interrupted tasks better than completed tasks. Invite content discovery by providing clear signifiers of additional content. Providing artificial progress towards a goal will help to ensure users are more likely to have the motivation to complete that task. Provide a clear indication of progress in order to motivate users to complete tasks.

RECOMMENDED READING AND RESOURCES

Aerssen, Benno van / Buchholz, Christian (2018): Das große Handbuch Innovation: 555 Methoden und Instrumente für mehr Kreativität und Innovation im Unternehmen, Vahlen-Verlag, München.

AIGA, Design business and ethics, 2007, AIGA.

Altschuler, Genrich Saulowitsch (1994): And Suddenly the Inventor Appeared: TRIZ, the Theory of Inventive Problem Solving, Technical Innovation Center, Worcester/USA.

Alvarez, Cindy (2014): Lean Customer Development: Building Products Your Customers Will Buy, O'Reilly, Sebastopol/USA.

Andler, Nicolai (2016): Tools for Project Management, Workshops and Consulting: A Must-Have Compendium of Essential Tools and Techniques, 3rd edition, Publicis Publishing, Erlangen/Germany.

Baumeister, Dayna (2014): Biomimicry Resource Handbook, Biomimicry 3.8, Missoula/USA.

Benedek, Joey / Miner, Trish (2010): Measuring desirability: New methods for evaluating desirability in a usability lab setting, in: Proceedings of Usability Professionals Association 2002 Conference, Orlando/USA.

Blank, Steve (2006): The Four Steps to the Epiphany: Successful Strategies for Products That Win, K&S Ranch Press, Palo Alto/USA.

Blank, Steve /Dorf, Bob (2012), The Startup Owner's Manual: The Step-By-Step Guide for Building a Great Company, K&S RANCH, Pescadero/USA.

Boyd, Drew / Goldenberg, Jacob (2013): Inside the Box: A Proven System of Creativity for Breakthrough Results, Simon & Schuster, New York/USA.

Brown, Tim (2009): Change by Design – How Design Thinking Transforms Organizations and Inspires Innovation, Harper Collins, New York/USA.

Brügger, Chris / Hartschen, Michael / Scherer, Jiri (2017): simplicity: Starke Strategien für einfache Produkte, Dienstleistungen und Prozesse, 2nd edition, Gabal-Verlag, Offenbach.

Buley, Leah, The User Experience Team of One: A Research and Design Survival Guide.

Buzan, Tony (2013): Mind Map Handbook: The ultimate thinking tool, HarperCollins, New York/USA.

Carlzon, Jan (1989): Moments of Truth, HarperBusiness, New York/USA.

Christensen, Clayton M. (1997): The Innovator's Dilemma: When new technologies cause great firms to fall, Harvard Business School Press, Boston/USA.

Christensen, Clayton M. / Hall, Taddy / Dillo, Karen / Duncan, David S. (2016): Competing against luck, HarperBusiness, New York/USA.

Christensen, Clayton M. / Raynor, Michael E. (2003): The Innovator's Solution: Creating and Sustaining Successful Growth, Harvard Business School Press, Boston/USA.

Cohn, Mike (2004): User Stories Applied: For Agile Software Development, Addison-Wesley Professional, Boston/USA.

Colborne, Giles, Simple and Usable Web, Mobile, and Interaction Design.

Cooper, Brant / Vlaskovits, Patrick (2014): The Lean Entrepreneur: How Visionaries Create Products, Innovate with New Ventures, and Disrupt Markets, John Wiley & Sons, Hoboken/USA.

Cooper, Robert G. (2011): Winning at New Products: Creating Value Through Innovation, 4th edition, Basic Books, New York/USA.

Curedale, Robert (2013): design thinking – process and methods manual, Design Community College, Topanga/USA.

Day, George S. (2007): Is it real? Can we win? Is it worth it? Managing risk and reward in an innovation portfolio, in: Harvard Business Review, 85, 12, S. 110 - 120.

De Bono, Edward (1972): PO: A Device for Successful Thinking, Simon & Schuster, New York/USA.

De Bono, Edward (2016): Six Thinking Hats, Penguin Books, London/UK.

Design Council UK (2005): The Design Process, https://www.designcouncil.org.uk/news-opinion/designprocess-what-double-diamond, Zugriffsdatum: 11.06.2018.

Eaton, Marcia Muelder, Aesthetics and the good life, 1989, Associated University Press

Ellison, David, Ethics and aesthetics in European modernist literature, 2001, Cambridge University Press

Fenner, David EW (Ed.), Ethics and the arts: an anthology, 1995, Garland Reference Library of Social Science

Flanagan, John C. (1954): The critical incident technique. Psychological Bulletin, 51, 4: 327 - 358.

Fritzpatrick, Rob (2013): The Mom Test: How to talk to customers & learn if your business is a good idea when everyone is lying to you, CreateSpace, New York/USA.

Furr, Nathan / Dyer, Jeff (2014): The Innovator's Method: Bringing the Lean Start-up into Your Organization, Harvard Business Review Press, Boston/USA.

Gadd, Karen (2011): TRIZ for Engineers: Enabling Inventive Problem Solving, John Wiley & Son, Chichester/UK.

Gini, Al (Ed.), Case studies in business ethics, 2005, Prentice Hall

Goller, Ina / Bessant, John (2017): Creativity of Innovation Management, Rotledge, Abingdon-onThames/UK.

Gordon, William (1961): Synectics: The development of creative capacity. Harper, New York/USA:

Gothelf, Jeff and Josh Seiden, Lean UX: Applying Lean Principles to Improve User Experience.

Gray, Dave / Brown, Sunni / Macanufo, James (2010): Gamestorming: A Playbook for Innovators, Rulebreakers, and Changemakers, O'Reilly Media, Sebastopol/USA.

Johnson, Jeff, Designing with the Mind in Mind.

Kelley, Tom / Kelley, David (2014): Creative Confidence: Unleashing the Creative Potential within us all, HarperCollins, London/UK.

Kelley, Tom/Littman, Jonathan (2001): The Art of Innovation: Lessons in Creativity from IDEO, America's Leading Design Firm, Crown Business, New York/USA.

Kim, W. Chan/ Mauborgne, Renée A. (2015): Blue Ocean Strategy, Expanded Edition: How to Create Uncontested Market Space and Make the Competition Irrelevant, expanded edition, Harvard Business school Publishing, Boston/USA.

Klein, Gary (2007): Performing a Project Premortem, in: Harvard Business Review. 85, 9, S. 18 - 19.

Koltze, Karl / Souchkov, Valeri (2017): Systematische Innovation – TRIZ-Anwendung in der Produkt- und Prozessentwicklung, 2. Auflage, Hanser Verlag, München.

Krug, Steve, Rocket Surgery Made Easy.

Kuang, Cliff and Robert Fabricant, User Friendly: How the Hidden Rules of Design are Changing the Way We Live, Work and Play.

Kumar, Vijay (2012): 101 Design Methods: A Structured Approach for Driving Innovation in Your Organization, John Wiley & Sons, Hoboken/USA.

Kumar, Vijay / Whitney, Patrick (2003): Faster, Cheaper, Deeper User Research, in: Design Management Journal: 50 - 57.

Layton, Mark C. (2012), Scrum For Dummies, John Wiley & Sons, Hoboken/USA.

Levitt, Theodore (1986): The Marketing Imagination, Free Press, New York/USA.

Lewrick, Michael / Link, Patrick / Leifer, Larry (2018): The Design Thinking Playbook: Mindful Digital Transformation of Teams, Products, Services, Businesses and Ecosystems, John Wiley & Sons, Hoboken/USA.

Liedtka, Jeanne / Oglivie, Tim (2011): Designing for Growth: A Design Thinking Tool Kit for Managers, Columbia Univers. Press, New York/USA.

Lindberg, Tilmann / Gumienny, Raja / Jobst, Birgit / Meinel, Christoph (2010): Is There a Need for a Design Thinking Process?, in: Proceedings of Design Thinking Research Symposium 8 (Design 2010), Sydney, Australia, October 2010, pp. 243-254.

Marsh, Joel, UX for Beginners: A Crash Course in 100 Short Lessons.

Martin, Bella / Hanington, Bruce (2012): Universal Methods of Design: 100 Ways to Research Complex Problems, Develop Innovative Ideas, and Design Effective Solutions, Rockport Publishers, Beverly/USA.

Martin, John / Bell, Ros / Farmer, Eion (2000): B822 – Technique Library, The Open University, Milton Keynes/USA.

Maurya, Ash (2013): Running Lean - Das How-to für erfolgreiche Innovationen, O'Reilly Verlag, Köln.

McDonough, William and Braungart, Michael, 'Cradle to Cradle: Remaking the Way We Make Things', 2002

McKay, Everett N., UI is Communication.

Michalko, Michael (2006): Thinkertoys: A Handbook of Creative-Thinking Techniques, 2. Auflage, Ten Speed Press, Berkeley/USA.

Moore, Geoffrey A. (2014): Crossing the Chasm: Marketing and Selling Disruptive Products to Mainstream Customers, HarperCollins Publishers, New York/USA.

Norman, Don, The Design of Everyday Things.

Papanek, Victor, 'Design for the Real World: Making to Measure', 1971

Pauk, Walter / Owens, Ross J.K. (2013): How to Study in College, 11. Auflage, Cengage Learning, Wadsworth/USA.

Paul, Celeste Lyn (2008): A Modified Delphi Approach to a New Card Sorting Methodology."PDF Journal of Usability Studies, 4, 1, Seite 7 - 30.

Plattner, Hasso / Meinel, Christoph / Weinberg, Ulrich (2009): Design-Thinking, mi-Wirtschaftsbuch, München.

Puccio, Gerard J. / Murdock, Mary C. / Mance, Marie (2011): Creative Leadership: Skills That Drive Change, 2nd edition, Sage Publications, London/UK.

Reichheld, Frederick F. (2003): The number one you need to grow, in: Harvard Business Review, 12: 47 - 54.

Reynolds, Thomas J. / Gutman, Jonathan (1984): Advertising is Image Management: Translating Image Research to Image Strategies, in: Journal of Advertising Research, 24, 1, S. 27 - 38.

Reynolds, Thomas J. / Gutman, Jonathan (1988): Laddering theory, method, analysis, and interpretation,in : Journal of Advertising Research, 28, S. 11 - 31.

Rhode, Mike (2012): The Sketchnote Handbook: the illustrated guide to visual note taking, Peachpit Press, Berkeley/USA.

Ries, Eric (2012): Lean Startup, Redline Verlag, München.

Roam, Dan (2009): The Back of the Napkin (Expanded Edition): Solving Problems and Selling Ideas with Pictures, Penguin Group, London/UK.

Ross, Jim (2011): Comparing User Research Methods for Information Architecture, in: https://www.uxmatters.com/mt/archives/2011/06/comparing-user-research-methods-for-informationarchitecture.php; date of access: 15.10.2018.

Rubin, Kenneth S. (2012): Essential Scrum: A Practical Guide to the Most Popular Agile Process (AddisonWesley Signature): A Practical Guide To The Most Popular Agile Process, Addison-Wesley Professional, Boston/USA:

Schlicksupp, Helmut (2004): Ideenfindung, 6. edition, Vogel Business Media, Würzburg/Germany.

Schwaber, Ken and Sutherland, Jeff (2016), The Scrum Guide, in: http://www.scrum guides.org, Zugriffsdatum: 12.09.2017.

Shostack, Lynn G. (1984): Designing Services That Deliver, in: Harvard Business Review, 01/1984.

Sibbet, David (2010): Visual Meetings: How Graphics, Sticky Notes and Idea Mapping Can Transform Group Productivity, John Wiley & Sons, Hoboken/USA.

Takeuchi, Hirotaka / Nonaka, Ikujiro Harvard (1986), The New New Product Development Game, in: Harvard Business Review, 64, 1, Boston/USA.

Tidwell, Jenifer, Charles Brewer and Aynne Valencia, Designing Interfaces.

Tognazzini, Bruce (2014): First Principles of Interaction Design (Revised & Expanded), https://asktog.com/atc/principles-of-interaction-design/; Date: 18.10.2018.

Travis, David and Philip Hodgson, Think Like a UX Researcher: How to Observe Users, Influence Design, and Shape Business Strategy.

Ulwick, Anthony W. (2005): What customers want, McGraw Hill, New York /USA.

United Nations, Global Compact the Ten Principles, www.unglobalcompact.org/AboutTheGC/TheTenPrinciples/index.html

Vulling, Ramon / Heleven, Marc (2017): Not Invented Here – cross-industry innovation, 3rd edition, BIS Publishers, Amsterdam/The Netherlands.

Wake, Bill (2003): INVEST in Good Storys, and SMART Tasks, in: http://xp123.com/articles/invest-in-goodStorys-and-smart-tasks, date of access: 12.09.2017.

Wallas, Graham (1926): Art of Thought, Harcourt, Brace and Company, New York/USA.

Wharton, Cathleen /Rieman, John /Lewis, Clayton /Polson, Peter (1994): The Cognitive Walkthrough Method: A Practitioner's Guide, in: Nielsen, Jacob / Mack, Robert L. (Hrsg.): Usability Inspection Methods, John Wiley & Sons, Inc., New York/USA.

Woodruff, Robert B. / Cadotte, Ernest R. / Jenkins, Roger L. (1983): Modeling Consumer Satisfaction Processes Using Experience-Based Norms, in: Journal of marketing research, 20, 3: 296 - 304.

Young, Indi (2008): Mental Models: Aligning Design Strategy with Human Behavior, Rosenfeld Media, New York/USA.

TOOLS AND SOFTWARE FOR UX DESIGN

Here's a brief description of each UX design tool that showcases its best use case and standout features.

FIGMA

Best UX design tool for ease of collaboration

Now part of the Adobe empire, Figma has a reputation for creating excellent design tools that empower rapid prototyping and development.

Figma helps businesses create, test, and efficiently deliver new product designs. Using Figma's pen tools, designers can draw in any direction with vector networks and generate arc designs. They can pin files for fast access, track contributors, add context notes, and perform collaboratively in real time. The application helps users build prototypes, create design transitions, and define interactions.

Collaboration tools such as diagrams, sticky notes, audio discussions, and online whiteboards also make brainstorming easy for teams.

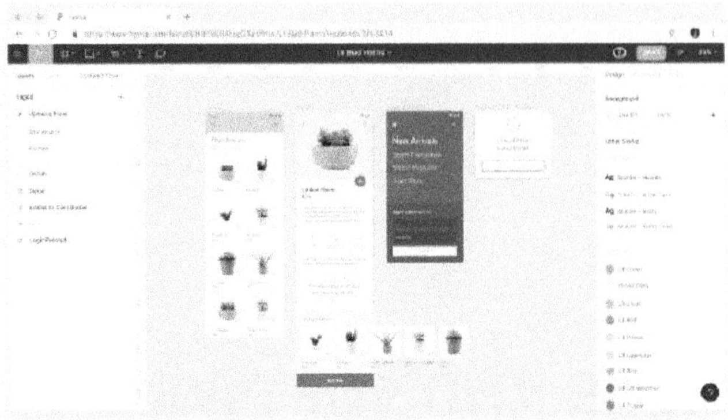

Figma gives designers a clear canvas to work on.

Figma Standout Features and Integrations

Features include advanced collaboration tools, vector networks, components, prototyping, design system management, version control, version history, audio conversations, team libraries, content management, overlays, automated provisioning, on-canvas commenting, plugins, and cross-platform compatibility.

Integrations include Axure, Bubble, Confluence, Flinto, Maze, Microsoft Teams, Pendo, Principle, ProtoPie, Sprig, and Zeplin.

Pros and cons

Pros:

- Quality plugins
- Drag-and-drop prototyping
- Cross-platform support

Cons:

- Steep learning curve
- Commenting can be confusing

UXCAM

UXCam allows you to record, analyze and share sessions and events with the aim of uncovering app usage patterns. The software captures every micro-interaction in your app in real time, then converts all data points into high-fidelity reports for further analysis.

UXCam helps product companies scale by leveraging contextual analytics, giving every stakeholder the right kind of UX metrics. Product teams get to understand the reasons behind user drop-offs and uninstalls, as well as discovering emerging user trends.

The growth team gains deep insights into customer in-app journeys and can analyze specific user segments. Members of the engineering team get real value, too. They get to the root cause of bugs and app crashes, ensuring high-quality development and release cycles.

UXCam Standout Features and Integrations

Features include session replay analysis, heatmaps, user analysis, screen analysis, user journey analysis, custom reports and dashboards, and crash analytics.

Integrations include Amplitude, Android, Firebase Crashlytics, Firebase Google Analytics, Intercom, iOS, MixPanel, React-native, Segment, and Xamarin.

Pros and cons

Pros:

- Helpful heatmaps
- Old-school design
- Instant insights

Cons:

- Number of recordings limited
- Session recordings sometimes fail

MARVEL

Using Marvel tools, you can wireframe, generate design specs, and connect integrations that enhance your workflow. The software makes it easy to create both low-fidelity and high-fidelity designs.

You can also draw app screens on paper, take photos, or add mockups from the cloud. Alternatively, you can draw directly on the screen. Just link each screen to form your app demo, then press play. Prototypes can be shared by email, SMS, or Twitter.

Features include design prototyping, a UI kit library, animations, responsive web design, version history, prototype sharing, commenting, and feedback.

Integrations include Ballpark, Confluence, Dropbox Paper, Jira, Microsoft, Niice, Sketch, Smartmockups, YouTube, and ZeroHeight.

Marvel gives you precise control over all elements of your designs.

Pros and cons

Pros:

- Excellent Sketch integrations
- Updated regularly
- Great for remote teams

Cons:

- No offline option
- No animations

UXPIN

The software enables you to gather user insights and feedback quickly. You can build interactive designs fast, then gather feedback by observing how end-users click through the designs.

UXPin

You can invite team members and other stakeholders to collaborate, import files from other design tools, and make your work interactive. You can also take advantage of the pre-built libraries, and user flows (complete with elements, colors, text styles, and icons).

UXPin Standout Features and Integrations

Features include built-in design elements, easy mockups, comments, auto layouts, and online user testing.

Integrations include Desktop.com, Jira, Miro, Rambox, Shift, and Sketch.

Pros and cons

Pros:

- Great for sharing projects and mockups
- Easy to implement basic prototypes
- Option to upload custom fonts

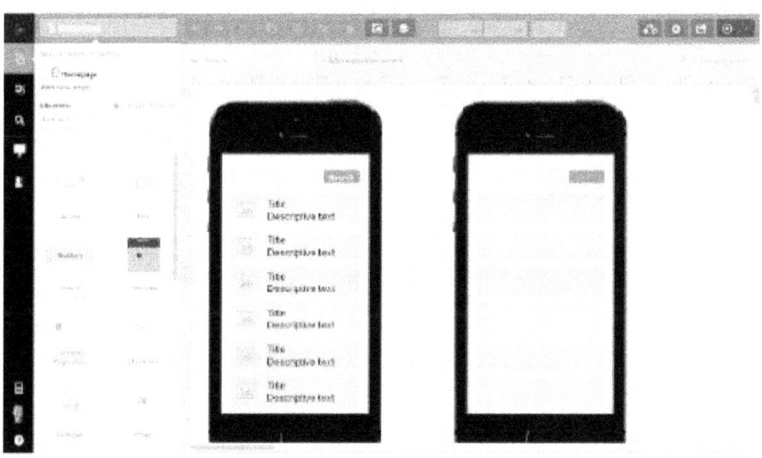

Cons:

- The platform can be slow
- Limited video integration

JUSTINMIND

The software makes it easy to improve user experience through visual designs, web interactions, and mobile gestures. Using the export and documentation tools, you can enable users to generate standard documents and export them into HTML. The platform also allows designers to publish UI designs with a single click, then invite colleagues to provide feedback.

Justinmind

The software allows you to create clickable prototypes, then work through to fully-functional simulations—all without typing a single line of code. You can design full interactions of your web and mobile products, including advanced interactions, animations, transitions, and interactive UI elements.

Justinmind Standout Features and Integrations

Features include pre-installed user interface kits, animations, transitions, effects, templates, forms, data lists, collaboration, app testing, and flow scenario management.

Integrations include Adobe Illustrator, Adobe XD, Figma, Jira, Microsoft TFS, and Sketch.

Pros and cons

Pros:

- Great for fast prototyping
- Ability to link/add Photoshop files
- Easy to share designs

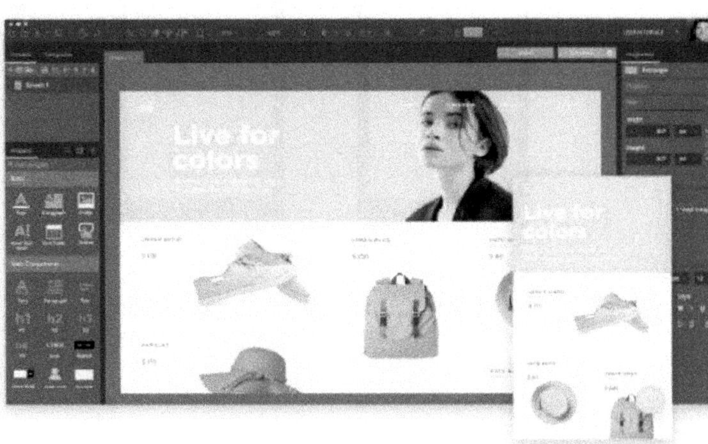

Cons:

- Limited integrations
- Needs more tutorials

WONDERSHARE MOCKITT

Wondershare Mockitt is an all-in-one online design, prototyping, and collaboration platform which aims to help developers create better products faster.

This UX design tool is perfect for creating interactive and animated prototypes that showcase your ideas effectively. You can create a life-like experience, leveling up your workflow by creating multiple artboards and instant interactions.

Formatted annotations help you understand the logic behind every interface design decision, while the real-time collaboration features allow you to share, edit, and comment in real time. The extensive library of templates and components helps you build prototypes faster.

Wondershare Mockitt Standout Features and Integrations

Features include a drag-and-drop functionality, a widget library, responsive design, version history, prototype sharing, and customizable templates.

Integrations include Asana, Box, Confluence, Dropbox, Google Drive, GitHub, Jira, Microsoft Teams, Slack, and Trello.

Pros and cons

Pros:

- Rapid prototyping
- Convenient developer handoffs
- No coding knowledge required to design or prototype

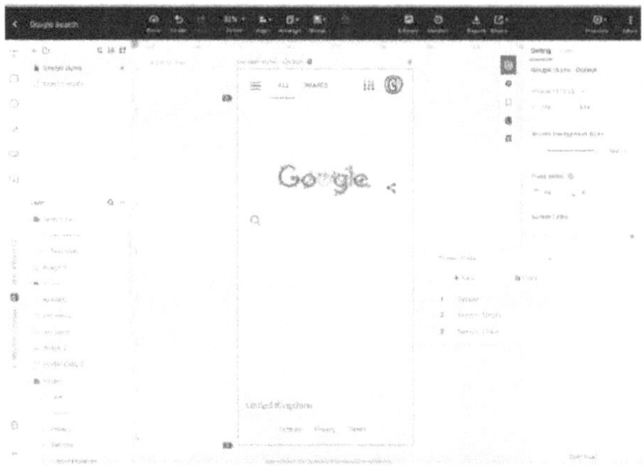

Wondershare Mockitt is a popular app and prototyping tool.

Cons:

- Smaller user base
- Occasional minor bugs

FREEHAND BY INVISION

Freehand by InVision is a digital product design platform that helps development professionals create and manage prototypes. The software provides a digital dashboard, allowing users to collaborate, test, and experiment with design templates and ideas.

invision

Freehand

The multiplayer whiteboard provides a collaborative workspace for teams to get work done, either in real-time or asynchronously. Using InVision Freehand, designers can streamline and automate workflows or develop prototypes.

The built-in shared design libraries help professionals work collaboratively, using tools such as instant playback, mirroring mobile devices, and editing timelines. Users also get library access with push/pull changes, UX components, and version rollback.

InVision Freehand Standout Features and Integrations

Features include visual collaboration tools, presentations, prototype creation, digital whiteboards, wireframing, planning, and feedback management.

Integrations include Asana, Basecamp, Confluence, DropBox, Jira, Sketch, Slack, Teamwork, Trello, and Microsoft Teams.

Pros and cons

Pros:

- Wide variety of templates
- Strong asset sharing capabilities
- Interactive prototyping

Cons:

- More integrations needed
- Navigation can be confusing

InVision's Freehand provides templates to help you create designs faster.

TREEJACK

Treejack empowers you to identify where and why people get lost when consuming your content, then take action to fix the issues.

Treejack

Using this tool, you can evaluate the searchability and hierarchy of your content, whether it's located on the web, in an app, or inside an intranet. You can test, iterate, and validate your design decisions, building out a digital experience that's intuitive and simple to navigate.

The software allows you to test how easily users can find the content they want. You can deploy the tree testing tool to build a website structure based on data, not assumptions. It's easy to test which labels and hierarchy make sense to your users and place elements where people expect to find them.

Treejack Standout Features and Integrations

Features include multiple iterations, design validation, automated insights, multiple visualization methods, user testing, and benchmarking.

Integrations with other software tools are available through connectors such as Zapier.

Pros and cons

Pros:

- Great for testing hierarchies
- Closely matches actual user behavior
- Ability to drill down through multiple levels

Cons:

- Relatively high entry pricing
- Limited integrations

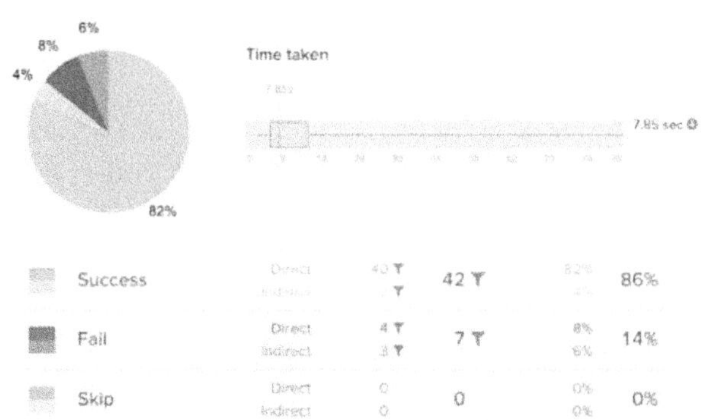

Treejack shows you the impact of changes you make.

SKETCH

Sketch is a cloud-based design tool that helps businesses create vector graphics and icons, collaborate with colleagues, and modify design topography or fonts—all through a single, unified platform.

It allows users to automate workflows, share prototype links, receive design feedback, and collaborate with internal and external stakeholders. Created for Mac users, Sketch also supports data export, project management, and reporting.

The software handles data synchronization activities and helps designers create and store symbols and layer styles in a centralized repository. It also offers rapid prototyping, powerful vector editing, shared libraries, and control over color profiles.

Sketch Standout Features and Integrations

Features include vector editing tools, UI prototyping, color variables, a symbol library, reusable elements, and overlays.

Integrations include Crystal, Drafta, Droplr, Flinto, Frontify, Lokalise, Marvel, Maze, Origami, Proto.io, and Zeplin.

Pros and cons

Pros:

- Excellent training resources
- Cost-effective
- Updated frequently

Cons:

- Only supports Mac users
- Limited prototyping features

Sketch helps designers create visually-stunning designs

FRAMER

Framer is a development platform that allows you to create realistic, interactive UI and UX designs for any app or website.

Framer

Using this software platform, you can collaborate with copywriters, developers, and other designers on all your UI and UX designs in real-time. The multiplayer features allow collaboration with colleagues on everything from wireframing to handoff.

All designs made in Framer are realistic from the start, with interactivity built into everything you create. Thanks to the interactive designs, you can spend more time designing and get quicker results from user testing. Team members can leave comments and respond to all feedback directly from the canvas.

Framer Standout Features and Integrations

Features include interactive prototyping, code components, design collaboration, UI kit library, design previews, responsive design, and templates.

Integrations include Copy Clipboard, Eventbrite, Giphy, Gumroad, Instagram, OpenTable, Product Hunt, Spotify, TrustPilot, and Twitter.

Pros and cons

Pros:

- Excellent animation features
- Powerful interaction elements
- High-fidelity prototypes

Cons:

- Steep learning curve
- Needs more sharing options

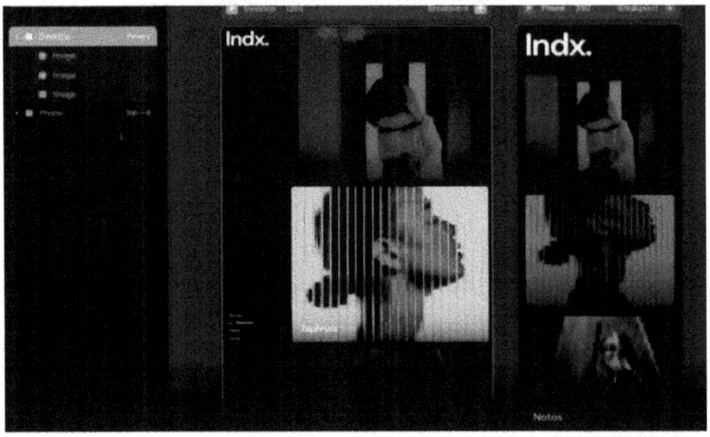

Here are a few more worthwhile options that didn't make the best UX design tools list:

1. **Proto.io**

Best UX design tool for drag-and-drop prototyping

2. **VisualSitemaps**

Best for auto-generating visual sitemaps

3. **Balsamiq**

Best UX design tool for advanced wireframing

4. **UXtweak**

Best UX design tool for UX research

5. **Visily**

Best UX design tool for fast app wireframing

6. **Antetype**

Best UX design tool for fully-interactive prototype

7. **Axure**

Best UX design tool for building functional prototypes

8. **Flowmapp**

Best UX design tool for website design

9. **Adobe XD**

Best UX design tool for the Adobe ecosystem

10. **Origami Studio**

BEST UX DESIGN TOOL FOR TAPPING INTO NATIVE HARDWARE APIS

Selection Criteria for UX Design Tools

The selection of the top UX design tools on the market is informed by my firsthand experience trying and researching various tools, ensuring that researcher can recommend those that effectively balance power and usability. Here's how researcher approach this decision-making process:

UX Design Tools Core Functionality (25% of final scoring): To be considered for inclusion on my list of the best UX design tools, the solution had to support the ability to fulfill common use cases. These include:

- Creating and testing interactive prototypes
- Facilitating real-time collaboration among design team members

- Integrating user feedback directly into the design process
- Ensuring designs are responsive and accessible across all devices
- **Managing project versions and history** for easy reference and rollback

Additional Standout Features (25% of final scoring): This part of the evaluation focuses on finding innovation in functionalities beyond the basics, such as advanced prototyping and AI-powered design assistance. Tools that offer unique features enhancing workflow and creativity receive higher scores.

- Advanced prototyping capabilities that mimic complex interactions and animations, as seen in tools like Figma and Adobe XD.
- AI-powered design assistance for generating design elements and suggesting improvements, enhancing efficiency.
- Comprehensive user testing platforms integrated within the tool, enabling designers to conduct and analyze tests without leaving the design environment.
- Robust version control systems that go beyond simple undo functions, allowing for detailed tracking of changes and team contributions.
- Exceptional integration with developer tools to ensure a smooth handoff from design to development, exemplifying the seamless workflow between tools like Sketch and Zeplin.

Usability (10% of final scoring): Usability testing focuses on evaluating each tool's learning curve, interface design, and workflow customization, with special attention paid to if the tool is intuitive to use and provides quick adaptation for new users.

When evaluating usability, prioritize:

- Intuitive interface design that minimizes the learning curve for new users.
- Customizable workflows that can be tailored to the specific processes of a design team.
- Efficient navigation and shortcut options that speed up the design process without sacrificing precision.

Onboarding (10% of final scoring): This section of the evaluation primarily assesses the availability and quality of training materials, templates, and interactive tours. Comprehensive onboarding resources contribute to higher scores.

To determine if a tool offers effective onboarding, look for:

- Comprehensive training materials, including videos, tutorials, and interactive product tours.

- Pre-designed templates and UI libraries that help new users start projects with ease.
- Community forums and in-app support such as chatbots for real-time assistance.

Customer Support (10% of final scoring): Here, the evaluation examines the responsiveness and effectiveness of support channels, including self-service resources. Overall, tools are tested on support quality, with higher scores for better service.

The standards for superior customer support include:

- Responsive support teams available through multiple channels (email, chat, phone).
- In-depth knowledge bases and FAQs for self-service troubleshooting.
- Active user communities for peer support and networking.

Value For Money (10% of final scoring): Here, the evaluation focuses on pricing transparency and the balance of features versus cost. Tools with free trials or demos that significantly contribute the the platform's perceived value will receive higher scores.

For this criteria, consider:

- Transparent pricing models with clear distinctions between different tiers and features.
- Free trials or demo versions that allow users to test the tool before committing financially.
- The balance of advanced features against the cost, ensuring that higher-priced plans justify their expense with significant added value.

Customer Reviews (10% of the final scoring): This criterion analyzes feedback across platforms for insights into user satisfaction and performance. Consistency in positive reviews leads to higher scores.

Altogether, evaluate:

- Consistency in customer satisfaction across various review platforms.
- Specific feedback on usability, performance, and support.
- Testimonials from users in similar industries or with comparable project needs.

Scores from each criterion are combined according to their weightings to derive a final score out of 100. This score is then translated into a star rating, with 5 stars indicating exceptional performance and 1 star indicating significant areas for improvement. This process ensures that the tools meet a wide range of design requirements and offer exceptional value and user satisfaction.

Trends in UX Design Tools for Future

In future, UX design tools and technologies have continued to evolve towards creating more intuitive, user-centered digital experiences. These trends reflect the shifting needs and challenges within the UX design and product management communities.

- **Generative Design and AI Integrations:** Naturally, the rise of AI tools is first on the list. Tools like Figma and Canva are increasingly incorporating AI to automate design processes, enabling rapid prototyping and generative design. This trend underscores a move towards efficiency and creativity, allowing designers to generate visual images and concept art swiftly.
- **Accessibility and Inclusivity:** Tools are also focusing more on creating designs accessible to a broader range of users, reflecting a growing awareness of inclusivity in digital products. This includes anticipatory design techniques aimed at streamlining user experiences and guiding users towards desired interactions with minimal cognitive load.
- **Interactive Animations and Microinteractions:** The rise of no-code tools like Rive for creating engaging, responsive interactive animations without extensive coding knowledge indicates a shift towards more dynamic user experiences. This trend highlights the importance of adding depth and intuitiveness to interfaces through interactive elements.
- **Immersive AR/VR Experiences:** Augmented Reality (AR) and Virtual Reality (VR) are being more commonly integrated into UI/UX design, suggesting a trend towards more immersive digital experiences. This involves using AR elements in applications to provide richer user experiences or creating entirely new interfaces in VR .
- **Buttonless Interfaces and Advanced Interaction Methods:** The movement towards buttonless user interfaces, utilizing voice commands, gestures, and other natural interaction methods, reflects a broader trend of technological advancement in UI design. This approach aims at creating seamless, intuitive user experiences.

These trends not only reflect the evolving digital ecosystem but also the industry's commitment to creating more personalized, intuitive, and inclusive user experiences. Designers and product managers must stay abreast of these developments to effectively address the complex challenges and opportunities presented by the ever-changing market demands.

INDEX

www.ingramcontent.com/pod-product-compliance
Ingram Content Group UK Ltd.
Pitfield, Milton Keynes, MK11 3LW, UK
UKHW050948290926
15470UKWH00005B/1713

9 781787 153042